PLAYING WITH POWER!

Nintendo® NES CLASSICS

8

10

18

30

34

40

52

64

90

106

130

140

170

196

248

278

284

FOREWORD

By Don James

Executive Vice President, Operations

Nintendo of America Inc.

Just out of college, I was picking up a letter of recommendation for the work I had done designing a coin-op cabinet for Far East Video, which had become the fledgling Nintendo of America. They offered me a position as a warehouse manager and I thought, "Sure, it's a job." That was 35 years ago.

One of my first memories as a Nintendo of America employee is looking at a game called Donkey Kong in our lobby, and along with our President, coming up with the name Mario for the main character, who was then called Jumpman. Yeah, I'm one of the two guys who named Mario.

We took a big gamble kick-starting the US home video game industry after it had crashed in the early 1980s. It took a lot of time and effort by many loyal and dedicated Nintendo employees. I was one of the employees who moved to New Jersey for three-and-half months to launch the Nintendo Entertainment System into the New York market. It was an experience I will never forget.

The Nintendo warehouse was located in Hackensack, NJ and it was, to say the least, sparse on amenities. There were rats and snakes inside the building, and we even had a barrel of some sort of dangerous, toxic substance roll into the parking lot, which an individual in a hazmat suit had to come and take away. Hence we all referred to our warehouse affectionately as "Rats and Snakes and Toxic Waste."

A small team built the Point of Purchase displays at night, loaded them into vans with NES Deluxe Bundles, and delivered them to retail outlets. Every morning we would all gather at a huge map of the New York area, which included Long Island and New Jersey, and plan the routes each of our four vans would take. The vans left full and returned empty, only to repeat the whole process the next day. In those three-and-a-half months, we worked 18 hours a day, 7 days a week.

When we were adapting the Japanese Famicom into what would become the Nintendo Entertainment System, I remember standing in the warehouse, which was filled with coin-op arcade games, and talking to our VP of sales. He said, "Don, do you have any idea what will happen to the company if this product takes off?" At the time I didn't think much about it, but looking back, it was the start of a truly epic journey for myself and the many fans of Nintendo's products and characters.

In the years since, many chapters have been added to the Nintendo story. We've come a long way since the days of Rats and Snakes and Toxic Waste. With this book, and the release of the Nintendo Entertainment System: NES Classic Edition console, I am excited to relive some of my own memories of those exciting early days. I hope you are, too!

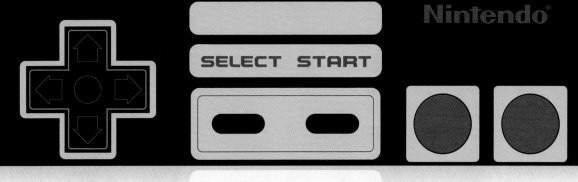

INTRODUCTION

By Nick von Esmarch

Two-tone gray with red and black accents: this seemingly simple color scheme is immediately recognizable to nearly any gamer, even now—even to those of us who were born years after the Nintendo Entertainment System launched. But why? Why, after decades of technological leaps and bounds, does this iconic video game console still hold such a cherished spot in our collective memory? Put simply: the NES changed everything.

Trust us; those of us who were there remember what gaming was like before the NES. After the industry crash of 1983, video games were thought to have been a fad. Not by those of us who played games, of course; but the companies that published them, the retailers that sold them, and the media outlets that covered them all seemed convinced that the heyday of video games had come and gone. The thought might be laughable now, but those of us who were there know how close it came to being true.

It wasn't just the most popular console of its time; the NES managed to revitalize and reshape an entire industry. For that reason alone, the NES deserves to be celebrated decades later. It helped define a generation of gamers, and its influence can still be felt to this day. If you need an example, just take a look at the NES Game Pad: a Directional Pad on the left with buttons on the right. It changed the way we interacted with games, and it established what most gamers have come to expect from a controller. At one time, every console that hit the market did so with its own unique (and often bizarre) controller. Offerings incorporated joysticks, dials, and keypads in various combinations and configurations. Mastering a new controller took nearly as much time as mastering a new game, and playing on an unfamiliar console was always a disadvantage during a round of competitive gaming. But the NES Game Pad changed all of that. Its influence can be seen in virtually every controller that's hit the market in the last 30 years. Thanks to the Game Pad, players instinctively know how to pick up and play nearly any game on any console.

For many of us, it now takes only a few minutes to feel comfortable with a new game. And that wasn't always the case.

Of course, the popularity of the NES wasn't just about color schemes and controllers. Our love for this system is built on its library of now-classic games. From the day it launched, the NES offered something for everyone. And as its library grew, so did its popularity.

The NES offered plenty of games for fast-twitch players; there were scores of options for players who could turn a single quarter into an entire day in the arcade. But there were also plenty of titles for the rest of us, too. In many cases, conquering a game was more about knowledge than reflexes. Some games could be mastered by anyone with a mind to do so—anyone willing to learn where the available power-ups were located, the order in which they should be collected, and the best times to use them. A missed jump didn't seem quite so disastrous if you knew where those extra lives were hidden. A room filled with hostiles didn't seem so overwhelming if you knew the weaknesses of each enemy. A stray shot didn't matter so terribly when you knew that extra ammunition was stashed just around the corner. Those of us who weren't blessed with remarkable skill could rely instead on preparation and persistence. We were still free to chase the bragging rights that came with high scores and endurance runs, but the NES also offered games that were deeper than we'd come to expect.

This diversity helped give the hobby a much broader appeal, and it allowed the NES to grow a fan-base unlike anything the industry had ever enjoyed in the past.

Gamers might now be preoccupied with frame rates, load times, and console exclusives, but that wasn't always the case. Back then, it seemed that our collective focus was squarely on the games, and all of the biggest games were on the NES. The same notebooks we used in class also contained our hand-drawn maps of Brinstar and Norfair. Graph paper squares were filled-in with colored pencil to create pixel-by-pixel reproductions of Goombas, Nettlers, and Octoroks. Secret passages and hidden rooms were discussed over sack lunches. After school, players exchanged hard-earned passkeys to help each other complete particularly challenging games. Before long, it seemed as though everyone had an NES at home, and everyone had at least one game they knew inside and out.

Those of us who grew up with the NES now count ourselves as the first generation of life-long gamers. Many of us have sons and daughters of our own, and we're eager to share with them the games we remember from our own childhoods. And why not? These titles aren't just touchstones in gaming history—they're every bit as entertaining as we remember. A few minutes with an old favorite is enough to make any NES fan remember exactly why they started gaming all of those years ago.

THE INSIDE STORY OF THE NES

THE INS
THE NES
From the outside, the NES Control Deck
like a simple box—a few buttons, a few jac
red light. But appearances can be decept
following pages we'll open up the hardwa

THE NES CONTROL DECK

From the outside, the NES Control Deck (CD) looks like a simple box—a few buttons, a few jacks, a little red light—but appearances can be deceptive. In the following pages we'll open up the hardware and see what goes on inside that world of amazing precision and blinding speed. Our tour into the electronic maze behind with a look at how the CD communicates with the world through Game Paks, Controllers, and your TV.

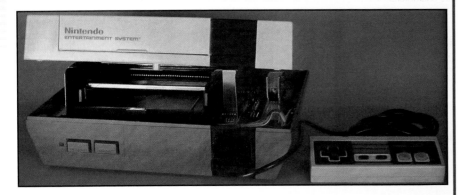

72 Pin Connector

Like all computers, the NES receives information from software. In this case, that means Game Paks. When you slide your Game Pak into the Control Deck, the open end slips into the 72 Pin Connector. It's like plugging in your telephone so you can receive calls. Information passes from the microchips inside the Game Pak through the 72 Pin Connector and into the Central Processing Unit (CPU) of the Control Deck or into the Picture Processing Unit (PPU), depending on the information and which Pin Connectors are accessed. If lint or dust gets into the 72 Pin Connector, the signals may not get through and it seems like the Game Pak isn't working.

RF Modulator

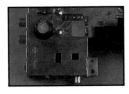

Did you know that your NES Control Deck is like a television station? The signal sent by the CD to your TV to create the image of Mario and other characters is the same broadcast by TV stations. The signal is called RF or Radio Frequency and it is generated by the RF Modulator inside the CD. But when the PPU creates video information, it sends a Composite Video Signal—the type of signal computer monitors can read. Most TVs receive RF signals, however, so the RF Modulator translates the Composite Signal and sends it to the TV. Strangely enough, once the TV receives the RF information, it translates it back into Composite Video Signals in order to display the picture.

Controllers

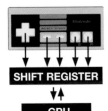

The Control Deck is also connected to the outside world through the Controllers. When the CPU needs controller information, it sends a message to a chip in the Controller called the Shift Register. The Shift Register reads the position of every button, either On or Off, then reports back to the CPU on the On or Off status of each button. Although it seems like this might take a long time, actually it all happens in less than a sixtieth of a second—much faster than the human eye can discern. The result is that characters seem to jump at the push of a button.

THE COMPUTER BRAIN

Every aspect of the game, from the picture that appears on the screen to the rules that determine how high a character jumps is controlled by two powerful components— the PPU and CPU. Let's take a peek.

The PPU

The Picture Processing Unit, like the CPU, is located on the main integrated circuit board of the CD. If you opened up your Control Deck, which you should never do, you'd find that it seems to be upside down. The PPU takes digital information from the CPU and Game Pak and converts it into Composite Video Signals that specify the color of every pixel on your TV screen. Sixty times every second the PPU redraws the entire screen in still frames, just like the multiple still frames of a motion picture. Because this happens so fast, it seems as if characters on the screen are actually moving.

The CPU

The Central Processing Unit is like a tiny switchboard with thousands of calls coming in and going out at the same time. For instance, every sixtieth of a second, or V-Blank period, when an image has been completely drawn on the screen, the CPU checks for commands called Interrupts. The Interrupt from the Game Pak may instruct the CPU to ask for the current position of all Controller buttons, or it may run some other routine, such as sending out a sound effect command. If you imagine the Game Pak as a cook book, the CPU would be the cook who follows the instructions—for every dish in the book at the same time.

STORY OF NES

OL DECK

HARDWARE TECHNICAL ARTICLE

THE COMPUTER BRAIN

Every aspect of the game, from the picture that appears on the screen to the rules that determine how high a character jumps is controlled by two powerful microchips—the PPU and CPU. Let's take a peek.

de that world of amazing precision d. Our tour into the electronic maze at how the CD communicates with Game Paks, Controllers and your TV.

NES MOTHERBOARD

Here's an article that originally appeared in Volume 22 of Nintendo Power magazine. Technology has come a long way since then, but the principles are remarkable familiar—and the story behind the circuits is still fascinating. So, if you remember blowing the dust out of your Game Pak—or even if you don't—read on, and enjoy how it used to be!

THE NES AT PLAY

Characters

Although Mario and other characters usually seem pretty solid, they are actually composed of several characters. Super Mario consists of eight separate characters, but they are all programmed to appear in a sequence that makes them seem like one unit. Backgrounds are also made up of many separate characters. In fact, every screen has 960 characters!

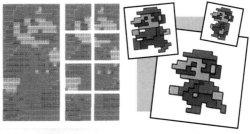

Scrolling

The PPU may display only 960 characters, or one screen at a time, but it actually stores twice that amount. In a one-way scroll, new characters constantly replace old characters behind the scroll. This is why in games like Super Mario Bros. the screen can scroll only one way. In Metroid, however, scrolling occurs in two directions and new characters are continually added in the direction of the scroll.

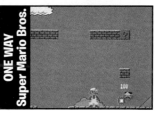

ONE WAY Super Mario Bros.

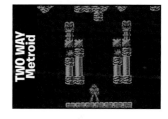

TWO WAY Metroid

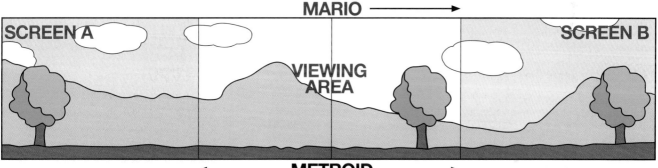

MARIO →

SCREEN A

VIEWING AREA

SCREEN B

← METROID →

RF Vs. RGB

Why do RGB (Red, Green, Blue) monitors seem to have clearer, sharper pictures than standard television monitors? Information can be lost or distorted by interference during RF transmission. But the RGB signal goes straight from CPU to the color guns of the monitor.

RF

The NES sends RF signals to the TV, but can also send Composite Video using the AV Cables.

RGB

Arcade games like the original release of *Punch-Out!!* use RGB, and the resulting picture is generally better.

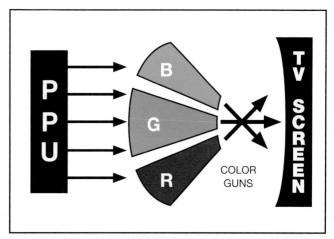

INTO THE FUTURE

Super Nintendo 16-bit chip.

Just as in the rest of the computer industry, video game technology is racing forward. New 16-bit game systems like the upcoming Super Nintendo are leading the way, but what is the real difference between the new systems and the traditional 8-bit systems like the NES and Game Boy? Speed of processing is the main difference. In an 8-bit system you can describe 256 individual things such as colors, whereas in a 16-bit system you can describe 65,536 individual things. The possibilities are tremendous, but the final result, as always, depends more on creative programming than the speed of the microprocessor.

THE LAUNCH OF THE NINTENDO ENTERTAINMENT SYSTEM

October 18, 1985 – The day the Nintendo Entertainment System launched in North America. Known as the Family Computer ("Famicom") in Japan, the NES released quietly in the US with a total of 17 launch titles.

Nintendo started in 1889 as a manufacturer of cards for a popular card game known as "Hanafuda," or "Flower Cards." They continued to manufacture cards for decades, but eventually moved toward creating and manufacturing toys in the 1960s. When the arcade boom hit in the '70s, Nintendo decided to try their hand at game development. They released a variety of arcade titles with moderate success, but they wouldn't become a big name in the game industry until the release of the arcade megahit *Donkey Kong* in 1981.

Arcade games were major hits in the late '70s, but began to simmer in the early '80s.

The big names in gaming and electronics at the time had moved on to bringing the arcade experience to the American home, where they were met with massive success. But by the time Nintendo had released the NES, the game industry was on shaky ground.

A wave of poor-quality games left consumers wary of purchasing any new games or home consoles that hit the store shelves. Video games were also considered a burden for retailers at the time, since it's said that most of them had large bargain bins filled to the brim with old games and consoles. Rumor has it that Nintendo had to market the NES as a toy, instead of video game console, in order to convince retailers to sell it. (Check out our Peripherals chapter for details.)

The NES released quietly and with only a small number of consoles produced. There were 17 titles available at launch, but they weren't enough to sway American consumers—at least not right away.

It took time, but eventually the NES became a smash hit that reignited the game industry and set the standard not only for quality games, but for entire genres. Today the NES is known and beloved by game enthusiasts the world over. Incredible games were created for the system, and several started entire franchises that have lived on for decades.

Join us as we relive the NES era: a time of Nintendo Power magazines, game paks, and summers well spent.

FIRST-PARTY NES TITLES: LAUNCH DAY

▶ 10-Yard Fight

"You're the quarterback in this amazingly real football game!

Enjoy realistic grid-iron action as you move your team up and down the field to victory! Run, pass, kick, punt—you call the plays in this true-to-life football. Play against the computer, or against a friend, for hours of real football action. The sights, the sounds, and the plays are so real, you'll think you're right on the 50-yard line!"

▶ Baseball

"The most realistic baseball game outside of a ballpark!

It's the bottom of the ninth. You're at the plate. Here comes the pitch. You swing—it's a smash deep into centerfield! A home run! It's Nintendo BASEBALL. A game so real, you'll think you're in the majors. You control the swing of the bat. The speed of the pitch. The hits, the steals, the double-plays! Play against a computer opponent or challenge a friend. Nintendo's state-of-the-art graphics and realistic game play will have you really believing you're playing baseball. Just add peanuts, popcorn, and crackerjacks for the time of your life!"

▶ Clu Clu Land

"The evil Sea Urchin has hidden all the gold in Clu Clu Land.

Are you clever enough to unravel the mystery of Clu Clu Land? It's up to you to find the gold before time runs out! But beware. The Sea Urchin will do everything in his power to stop you. He'll set up traps to trick you, or bounce you against the Rubber Trap and land you flat on your back! If you can control the Sea Urchin by stunning him with electric shockwaves, you just might find out where he's hidden the gold and move on to an exciting bonus round!

▶ Duck Hunt

"Take aim, fire, and score! It's DUCK HUNT!

Your trusty hunting dog wades into the marshes to flush out your prey. Your fingers tighten around your Zapper™ light gun. Suddenly, there's a duck in the air! You've only got three shots to bag this duck, and if you miss, even your dog laughs at you! But become a sharp-shooter, and you'll progress to the next round where two ducks fly up at the same time. And then you're on to the ultimate challenge: Clay Shooting. Where you'll compete in a wild clay-pigeon shooting contest! Play DUCK HUNT and discover you can have lots of laughs and be challenged at the same time."

▶ Excitebike

"Design your own motocross course for a different racing challenge every time!

This thrilling Nintendo Programmable game lets you vary the obstacles, change the sequence of events, and increase the racing challenge time and time again! You'll start out in a Nintendo-designed preliminary race, and move through a series of increasingly difficult challenge races! You'll face crazy curves, hairpin turns, daredevil jumps, and some very fierce motocross competition, as you race your bike toward the checkered flag. This thrilling test of driving strategy and skill will keep you riveted to the screen for hours!"

▶ Golf

"From tee to green, you've never played golf like this!

Nintendo GOLF lets you choose your clubs, change your stance, control your swings—even select the angle of impact! You'll view the hole from both close up and far away, judge the changing conditions of the green, and measure the wind velocity! But watch out. When the wind changes, so does the flight of your ball! With Nintendo's state-of-the-art graphics and realistic game play you'll really believe you're on the fairways. So play Nintendo GOLF, because there's not a video golf game on par with it anywhere!"

Gyromite

"This game is so intense you can't play it alone!

You'll need R.O.B.™—the World's first Robotic Operating Buddy—to play this action-packed game! You've got to keep R.O.B.'s gyroscope spinning in order to help a mad scientist deactivate all the dynamite in his laboratory. You'll move columns up and down to speed the scientist on his way while trying to avoid the lethal Smicks. And you'll get him to his dynamite even faster if you can get R.O.B. to spin two gyros at the same time! But don't take your eyes off the scientist, because anything can happen in GYROMITE! Where two hands and one pair of eyes aren't always enough!"

Hogan's Alley

"Are you tough enough to join the FBI?

You need split-second timing and sharp-shooting accuracy to join the FBI. Have you got what it takes? Prove it! Use your Zapper™ light gun to shoot the gangsters in the FBI line-up *without* hitting the innocent bystanders. Hit the gangsters and you'll score enough points to move to the next location: Hogan's Alley. Here's where the going gets rough. The gangsters pop in and out of windows, doorways, and shadows, and are visible for a shorter amount of time. Beat the gangsters this time around and you'll move to the Trick Shoot round. How long can you keep the tin cans hopping in the air? Keep them up there long enough, and you'll score enough points to become a full-fledged Agent in this exciting Nintendo Light Gun game!"

Ice Climber

"It's only you and an ice hammer as you make your way to the top of the mountain!

If you can break through 8 levels of treacherous arctic ice, you'll reach the top of the mountain! But watch out. The Nitpickers, Condors, and Polar Bears don't want you up there. And they've got a bag of tricks that will test every ounce of your strength and courage. Are you going to let them stop you? No way! There are 32 mountains to choose from and endless thrills as you fight these arctic creatures alone or with a friend, and ascend to the top of the mountain in ICE CLIMBER!"

Kung-Fu

"Kick, jump, and punch your way to victory in KUNG FU!

You'll need lightning-fast reactions to knock out the Knife Thrower, stop the Stick Fighter, and trip-up the evil Tom Tom Brothers in this action-packed martial arts contest! Are you sure you're tough enough? Because it'll take all your strength and skill to master the moves in KUNG FU, beat your opponents, and rescue the fair Sylvia who's held captive on the top floor! The action is non-stop, and just when you think you've got your enemies licked there's always a Giant, a Snake, or a fire-breathing Dragon to contend with in KUNG FU!"

Pinball

"Be a pinball wizard, right in your own home!

Bank off bumpers, flip double flippers, even win a bonus—in Nintendo's lightning-fast PINBALL! You'll have the time of your life as you flip from upper to lower game screens, rack up points to beat your opponent, and, if you're lucky, progress to the bonus round where you'll save the falling maiden in this video version of the real thing!"

Soccer

"You've got to be fast on your feet to keep up with Nintendo SOCCER!

Enjoy World Cup action as you move your team up and down the field to victory! Perform Kickoffs, Throw-ins, Goal kicks, and Corner kicks—just like in a real soccer match. You can choose a computer team or a friend as your opponent. Then select a skill level from 1-5. You'll love Nintendo's state-of-the-art graphics and realistic game play, and of course, the head-to-head competition that you'll control just with your fingertips! If you miss out on this exciting Nintendo game pak, you'll be kicking yourself!"

Stack-Up

"Here's a high-tech, high-strategy juggling act that's loads of fun!

Are you up to the challenge? You've got to get R.O.B.—the World's first Robotic Operating Buddy—to stack a pile of colored discs to match the colored pattern on the screen. This exciting Robot game can be played in several ways. In the Direct mode, you have to match the pattern in the shortest number of moves. In the Memory mode, you can program up to 100 Robot moves as you try to match the pattern. In the Bingo mode, on screen alien beings keep changing the pattern, preventing you from completing your mission! Inside you'll find five colored discs and five disc holders along with the game pak. Everything you need to play STACK UP!"

Super Mario Bros.

"Do you have what it takes to save the Mushroom Princess?

You'll have to think fast and move even faster to complete this quest! The Mushroom Princess is being held captive by the evil Koopa tribe of turtles. It's up to you to rescue her from the clutches of the Koopa King before time runs out. But it won't be easy. To get the princess, you'll have to climb mountains, cross seas, avoid bottomless pits, fight off turtle soldiers and a host of black magic traps that only a Koopa King can devise. It's another non-stop adventure from the SUPER MARIO BROS.!"

Tennis

"Whether it's singles or doubles you'll love the non-stop action of this amazingly real tennis game!

Slam a serve, fire a blazing backhand, smash a forehand volley— you call the shots in Nintendo TENNIS! Nintendo lets you choose an opponent from five different skill levels. So as your game improves, so does your playing partner! Plus, you can actually gauge the speed of your serve! The better your timing, the faster it moves across the net. You'll have hours of fun rushing the net, playing the baseline, or roaming the court. With Nintendo's state-of-the-art graphics and realistic game play, you'll really believe you're at center court!"

Wild Gunman

"Take on the fastest guns on the West in WILD GUNMAN!

Your palm sweats as you grip your Zapper™ light gun. The Outlaw's eyes flash. He yells "Fire!" And suddenly you're in the middle of a Wild West shootout! Get the Outlaw before he gets you, and you'll win a reward! But watch out—the more you win, the tougher it becomes, because this gunman has some very nasty friends. You can take on one Outlaw, two Outlaws—or the whole wild gang. Are you up to the action? Because it's fast and furious in this quick-on-the-trigger Nintendo Light Gun game!"

Wrecking Crew

"Here's an off-the-wall demolition game you design yourself!

This amazing Nintendo Programmable game lets you design your own building, place obstacles wherever you want them, and then blow everything to smithereens! You can play the game as designed by Nintendo, or you can be the game designer and build a different maze of barriers to tear down every time. You'll have hours of fun demolishing monsters like Gotchawrench and Eggplant Man, and blowing up a building you built yourself, in this off-the-wall demolition."

EXCITEBIKE

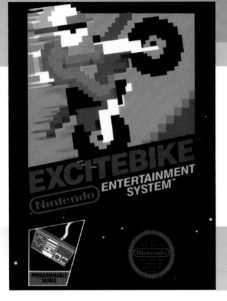

Developers:
Nintendo R&D1

Director:
Shigeru Miyamoto

Producer:
Takahara Harada

Composer:
Akito Nakatsuka

Original Release Date:
November 30, 1984 Famicom
JP; October 18, 1985 NES US

SUMMARY

The exciting game of motocross is played right in your own home on your television set. The techniques used for super jumps, wheelies, and blocks are almost the same as those used in an actual stadium motocross meet.

Excitebike features both a preliminary game and a regular game. To participate in a regular game, you must first win a national challenge race. There are one to five courses in a national challenge race and you can start from any of them.

There are also five courses for a regular game. If you win at the first one, your rank goes up from two to five, in order of sequence. Choose from Course Two to Five of the preliminary courses and, if you win, your rank increases with each regular game.

Skillfully guide your bike over the course by pushing up and down on the control pad. A jump ramp appears periodically. When this happens, press Left on the Directional Pad to raise the front wheel for a good jump. Will you become a supercross champion?

HOW TO

Just like actual motocross, Excitebike is complex. You must watch your engine's temperature, learn to jump off ramps properly, and use your turbo boost effectively to become the motocross champ.

Accelerating and Braking

Press the A Button to control the bike's speed and avoid obstacles or pass competitors. You can also press the B Button to engage turbo to get a speed boost.

Cool Down at Arrow Signs

During races you come across arrows on the ground. Guide your bike over these to reduce the engine's temperature. Turn on the turbo while the engine is cooling off to improve your chances of winning!

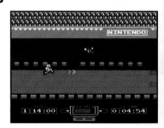

Avoiding Engine Overheating

Pay attention to the engine's temperature at the bottom of the screen. It's fine as long as it stays in the green range, but your bike will overheat and stop if the gauge goes into the red zone.

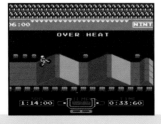

Practice Mode

A target time is indicated in the practice mode. If you complete the course time, your time becomes the new target time for the course.

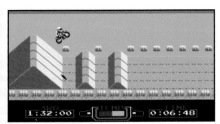
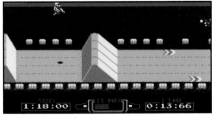
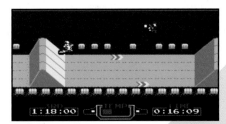

High Jumping

When you must jump over high obstacles or use the ramp, push left on the Directional Pad to raise up the front wheel and jump. Keep your front wheel up while you're in the air to go even higher and make it easier to clear any obstacles ahead.

Long Jumping

This is the most effective jump during the race. When you come to a jump ramp or an obstacle, raise your front wheel up and go full speed ahead. Try to match the angle of the jumping bike to the angle of the landing spot to land without losing any speed.

Get Back Up

If you bump into a rival motocrosser or make a bad landing from a jump during the race, your bike will overturn. When this happens, get back up faster by hitting the A Button repeatedly. Use this technique to achieve your best time and win the prize!

TRACKS

There are two "Selections" on the Main menu, both of which determine whether you race other motocrossers or not. Selection A is simply time trials. You race against the clock to beat the third place time, which is shown at all times during the race in the bottom-left corner of the screen. Beat that time to advance. If you go over that time, you get a "Game Over."

If you choose Selection B, you race on the same tracks as Selection A, but have other racers on the track to potentially knock you off your bike. Beating the clock is still the goal here, but it's a lot harder to accomplish with so many other racers on the track.

After beating the time in a race, you must race on that track a second time, but with a lower time-to-beat and with new obstacles on the course. The second time around is much more challenging than the first, so it might take a few tries to get past each track. Just keep practicing and you'll beat it eventually! See if you can get through all of the tracks in one try!

Design Mode

Design Mode is a feature of this game that allows you to design your own favorite layout.

Select the Design Mode from the Title screen and press Start. Then choose the Design Mode again to set up the course layout. Move the motocrosser forward with the A Button to the desired location, then select an obstacle from "A" to "S" and place it on the track using the B Button. To Erase a hurdle, select "CL" and press the B Button.

You can also establish the number of laps for the course—from one to nine laps—by pressing Up and Down on the Directional Pad.

The Pieces

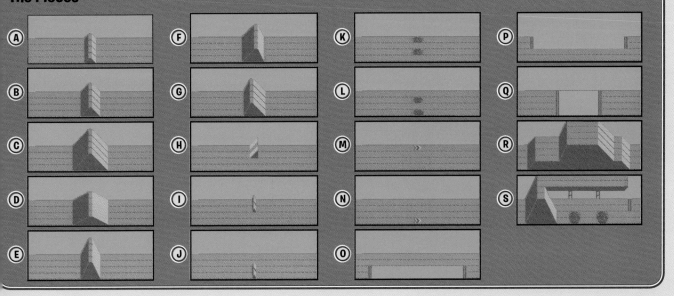

ICE CLIMBER

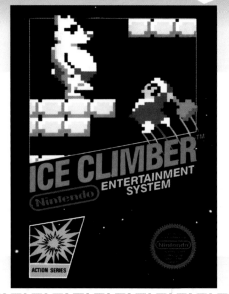

Developer:
Nintendo R&D1

Director:
Kenji Miki

Designer:
Masayuki Uemura

Composer:
Akito Nakatsuka

Original Release Date:
January 30, 1985 Famicom JP;
October 18, 1985 NES US

SUMMARY

Do you have what it takes to reach the top of an ice-covered, creature-infested mountain? How about 32 of them? Play as Popo and prove you've got the sharp reflexes, steady hands, and steely determination of an expert climber. Or team up with a friend to tackle each mountain as Popo and Nana. To succeed, you'll need to execute daring jumps, dodge falling icicles, fend off hostile creatures, and more. Keep your climber safe (and the game going) to achieve your highest possible score as you conquer increasingly difficult mountains.

HOW TO PLAY

Use the Directional Pad to move Popo (or Nana) left and right, respectively. Press the A Button to jump and press the B Button to swing your hammer. Press the Start Button to pause and resume the action during gameplay.

On the Main menu, press Up or Down on the Directional Pad to select your starting mountain. Use the Select Button to cycle between available game modes, and press the Start Button to begin the game.

Controller 2

During a 2-Player game, controlling Nana is exactly like controlling Popo: use the Directional Pad to move, press the A Button to jump, and press the B Button to swing your hammer. However, the Start Button and Select Button are only functional on Controller 1.

Game Modes

Ice Climber offers two game modes:

A 2-Player game requires the use of a second controller. The player using Controller 1 plays as Popo, while the player using Controller 2 plays as Nana. 2-Player games can be cooperative or competitive, depending on how the players use their respective characters.

A Precarious Partnership

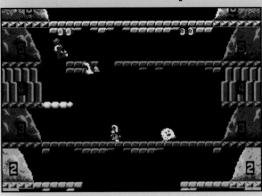

Popo and Nana make a great team, but they can also work against each other. If you're feeling cooperative, avoid climbing too far ahead of your partner, and look for opportunities to protect your ally from hostile creatures. Feeling competitive? Prove your superior climbing skills by outscoring your opponent as you race to the top of the mountain.

Progressing through the Game

Mountains

Ice Climbers takes place across 32 different mountains, each of which is divided into eight numbered floors and a large bonus stage. To conquer a mountain, you must climb past all eight floors and enter the bonus stage. From that point on—whether or not you successfully complete the bonus stage—you're guaranteed to move on to the next mountain in the sequence.

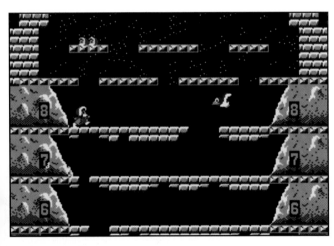

Numbered Floors

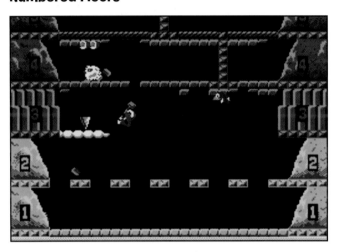

Although bonus stages can be very challenging, a mountain's numbered floors hold its greatest dangers. Until you overcome Floor 8 on a given mountain, taking damage or falling off the screen results in the loss of your climber. A mountain is considered conquered the moment you've overcome all eight of its numbered floors and entered the bonus stage.

An Endless Challenge

Once you've conquered Mountain 32, you're transported to Mountain 33. However, this is simply a more challenging version of Mountain 01; from this point on, the sequence repeats, and your adventure takes place across previously conquered mountains.

Game Over

You start a 1-Player game with a total of four Popos—one in play and three in reserve. When Popo collides with an enemy, touches a hazard, or falls off the bottom of the screen, he disappears and a new Popo takes his place. When you run out of Popos, the game ends and you're returned to the Main menu.

A 2-Player game follows similar rules. Player 1 starts out with a total of four Popos; Player 2 begins with four Nanas. The game ends when all Popos and Nanas have been lost.

Bonus Stage

Each time you conquer a mountain's eighth floor, you begin a bonus stage. In a bonus stage, your primary goal is to reach the Condor above the mountain within the allotted time. Each bonus stage also contains vegetables that you can collect for extra points. A bonus stage ends when you grab on to the Condor, fall off the screen, or run out of time. There's no penalty for failing to clear a bonus stage—falling (or running out of time) doesn't cost you a climber, and you'll receive credit for any vegetables you managed to collect before leaving the mountain.

Basic Gameplay

Moving

Use the Directional Pad to move left and right. Release the Directional Pad to stand still. Be aware that it takes longer to stop or change direction when moving on icy platforms. Unless an obstacle (like a pillar) is blocking your path, you can also move past the border of the area to appear on the opposite side of the screen.

Jumping

Use jumps to leap over enemies, move between platforms, or destroy overhead blocks. During a jump, your climber's hammer is automatically raised above his or her head—this means that each jump also serves as an upward attack.

Striking

Perform strikes to damage enemies and objects directly in front of your climber. Use strikes to defeat Nitpickers, stun Toppies, or shatter chunks of ice—just know that you cannot perform strikes while jumping or falling.

CHARACTERS AND OBJECTS

Climbers

Popo

With his blue parka, trusty hammer, and impressive jumping skills, Popo is more than a match for any mountain. Popo is the only hero who appears in a 1-Player game. In a 2-Player game, the player using Controller 1 controls Popo.

Nana

Apart from her signature pink parka, Nana possesses all the same skills and equipment as her climbing partner. Nana appears only in 2-Player games, and is always controlled by the player using Controller 2.

Creatures

Topi

These shaggy creatures are often found on numbered floors. Toppies aren't inherently aggressive, but that doesn't mean they aren't dangerous—colliding with a roaming Topi will cost you a climber. Strike a Topi with your hammer (rendering it temporarily harmless), or simply keep your distance from these troublesome critters.

Toppies also tend to repair and maintain their habitats. Each time a patrolling Topi encounters a gap, it races to the nearest cave and emerges with a large chunk of ice. If left to its own devices, a Topi will use chunks of ice to patch each and every hole on its floor.

Point Value: Topi
Toppies can be stunned, but they can't be defeated. No points are awarded for striking a Topi.

Nitpicker

These troublesome birds are fiercely territorial and surprisingly persistent. Colliding with a Nitpicker will cost you a climber, and dodging a Nitpicker usually results in the enemy circling back around for another pass. Use a well-timed hammer strike to knock a Nitpicker out of the air, or move directly under a Nitpicker and jump straight up to hit the bird with an upward attack.

Point Value: Nitpicker
You receive 800 points for each Nitpicker you defeat during a climb.

Polar Bear

The Polar Bear enjoys nothing more than pestering struggling climbers. This meddling bear shows itself only after you've spent a significant amount of time on a mountain—the longer you linger on a mountain's numbered floors, the more likely it is you'll encounter a Polar Bear. Soon after it appears, the Polar Bear leaps into the air and crashes down with enough force to push the lowest visible floor off the screen. Move quickly to reach safe ground before that happens.

If you're fast enough, you can interrupt a Polar Bear's attack by striking it with your climber's hammer. A successful hit stuns the creature, forcing it to leave the mountain. However, this retreat is temporary. Given enough time, a foiled Polar Bear will return and attempt another attack.

Point Value: Polar Bear
No points are awarded for driving a Polar Bear from the mountain.

Condor

This massive bird not only keeps bonus stages stocked with vegetables, it also circles the peak of each mountain you climb. Once you reach the top of a mountain, jump up and grab on to the Condor to earn some serious bonus points.

Point Value: Condor
The points awarded for reaching a Condor vary depending on how many mountains you've already conquered.

Hazards

Topi Ice

Toppies use chunks of ice to fill any holes in their respective floors. Upon reaching a gap, a single chunk of Topi ice can fill a gap up to two blocks wide. Colliding with one of these jagged bits of ice before it's converted into terrain costs you a climber. You can simply keep your distance—allowing a Topi to complete its repairs—or you can destroy an ice chunk by striking it with your climber's hammer.

Point Value: Ice
You receive 400 points for each piece of Topi ice you destroy during a climb.

Icicle

Icicles sometimes form below clouds or blocks of terrain. Soon after it appears, an icicle breaks loose and falls straight down. Although it's possible to destroy a falling icicle, it's generally easier (and much safer) to simply move out of its path. If you spot water accumulating overhead, step aside—it won't be long until that water freezes into a fully formed icicle.

Point Value: Icicle
No points are awarded for destroying an icicle.

Vegetables

Each bonus stage contains four vegetables that you can collect for extra points. Your starting mountain (the mountain you selected on the Main menu) always features eggplants. Subsequent mountains offer carrots, cabbages, cucumbers, corn, turnips, pumpkins, Chinese cabbages, potatoes, and mushrooms—in that order. Once you've successfully completed 10 mountains, eggplants reappear and the cycle repeats.

Eggplant

Carrot

Cabbage

Cucumber

Corn

Turnip

Pumpkin

Chinese Cabbage

Potato

Mushroom

Point Value: Vegetables
The points awarded for collecting a vegetable vary depending on how many mountains you've already conquered. However, collecting at least one ear of corn during a bonus phase always adds an extra climber to your reserves.

TERRAIN

Climbing is all about negotiating tricky terrain, and each mountain features its own combination of vital footholds and troublesome obstacles. A proper understanding of terrain helps you identify the fastest and easiest path to the top of a mountain.

Floors

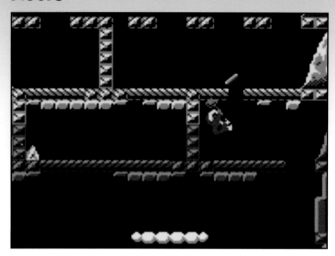

Some floors can be broken, while others are impenetrable. Some floors allow you a chance to stop and catch your breath, while others carry unsuspecting climbers to nearby gaps. Luckily, each type of floor features its own distinct appearance.

Color-Coded

A floor's color indicates whether it's made of grass (green), dirt (brown), or ice (blue). Icy floors offer less traction than floors made of grass or dirt, increasing the time it takes for a running climber to stop or change direction.

Standard Floors

Standard floors rank among the most reliable footholds a climber could hope to find on a mountain. As luck would have it, they're also quite common.

Breakable Floors

Breakable floors are made up of destructible blocks of terrain. To create a hole in a breakable floor, simply stand below it and jump—your hammer does the rest!

Unbreakable Floors

Unbreakable floors are made up of indestructible beveled blocks. They serve as excellent footholds, but also make effective obstacles. When you reach an unbreakable floor, your only option is to find a path around it.

Moving Floors

Moving floors act like conveyer belts. If a climber stands on a moving floor, it won't be long before he or she is carried to a nearby gap and dropped to the floors below. In many cases, you can counteract the effect of a moving floor by running in the opposite direction. However, some moving floors are faster than others.

When running isn't enough to overcome the pull of a moving floor, perform a series of jumps to minimize the floor's effect on your climber.

Breakable Moving Floors

Breakable moving floors feature a pattern of uniform diagonal lines. If the lines are angled downward from left to right, the floor moves to the right. If the lines are angled downward from right to left, the floor moves to the left. To create a hole in a breakable moving floor, jump up and hit it from below.

Unbreakable Moving Floors

Unbreakable moving floors feature a pattern of irregular diagonal lines over a row of indestructible beveled blocks. Again, the diagonal lines indicate in which direction a floor moves: if the diagonal lines are angled downward from left to right, the floor moves to the right. Otherwise, it moves to the left.

Clouds

In lieu of solid ground, passing clouds can make serviceable (but temporary) footholds. Some clouds move much faster than others, but even the slowest cloud offers only enough time for a jump or two before it carries your climber out of position. A cloud always passes through at least one obstacle before it reaches the border of the area, ensuring that any onboard climbers are knocked off a cloud before it reappears on the opposite edge of the screen.

In most cases, clouds serve as helpful platforms. However, clouds that pass along floors can scoop up unsuspecting climbers, carrying them away from hard-earned footholds or into nearby hazards. It's also worth noting that a climber can't pass through the bottom of a cloud—colliding with an overhead cloud interrupts your climber's jump, increasing the chances of a costly fall.

Big Cloud

In general, the larger the cloud, the easier it is to jump onto.

Group of Clouds

You'll sometimes encounter a group of clouds moving as a single unit.

Small Cloud

Landing on a small cloud takes precision timing—particularly if it's moving quickly.

Pillars

Pillars are essentially indestructible walls. They feature the same beveled blocks found in other unbreakable terrain—just stacked vertically!

SCORING

Destroying Terrain

Destroying a block of terrain is always awarded with points, but the value for each block varies by mountain. To determine the exact value of a given block, multiply the number assigned to your current mountain by 10 points. This means that destroying a block of terrain on Mountain 01 is worth 10 points, while destroying a block on Mountain 32 is worth 320 points.

Point Values: Destroying Terrain

Location	Point Value (Per Block)
Mountain 01	10
Mountain 02	20
Mountain 03	30
Mountain 04	40
Mountain 05	50
Mountain 06	60
Mountain 07	70
Mountain 08	80
Mountain 09	90
Mountain 10	100
Mountain 11	110
Mountain 12	120
Mountain 13	130
Mountain 14	140
Mountain 15	150
Mountain 16	160
Mountain 17	170
Mountain 18	180
Mountain 19	190
Mountain 20	200
Mountain 21	210
Mountain 22	220
Mountain 23	230
Mountain 24	240
Mountain 25	250
Mountain 26	260
Mountain 27	270
Mountain 28	280
Mountain 29	290
Mountain 30	300
Mountain 31	310
Mountain 32	320

Because you can start your game on any mountain—and because you'll never run out of new climbs to attempt—the ultimate goal of *Ice Climber* is to score as many points as you can before you run out of climbers. Each time you conquer a mountain, any points you earned during your climb are added to your total score. Bonus stages offer the best opportunities to earn points, but there are a few other ways to boost your score throughout each climb.

Fixed Point Values

Some actions award a set amount of points, no matter when or how you perform them:

- You receive 400 points for each piece of Topi ice you smash.
- You receive 800 points for each Nitpicker you defeat.

Variable Point Values

Actions like destroying terrain, collecting vegetables, or grabbing a Condor reward different point values, depending on when or how you perform them.

Collecting Vegetables

The number of points awarded for collecting a vegetable varies based on how many bonus stages you've already reached. This means that while progressing through mountains yields more valuable vegetables, the specific mountain has no effect on how many points are awarded for collecting a vegetable.

Point Values: Collecting Vegetables

Location	Point Value (Per Vegetable)
First bonus stage	300
Second bonus stage	500
Third bonus stage	600
Fourth bonus stage	700
Fifth bonus stage	800
Sixth bonus stage	1000
Seventh bonus stage	2000
Eighth bonus stage	3000
Ninth bonus stage	4000
Tenth+ bonus stage	5000

Grabbing the Condor

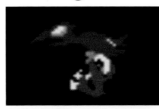

As with collecting vegetables, the number of points awarded for successfully grabbing a Condor varies based on how many bonus stages you've already reached in your current game.

Point Values: Grabbing the Condor

Location	Point Value
First bonus stage	3000
Second bonus stage	5000
Third bonus stage	6000
Fourth bonus stage	7000
Fifth bonus stage	8000
Sixth bonus stage	10,000
Seventh bonus stage	20,000
Eighth bonus stage	30,000
Ninth bonus stage	40,000
Tenth+ bonus stage	50,000

TIPS AND TRICKS
General Tips

Breakable floors often feature some sections that are thinner than others. When you need to create a hole, you can save a bit of time by attacking these weak spots. This tactic is especially useful when you need to break through terrain before a cloud carries you out of position.

Popo (and Nana) can jump much farther vertically than horizontally. Before you attempt a running leap, check for overhead obstacles that might knock you out of the air mid-jump. Precision jumping is the key to effective climbing, so take some time to master various jumps on early mountains. With a bit of practice, you can learn to identify which footholds offer the easiest route up any mountain.

When you attack an enemy, make sure that only your climber's hammer makes contact with your target. This is especially important when you use an upward attack to clear out a Nitpicker or icicle.

When a replacement climber first appears on a mountain, he or she is invulnerable to damage. This effect lasts until you take control of your climber, giving you plenty of time to decide when and how to resume your climb.

Just because an obstacle is blocking your path, don't expect it to hinder your enemies. Toppies can slip right past pillars, and Nitpickers have no problem flying around unbreakable floors.

Smashing Topi ice is a great way to earn some extra points, but it's sometimes best to let a Topi complete its repairs—new terrain can serve as extra footholds, reducing the chances of a costly fall.

Once it reaches a gap, Topi ice takes the basic form of the surrounding terrain. However, a patched area is always breakable. For example, if a Topi fills an existing gap in an unbreakable moving floor, the patched area appears as a breakable moving floor.

Remember that collecting at least one ear of corn from a bonus stage adds an extra climber to your reserves. The fifth bonus stage you reach always contains corn, and you won't find more until you reach your fifteenth bonus stage. Your reserves never display more than three climbers, but don't worry—any additional climbers you manage to earn appear when they're needed.

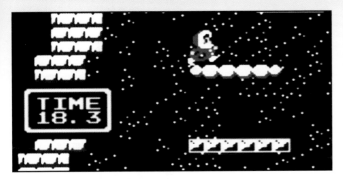

During a bonus stage, reaching the Condor is always worth far more points than collecting all the available vegetables. If you're in danger of running out of time, consider abandoning any remaining vegetables to improve your chances of reaching the top of the bonus stage.

2-Player Tips

Scores for each player are kept separately, so points are awarded only to the player who earned them. If you're playing cooperatively, consider sharing high-value targets like vegetables with your climbing partner. This is especially important if a bonus stage contains corn—a player who fails to collect at least one ear of corn won't receive an extra climber.

During cooperative play, try to stay within a floor or two of your climbing partner. The terrain shifts to keep pace with the leading climber—moving too quickly can force your partner off the screen, costing them one of their climbers. Of course, outpacing your opponent is the simplest way to gain an advantage during competitive play.

Two climbers can't occupy the same space at the same time, and mid-air collisions cause climbing partners to bounce away from each other. During cooperative play, try to give your partner enough space to move freely. During competitive play, you can use this feature to prevent your opponent from reaching his or her intended footholds.

If your partner is having trouble making a high jump, use your climber to give them a boost. Move under an airborne ally and jump straight up—a properly timed collision can launch your partner to new heights.

SUPER MARIO BROS.

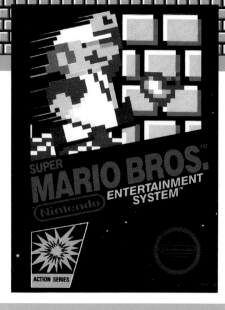

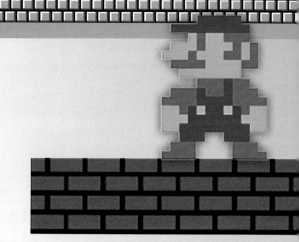

Developer:
Nintendo R&D1

Director:
Shigeru Miyamoto

Designers:
Shigeru Miyamoto, Takashi Tezuka

Programmers:
Toshihiko Nakago, Kazuaki Morita

Composer:
Koji Kondo

Original Release Date:
September 13, 1985 Famicom JP;
1985 NES US

SUMMARY

"One day the kingdom of the peaceful Mushroom People was invaded by the Koopa, a tribe of turtles famous for their black magic. The quiet, peace-loving Mushroom People were turned into mere stones, bricks, and even field horse-hair plants, and the Mushroom Kingdom fell into ruin.

"The only one who can undo the magic spell on the Mushroom People and return them to their normal selves is the Princess Toadstool, the daughter of the Mushroom King. Unfortunately, she is presently in the hands of the great Koopa turtle king.

"Mario, the hero of the story, hears about the Mushroom People's plight and sets out on a quest to free the Mushroom Princess from the evil Koopa King and restore the fallen kingdom of the Mushroom People.

"You are Mario! It's up to you to save the Mushroom People from the black magic of the Koopa!"

LEVELS

Super Mario Bros. has all sorts of challenges to overcome and plenty of secrets to find. We've picked the toughest and most secret-heavy stages to cover in this section. If you've wondered how to beat one of King Koopa's many castles, or where to find the ultra-secret Warp Zones, wonder no more! We've got you covered.

World 1-1

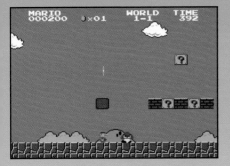

1 You'll meet your first Goomba here. Stomp him! Just make sure there aren't any Blocks overhead when you do!

2 Stand on the sixth Block from the edge of the last pipe and jump! A 1-Up appears!

3 This is where you meet your first Koopa Troopa. Use the same tactics you used on the Goombas and jump on its head! Just watch out! If you hit it while it's in its shell, it can bounce back at you.

World 1-2

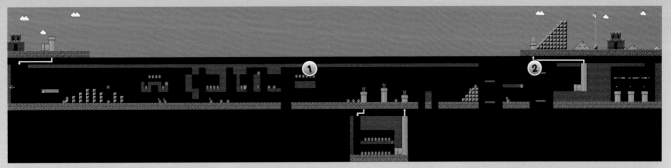

1 Hop onto the Block to the left of the pit, then jump to Blocks to the right of the pit. Head to the far-right side of the Block and jump up. You reveal a hidden 1-Up! Now immediately try to punch out the Block to the right of the 1-Up to get it to drop. If you don't, you must race the 1-Up to a pit near the end of the level.

2 When you reach the platforms moving vertically, you can jump on the one to the right and use it to jump onto the Blocks above the exit pipe. Keep heading right to find your first Warp Zone! Use this location to immediately warp to Worlds 2, 3, or 4.

World 1-4

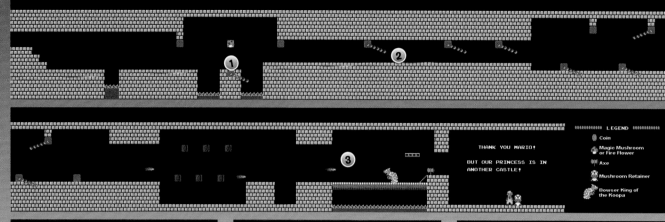

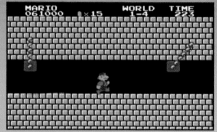

LEGEND

1 This Fire Bar rotates! Beginners should jump over it and ignore the "?" Block next to it. Experts can go for the Power-Up inside the "?" Block, if they are feeling daring. Note that the Power-Up will come out of the Block to the right, so make sure to plan accordingly.

2 These Fire Bars may look difficult, but they're actually a breeze to get past. Watch your timing, and run when the bars are horizontal.

3 There are two ways to defeat the horrible King Koopa: either pummel him with fireballs as Fiery Mario, or get past him and grab the axe behind him. If you want to reach the axe, run and jump on the platform above him or run underneath him when he jumps. Jumping over him is usually the better strategy.

World 2-1

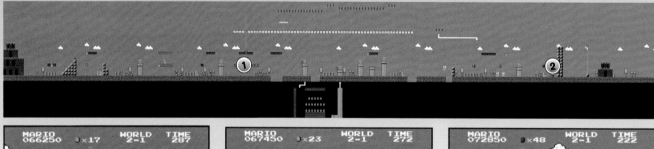

1 You can find a beanstalk leading to Coin Heaven in this stage. Just hit the Block shown in our screenshot, climb the beanstalk, and a wealth of coins will be within your grasp.

While riding on the platform, make sure to let go of any coins that you miss while jumping. Jumping back for a missed coin almost certainly guarantees that you miss even more coins up ahead.

2 You encounter a new type of obstacle here: the spring. We say obstacle, but it's really a traversal tool that helps Mario reach new heights. The reason we've even referred to them as obstacles is because managing them can be extremely dangerous, especially when next to a pit. You must use precise timing while on a spring if you want to actually launch into the air. It's incredibly easy to jump on a spring thinking you're about to rocket into space, but instead short hop directly into an enemy or a pit. Make sure to give a spring a few practice bounces before using it to launch over an obstacle. You need to get your timing right before the main event!

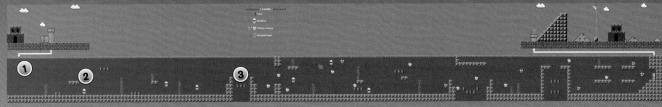

World 2-2

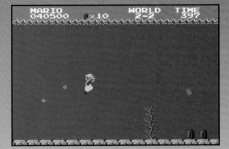

① World 2-2 is your first swimming stage in Super Mario Bros. and you'll immediately notice how differently Mario controls under water versus on dry land. Press jump to swim upward, or don't press it to slowly sink to the bottom of the screen. There are a ton of new underwater hazards to contend with in stages like these, so get good and comfortable with swimming before you progress through the level.

② One of the new underwater enemies you meet is a tricky squid named "Blooper." Bloopers always fight to be on the same level as Mario, so they sink when Mario is below them and quickly swim upward when Mario is above them. When they travel in groups, they can be a particular pain to get around. You must constantly predict where they are going to move to get around them.

③ Underwater pits are just as deadly as pits on dry land, with one little caveat: they drag Mario down as he swims over them. That means you must prepare to swim aggressively whenever over a pit to keep Mario from being pulled to the Davy Jones' Locker. Calculate the risk before trying to nab those all-too-tempting golden coins hovering above each pit.

World 2-4

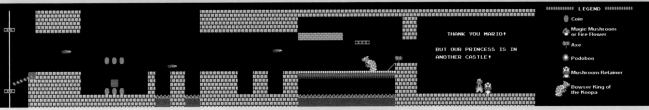

THANK YOU MARIO!

BUT OUR PRINCESS IS IN ANOTHER CASTLE!

●●●●●●●●● LEGEND ●●●●●●●●●

- 🪙 Coin
- 🍄 Magic Mushroom or Fire Flower
- 🪓 Axe
- 🔥 Podoboo
- 👤 Mushroom Retainer
- 🐢 Bowser King of the Koopa

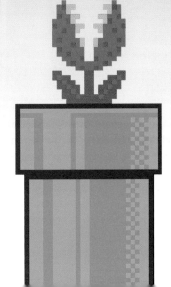

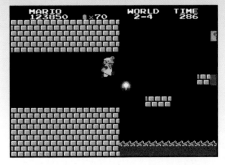

① Watch for the Podoboos when you jump onto these Blocks above the pit. The "?" Block contains a Power-Up, but it can be tricky to get. Jump from the far-right Block in the center Block set to reach it safely.

② Here are a few points to help you successfully negotiate the lifts. Before you jump, get to the edge. If you're not right at the edge, you'll bump your head on the roof and fall into the bottomless pit. You also have to be quick to avoid the Fire Bars.

World 3-1

(1) World 3-1 is the best place to obtain unlimited 1-Ups. Get to the stairs at the end of the stage and jump on the second Koopa Troopa. Leave it in its shell, then jump on the left side of its shell to knock it into the step. If your timing is perfect, Mario will bounce off the shell automatically and you earn unlimited 1-Ups.

World 3-4

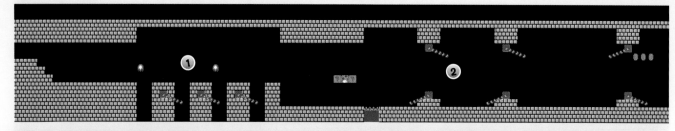

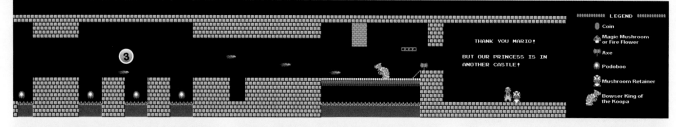

THANK YOU MARIO!

BUT OUR PRINCESS IS IN ANOTHER CASTLE!

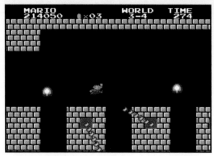

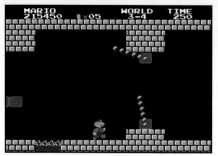

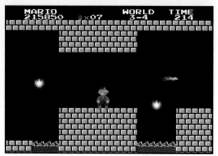

(1) Podoboos are shooting out of these pits, so proceed with the utmost caution. Time your jumps carefully and cross the area when the Fire Bars are pointing down.

(2) These four Fire Bars are rotating in different directions. Needless to say, they are deadly! Stay to the left and observe them for a moment. Learn their patterns, then carefully jump ahead.

(3) These pits all contain Podoboos and King Koopa's fire breath is headed your way. If things get too hot, seek refuge in the small alcove to the right of the pits.

World 4-2

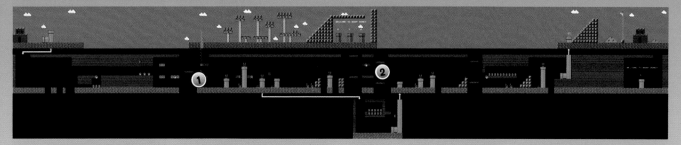

(1) There are two different Warp Zones in World 4-2; the area under this Block set leads to the first one. There are several hidden Blocks here and one of the visible Blocks conceals a beanstalk that takes you to the Warp Zone. You must hit the hidden Blocks in order to reach the beanstalk, so carefully analyze our screenshots to see when and where to hit them.

This Warp Zone provides access to Worlds 6, 7, and 8.

(2) The second Warp Zone can be found just like the first Warp Zone from World 1-2. As soon as you reach these platforms, jump onto the top of the level and head to the right. You eventually come to a lone pipe that leads to World 5.

VINTAGE ADVICE

Some of the tips in this chapter came from an issue of Nintendo Power magazine from back in the day! Do you remember reading this Counselor's Corner feature?

World 4-4

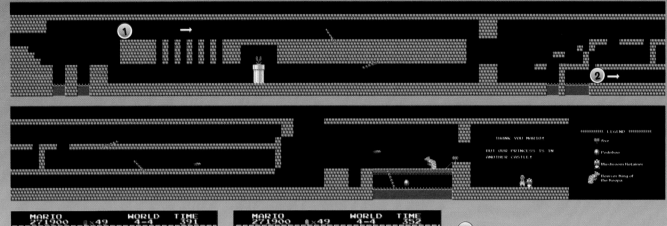

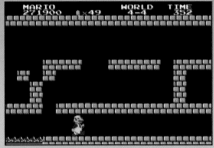

① There are two paths you can choose from at the start of this Castle stage. The lower hall is a trap. You'll be stuck there with no hope of escape. Use the top route and follow it to safety!

If you don't take the correct route, you'll be doomed to repeat this stage!

② When you reach this fork, make sure to take the lower path, which leads straight to King Koopa.

World 5-4

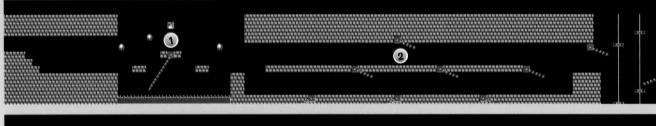

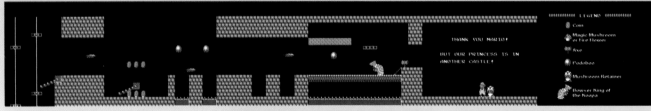

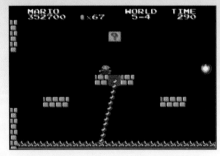

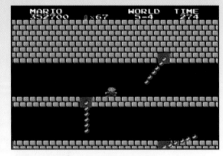

① This Fire Bar is twice as long as usual! No matter where you stand on the Blocks, it will get you. The only way to clear it is to jump over it with precise timing. If you get stuck, jump on the "?" Block, and jump as the Fire Bar approaches.

② These Fire Bars are very close together. Clear them one at a time.

World 6-4

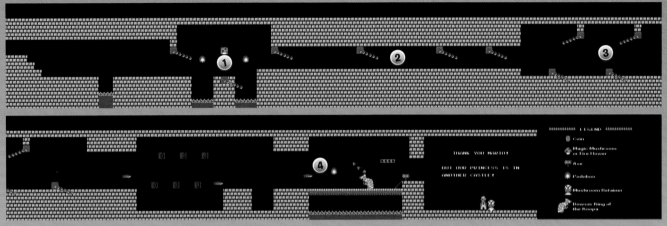

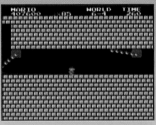
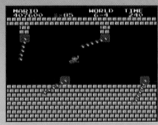
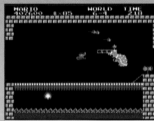

1 You'll find this situation familiar, but the Fire Bar rotates to the left. And the Podoboos appear more frequently. It's a challenging combination!

2 You must contend with a low ceiling and Fire Bars that rotate to the left! Clear the Fire Bars one at a time.

3 This is like World 5-4, but far more challenging. The upper and lower Fire Bars rotate in different directions. Jump when the lower Fire Bar is moving toward you and the upper Fire Bar is moving away.

4 Starting in this world, the evil Bowser comes equipped with hammers. It's much more difficult to survive because the hammers can hit you on top of the lift. Beware!

World 7-4

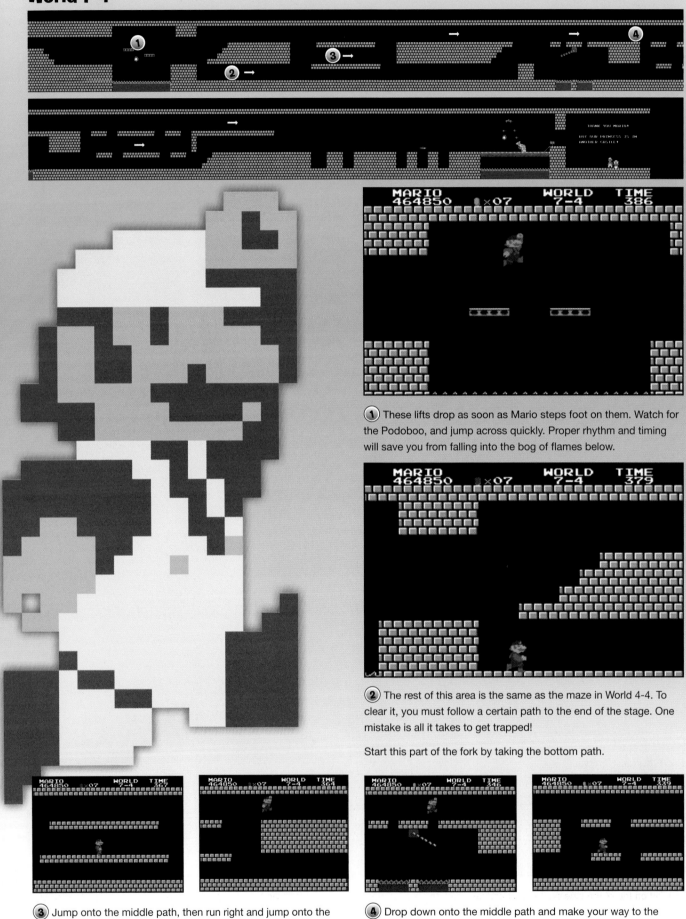

① These lifts drop as soon as Mario steps foot on them. Watch for the Podoboo, and jump across quickly. Proper rhythm and timing will save you from falling into the bog of flames below.

② The rest of this area is the same as the maze in World 4-4. To clear it, you must follow a certain path to the end of the stage. One mistake is all it takes to get trapped!

Start this part of the fork by taking the bottom path.

③ Jump onto the middle path, then run right and jump onto the upper path ahead.

④ Drop down onto the middle path and make your way to the right. Jump up onto the upper path ahead and you're home free!

World 8-2

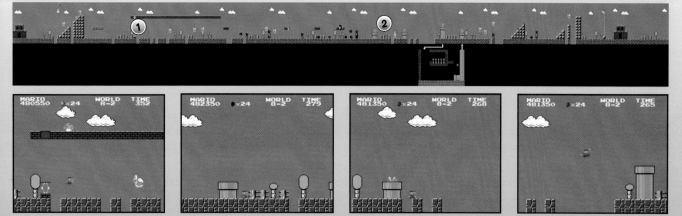

① There's a 1-Up in the Block directly above the spring. Break the Block to the right of the 1-Up Block to have it drop down to your level. If you're not Super Mario, you must follow the 1-Up to the right until it falls off of the row of Blocks.

② There are two ways to clear these pits. The first is to stand near the left pipe and make a running jump over the second pipe. When Mario lands, immediately make another jump from the second tiny flat.

Another way is to get down on the first tiny flat and make a running jump over the pits. No matter which way you choose, timing and the length of your jumps determine your fate.

World 8-4

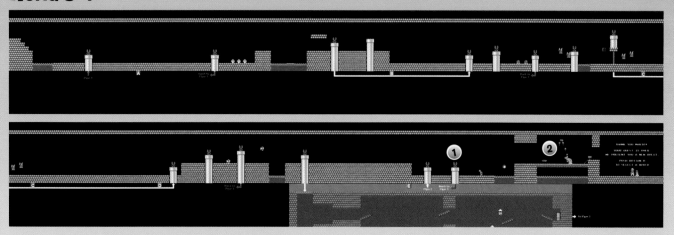

This castle scene is divided into five zones. Three out of the five do not lead to anywhere. Use the pipe to reach the next zone. Some pipes take you to the beginning of the stage, instead of letting you through to the next zone. This stage is truly a maze!

Use the map to find the path through this treacherous level. Note that walking past the B zone takes you back to A; walking past the C zone takes you back to B; and walking past the E zone takes you back to D. Choose the pipes shown on the map to go directly to the King of Koopas himself, Bowser!

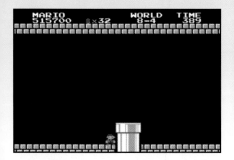 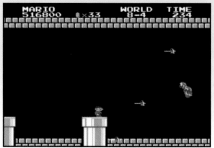 

① Get on top of the pipe on the right and take time to observe the movement of the Hammer Bros. If they don't throw their hammers while they jump, it's a good time to make your move. Use a running jump to get behind them and quickly jump over the lava pit.

② The only thing that stands between you and Princess Toadstool is Bowser! You know how to beat him—you've been training for this moment! Defeat Bowser and save the princess! You can do it!

THE EARLY PERIOD (1986)

During 1986, Nintendo's focus was to bring arcade-quality experiences to the console market with the NES. It was during this time that we saw ports of popular arcade titles like *Donkey Kong, Balloon Fight,* and the original *Mario Bros.*

But not all of the titles released during this time were arcade ports. Nintendo also released a Light Gun title *Gumshoe,* a motorcycle racing game called *Mach Rider,* a two-player competitive fighting game called *Urban Champion,* and several others. Nintendo also started developing relationships with third-party developers who would later become creators of some the system's most memorable titles.

This was a year of growth for Nintendo. Whether or not the NES would be a success in North America was proven this year with consoles sales reaching over a million total consoles sold. It was the start of something big. Nintendo had begun to turn people's feelings around toward video games and that positive turn would only grow exponentially from here.

Donkey Kong
June 1986

"Can you save Mario's girl from the clutches of Donkey Kong?

Donkey Kong has kidnapped Pauline and taken her to the top of a construction site! It's up to you to help Mario save Pauline before time runs out. But it won't be easy. Donkey Kong will do everything in his power to stop you. He'll throw barrel bombs, flaming fireballs, and everything else he can get his hands on. So if you're looking for action, don't monkey around. Get the original DONKEY KONG from Nintendo Arcade Classics Series."

Donkey Kong Jr.
June 1986

"Can Donkey Kong Jr. save his papa from Mario's prison?

Mario has gone mad! He's turned the tables on Donkey Kong and locked him in a cage. It's up to you, as Donkey Kong Jr., to rescue your father by stealing Mario's set of keys. But it won't be easy. You'll have to fight off ape-eating Snapjaws, jump onto moving islands, and break through a jungle of vines to get to the keys that will free Donkey Kong. Can you handle the action? Because this off-the-wall monkey business will have you going bananas!"

Donkey Kong Jr. Math
June 1986

"Learning is fun when you make a game of it!

Are you good with numbers? Well, here's your chance to prove it. Use your brains to help Donkey Kong Junior add, subtract, divide, and multiply correctly. And to make it more of a challenge, you'll have to climb up chains, jump on islands, and choose the right answers in the least amount of time! Play against the computer, or challenge a friend. Either way, you'll learn a lot, and no one will ever make a monkey out of you. At least when it comes to numbers."

Donkey Kong 3
June 1986

"Look out for flying coconuts! Donkey Kong is on the loose!

Donkey Kong is at it again! This times he's loose in the greenhouse. And he's got company: A swarm of pesky bees. It's up to you to get Donkey Kong out of the greenhouse and exterminate the bees—without hurting the flowers. But that's easier said than done. Because Donkey Kong has plenty of coconuts to hurl at you. And those bees know just where to sting you so it hurts. But if you keep your wits about you, you'll score lots of points and have lots of laughs in the best Donkey Kong of them all—DONKEY KONG 3."

Mario Bros.
June 1986

"You'll need lightning-fast reactions to get out of this pipeline adventure alive!

Mario and Luigi are doing some underground plumbing when all sorts of weird creatures come flying out of the pipes. Turtles, crabs—even fighterflies—attack the helpless Mario Bros. It's up to you to kick, punch, and knock out these sewer pests before time runs out! But beware. Just when you think you got rid of them, they come back for more! Play against the computer, or with a friend—either way, this is one underground classic you'll want to play time and time again!"

Popeye
June 1986

"Now you're the King of Spinach in a battle for Olive's love!

Are you ready to climb ladders, jump landings, eat spinach, and punch out Brutus, Seahag, and the flying Bernard? Because that's what it takes to win Olive Oyl's hand in marriage. You'll score points by defeating your enemies and collecting the "love tokens" Olive drops from her window. The more you collect, the more points you'll score and the faster you'll win her love. But watch out. Around every corner lurks another jealous suitor. You'll have to think with your head as well as your heart to win this fast action love affair!"

Balloon Fight
August 1986

"You'll need lightning fast reactions to win this battle in the sky!

Take to the skies! It's BALLOON FIGHT. You'll score lots of points and have loads of fun when you burst enemy balloons and send their parachutes crashing into the sea. But beware. These hot-air invaders have an amazing ability to land safely, blow up another balloon, and come back stronger than before! What's more, if you fly too low you'll be devoured by man-eating sharks! Challenge them alone if you think you're up to it, or team up with a friend. Either way, you'll have the time of your life fighting off your opponents in the sky and avoiding those hungry sharks below in BALLOON FIGHT!"

Gumshoe
August 1986

"You'll have to shoot fast to get out of this Light Gun game alive!

Jennifer's been kidnapped! Now's your chance to prove you're a sharp-shooting detective by helping Jennifer's father find the five diamonds that will pay her ransom. You'll use your Zapper light gun to blow away anything that gets in your way. But even with the Zapper, this case will be hard to crack. Because not only are the diamonds hard to find, but you only have 24 hours to find them! What's more, you'll have to think fast and shoot even faster, because ferocious monsters, diving airplanes, and hungry man-eating sharks will stop at nothing to prevent you from getting to the diamonds. Think you're a sharp shooting detective? Well, you'd better be. Because if you're not, it's curtains for you in this quick-on-the-trigger Nintendo Light Gun game!"

Mach Rider
August 1986

"It's a thrilling race to save the planet—on a course you can create yourself!

Grip the handles of your futuristic motorcycle. Feel the freezing wind crack against your cheeks. Suddenly you're off! Riding at speeds up to 500 miles per hour in a desperate race to save the planet. You'll love every hair pin curve because you've created this daredevil course yourself. Along the way you'll be challenged by an endless array of ruthless villains who will do everything in their power to destroy you and your planet. You'll defend yourself with a specially mounted Power Blaster. But watch out! The action is fast. The danger is imminent. Design your own course or ride one of ours, in this lightning fast Nintendo Programmable game!"

Urban Champion
August 1986

"Think you're tough, huh?

Well, you'd better be. Because you've got to be quick on your feet and fast with your hands to knock your opponent off the screen and become the next URBAN CHAMPION. Play by yourself or challenge a friend, either way you'll have a knockout time defeating the toughest guys in the neighborhood in URBAN CHAMPION."

BALLOON FIGHT

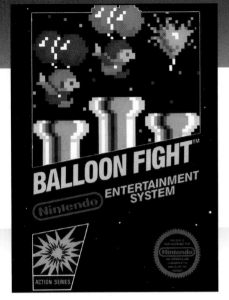

CREATORS

Developer
Nintendo R&D1

Director
Yoshio Sakamoto

Programmer
Satoru Iwata

Composer
Hirokazu Tanaka

Original Release Date
1984 Arcade JP; August
1986 NES US

SUMMARY

You play as the Balloon Fighter: a man with a dream of flight! With two balloons strapped to your back, you're free to take flight and soar through the skies. Or you would be if it weren't for a group of territorial Birds that want to blast you out of the sky.

Balloon Fight is a physics-based action game through and through. You contend with intertia and momentum just as much as enemies and obstacles. The faster you move in one direction, the harder it is to change directions. It's because of these elements, and the charming music and character designs, that *Balloon Fight* has stood in the hearts of those who've played it as a true classic. Even after a years-long hiatus, we came back to this game and found it just as gripping to chase high scores as we did the first time we played it.

HOW-TO

You start the game with two balloons. Your goal is to fly through each Phase and pop the balloons of all the enemies without having your balloons popped in the process. If you have a balloon popped, it stays popped until you lose the second balloon and start with a new man, or until you reach one of the Bonus Phases that appears every fourth Phase.

Flying and Fighting

To fly, you have to flap. How fast you flap depends on what button you press and how fast you press it. Holding the B Button allows you to flap swiftly, while tapping the A Button performs a single flap per press.

To get into the air quickly, hold B if the sky above you is clear of enemy Birds. But if things are a little tight and you need to maneuver between several Birds and obstacles, tapping the A Button is your best bet.

In order to complete each Phase, you must defeat all the Birds on the screen. To do this, pop their balloons by landing on them. The Birds can return the favor, so position yourself above the Birds whenever possible.

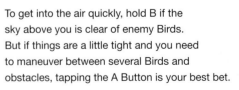

Controls

Directional Pad: Used to move left or right. Up and down have no function in this game.

A Button: Flap once for every press. Used for more precise flying.

B Button: Hold to continuously flap. Used to flap swiftly and fly through the air faster.

Start Button: Used on the Main Menu to start the game. Also used to pause the game during gameplay.

Select Button: Used to select the game mode while on the Main Menu.

Bird Tiers

If a Bird succeeds in repumping its balloon, it progresses the next tier of Bird.

Red Birds > Green Birds > Yellow Birds

Yellow Birds are the apex predator in this game, so once a Bird achieves yellow status, its progress stops, even if it repumps its balloon.

Once you've popped a Bird's balloon, the Bird parachutes down to the ground. After it lands, if left alone for too long, it pumps up another balloon. If it succeeds, it becomes a tougher Bird, making your job of clearing the screen that much harder. To prevent this, hit the Bird's parachute while it's falling, or hit the Bird while it's on the ground. It's also possible for a parachuting Bird to fall into the water found at the bottom of each Phase. If that happens, the Bird is defeated, same as if you had stomped on it yourself, but you don't gain any points for the defeated Bird.

Enemies and Obstacles

The world is a dangerous place for a Balloon Fighter. This section includes descriptions for all enemies and obstacles you encounter during your time with *Balloon Fight*.

Red Birds

Red Birds are, without a doubt, the easiest enemy in the game. Their strategy involves apathetically flapping around in place, maybe drifting a little to the left or right, but ultimately being completely aimless. Perhaps they are pacifists trying to bring the Bird/Balloon Fighter conflict to an end through talk instead of combat. Maybe they are simply looking to observe the world from the air and got caught in this aerial battle. Or maybe they just don't have the confidence to pop the Balloon Fighter's balloons and instead float pensively, hoping one day to have the boldness to fight like their brothers in arms. Whatever their motivation, they pose little threat to you so long as you don't fly directly below them.

Green Birds

It's said the Green Birds are Red Birds who tapped into their own ambitious nature. While not of the same caliber as the all-too-deadly Yellow Bird, the Green Birds make a concerted effort to bring down the Balloon Fighter. Instead of listlessly drifting through the air, the Green Birds slowly drift in your direction. They are easy enough to avoid and defeat, but if they group up with any other Bird-types, they can be a real bother.

Yellow Birds

Barons of the skies, the Yellow Birds are as deadly as they are pastel. They chase down the Balloon Fighter with unending fervor and energy. They are faster than the other Bird-types, smarter, and maneuver as well as the Balloon Fighter. Expect them to contantly fight for height advantage and to always be directly above you. Take your time dispatching groups of them; they love popping your balloons as you drop in to finish off one of their ranks. Always keep these fiends in the corner of your eye, or fall to their aggressive style like so many before you.

The Giant Fish

Below the surface of the water lurks a creature of unending hunger, a monster whose stomach can never be filled. We speak, of course, of the Giant Fish. This scaly scavenger roams the map, back and forth, looking for its next meal. If you happen to be just above the water as it passes by, it leaps out at you. If it grabs you, it pulls you under and takes a life immediately, regardless of how many balloons you have. The Giant Fish also attacks any Birds that get near it, so it's as much friend as foe.

Lightning Ball

Clouds exist in every Phase, and while they seem completely harmless, they hide a dark secret—or should we say a *light* secret? As you play a Phase, every once in a while, a cloud begins to flash. Once that happens, expect a lightning bolt to strike from the cloud and leave a Lightning Ball bouncing around the screen. Contact with the Lightning Ball means an instant life loss for the Balloon Fighter. The Ball bounces around the screen in diagonal directions until it drops into the water. It's easy enough to dodge by itself, but when you have several Birds on the screen as well, the Lightning Ball can be a real pain to deal with.

Flippers

Flippers can't harm the Balloon Fighter directly, but they can change the tide of battle in an instant. Touching a Flipper shoots the Balloon Fighter off in a semi-random direction, which can block you from finishing off a Bird, or can send you rocketing into peril. The good news is that Flippers also affect any Birds that touch it. Keep your distance from Flippers to avoid the trouble they produce.

Game Modes

There are technically three game modes, but A and B are the same game with one and two players, respectively.

Games A and B

In Games A and B, you must pop the balloons of all Bird enemies to progress to the next Phase. There are 16 total Phases to complete. Once you've completed all 16, the game jumps back to Phase 1, and you get the chance to play through again. Play through the Phases over and over to reach the highest scores possible.

Game B adds a second Balloon Fighter to the game, allowing you to play through with a friend. Just be careful! The two players can pop each other's balloons, making the Balloon Fighter the deadliest enemy of all!

Scores (Games A and B)

Pop the enemy's balloon: 500-1000 points

Pop the other player's balloon (in a two-player game): 1000 points

Destroy an enemy's parachute while it's still in the air: 1000-2000 points

Hit the enemy while it's on the ground (after popping its balloon): 750-1500 points

Pop a bubble: 500 points

Pop a balloon during a Bonus Phase: 300-700 points

Pop every balloon during a Bonus Phase: Perfect score bonus, 10,000-30,000 points

Phases

There are 16 Phases to play through in *Balloon Fight*, but the game doesn't end once you've completed them all. After completing all 12 regular Phases and four Bonus Phases, the game starts over at Phase 1. This allows you to continue achieving higher and higher scores to beat your own records.

This section includes screens for each of the game's 16 Phases, so you can learn about what's coming before you face it. We list the types of enemies and obstacles you contend with in each Phase, providing everything you need to reach your highest scores possible.

Phase 1

Red Bird(s) x 3

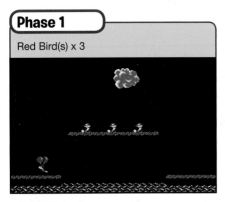

Don't Delay!

The Birds always start every mission without balloons. If you're quick, you can defeat a few of them before they take flight.

Freedom of Flight

An important mechanic to keep in mind while playing *Balloon Fight* is the ability to wrap around the screen. Whenever you reach the left or right side of the screen, you fly on through and appear on the opposite side. This allows you to utilize more free space while you try to get away from, or on top of, enemies in any given Phase.

Phase 2

Red Bird(s) x 2   Green Bird(s) x 3

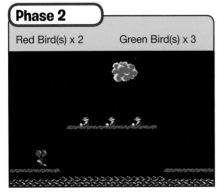

Bird-Watching

Green Birds move at the same speed as Red Birds, but unlike Red Birds, they try to pop your balloons. They don't do so with any real conviction, so don't expect them to try too hard to reach you, but don't underestimate them either.

Walk, Don't Run

While *Balloon Fight* is all about flying, sometimes walking on the ground or platforms is a boon. Your walking speed matches your top speed in the air, and you don't have to wrestle with the flight physics. To make a quick getaway, or to reposition yourself, keep walking in mind.

Phase 3

Red Bird(s) x 1   Yellow Bird(s) x 2
Green Bird(s) x 2

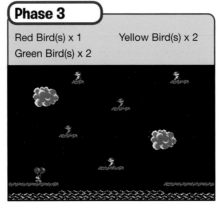

Bird-Watching

Yellow Birds are the true foe of *Balloon Fight*. They're swift and highly aggressive. They always work to stay above you, and in groups they can be positively devastating. Proceed with extreme caution and cleverness, don't do anything reckless, and take your time eliminating them; rushing in is a surefire way to get your balloons popped.

Bonus Phase

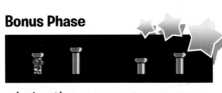

Jackpot!

You encounter a Bonus Phase after every three regular Phases. In Bonus Phases, your job is to pop balloons as they emerge from the pipes scattered along the bottom of the screen. There are 20 balloons in all, and popping all 20 gives you a massive boost to your score.

In this Phase, the balloons are worth 300 points apiece, and popping all 20 grants you a bonus of 10,000 points.

Phase 4

Red Bird(s) x 3   Yellow Bird(s) x 1
Green Bird(s) x 1

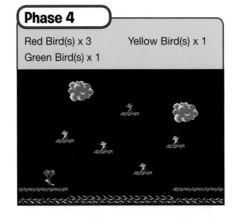

Phase 5

Red Bird(s) x 2   Yellow Bird(s) x 1
Green Bird(s) x 3

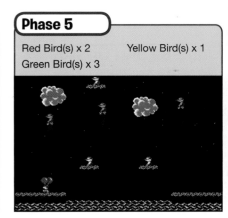

Phase 6

Red Bird(s) x 1   Yellow Bird(s) x 4

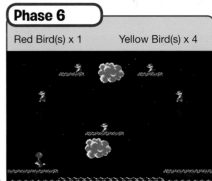

A Test of Endurance

This is one of the hardest Phases in the game, without a doubt. Four Yellow Birds litter the top of the screen, so not only do you have an excess of the game's hardest enemy, but they all start on the high ground.

Patience is key here, so play defensively and take your time. If you manage to knock a Yellow Bird down, don't race after it unless you're confident you can take it out without losing a balloon. The Yellow Birds love to swoop in as you drop in on a downed Bird, and with this many of them, you can lose a man in an instant if they get on top of you.

Bonus Phase

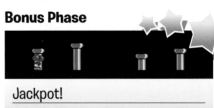

Jackpot!

In this Phase, the balloons are worth 500 points apiece, and popping all 20 grants you a bonus of 15,000 points.

Phase 7

Red Bird(s) x 1	Yellow Bird(s) x 2
Green Bird(s) x 3	Flipper(s) x 1

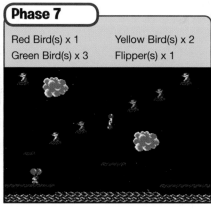

Flippers

Flippers bounce and redirect both the Balloon Fighter and the Birds whenever touched. This makes it more difficult to reach a parachuting Bird that passes through the Flipper, but can also throw a Yellow Bird off your trail.

Phase 8

Red Bird(s) x 2	Yellow Bird(s) x 2
Green Bird(s) x 2	Flipper(s) x 1

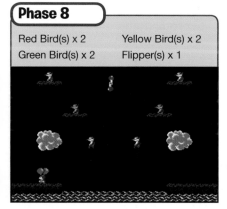

Phase 9

Red Bird(s) x 3	Yellow Bird(s) x 1
Green Bird(s) x 1	Flipper(s) x 2

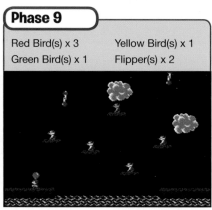

Bonus Phase

Jackpot!

In this Phase, the balloons are worth 700 points apiece, and popping all 20 grants you a bonus of 20,000 points.

Phase 10

Green Bird(s) x 2	Flipper(s) x 4
Yellow Bird(s) x 4	

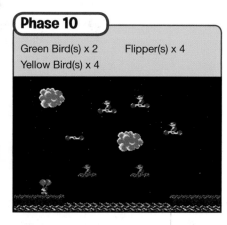

Phase 11

Red Bird(s) x 2	Yellow Bird(s) x 2
Green Bird(s) x 2	Flipper(s) x 1

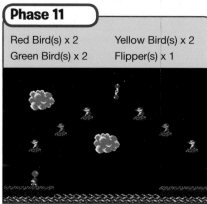

Phase 12

Red Bird(s) x 4	Yellow Bird(s) x 1

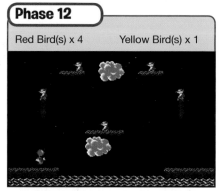

Bonus Phase

This Phase marks the final stage in the game. After this, you start back at Phase 1 and play through the game again to keep building your high score. Keep it up and smash through your personal bests!

Jackpot!

In this Phase, the balloons are worth 700 points apiece, and popping all 20 grants you a bonus of 25,000 points.

Future Fortune

Bonus Phases still appear every fourth Phase, but they are all now worth 30,000 points for a perfect score and 700 per balloon.

Balloon Trip

Balloon Trip is a never-ending autoscroller that removes all enemies from the game except for the Giant Fish, and provides an endless supply of Lightning Balls and balloons. Your job is to pop the balloons while avoid the Lightning Balls for as long as possible.

Put your *Balloon Fight* skills to the test and see how long you can last in this alternate mode of the game!

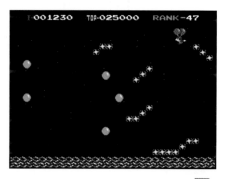

Scores

Pop a balloon:
300-700 points

Pop a bubble: 500 points

Pop 20 balloons in succession: All balloons turn orange

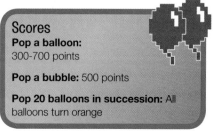

DONKEY KONG

Developer:
Nintendo R&D1

Director:
Shigeru Miyamoto

Producer:
Gunpei Yokoi

Composer:
Yukio Kaneoka

Original Release Date:
July 9, 1981 Arcade JP;
July 15, 1983 NES JP
(June 1, 1986 US)

SUMMARY

Can you save Pauline from the clutches of Donkey Kong? Help Mario scale the construction site and come to the rescue! Dodge the fireballs and barrels that Donkey Kong hurls down the ramps and ladders to thwart your efforts.

PLAYING DONKEY KONG

Use the Directional Pad to move Mario left or right. Press Up or Down while standing in front of, or above, a ladder to climb it. Press the A Button to jump and the Start Button to pause the game.

Game Modes

You must choose one of the four options at the Main menu to start the game:

Game A of both 1-Player and 2-Player is considered the beginner difficulty, while Game B is for experts.

Selecting a 2-Player game mode means you take turns switching the controller whenever one of you loses a Mario. Compete to see who can achieve the highest score before getting a game over, and determine who the real Donkey Kong champion is!

Scoring

At its core, *Donkey Kong* is a game all about high scores. Complete all three of the game's levels, and you'll be sent back to the first stage to start over and keep raising that high score. Here are the ways you build your score in *Donkey Kong*.

Picking Up Pauline's Possessions

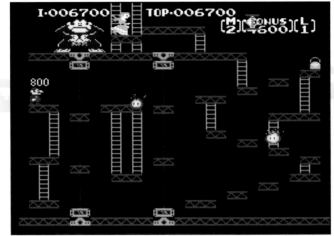

Gain points by picking up things dropped by Pauline (her Parasol and Purse). Each one lands you 800 points!

Stage Bonus

The Stage Bonus window appears in the top-right corner of the screen. The bonus continuously ticks down as you play the level. When you reach Pauline in any given stage, the Stage Bonus stops and you are given the points currently shown in the window. At the start of the next stage, the Stage Bonus total restarts and begins ticking down once again. If you want the highest bonus possible, hurry to complete stage. If the bonus runs out, Mario loses a life, so don't delay!

Jumpman

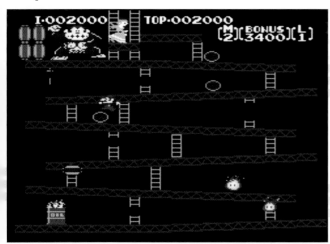

Mario's original name was Jumpman, and you can see why in *Donkey Kong*. He can't attack enemies without a hammer, so he relies on his sky-high jumping to avoid foes and progress through each stage. Jumping over barrels nets Mario 100 points per jump—the perfect combination of form and function!

Hammerman

Pick up one of the hammers in Stages 1 and 3 and start hitting the fireballs or barrels with it. You earn 500 points for each one you destroy.

Handyman

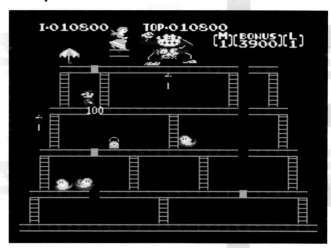

To complete Stage 3, you must pull all the bolts out of the girders. But removing them also has the benefit of scoring you an additional 100 points per bolt.

Extraman

Loops

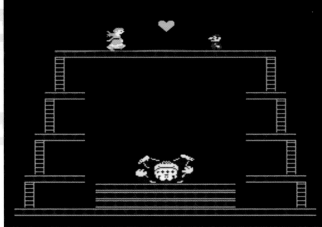

Reach a total of 20,000 points to gain an extra life! Every 20,000 points after that results in yet another extra life.

If you succeed in finishing Stage 3, the game loops back to Stage 1. As you complete loops, your enemies increase in number and speed, but so does the Stage Bonus total. Keep going to reach the highest score possible!

Beware!

The following spell the end for Mario:

- When Mario touches a fireball or barrel

- When a jack in Stage 2 hits Mario

- When Mario falls too far down

When all Marios are gone, the game is over.

CHARACTERS AND COLLECTIBLES

Mario's enemies include: Donkey Kong, fireballs, barrels, and jacks.

Mario

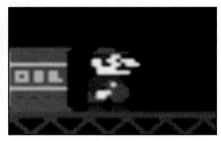

Mario is the hero of the game. He must climb up steel girders and avoid enemies to rescue Pauline.

Donkey Kong

The giant gorilla who kidnaps Mario's sweetheart awaits at the top of the steel girders.

Pauline

Pauline was kidnapped by Donkey Kong. It's Mario's mission to rescue her.

Hammer

Mario's tool of his trade. The hammer has the ability to destroy most enemies that come his way, but at the cost of mobility. You can't climb any ladders or jump while Mario holds the hammer.

Pauline's Possessions

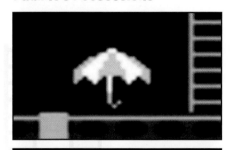

These are Pauline's lost articles. If Mario picks them up, you get 800 points!

Enemies

These enemies try to stop Mario from moving on. Either jump and dodge them or use your hammer to destroy them.

Level 1

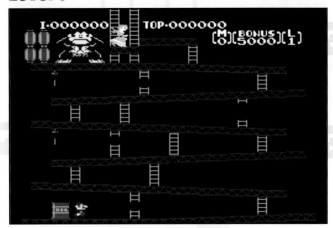

In this stage, Donkey Kong throws a never-ending barrage of barrels your way. If the barrels land in the flaming can at the start of the level, they create little fire monsters that slowly shuffle their way toward Mario.

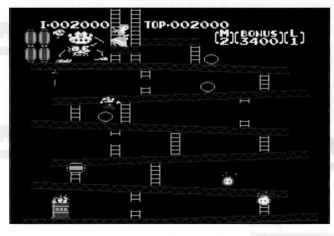

As Mario proceeds, several barrels thrown by Donkey Kong come rolling by. Jump over them and press on. You get 100 points for each barrel you successfully jump over. Be careful around ladders when a barrel is above Mario. The barrels roll down the ladders and knock Mario out if he's climbing one.

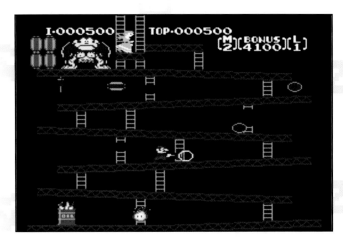

A hammer is available in one of two places in this stage. Find the right place, get the hammer, and use it to break the barrels. However, you can't climb the ladder while you hold the hammer.

Pay attention to the bonus points shown on the upper-right corner of the screen. As time passes, these bonus points decrease. The sooner you finish the level, the more bonus points you keep.

Level 2

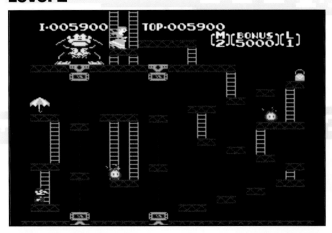

In this stage, use a ladder and an elevator to cross over to the floating girders. Jacks and fireballs try to stop Mario from proceeding.

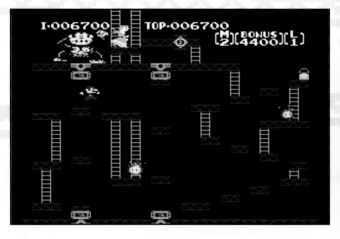

Make careful use of the elevator to cross from one steel girder to another. Mario can jump as high and as far as the width of two girders. Any more than that in any direction and Mario's done for.

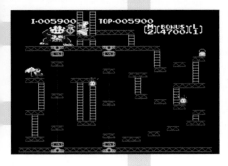 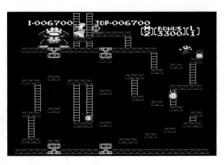

Grab the umbrella from the upper-left corner of the screen or the purse from the upper-right and get 800 points for each item. Avoid the fireballs and jacks when you go for the purse.

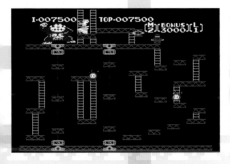 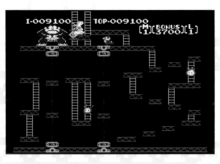

The jacks come down in a set pattern, which makes it easy for you to avoid them. Wait in front of the position where the jack will bounce (as seen in our screenshot). When it passes you, it's safe to go back and climb the ladder.

Level 3

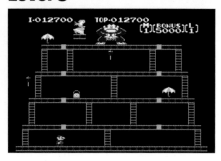

You must undo the eight yellow bolts that connect the steel girders. Successfully remove all eight of them to save Pauline from Donkey Kong's clutches.

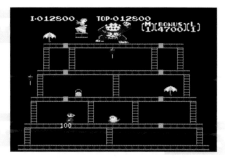

The steel girders that make up this stage are connected by eight bolts. Remove them all while avoiding the attack of the fireballs.

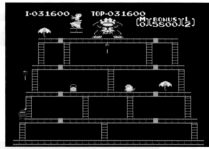

You find two hammers in this stage: one just below Donkey Kong and another in the middle-left section of the stage. Use a hammer to destroy the fireballs. Remember that you cannot jump while holding the hammer.

The number of attacking fireballs increases, so undo the bolts quickly. The shortest route to all the bolts is to go upward from the lower-left corner, and then downward from the upper-right.

DONKEY KONG JR.

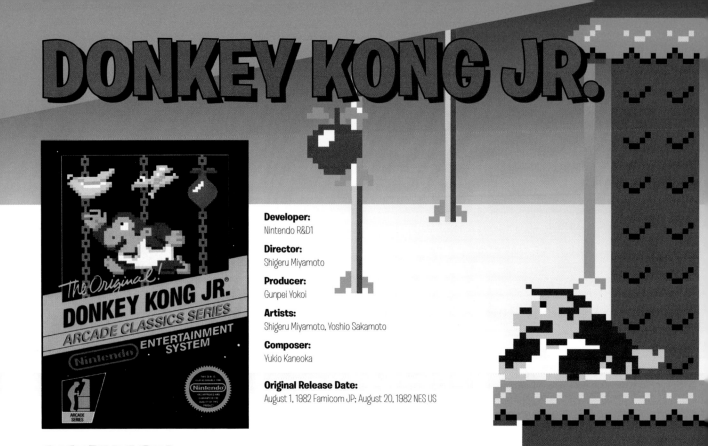

Developer:
Nintendo R&D1

Director:
Shigeru Miyamoto

Producer:
Gunpei Yokoi

Artists:
Shigeru Miyamoto, Yoshio Sakamoto

Composer:
Yukio Kaneoka

Original Release Date:
August 1, 1982 Famicom JP; August 20, 1982 NES US

SUMMARY

Donkey Kong has been captured by Mario, and Junior is determined to do something about it. Take control of this heroic ape as he climbs, slides, and jumps his way to the keys he needs to thwart Mario's plans. Don't expect it to be easy, though! Mario and his minions are determined to keep Donkey Kong behind bars.

HOW TO PLAY

Use the Directional Pad to move Junior in the corresponding direction. Press the A Button to jump. Press the Start Button to pause and resume the action during gameplay. Press the Start Button to pause and resume the action during gameplay. On the Main menu, press Select to cycle through available game modes, and press Start to begin the game.

Game Modes

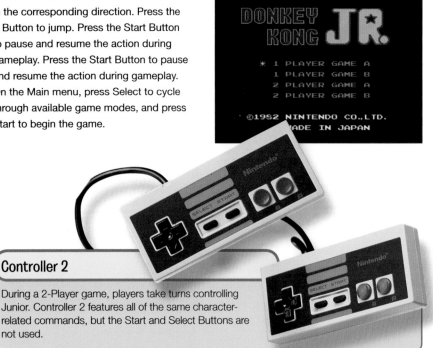

Donkey Kong Jr. offers four different game types:

Game A represents the beginner difficulty. Game B represents expert difficulty: enemies appear at a faster rate and are more difficult to avoid. Both difficulty settings are available in 1-Player and 2-Player game modes.

A 2-Player game requires the use of a second controller. Players take turns controlling Donkey Kong Jr. A turn ends whenever a player completes a round or loses a Junior.

Controller 2

During a 2-Player game, players take turns controlling Junior. Controller 2 features all of the same character-related commands, but the Start and Select Buttons are not used.

Game Screen

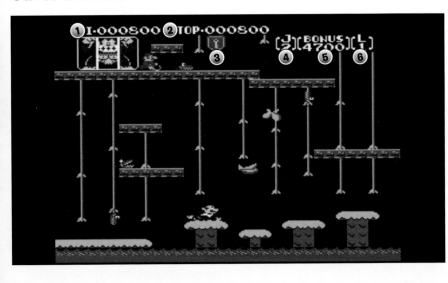

1. Your current score.

2. The highest score earned during the current session.

3. A key.

4. The number of Juniors left in your reserves. When you lose all your Juniors, the game ends.

5. The number of bonus points remaining. Bonuses decrease in value as time passes. If the bonus reaches zero before you complete the round, you lose a Junior.

6. Your current loop. Conquer all four rounds to complete a loop. The higher the loop, the greater the challenge!

Progressing through the Game

Rounds and Loops

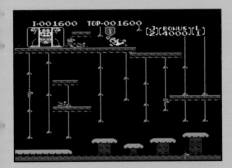

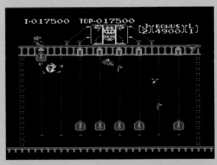

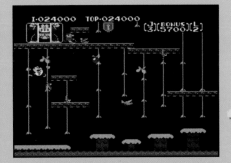

To free Donkey Kong, you must conquer four challenging rounds. In each of the first three rounds, your goal is to reach the key near the top of the screen. If you succeed, the round ends and the next round begins.

In the fourth round, you must push six separate keys into the locks near the top of the screen. When all six keys are in place, Donkey Kong is set free, and you're transported back to Round 1 to begin the process again. At this point, you've not only conquered all four rounds, you've also completed your first loop of the game.

All loops feature the same four rounds in the same order, but each new loop contains more challenging scenarios than the loops that preceded it—most notably, enemies move faster and appear more frequently. The more loops you complete, the more difficult the game becomes. Of course, as the challenge increases, so do the potential points you earn in each round!

Game Over

You start a 1-Player game with a total of three Juniors—one in play, and two in reserve. Each time Junior touches an enemy, falls too far, or fails to complete a round before the bonus reaches zero, he disappears. The stage then resets with a new Junior in the starting position. When you run out of Juniors, the game ends and you return to the Main menu.

In a 2-Player game, each player starts with a total of three Juniors. When a player runs out of Juniors, he or she is eliminated from the game. The game ends when both players have lost all of their Juniors.

Basic Gameplay

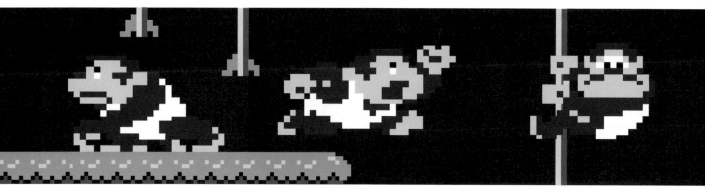

Walking

While Junior is on a floor or platform, press Left or Right on the Directional Pad to move him the corresponding direction.

Jumping

Perform jumps to move between platforms, leap over enemies, and grab on to vines or chains. Junior can jump only when he's on a floor or platform.

Climbing

While Junior is on a vine or chain, press Up on the Directional Pad to climb toward the top of the screen, and press Down to descend. Press Left or Right to move horizontally.

Shifting, Reaching, and Releasing

Depending on Junior's position, pressing Left or Right on the Directional Pad can have slightly different effects. He can shift to the opposite side of his current vine, reach away from his current vine, or release his grip on a vine.

For example, when Junior is clinging to a vine's left side, pressing Right on the Directional Pad simply causes Junior to shift his body to the vine's right side. However, pressing Left would cause Junior to reach out to the left.

When you make Junior reach toward a vine, he automatically grabs it, gripping both vines at once. From this position, pressing Left or Right on the Directional Pad causes Junior to release one of the vines he's latched on to.

Junior can reach out and/or release his grip whether or not there's a vine within range. You can use this to move Junior from vines to platforms, but a poorly timed release can result in a costly fall.

CAST & ITEMS

Main Characters

Junior

This determined little ape is on a quest to free Donkey Kong from his cage. Junior is the game's only playable character—in a 2-Player game, players take turns controlling Junior.

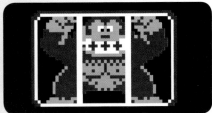

Donkey Kong

He's obviously more comfortable leading the charge, but this time around, Donkey Kong is forced to watch the action from behind bars. Can Junior free this iconic ape before it's too late?

Mario

Mario may be the hero of countless adventures, but he's also Junior's greatest antagonist. Now that he's captured Donkey Kong, Mario is determined to keep the troublesome gorilla imprisoned by any means necessary.

Enemies

Snapjaws

These small, lizard-like creatures can be found patrolling the platforms and vines of most stages. Blue Snapjaws can only descend vines—once a blue Snapjaw reaches the bottom of a vine, it falls off the screen. A red Snapjaw can move freely between vines and platforms. The only way to rid yourself of a red Snapjaw is to strike it with a piece of fruit.

Nitpickers

You encounter two different types of Nitpickers n your quest to free Donkey Kong. The white-bodied Nitpickers found in Round 2 drop eggs as they fly through the area. The larger, blue-bodied Nitpickers found in Round 4 don't drop eggs, but they do zigzag back and forth across the stage as they make their way toward the bottom of the screen.

Sparks

These enemies are found only in Round 3. While a red Spark always circles a single platform, blue Sparks use marked paths to drop down onto lower platforms.

Items

Fruit

Each round contains at least two pieces of valuable hanging fruit. When Junior touches fruit, it breaks free and drops straight down. A piece of falling fruit instantly defeats any enemies it touches, making it Junior's only weapon against Mario's minions.

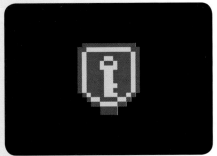

Keys

Every round contains at least one key. In the first three rounds, keys represent Junior's immediate goal—when he reaches the vine next to a key, he climbs onto the nearby platform and the round ends.

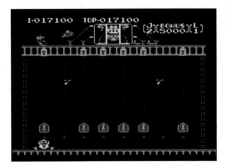

In Round 4, you find six keys hanging on chains. Push all six of the keys into their locks to free Donkey Kong and complete your current loop.

SCORING

Junior's objective might be to free Donkey Kong from his cage, but your priority will likely be achieving your highest possible score. The bulk of your points will almost certainly come from round bonuses, but there are a few other things you can do to boost your score during a game.

Bonus Points

Every round offers a bonus that decreases over time. The faster you complete a round, the more bonus points you receive. If you fail to conquer a round before the bonus expires, you lose a Junior.

In the first loop, round bonuses start at 5000 points. Each time you complete a loop, round bonuses increase by 1000 points—Loop 2 offers bonuses of 6000 points, Loop 3 offers bonuses of 7000 points, and so on. However, larger bonuses also decrease at a faster rate.

Fruit Attack

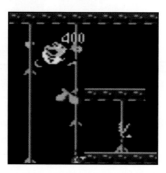

You receive 400 points each time Junior touches a piece of hanging fruit, and earn even more points when a falling fruit collides with one or more enemies. Taking out just one pest earns you an extra 800 points. If the fruit hits two foes, you receive 1200 points. If you manage to clear out three enemies with a single piece of fruit, you earn an impressive 1600 points.

Evasive Jumps

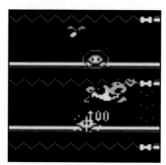

You receive 100 points each time Junior jumps over a Nitpicker or Spark. No points are awarded for jumping over Snapjaws.

Extra Junior

When your score reaches 20,000 points, an extra Junior is added to your reserves!

Key Use

You receive 200 points each time you insert a key into a lock. Locks appear only in Round 4, and you must activate all of them to successfully free Donkey Kong.

RECOMMENDED TACTICS

General Tips

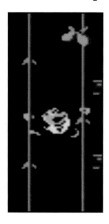

When Junior is gripping two vines at once, he can climb upward at a much faster pace. However, he descends much faster when he's gripping a single vine.

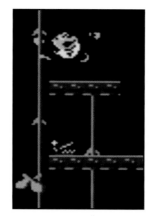

While Junior is reaching away from a vine, he can't climb or descend.

It takes longer for Junior to walk across floors or platforms than it does to move across a row of closely grouped vines.

Junior is an impressive climber, but he can fall only a short distance without taking damage. Make sure a drop is safe before allowing Junior to step over a ledge or let go of a vine.

Round 1

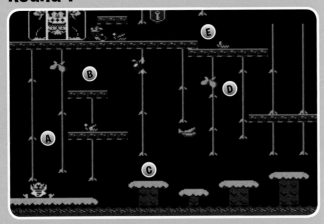

This round takes place on a good mix of vines and platforms. You find a couple of red Snapjaws patrolling the area, but expect to encounter many more enemies. During your time in Round 1, Mario releases blue Snapjaws into the area—each crack of Mario's whip signals the appearance of a new enemy, so stay alert as you make your way up to the key.

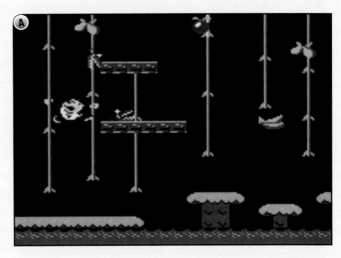

When the round starts, climb up the vines above your starting position. Try to utilize both vines (for a faster climb), but be prepared to move away from incoming Snapjaws.

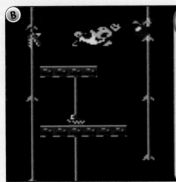

Alternate Route

The platform at Point B is sometimes occupied by a red Snapjaw. When this happens, it's usually best to utilize the lower platform. This means abandoning at least one piece of fruit, but the time you save should result in a larger bonus when you finish the round.

If possible, climb up to the platform at Point B—this makes it much easier to claim the first two pieces of fruit. Move to the right and jump across to the next vine.

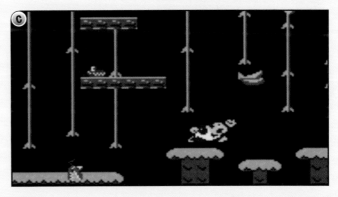

Slide down to the island at Point C, then jump across the islands to the right. Grab the first free vine (the ideal vine varies based on Snapjaw positions). Once you've latched on, use the vines to claim the remaining fruit as you make your way up to Mario's floor.

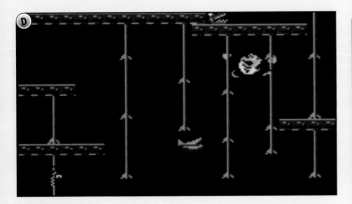

As you move between vines, watch for newly summoned enemies. It's not always easy to predict which vine a Snapjaw will choose, so avoid lingering too close to Mario's floor. Leave enough space to react to a descending Snapjaw.

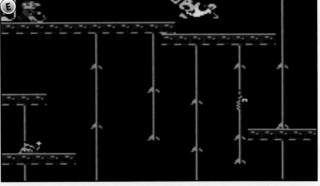

You need a bit of space to clear the step at Point E. Remember to jump during your approach—a late jump will simply cause you to bounce off the step. Once you've overcome this obstacle, hop over any newly summoned Snapjaws on your way to the key.

Round 2

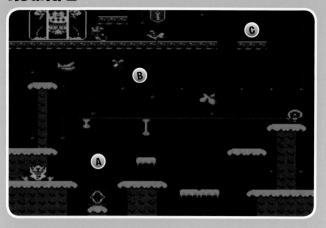

This round features chains instead of vines, but it also includes a couple of unique elements. In addition to a jump-boosting springboard and some moving islands, you also find two retracting grips attached to a long cable. Time each jump to make sure your intended foothold is in place when you land, and watch out for the Nitpickers Mario sends your way. Each time one of these pesky birds is summoned, it swoops down through the gap in the top floor and flies to the left. Don't think that staying low will keep you safe—these Nitpickers can drop eggs as they fly!

Alternate Route

If you're having trouble mastering the high jump, make your way to the chains near the screen's right edge. Climb up to the floating platform, latch on to a retracting grip, and drop down on the moving island from above.

You can save a lot of time by utilizing the springboard at Point A. When the round starts, move near the springboard and watch the moving island to the right. Jump onto the springboard as the island approaches, and then jump again just before the springboard launches you into the air. With proper timing, this spring-assisted high jump should carry you straight to the moving island.

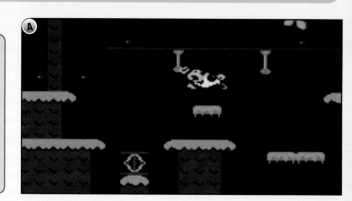

From the moving island, jump onto the leftmost retracting grip—just make sure that the grip is both in range and extended before you try to grab it. Ride back to the left and climb onto the chain near the end of the line.

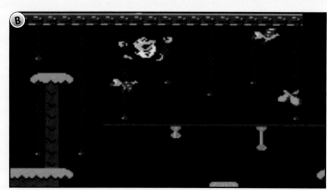

After a Nitpicker swoops through the gap, it flies to the left at a random elevation. Climb up and down the chains to avoid these enemies—just remember that the closer you get to the gap, the less time you have to react to an incoming Nitpicker.

Use the chains along the screen's right edge to climb up to Mario's floor. Hop over the gap and make your way to the chain just past the key. As you do, jump over any Nitpickers Mario sends your way.

Round 3

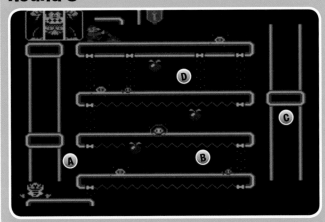

Round 3 features four long platforms stacked between two sets of vine-like wires. You must follow a serpentine path to the key, moving back and forth across the screen as you make your way toward Mario's platform, while encountering some electrifying enemies. There's a red Spark circling each platform, and blue Sparks enter the fray each time Mario pulls his lever. Pay special attention to the dotted lines that run between platforms; blue Sparks can move along these marked paths.

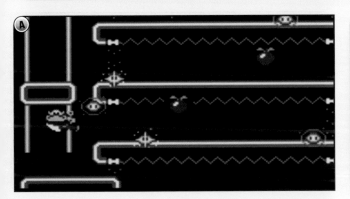

Because there's really only one path to the key, enemy positions will dictate when you should move from the safety of a wire. Always make sure your landing spot is clear of Sparks before you move onto a platform.

Leaping over enemies is often necessary, and it's a great way to earn a few extra points. However, before you jump over an approaching Spark, check the area directly above you. If jumping will send you into an overhead enemy, you might have to make a momentary retreat.

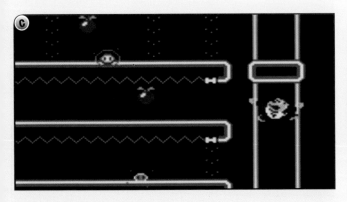

Grip both wires during each climb. The faster you reach the key, the more bonus points you'll receive!

The platform just below Mario's floor can be tricky. You must pass through four marked paths, and there's no way to tell which one a newly summoned blue Spark might choose. Time your approach to ensure that you're able to slip under (or jump over) any approaching Sparks. Once you reach the last set of wires, climb up and jump over any incoming Sparks on your way to claim the key.

Round 4

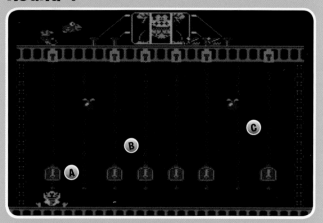

Instead of reaching a key, the fourth round tasks you with using keys to unlock Donkey Kong's cage. Climb under the keys to push them up toward their locks; click all six keys in place to free Donkey Kong. Of course, this seemingly simple goal is complicated by some red Snapjaws and a series of large Nitpickers. Be careful! Once Mario summons a Nitpicker, it flies back and forth across the screen, dropping a bit lower with each turn.

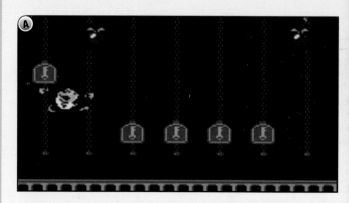

When the round starts, jump onto the chain directly above you and begin pushing the first key toward its lock. Remember that climbing upward is always faster while you're gripping two chains at once. This also makes it easier to collect the first piece of hanging fruit. Depending on your chosen difficulty and/or current loop, you should be able to get the first key in place before a single Nitpicker reaches your location.

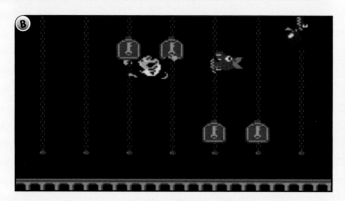

When two keys are on adjacent chains, try to push both of them into their locks at the same time. If an approaching Nitpicker forces you to descend, release your grip from one chain just long enough to slide out of danger.

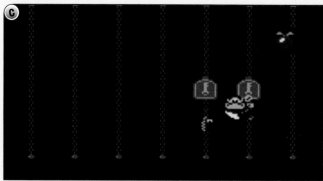

Patrolling Snapjaws can also force you to abandon a key mid-climb. When this happens, it's usually best to simply wait for the Snapjaw to move past you, and then resume climbing both chains.

As you deal with the last key, keep a watchful eye on swooping Nitpickers. By the time they turn toward you, you won't have much time to react. Be ready to move!

Place all six keys into their locks to free Donkey Kong from his cage, conquer Round 4, and begin the next loop of the game.

A BLAST FROM TECHNOLOGY'S PAST

This is a reboot of an article originally published by Nintendo back in January 1991 about how Game Paks work. We're presenting it again now for your entertainment, so soak up all the nostalgia it brings back. And, who knows, you might even learn something!

Have you ever wondered how those small cartridges that you stick into your NES called Game Paks create all of those different, incredible and immersive adventures? In the following pages, we'll tell you everything you need to know about ROMs, RAM, MMCs, and other elements that help create the amazing experiences you find in your NES Game Paks.

IT ALL BEGAN WITH NROMS

Let's start at the beginning. Computers like the NES Control Deck are impressive machines. You can do everything with them from designing spacecrafts to rescuing Princess Toadstool from the evil clutches of King Koopa. But even the most powerful super computers are useless without programs to run on them. Game Paks, of course, are really just programs that your NES Control Deck can run. As you also probably know, programs consist of stored bits of data, or memory, in the form of numbers. What you might not know is how that memory is stored in your Game Paks, or that different games use different types of components. Why all the differences? Because the NES was designed so that the latest technology could be used in each new generation of Game Paks. It's like an RC car: when a faster motor comes out, you buy one and slap it in your old racer. That's how games can get bigger and better while your Control Deck stays the same.

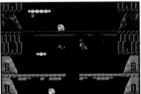

For several years in a row, the max memory size on silicon chips has doubled every year. Back in '85, the 256k X 64k of Super Mario Bros. was considered big.

In 1985, the first NES games appeared using the NROM. ROM, which stands for Read Only Memory, is like a book with words that can't be changed or added to. By today's standards, the two microchips—one for the program and one for characters—were rather small. The Program ROM's maximum memory size was 256k and the Character ROM's max memory was 64k. Of course, small is a relative term. 256k means 256,000 bits of information. Actually, one k equals 1024 bits, so 256k is a bit larger than 256,000 bits. But size isn't everything.

Down To Basics
NROM Game Pak

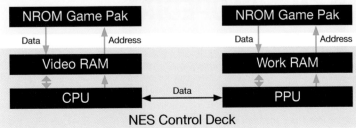

This diagram shows how NROM memory is used. The PRG contains game rules, like how high Mario jumps, while the CHR has information about what Mario looks like. Work RAM stores game data, like your score.

STEPPING UP WITH THE UNROM

It wasn't long before Nintendo started looking for ways to expand the capabilities of the NES. The UNROM was one result. The UNROM Game Pak has a PRG ROM and a RAM chip. RAM means Random Access Memory. It's a place to store information until it's needed, like a filing cabinet. Background and moving object characters for the current area of the game are stored in RAM, which is a more versatile method than storing everything in a ROM. The UNROM allows greater memory size and a process called Bank Switching, which we will cover next.

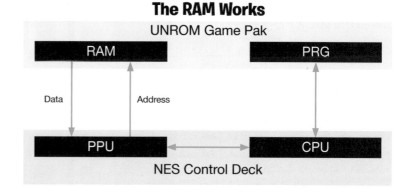

The RAM Works

MMCS: CUSTOM CRAFTED FUN

To understand Bank Switching, picture a game program as one page in a storybook. The first thing you'll notice is that you can only write so much on a single page. A one-page story might be okay, but if you want to expand the story, you'll need to add more pages. It's the same with games. Program size is limited, but you can add programs to the chip. Bank Switching allows you to have several programs in one chip. When a new area of the game is reached, you'll automatically switch to the appropriate program, which is useful in big games with many variations or worlds.

An even bigger revolution came along in the form of Memory Management Controllers, or MMCs. An MMC is a custom designed set of circuits in a chip that allow specialized functions. Some of the circuits, which are also called Logic Gates, increase the speed or efficiency of computations. Others direct the program to specific locations in memory, sort of like doors that open if you have the right key. The UNROM used off-the-shelf Logic Gates, which took up a lot of space. MMCs are more compact, cheaper, and they also allow larger program and character memory size. Some of the other benefits include being able to scroll in different directions and the use of battery backed up RAM, which can save your game progress from one play session to the next. When the first wave of games with MMCs hit, they made quite a splash. *The Legend of Zelda*, *Metroid*, and *Kid Icarus* opened up vast new worlds of NES fun and challenge. Most new games today use MMCs, and newer and better MMCs are under development all the time. Next we'll show you an encyclopedia of MMCs currently in use and some of their special features.

Games such as Kid Icarus became possible with the introduction of specialized MMCs.

It's Only Logical

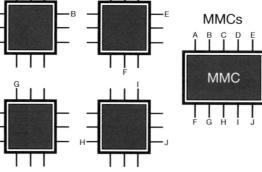

Logic Gates are like a buffet dinner. Your choices are great, but you only want dessert, everything else just takes up space and is wasted. With MMCs you jump straight to the dessert table.

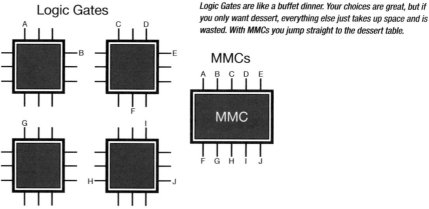

MMC ENCYCLOPEDIA

There are several different types of MMC. In this section, we'll give you a breakdown of each one.

MMC1

The first MMC chip to be used for the NES is still the most popular today. Many of the classic games like *The Legend of Zelda* and *Metroid* became possible only after the MMC1 was developed. In *Metroid*, for instance, much of the challenge and excitement comes from the ability of the game to scroll both horizontally and vertically. That kind of change of pace keeps a game fresh and exciting all the way to the end. Extra memory can also translate into more worlds and enemies.

MMC2

To date, only one game has been designed for use with the MMC2, but that game is one of the biggest hits of all time: *Punch-Out!!* is unique in several ways. First, the opponents are big

characters. You can actually see expressions on their faces or subtle movements of their feet or hands, which are often signals to throw a punch. Second, the game program has a great number of variations, which requires extra memory.

MMC3

Along with additional memory size, the MMC3 allows some great innovations like the split screen scrolling in Super Mario Bros. 3. The scoreboard at the

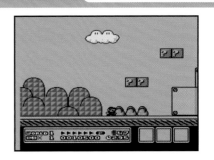

bottom of the picture is actually a second screen, which stays put even as Mario sprints from left to right. It's made possible by a timer function that was specially built into the MMC3.

MMC5

The latest advances, including an improved battery back up system, better color definition, and partial screen scrolling are made possible by the MMC5. Some of these improvements are due to a customized mathematics module that frees up the Control Deck's CPU from some repetitive functions such as running an internal clock. It also allows a vertical split screen scroll, which means you can have a side bar of information while the scrolling action of the game continues. Memory size for the MMC5 shoots up to 8 Megs. With a single Meg equaling 1,048,576 bits, that's a lot of memory. As for saving games, with the MMC5 you won't have to push RESET on your Control Deck while pushing POWER when you want to quit.

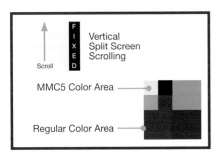

To see how color definition is improved in more advanced NES titles, study this Color Area illustration. Each Color Area can have up to four different colors, but with the MMC5 the color area is smaller. In the same space where older games had one Color Area with four possible colors, the MMC5 allows four Color Areas with 16 possible colors.

Battery Paks

In the early days of NROMs, if you wanted to finish a game you to do it during one play session. That limited the complexity of games, because no matter how good a game is, players are only human

and have to stop and eat or sleep every so often. In a RAM chip, where game information is stored, memory takes the form of switches that are either turned on or off. If a switch is on, it represents the digit one, and if it's off, it represents zero. Together, the ones and zeroes make up numbers, which is how computer information is stored. Without the power turned on, all the switches are deactivated and the information is lost. By putting a battery in the Game Pak, game data can be stored as long as the life of the battery—about five years.

Compression

Compression is a programming technique that allows a programmer to pack as much information as possible into a limited memory space. This is one reason why memory size alone doesn't tell the whole story.

PUTTING IT ALL TOGETHER: BEHIND THE MASK ROM

One of the most common misconceptions about NES games is that you can record and erase them like tape cassettes. Erasable and/or Programmable ROMs do exist (EPROMs and PROMs), but they are very expensive and are chiefly used for NES research and development. To reduce costs, NES Game Paks use what is called a Mask ROM. The process begins by converting the game program into an actual integrated microcircuit. Using a photographic process, the circuit is reproduced on thin silicon wafers, so the game information isn't just stored in the chip, it's part of the chip. Then the wafers are sandwiched together and attached to connector pins. Below are the two most common configurations of Mask ROM chips. The major difference is that the Flatpack Chip is small and more compact, so it can fit inside Game Boy Paks.

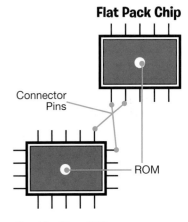

The Bottom Line

As you've seen, Game Paks are not all created equal. Some have special built-in features that allow greater variety in game design. But the measure of any great game is not memory size or whether it uses a MMC1 or MMC5. The real test is whether or not it's fun to play. Dr. Mario, a 256k X 256k game, requires less memory than many other new games, but once you start playing, it's almost impossible to stop. Remember: it's the stuff that memory is made of that counts.

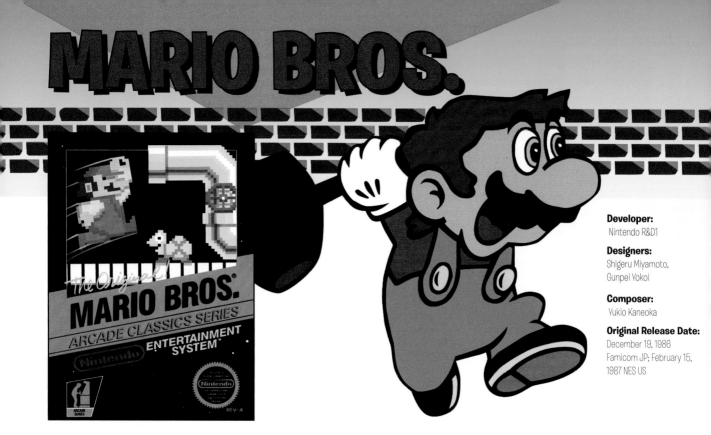

MARIO BROS.

Developer:
Nintendo R&D1

Designers:
Shigeru Miyamoto,
Gunpei Yokoi

Composer:
Yukio Kaneoka

Original Release Date:
December 19, 1986
Famicom JP; February 15,
1987 NES US

SUMMARY

Play alone as Mario, or team up with a friend as Mario and Luigi to best baddies in this underground adventure. Face countless waves of enemies as you clear the sewers of unwanted pests. Test your mettle as you jump, punch, and kick your way through phase after phase of action to achieve your highest possible score.

HOW TO PLAY

Use the Directional Pad to move Mario (or Luigi) left and right. Press the A Button to jump. Press the Start Button to pause and resume the action during gameplay. On the Main menu, use the Select Button to cycle through available game modes, and use the Start Button to begin the game.

Game Modes

Mario Bros. offers four different game types:

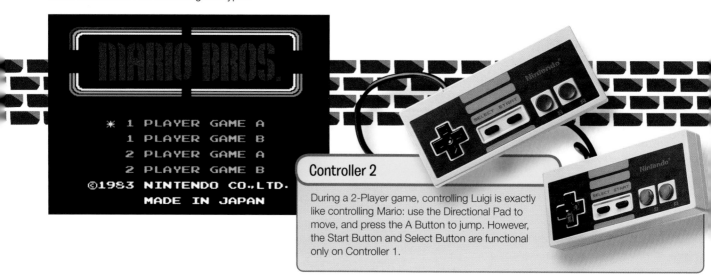

Controller 2

During a 2-Player game, controlling Luigi is exactly like controlling Mario: use the Directional Pad to move, and press the A Button to jump. However, the Start Button and Select Button are functional only on Controller 1.

Game A represents the beginner difficulty. Game B indicates expert difficulty: enemies appear sooner, move faster, and recover more quickly. Both difficulty settings are available in 1-Player and 2-Player game modes.

A 2-Player game requires the use of a second controller. The player using Controller 1 plays as Mario, while the player using Controller 2 plays as Luigi. 2-Player games can be cooperative or competitive, depending on how the players use their respective characters.

Friends or Foes?

A 2-Player game offers plenty of opportunities for teamwork, but it also presents a number of ways for players to thwart each other's efforts.

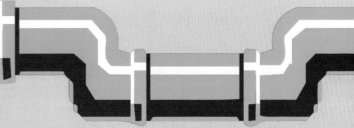

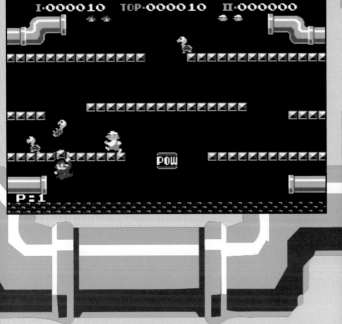

The simplest way to cooperate is to have one player punch critters while the other character kicks them. This helps ensure that flipped enemies are defeated before they have a chance to recover.

For those who prefer a bit of competition, there are multiple ways for two players to impede each other's progress. For example, you can punch a flipped critter to revive it as your opponent moves in to deliver a kick.

Phases

Standard Phases

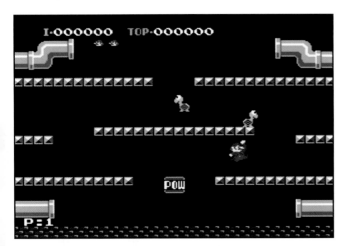

The object of a standard phase is to defeat all turtles, crabs, and fighter flies that appear in the area. If you succeed, the current phase ends and the next phase begins.

During standard phases, critters emerge from the pipes at the top of the screen. Left to its own devices, a critter will travel in a set direction, dropping a bit closer to the ground each time it reaches the edge of a platform. Once on the ground, an untouched critter enters one of the available pipes and returns to the top of the screen to repeat the process.

To clear a critter from the area, you must first flip the target enemy, and then kick it into the water. Flipping a critter usually involves punching the platform beneath your target. Available POW Blocks can also be used to flip critters. Kicking a critter is simply a matter of touching a flipped enemy before it recovers.

Game Over

Clearing critters is dangerous work, and it takes a lot of skill to keep the Mario Bros. out of harm's way. You start a 1-Player game with a total of three Marios—one in play and two in reserve. When Mario takes damage, he disappears and is replaced with a new Mario. When you run out of Marios, the game ends and you return to the Main menu.

A 2-Player game works much the same way as a 1-Player game. Player 1 starts out with a total of three Marios; Player 2 begins with three Luigis. The game ends when all Marios and Luigis have disappeared.

Bonus Phases

During a bonus phase, your goal is to collect 10 coins within a 20-second time limit. As you progress through the game, bonus phases feature new elements like slippery, ice-covered platforms. The first bonus phase appears during Phase 3, after which point a bonus phase appears each time you clear four standard phases.

Basic Gameplay

Moving

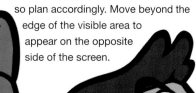

Use the Directional Pad to move left or right. It takes a moment to reach top speed, come to a stop, or change direction while running, so plan accordingly. Move beyond the edge of the visible area to appear on the opposite side of the screen.

Jumping

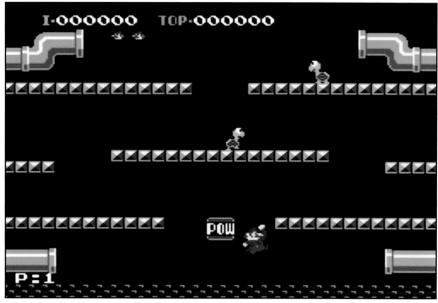

Jump to move between platforms, leap over enemies, or punch objects above you. Jump while moving to leap in the corresponding direction.

Punching

Jump up and hit a platform to deliver a punch to all enemies or objects within the affected area. Use punches to damage or flip enemies, collect coins, or activate POW Blocks. You can also punch a stunned enemy to flip it back onto its feet.

Kicking

Touch a flipped critter to automatically kick it into the water. This clears the pest from the area and takes you one step closer to completing the phase.

CHARACTERS AND ITEMS

Heroes

Who would be willing to battle endless waves of subterranean baddies? Why, the Mario Bros., of course! No job is too big or too dangerous for these two brave heroes.

Mario

Armed with only his jumps, punches, and kicks, Mario is tasked with clearing out the pesky critters plaguing the sewers. Mario is the only hero that appears in a 1-Player game. In a 2-Player game, the player using Controller 1 controls Mario.

Luigi

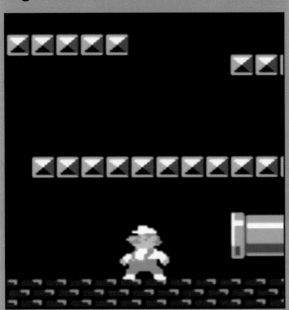

Like Mario, Luigi is responsible for keeping the sewers clear of crafty critters. Fortunately, he's every bit as capable as his brother. Luigi appears only in 2-Player games, and is always controlled by the player using Controller 2.

Critters

Turtles, crabs, and fighter flies are mandatory targets—a phase ends only once all of these enemies have been cleared from the area. Critters can be touched only while they're flipped on their backs; making contact with an upright critter damages Mario (or Luigi), causing the unfortunate hero to vanish from the area.

Flipping a critter onto its back leaves it temporarily stunned and vulnerable to attack. If you fail to kick a flipped critter before it recovers, the irritated enemy hops back to its feet and moves at a noticeably faster pace; a critter that recovers from being flipped a second time moves even faster. When only one critter remains in a phase, it becomes instantly enraged, moving at top speed until it's defeated.

Different critters move in unique ways, and at different speeds. Like Mario and Luigi, these pesky critters can move past the border of the area, after which they appear on the opposite edge of the screen. It's also important to note that a critter changes direction whenever it walks into a character or coin.

Turtle

Making their debut in Phase 1, turtles are the first critters you encounter in the sewer. If left alone, a turtle will walk straight ahead at a relatively low speed, dropping between platforms until it finds its way to the ground. Land a single punch on a turtle to flip it over and leave it vulnerable to a kick.

Crab

Crabs first appear in Phase 4. Like turtles, these scuttling foes travel straight across flat surfaces. However, crabs move considerably faster, and you must punch a crab two times before it becomes vulnerable to a kick. The first punch simply angers a crab, causing it to move more quickly; the second punch flips the crab, leaving it stunned for a short time.

Fighter Fly

Fighter flies first appear in Phase 6. Rather than moving along flat surfaces, these tricky enemies use their wings to hop short distances. To flip a fighter fly onto its back, you must punch the critter just as it lands.

Additional Enemies

Turtles, crabs, and fighter flies aren't the only enemies you encounter in the sewers. Freezies and fireballs are every bit as dangerous as roaming critters—a single touch from one of these enemies will cause Mario (or Luigi) to disappear from the area.

Unlike critters, freezies and fireballs don't need to be defeated to complete a stage. However, each of these additional enemies can be defeated with a well-timed punch, making the area a bit safer—and netting you some extra points in the process!

Freezies first appear in Phase 9. Fireballs show up whenever you spend a significant amount of time in a single phase—the longer you take to complete a phase, the more fireballs you can expect to encounter.

Freezie

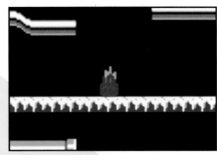

Once a freezie emerges from a pipe, it slides across flat surfaces, dropping down along the platforms until it stops at a randomly selected spot. Soon after this happens, the target platform is covered in ice and the freezie vanishes. Ice-covered platforms offer far less traction than standard surfaces, increasing the time it takes for Mario (or Luigi) to come to a stop or change direction. Punch a freezie before it vanishes to clear it from the area and keep the platforms ice-free.

Green Fireball

Green fireballs can appear at either edge of the screen—usually in-line with a hero's current position. These enemies utilize an uneven twirling motion as they travel horizontally across the area. A green fireball vanishes when it reaches the edge of the screen, but it usually doesn't take long for another fireball to appear.

In most cases, the best way to avoid a green fireball is to move vertically: drop down from the edge of your current platform or jump up to the platform above you. You can destroy a green fireball with a well-timed punch, but it's often safer to simply avoid the roaming hazard and wait for it to disappear.

Red Fireball

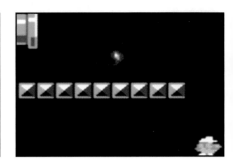

Red fireballs always appear near the pipes at the top of the area. They're considerably slower than green fireballs, but they travel diagonally, changing direction as they bounce off platforms or reach the edge of the screen. This means that a single red fireball can roam throughout the entire area. To destroy a red fireball, punch it just as it lands on a platform. Otherwise, keep your distance as you work to complete the phase.

Items

Although you face your share of dangers underground, you also discover a few useful items. Collect coins to boost your score, and use POW Blocks to help even the odds in the fight for the sewers.

Coin

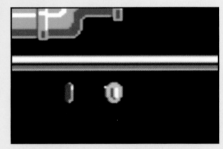

Each time you kick a critter into the water, a coin emerges from one of the pipes near the top of the screen. During a standard phase, a coin behaves similarly to a turtle or crab: it travels along flat surfaces, moves beyond the area's border to reappear on the opposite edge of the screen, and changes direction whenever it comes into contact with an enemy or object. However, coins move fairly quickly, and they never return to the upper platforms. Once a coin enters a ground-level pipe, it's gone for good.

Collect coins by touching them or by punching them through platforms. When you defeat a phase's last critter, any remaining coins vanish from the area.

POW Block

Punching a POW Block essentially delivers a punch to every enemy and item on every horizontal surface in the area. This means that a well-timed punch of a POW Block can flip multiple critters, collect available coins, and eliminate roaming freezies and fireballs. However, it's important to note that the impact will have no effect on enemies that are airborne (or falling), and that punching a POW Block will flip any stunned critters back to their feet.

A POW Block can be punched only three times before it vanishes. With the exception of the first bonus phase (Phase 3), each one begins with a new, fully charged POW Block.

Scoring

Mario Bros. is an endless adventure—no matter how many phases you complete, there's always more work to be done. This means that achieving the highest possible score will likely be your focus. Fortunately, you have plenty of opportunities to earn points during your time underground.

Flipping Critters

Each time you flip a turtle, crab, or fighter fly on its back, your score increases by 10 points.

Kicking Critters

Kick an upturned critter to clear it from the area, gaining 800 points in the process. You can also clear vulnerable critters in quick succession to earn bonus points. For example, kicking four overturned enemies in a row yields 800 points for the first critter, 1600 points for the second, 2400 points for the third, and a whopping 3200 points for the fourth critter in the series.

Bonus Coins

Collect a coin before it vanishes to earn an extra 800 points.

Defeating Freezies

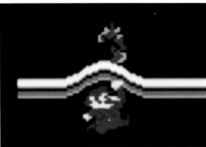

Punch a freezie before it overtakes a platform to earn 500 points.

Extinguishing Fireballs

Land a punch on a roaming fireball to boost your score while making the sewers a little bit safer. Extinguishing a green fireball is worth 200 points, while destroying a red fireball grants 1000 points.

Perfect Bonus

Collect all 10 coins during a bonus phase to earn some serious bonus points. Successfully clearing the first bonus phase grants you 3000 points; all subsequent bonus phases offer Perfect Bonuses worth 5000 points. Best of all, these bonus points are granted in addition to the points you earn from collecting the available coins.

AN EXTRA HERO
Scoring points does more than just give you bragging rights. Earn 20,000 points to add an extra Mario (or Luigi) to your reserves!

TIPS AND TRICKS

General Tips

Punching directly under a critter launches it straight up into the air, punching just behind a critter launches it forward, and punching just ahead of it launches your target backward. Precision punching is the key to clearing a phase as quickly and safely as possible. For example, if a turtle is approaching the edge of a platform, punch behind it so that it lands near your position, and then follow up with a quick kick. When you deliver your first punch to a crab, aim just ahead of your target to knock it back, and then punch it again as it moves back into range.

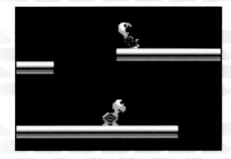

A stunned critter flashes between two color schemes just before it recovers. Use this warning sign to gauge whether you should retreat or attempt a last-second kick.

If you don't think you can reach a stunned critter in time to kick it, it's sometimes best to punch it instead. Doing so flips your target back onto its feet, but it also prevents the critter from growing angrier.

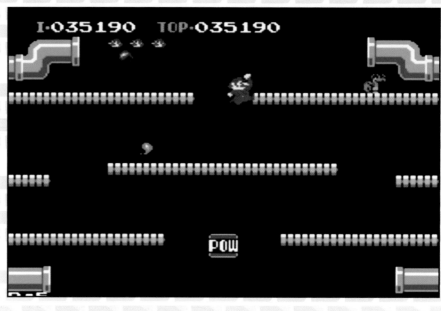

Look before you leap! You can't change direction in mid-air, so make sure you're moving at the proper speed—and in the proper direction—before you commit to a jump.

Use POW Blocks sparingly. They're great for emergencies (or for flipping groups of critters for valuable kick combos!), but POW Blocks also serve as useful platforms. Depleted or destroyed POW Blocks are replaced only during bonus phases, so plan accordingly.

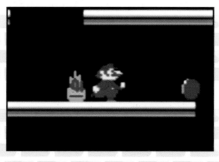

You earn a lot of extra points by hunting fireballs or performing kick combos, but the surest way to achieve a high score is to keep the game going as long as possible. It's often better to keep your hero safe than to attempt a risky maneuver.

When a new Mario (or Luigi) is brought in from your reserves, the hero appears on a small platform near the top of the screen. This platform can remain in the area for up to 10 seconds, but it vanishes the moment you take control of your hero. Each time you rejoin the fray, take a moment to assess nearby threats and carefully plan your first move.

2-Player Tips

During cooperative play, consider assigning specific tasks to each player. Put one player in charge of punching critters while the other player kicks them to complete phases as quickly and safely as possible.

Player scores are kept separately, meaning that points are awarded only to the player who earns them. If you're playing cooperatively, consider swapping responsibilities between phases to ensure that you and your partner can boost your respective scores throughout the game. When you're playing competitively, look for chances to thwart your opponent's attempts at high-value maneuvers like kicking critters or collecting coins.

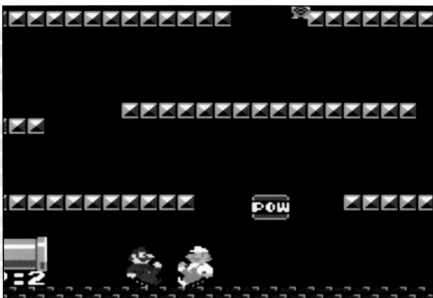

Mario and Luigi can bump into each other, so try to stay out of your partner's way during a cooperative game. During competitive play, you can use this feature to block your opponent's path or push them into approaching enemies.

If you find yourself being pushed toward an enemy, don't bother trying to push back. It's much more effective to simply jump over your opponent. A properly timed escape will not only get you out of harm's way, but it can also send your opponent rushing into the approaching threat.

The POW Block also affects heroes. During a competitive game, use POW Blocks to launch your opponent into the air while stunned critters are flipped back onto their feet. Remember that each POW Block can be used only three times—during a cooperative game, communicate with your partner to ensure that a POW Block is used only when it benefits both players.

THE MIDDLE PERIOD
(1987-1989)

The NES truly hit its stride during this period. Most of Nintendo's most popular NES hits are released at this time—titles such as *Metroid*, *The Legend of Zelda*, *Kid Icarus*, *Zelda II: The Adventure of Link*, *Super Mario Bros. 2*, *Punch-Out!!*, and many more. Nintendo also received incredible support in the form of third-party titles at this time; the number of games that were released in this short time period is absolutely staggering.

While this era produced some of Nintendo's most cherished classics, the NES still had more to give on a technical level. It wasn't until the next and final period that the NES was pushed to its limits.

During this period, the popularity of the NES went through the roof. The system boomed and saw near-endless support in the way of new titles from both third-party developers and Nintendo itself. By the time this period ended there were more Nintendo consoles in homes than any other console before it.

Pro Wrestling
March 1987

"Now real wrestling action is at your fingertips!

It's a reverse bulldog, a double noggin-knocker, a leap off the top turnbuckle—it's pure pandemonium! Welcome to the world of Nintendo Pro Wrestling. Where you take on six of the meanest, baddest, most rotten guys around. With names like The Amazon, Giant Panther, and Kin Corn Karn. You'll begin the match by choosing a wrestler and an opponent—either the computer or a friend. Then with a flick of the wrist you'll perform drop-kicks, body-slams, head-locks and dozens of other bone-crunching moves designed to annihilate your opponent. But be warned. Each wrestler has his *own* arsenal of back-breaking moves. Which means you'll have to think fast and move even faster to pin your opponent, hold him for a three-count, and become champion of Nintendo Pro Wrestling!"

Slalom
March 1987

"Hit the slopes of Mount Nasty for the challenge of your life!

The freezing wind crack against your face. The tension mounts. Suddenly, you're off! Speeding through the gates on one of Nintendo's 24 snow-covered runs. Welcome to SLALOM! Where you feel every bump, every jump, every death-defying turn, just like in a real slalom race! Along the way you'll dodge other competitors, trees, sledders—even snowmen—as you speed down mountains like Snowy Hill, Mount Nasty, and Steep Peak in a heart-pounding race against the clock. Challenge the moguls and execute trick jumps. You'll find SLALOM just as thrilling and *dangerous* as the real thing!"

Volleyball
March 1987

"Here's your chance to bump, set, and spike your way to victory!

Slam the perfect serve. Spike the game-winning point. Make the save that saves the game! It's all up to you. Because you call the shots in Nintendo VOLLEYBALL. You'll start by selecting a team from the country of your choice. As Captain, you'll lead your team through a fast-paced warm-up round, then quickly move into the heat of real volleyball competition. You'll decide when to spike, when to lob, when to make a diving save—everything just like the captain of a real volleyball team! Play against a friend or challenge the computer. Either way, Nintendo's true-to-life graphics and realistic game play will bring all the fun and excitement of volleyball right into your home!"

Kid Icarus
July 1987

"Get ready for the action and adventure of Greek Mythology translated to the Video Age.

Far away in a kingdom called "Angel Land" the evil goddess Medusa has stolen the Three Sacred Treasures and imprisoned the goddess of light, Palutena. As Kid Icarus, your mission is to find the treasures, destroy Medusa, and rescue Palutena from the depths of the Palace in the Sky. To find the treasures you'll travel through ruins collecting weapons and storing power for use in combat against creatures of Medusa's army. Use your bow and arrow to ward off gatekeepers of the Underworld, Overworld, and Skyworld as you strive toward your battle against Medusa. Will you survive to restore Palutena's light and return it to "Angel Land"? Only you know."

The Legend of Zelda
August 1987

"Welcome to THE LEGEND OF ZELDA. Where the only sound you'll hear is your own heart pounding as you race through forests, lakes, mountains, and dungeonous mazes in an attempt to restore peace to the land of Hyrule. Along the way, you'll be challenged by Tektites, Wizzrobes, and an endless array of ruthless creatures who'll stop at nothing to prevent you from finding the lost fragments of the Triforce of Wisdom. But don't despair. With a little and a lot of courage, you'll conquer your adversaries, unite the Triforce fragments, and unravel the mystery of THE LEGEND OF ZELDA!"

Metroid
August 1987

"It's you against the evil Mother Brain in the thrilling battle of Metroid!

You're inside the fortress planet Zebes. The planet of endless secret passageways where the Metroid are multiplying. Left alone the Metroid are harmless. But in the wrong hands they could destroy the galaxy. It's up to you to prevent the Mother Brain that controls Zebes from using the Metroid for evil purposes. But that won't be easy. You'll have to use your spacesuit to absorb valuable energy for your search to gain the use of power items like the Ice Beam, Wave Beam, High Jump Boots, and Varia Suit. If you survive, it will be you and your acquired powers against the Mother Brain."

Punch-Out!!
October 1987

"Who'll be the champ in the World Video Boxing Association?

Punch-Out!! It's 13 tough matches in the minor, major, and world circuits that lead to the final challenge—the World Video Boxing Association title fight. The ultimate bout against the newest WVBA Champ— Mr. Dream.

Practice your hook and take a quick jab. Try to stay light on your feet as you dance left, then right, dodging punches while you throw your own. Boxers from around the world like Piston Honda, Glass Joe, and Super Macho Man are all trying to knock you out of the ring.

You've trained for months for this moment. There's the bell. Shake hands and come out boxing!"

Rad Racer
October 1987

"Feel the awesome power of 3-D rally racing!

This is no ordinary game pak. This is Rad Racer. Nintendo's thrilling 3-D video game. Rad Racer comes action packed with revolutionary 3-D technology and 3-D glasses (they're free inside) that will have you really believing you're in the middle of a cross country rally race— cruising along at 200 miles per hour!

Rad Racer takes you through 8 treacherous race courses, including the Los Angeles Nightway, the San Francisco Highway, and the Grand Canyon. No matter what car and course you choose, Rad Racer's hair-pin curves, dare-devil turns, and realistic action will bring home all the fun and excitement of real rally racing. Think you're up to it? Then drivers start your engines. It's Rad Racer!

1988

Ice Hockey
March 1988

"Fast-paced action at the drop of the puck!

It's fast skatin', hip checkin', high scoring action. Lead your team into center ice, over the opponent's blue line. Pass over to the point and set up for the tip in—Score! Choose a country for you and your opponent, select a level of play, and face off at center ice to become the top goal scorer in Nintendo's Ice Hockey. Get charged with a penalty and test your defense. Or attack on a power play and use your puck handling skills to catch your opponents off guard. Either way, you can become a superstar in the league of Nintendo Ice Hockey."

World Class Track Meet
August 1988

"Surely you can trot past Turtle, but can you catch a Cheetah?

Run, jump, and race to your heart's content! This action-packed game turns your home into an exciting stadium! Using the Power Pad, we dare you to increase your physical ability and surpass your athletic goals. You'll compete against a runner in the Tournament Mode, and in 4 events for a total score in Olympic Mode. The top 6 winners' names and scores will appear on the electronic billboard. The top 3 winners will stand on the winners' platform. Compete against a computer or friends in an ultimate athletic challenge that could reward you the gold!"

Donkey Kong Classics
October 1988

"What's more fun than a barrel of monkeys? A Donkey Kong double feature!

In DONKEY KONG you'll duck barrel bombs and flaming fireballs as you help Mario save his girlfriend Pauline from the clutches of Donkey Kong. In DONKEY KONG JR., you'll join forces with these madcap monkeys to help Donkey Kong Jr. rescue his father from Mario's prison. Are you ready for laughter? You'd better be. Because this double dose of monkey business will have you rolling in the aisles!"

Super Mario Bros. 2
October 1988

"Mario's back! Bigger and badder than ever before!

This time it's a fierce action-packed battle to free the land of Subcon from the curse of the evil Wart. It's up to you, along with Mario, Luigi, Toad, and the Princess to fight your way through bizarre multi-level worlds and find him! This time you've got a brand new kind of power—plucking power—and now anything you find can be a weapon. But beware! You've never seen creatures like these! Shy Guys and Tweeters! Ninji and Beezos! You've never had an adventure like this! Only cunning and speed can save you now."

Anticipation
November 1988

"Now you're playing with brainpower.

Bored with board games? Tired of pursuing trivia? Had your fill of ethical questions? Then you're ready for ANTICIPATION. This zany, unpredictable, totally whacked-out *video* board game begins with a giant connect-the-dots puzzle. Suddenly, a video pencil starts connecting the dots and, before you know it, you're in a maddening race against the clock, trying to solve the puzzle. Is it an Igloo? A Penguin? A Pineapple? Whatever it is, you—and all your friends—will have a great time trying to guess what the pencil is drawing. Guess right and you'll get a crack at the *really tough* puzzles—no dots or clues, just the pencil drawing a picture. Think you're up to it? Then challenge your friends. Or take on the Computer. Either way, this off-the-floor board game will challenge you, excite you, and generally drive you crazy for years to come."

Super Mario Bros. & Duck Hunt
November 1988

"Take aim, fire and… save the Mushroom Princess?

Two of the very best video game entertainment experiences in one package! The Mushroom Princess is being held captive by the evil King Koopa. Rescue her before the time runs out in another non-stop adventure from the SUPER MARIO BROS.!

You've only got three precious shots when hunting these elusive ducks. Be a sharpshooter with the Zapper light gun or even your trusty old dog will laugh at you! Play DUCK HUNT and SUPER MARIO BROS. and discover you can have lots of laughs and be challenged at the same time."

Zelda II: The Adventure of Link
December 1988

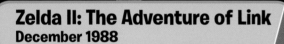

"The Hyrule fantasy continues…

The land of Hyrule is in chaos. As Link, you'll be sent on a treacherous journey to return six precious Crystals to their origins in six stone statues. Only by defeating the guardians of the six palaces will you gain passage to the seventh palace, take on the ultimate challenge that awaits you, and wake the Princess Zelda from her sleeping spell. On your way, helpful villagers you encounter will offer clues and secret messages invaluable in your quest. As you guide Link through the levels of Hyrule, close-ups and overviews will enhance your video vision. Are you up to the challenge?

In the tradition of the Legend of Zelda, the Adventure of Link is one of the most challenging video games we've ever created. To help you keep up with the action, Nintendo's exclusive Extended Playing Power means LINK is programmed to remember everything you find on your journey, so you never have to start your search empty-handed."

1989
Dance Aerobics
March 1989

"Hop, skip and jump your way into shape!

It's time to get up and get physical with Nintendo's DANCE AEROBICS. You and all your friends will have a blast working your way through 12 levels of aerobic conditioning and 64 separate aerobic routines. With DANCE AEROBICS, you'll feel better, you'll look better, and you'll have a lot of fun. So don't just stand there, get out your Power Pad and shake, rattle, and roll your way into a new you!"

Cobra Triangle
July 1989

"Speed and skill are all that can save you.

You're in the hot seat and it's full speed ahead into a river of danger.

Cobra Triangle! The challenge.

Logs jam the river. Whirlpools spin madly. You're under enemy fire, and it's a race against time!

And this is just the start!

Advance in the skill and work your way up through the seven stages of Cobra Triangle. Collect pods in mid-air as you rocket over jumps. Outmaneuver the enemy as you frantically speed exploding mines to the safety area.

You thought you'd seen it all.

And then! Speeding boats actually drag helpless swimmers away! You're the protector. It's up to you to outwit the enemy and sink their rotten boats… before it's too late.

Finally, you meet the monsters. Can you discover the secret of getting past them? And if you can, what dangers await you then?

Are you the one? Can you survive the Cobra Triangle?"

Dragon Warrior
August 1989

"Dragon Warrior… the epic beginning of a new era in video games.

Mere finger speed and sweat are no match for the challenges of this game. You will be required to use deductive reasoning, not a quick sword, to defeat your enemies.

All is darkness. The Dragon-lord has captured the Princess and stolen Erdrick's powerful ball of light.

You are Erdrick's heir. To you has fallen the most dangerous task— to rescue the King's daughter and recover the mystic ball of light.

Your mission is deadly, but it is your fate. Prophets have long foretold your coming.

Three keepers await your journey, each ready to aid you with a mystic item of great power.

Gather the three objects. Scribes will record your deeds. Use cunning and wisdom to choose your commands. Gain experience, weapons, and armor as you battle your way through the world. Rest if you must.

Search out the Dragon-lord's lair and face your destiny. In this role-playing adventure you are the Dragon Warrior!"

Faxanadu
August 1989

"Unlock doors of legend on your journey through Faxanadu.

You are the elves' last hope. Outside the town walls lurk monsters with the power to destroy anything in their path. Inside the walls, water and time are running out. Soon the ancient elf town of Eolis will vanish into eternity.

Only you can save Eolis. No one else dares to venture beyond the walls, onto the World Tree, where towns and fortresses precariously await the whims of fate at the hands of the Evil.

You are searching for the water source and for an antidote to the poison that makes the water undrinkable. To find them you'll need gold and food and magic, speed with a sword… and luck.

Every town holds a new mystery every fortress, a new danger. Merchants will sell you magic and valuable tools, but it's up to you to figure out what you need. Long, secret mantras help you slip through the mists, but will you survive the next challenge?

This is Faxanadu, the legend, the adventure—the incredible journey on the World Tree."

Tetris
November 1989

"The Soviet Game Sensation!

Your pulse quickens. Beams, boxes, zig-zags, and "L" shaped building blocks drop relentlessly down a narrow passage.

You quickly spin, shift, and align the shapes, then slide them in for a perfect fit.

It's challenging and the pace is demanding. But satisfaction comes as you position each block neatly into place.

Start at new heights for a tough contest. Pick the music and set your pace from 20 progressive skill levels."

Short Order & Eggsplode!
December 1989

"Eggsplode! is Eggciting!

This hen-house will keep you hopping!

It's your job to protect the chickens.

The sly fox and his giggling friend are planting bombs in the hen house.

Quick! Jump on the Power Pad to stop the Eggsplosion! But don't mistake an egg for a bomb or the chicken may give you a piece of her mind.

Eggstra good times are guaranteed!

Short Order Shenanigans!

Can you build a bigger burger?

Piggy, rabbit and mouse place their orders. Get hopping and see who can last the longest!

Keep their orders straight, match their steps, and you'll make hamburgers as tall as a house!

It's an entertaining romp for kids with an appetite for fun!"

To The Earth
November 1989

"Use your Zapper Light Gun to blast deadly UFOs, hurling meteors, and angry aliens on a cosmic battlefield!

You are on a mission to save the Earth. You are the commander of a high-speed astro cruiser.

Meteors are crashing. UFO's hurtle toward you at astro speed. Deadly alien vessels take a collision course.

Use your Zapper Light Gun to blast back. Your weapons snap and flash as wave after wave of extraterrestrials attacks! Saturn and Jupiter may hide more treacherous aliens.

Zoom past them, but don't relax your guard—not until you've fought your way… To The Earth!

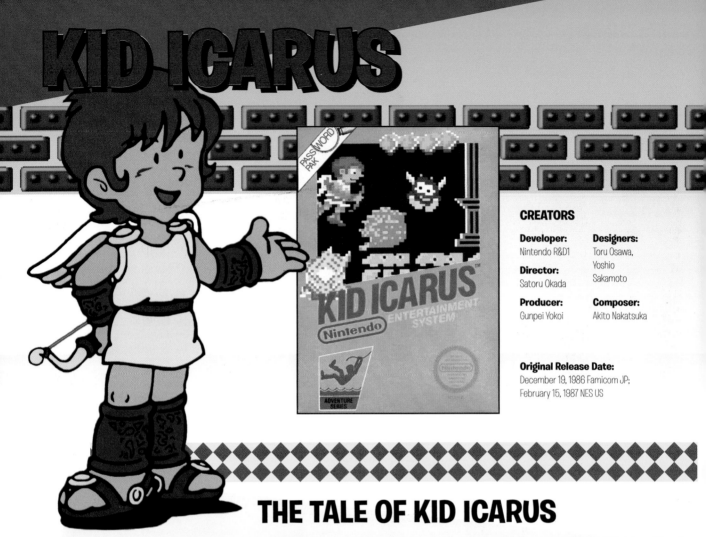

KID ICARUS

CREATORS

Developer:
Nintendo R&D1

Director:
Satoru Okada

Producer:
Gunpei Yokoi

Designers:
Toru Osawa,
Yoshio
Sakamoto

Composer:
Akito Nakatsuka

Original Release Date:
December 19, 1986 Famicom JP;
February 15, 1987 NES US

THE TALE OF KID ICARUS

Let us go back to the distant past, to an age when gods and man lived together in harmony. There was once a kingdom called Angel Land. This kingdom was ruled by two beautiful goddesses: Palutena, who administered light, and Medusa, who ruled darkness. Palutena lived in the Palace in the Sky and administered light so that man could live in happiness. And, bathed in this light, man grew food and lived in peace. Medusa, the goddess of darkness, was different. Medusa hated mankind. She took great pleasure in drying up the crops that man took great pains to grow, and in turning people into stone statues.

In her anger, Palutena changed Medusa into an ugly monster and banished her to the deep, dark Underworld. For this, Medusa promised to take over the Palace in the Sky where Palutena lived. So great was Medusa's anger that she joined forces with the monsters and evil spirits of the Underworld. Her army soon surpassed the strength of Palutena's, and a war between Palutena and Medusa began. Medusa led a surprise attack on Palutena's army; they barely managed to escape the ambush.

Palutena's army suffered major losses and was heavily defeated in the final battle. What's more, Medusa's army took the Three Sacred Treasures—the Mirror Shield, the Light Arrows, and the Wings of Pegasus—away from them. Almost all the warriors in Palutena's army were turned into stone statues, and Palutena herself was imprisoned deep in the Palace in the Sky. The peaceful realm of Angel Land came to be inhabited by foul and terrible monsters and was turned into a land of darkness ruled by the wicked Medusa. During her imprisonment in the depths of the Palace in the Sky, Palutena's Strength was drained to its last. As a last resort, she sought the help of an angel youth named Pit, who was held prisoner in a deep dungeon in the Underworld.

Pit was a valiant warrior who used to be in charge of Palutena's personal bodyguards. Armed with a bow and arrow brought to him through Palutena's magical Strength, Pit attempted to escape from the Underworld. The guard at this time was low in number, as Medusa's army had advanced to the Palace in the Sky. Pit succeeded in his escape and set out on his long adventure to rescue Palutena. Yet to defeat Medusa, he had to obtain the Three Sacred Treasures.

Will Pit be able to restore Palutena's light and return it to Angel Land? Only you can answer that question.

GETTING STARTED

Title Screen

From the Title Screen, press the Start Button to activate the Main Menu.

Main Menu

The Main Menu offers two options: **Start** or **Continue**.

Press the Select Button to choose either Start or Continue. If you choose Start, the game begins. If you choose Continue, the Password Screen appears.

Password Screen

Use the Directional Pad to select a letter or number. Press the A Button to confirm your choice. Use the B Button to backspace the register. When you finish the password, press the Start Button to continue your game.

GAME OVER

Pit's Endurance deceases each time he takes damage. When his Endurance runs out, the game ends and a password appears. Press the Start Button to immediately restart your game from the last checkpoint, or use the password to continue your game at a later time.

HOW TO PLAY

Basic Controls

Move

Press Left and Right on the Directional Pad to move Pit in the corresponding direction. When Pit is near a ladder, press Up to climb.

Jump

Press the A Button to make Pit jump. Perform jumps to move between platforms or leap over enemies.

Crouch

Hold Down on the Directional Pad to make Pit crouch. Crouching is used to dodge projectile attacks, but it also allows Pit to drop down from certain types of platforms. While Pit is crouching, press Left or Right to make him slide in the corresponding direction.

Aim

By default, Pit aims his bow in the direction he's facing. Hold Up on the Directional Pad to make Pit aim upward.

Attack

Press the B Button to shoot Pit's bow or swing an equipped Mallet.

Equip Mallet

Press the Select Button to equip a Mallet from Pit's inventory. Mallets can only be equipped in fortresses, and they should only be used to free Centurions from statues. Press the Select Button while a Mallet is equipped to put it away.

Displays

Screen Display

During gameplay, the screen display offers two useful pieces of information:

- The number of Hearts in Pit's possession
- Pit's current level of Endurance

Hearts are the currency of Angel Land. Use the Hearts you collect to buy useful items from Stores and Black Marketeers. Pit can hold up to 999 Hearts at a time.

Endurance indicates how much punishment Pit can sustain before he succumbs to his injuries. Red sections indicate remaining Endurance, while the blue section indicates lost Endurance. At the beginning of the game, Pit has only one bar of Endurance. You can unlock up to four additional bars of Endurance by achieving high scores.

Menu Display

During the game, press the Start Button to pause the action and open the Menu Display. This screen contains additional details about Pit's current status and your overall progress.

TOTAL

This is the amount of points you've earned since starting the game. Your total score updates each time you reach the checkpoint at the end of the stage.

SCORE

This is the amount of points you've earned since your last checkpoint. When you reach the next checkpoint, this number is added to your total score.

HEART

This is the number of Hearts in Pit's possession.

ENDURANCE

This meter shows Pit's current level of Endurance.

STRENGTH

This indicates Pit's current attack power. When the game begins, Pit's Strength is indicated by a single arrow. To improve this rating, Pit must perform well enough to impress the god of the Sacred Chamber. Each time Pit is deemed worthy enough, his Strength rating increases by one arrow, and his attacks become noticeably more powerful.

MAP

This slot is filled when Pit collects a fortress's Check Sheet. If Pit also has a Flaming Torch, the Check Sheet indicates his current location. If Pit has a Pencil, the Check Sheet indicates any locations that have already been visited. Once Pit leaves a fortress, the Check Sheet, Pencil, and Flaming Torch are discarded.

WEAPONS

This displays any enchanted Weapons currently in Pit's possession. If a Weapon is grayed out, it can't be used. This happens when a Weapon hasn't been activated, or anytime Pit is within a fortress.

TREASURES

This indicates how many of the Three Sacred Treasures Pit has collected. Pit must collect all three of these items before he's able to face Medusa.

INVENTORY ITEMS

The Menu Display also contains six slots for inventory items:

- Water of Life
- Mallets
- Angel's Feathers
- Flaming Torch
- Pencil
- Credit Card

When Pit acquires one of these items, it's automatically placed in the appropriate slot.

EXPLORING ANGEL LAND

Angel Land is divided into four distinct worlds:

1. Underworld **2.** Overworld **3.** Skyworld **4.** Palace in the Sky

The Underworld, the Overworld, and Skyworld each contain a fortress, and each fortress holds one of the Three Sacred Treasures. Unfortunately, each of these powerful artifacts is protected by one of Medusa's Gatekeepers. Pit's mission (and your objective) is to find and defeat each of the Gatekeepers, collect the Three Sacred Treasures, and use them to defeat Medusa in the Palace in the Sky.

Chambers

There are eight types of chambers scattered throughout Angel Land. Visit these chambers to find challenging battles, useful items, helpful merchants, and more. Most stages contain multiple chambers, so investigate any curiously located doors.

Mind the Doors

Chambers located in fortresses can be visited multiple times. Outside of fortresses, chamber doors are sealed the moment you leave.

Treasure Chamber

Each Treasure Chamber holds eight containers. Shoot a container to crack it open and see what's inside. Of course, there are a few things you should know before you begin raiding a Treasure Chamber:

- It costs five Hearts to shoot a container.
- When you collect a revealed item, all unbroken containers vanish.
- Most containers hold either a Big Heart or a Mallet.
- One container holds the God of Poverty.
- If you free the God of Poverty, all revealed items and unbroken containers vanish.
- If you break seven containers without revealing the God of Poverty, he leaves the Treasure Chamber. You can then break the final container to reveal a rare item left in his place.

Lucky Number Eight

When you manage to break all eight of a Treasure Chamber's containers, the last container contains one of four items:

- Angel's Feather
- Water of Life (Bottle)
- Water Barrel
- Credit Card

While most of these items can be also purchased from various merchants, clearing Treasure Chambers is the only way to find the elusive Credit Card.

Enemy's Lair

Every Enemy's Lair contains a sizable group of Specknoses. You don't receive any points for battling these enemies, but each Specknose you defeat drops a Big Heart. Of course, suffering damage depletes Pit's Endurance—and the Protective Crystal doesn't function within these chambers. Luckily, you're free to leave an Enemy's Lair at any time.

Store

Visit Stores to exchange the Hearts you've collected for useful items. Angel's Feathers are available in all Stores located outside of fortresses. Pencils and Flaming Torches are only found in Stores located within fortresses. Each Store only stocks three items at a time, but every Store offers at least one Water of Life item.

Possible Stock: Standard Store

Item	Price
Water of Life (Chalice)	210
Water of Live (Bottle)	350
Mallet	20
Angel's Feather	390

Possible Stock: Fortress Store

Item	Price
Water of Life (Chalice)	210
Water of Live (Bottle)	350
Mallet	20
Pencil	180
Flaming Torch	350

Rapid Restock

If you don't see the item you want in a fortress Store, exit the chamber and return to find a new selection of items waiting for you.

Black Marketeer

Like Stores, these chambers offer useful items for sale. The prices are a bit higher, but the Black Marketeer sells some items you can't buy anywhere else. Each Black Marketeer only stocks three items at a time, and these chambers are never found in fortresses.

Possible Stock: Black Marketeer

Item	Price
Water of Life (Bottle)	480
Water Barrel	500
Angel's Feather	450
Fire (Flaming Arrows)	600
Sacred Bow	500
Protective Crystal	700

Stolen Goods

An enchanted Weapon only becomes available for purchase after it's been stolen by a Pluton or a Pluton Fly.

Sacred Chamber

Each time you enter a Sacred Chamber, your recent performance is judged. If you've displayed exceptional skill since the start of the stage, the Sacred Chamber contains a god. After a brief greeting, the god offers an arrow; simply collect the arrow to increase Pit's Strength rating. If the chamber is empty, you must wait until you reach the next Sacred Chamber for another chance to increase Pit's Strength rating.

Sacred Training Chamber

Each time you enter a Sacred Training Chamber, a god summons a series of Monoliths for you to battle. Dodge or defeat these enemies until the god reappears. If you succeed, the god allows you to pick any one of the three enchanted Weapons.

Hot Spring Chamber

Hot Spring Chambers contain pools of revitalizing water. Jump into one of these pools to fill Pit's Endurance meter within a few seconds!

Hospital

These chambers are only found in fortresses, but they offer a vital service—whenever Pit is transformed into an eggplant, visit the nearest Hospital to remove the curse.

POWERING UP

Pit begins the game with a single bar of endurance, a Strength rating of one arrow, and a bow capable of short-range attacks. Luckily, there are several ways to improve Pit's combat abilities as you progress through the game.

Increasing Endurance

Pit's Endurance meter starts out with only one bar, but you can unlock up to four additional Endurance bars by reaching various score thresholds. The more enemies you defeat, the faster you add new bars to Pit's Endurance meter.

Endurance Levels

Level	Minimum Total Score
1 bar	0
2 bars	20,000
3 bars	50,000
4 bars	100,000
5 bars	200,000

Each time you reach a checkpoint, all the points you earned in the previous stage are added to your total score. Each time you earn a new bar, it's automatically added to Pit's Endurance meter.

Increasing Strength

When the game starts, Pit has a Strength rating of one arrow. To increase this rating, you must earn and collect new arrows from Sacred Chambers. There are several factors that determine whether or not a god appears in a Sacred Chamber; some of the actions you take improve your chances of receiving an arrow, while others count against you.

High-skill actions include:

- Defeating enemies that award points
- Collecting Hearts
- Collecting Mallets
- Earning or recovering an enchanted Weapon
- Purchasing inventory items

Note that some high-skill actions carry much more weight than others. In most cases, defeating an enemy worth 500 points is deemed much more impressive than defeating an enemy worth 100 points; earning an enchanted Weapon is far more impressive than purchasing an Angel's Feather. Put simply, the more high-skill actions you perform before you reach a Sacred Chamber, the better your chances of boosting Pit's Strength rating.

Low-skill actions include:

- Taking damage from enemies
- Firing arrows
- Breaking Treasure Chamber containers

Obviously, it isn't practical to avoid all low-skill actions. The idea is to weigh any risks against potential rewards. It's well worth raiding a Treasure Chamber if you emerge with a nice haul of items, and if a few arrows allow you to defeat an enemy, don't hesitate to shoot. Just remember to make up for each low-skill action with plenty of high-skill actions.

Activating Weapons

You can earn enchanted Weapons by completing challenges in Sacred Training Chambers. Each time you succeed, you can choose one of three powerful items: Flaming Arrows, the Sacred Bow, or the Protective Crystal. However, acquiring one of these items is just the first step—each Weapon you collect must be activated before it can be used.

Weapon activation is tied to Pit's Endurance meter. A newly acquired Weapon remains dormant (grayed out) until Pit's Endurance meets or exceeds a specific number of full bars. The minimum amount of Endurance needed to activate a particular Weapon depends on the order in which the three Weapons are chosen.

Weapon Activation

Position	Required Endurance
First Weapon	2 full bars
Second Weapon	3 full bars
Third Weapon	4 full bars

Once a Weapon has been activated, it no longer carries any Endurance requirements. Weapons can't be used in fortresses, so all Weapons are deactivated when Pit enters one of these stages. Once the fortress has been conquered, any previously activated Weapons automatically regain their power.

POWERING UP AND ENDINGS

When you complete the game, you receive one of five endings. To receive the game's happiest ending, you must complete four tasks by the time you defeat Medusa:

- Reach Pit's maximum Heart capacity (999 Hearts)
- Reach Pit's maximum Strength rating (5 arrows)
- Reach Pit's maximum Endurance level (5 bars)
- Acquire all three Weapons (Fire, Sacred Bow, Protective Crystal)

ITEMS

Weapons

These powerful items can be earned by completing the challenges found in Sacred Training Chambers.

	Fire (Flaming Arrows)	This Weapon adds a spinning fireball to every arrow Pit fires.
	Sacred Bow	This Weapon allows Pit's arrows to fly a bit faster and much farther.
	Protective Crystal	This Weapon produces two magic crystals that circle Pit, damaging any enemies they touch.

Sacred Treasures

These items must be recovered from Medusa's Gatekeepers. The Three Sacred Treasures can only be used when Pit reaches the Palace in the Sky.

	Sealed Casket	Each Sealed Casket you recover from a Gatekeeper contains one of the Three Sacred Treasures. Sealed Caskets are automatically opened when Pit is ready to confront Medusa.
	Mirror Shield	The Mirror Shield allows Pit to repel enemy projectiles.
	Light Arrows	Light Arrows allow for powerful, long-range shots.
	Wings of Pegasus	The Wings of Pegasus allow Pit to fly.

Hearts

As the currency of Angel Land, Hearts can be used to purchase items from Stores and Black Marketeers. These items almost always appear when an enemy is vanquished, and more powerful enemies tend to drop more valuable Hearts. Hearts disappear after a few seconds, so grab them as quickly as you can.

	Heart	Collect one of these to add a single Heart to Pit's funds.
	Half Heart	Collect one of these to add five Hearts to Pit's funds.
	Big Heart	Collect one of these to add 10 Hearts to Pit's funds.

Special Items

These items are very rare—don't pass one by without grabbing it!

	Harp	Touch a Harp to transform nearby enemies into Mallets. Any Mallets you collect can be used to break the Centurion statues found in fortresses.
	Arrow	These special arrows only appear in Sacred Chambers, and only when you've managed to impress the gods. Each arrow you collect increases Pit's Strength rating, making his attacks more powerful.
	Credit Card	The Credit Card can only be found in Treasure Chambers. This item gives you a line of credit at Black Marketeers. Once you purchase an item on credit, the Hearts you collect are automatically applied to your debt. You can't replenish your funds or make more purchases until the debt is paid off, so spend wisely!

Common Items

These items can be purchased from merchants and/or found scattered throughout Angel Land. But that doesn't mean they're easily acquired—some of these items can be very expensive.

	Mallet	Use Mallets to free Centurions trapped within fortress statues. Using a Mallet removes it from Pit's inventory, so collect as many as you can.
	Angel's Feather	An Angel's Feather is consumed when Pit falls off the screen. Instead of vanishing, Pit floats back up, which provides him with a short amount of time to reach a safe foothold.
	Water of Life (Chalice)	Chalices are consumed the moment they're collected. Grab one of these items to instantly refill one bar of the Endurance meter.
	Water of Life (Bottle)	Bottles are consumed when Pit's Endurance is completely drained. Consuming a Bottle refills one bar of Endurance, preventing Pit from succumbing to his injuries. By default, Pit can only carry one Bottle at a time.
	Water Barrel	The Water Barrel allows Pit to carry up to eight Bottles. This item can be purchased from Black Marketeers or found in Treasure Chambers.

Fortress Items

These items can only be found in fortresses. They're automatically removed from Pit's inventory each time a fortress is conquered.

	Check Sheet	Every fortress contains a Check Sheet for you to find. This item serves as a map of the fortress, but it requires a Pencil and/or Flaming Torch to be of use.
	Flaming Torch	This item is only found in fortress Stores. The Flaming Torch allows the Check Sheet to show Pit's current location. Without a Check Sheet, a Flaming Torch serves no purpose.
	Pencil	This item is only found in fortress Stores. The Pencil allows the Check Sheet to mark rooms that have already been visited. Without a Check Sheet, a Pencil serves no purpose.

ENEMIES

Common Enemies

These enemies are found throughout Angel Land.

	Name	Health	Attack	Heart Value	Point Value	Description
	Shemum	1	1	1	100	This snake-like creature slides along platforms, dropping down whenever it reaches a ledge.
	Specknose	1	2	10	0	The Specknose only appears in Enemy's Lairs. These creatures are swift and aggressive, but they aren't very durable. They drop Big Hearts, but you receive no points for defeating a Specknose.
	Reaper	10	2	10	500	These powerful enemies patrol platforms throughout Angel Land. If a Reaper spots you, it charges straight toward you while summoning a swarm of Reapettes. Shoot Reapers from behind, or slip past them while they're turned away from you. Either way, avoid being seen!
	Reapette	1	2	1	100	These creatures appear when a Reaper spots you. Reapettes aren't very durable, but they can deal significant damage. When these enemies appear, lure them to a relatively safe spot and shoot them down.
	Monolith	1-2	1-2	1	0	These enemies only appear in Sacred Training Chambers. Defeat or dodge these Monoliths to prove your worthiness and earn enchanted Weapons. Monoliths can materialize at any spot within a chamber, so it's usually best to stand your ground and shoot them as they appear. They drop Hearts, but you receive no points for defeating a Monolith.
	Eggplant Wizard	10	2	10	500	Eggplant Wizards only appear in fortresses. These fiends use their arcing projectiles to transform Pit into an eggplant. Once this happens, the only way to remove the curse is to visit an available Hospital. These enemies are also fairly durable—until you've boosted Pit's Strength rating, it's usually best to slip past an attacking Eggplant Wizard.

World 1: Underworld

	Name	Health	Attack	Heart Value	Point Value	Description
	Monoeye	1	1	5	300	Monoeyes almost always appear in groups. If you spot a lone Monoeye, you can be sure more are on the way. These enemies fly in irregular sweeping patterns, moving back and forth across the stage until they close in to attack. Wait for them to float into range, and then take them out one at a time.
	McGoo	1	1-2	5	300	This creature emerges from the ground, hurls a fireball, then sinks back out of sight. Luckily, it takes a moment for a McGoo to solidify. Shoot one just as it appears, and then crouch down to avoid its attack.
	Nettler	1	2	5	300	Once it gets close, a Nettler can duck under Pit's arrows. Stay back and shoot this enemy from a safe distance.
	Commyloose	2	1	5	300	These creatures attack in formation, leaping up from the bottom of the screen. A Commyloose must land between each pouncing attack—that's the best time to strike.
	Ganewmede (Blue)	1	1	5	300	These creatures only appear in the Underworld fortress. They tend to attack in large groups, so dodging them can be fairly difficult. Luckily, they aren't very durable.
	Ganewmede (Red)	2	2	10	500	Red Ganewmedes behave just like blue variants, but they're twice as powerful. They're only found in the Underworld fortress.
	Kobil (Blue)	2	1	1	100	These fortress-dwelling creatures are relatively slow. Shoot them before they have a chance to attack.
	Kobil (Red)	6	2	5	300	Red Kobils are stronger than blue Kobils, but they exhibit the same behavior. Stay back and shoot them from a safe distance.

	Name	Health	Attack	Heart Value	Point Value	Description
	Twinbellows	100	2	0	8,000	Located deep within the Underworld fortress, Twinbellows is the first Gatekeeper you face. This massive two-headed hound uses a sweeping stream of fireballs to attack its prey from a distance.

World 2: Overworld

	Name	Health	Attack	Heart Value	Point Value	Description
	Rokman	2	3	10	500	Once a Rokman appears, it drops straight down until it vanishes from sight. These creatures always appear in groups. Falling Rokmen can do serious damage, so take them out quickly.
	Girin	1	1	5	300	These burrowing bugs use the same tactics favored by McGoos—soon after a Girin appears, it launches a projectile and vanishes back underground. When you spot a set of Girin pincers poking out of the ground, get ready to duck.
	Minos	2	1	5	300	When a Minos attacks, it leaps up from below, floats in the air for just a moment, then falls back out of sight. If you discover you've wandered into Minos territory, stick to the high ground—the longer you have to spot a Minos, the better your chances of dodging it.
	Mick	2	1	5	300	These creatures are similar to the Monoeyes found in the Underworld, but they tend to be less elusive. When Micks attack, position yourself directly in their path, and then use a series of rapid arrow shots to clear them out before they reach you.
	Keron	3	1	5	300	These toad-like creatures utilize pouncing attacks. They aren't particularly swift, but Kerons are fairly durable. Until you've improved Pit's Strength rating, attack these creatures from a safe distance.
	Pluton	N/A	0	N/A	N/A	These thieving enemies use their pouncing attacks to snatch enchanted Weapons from Pit's inventory. Plutons can't be defeated, so evasion is your best option. Watch a Pluton as it approaches, then dodge past it as it prepares to strike. Weapons stolen by Plutons can be reacquired in Sacred Training Chambers or bought back from Black Marketeers.
	Snowman	10	1-3	10	500	These large, durable creatures attack by hurling snowballs. It's usually best to attack a Snowman from a distance. Touching a snowball costs Pit some Endurance, but touching a Snowman causes considerably more damage.
	Tamambo (Blue)	2	1	5	300	These enemies are only found in the Overworld fortress, and they always appear in large groups. Shoot them as they appear to prevent them from overwhelming you.
	Tamambo (Red)	3	2	10	500	Like the blue Tamambo, the red Tamambo only appears in the Overworld fortress, and it always attacks in groups. However, a red Tamambo is a bit stronger than its blue counterpart.
	Shulm (Blue)	3	1	1	100	Shulms only appear in the Overworld fortress. They move fairly slowly—just stand back and shoot them from a distance.
	Shulm (Red)	8	2	5	300	Red Shulms are noticeably tougher than blue Shulms, but they're otherwise the same. Keep your distance and take these creatures out before they can attack.

	Name	Health	Attack	Heart Value	Point Value	Description
	Hewdraw	200	3	0	8,000	This leaping serpent serves as the Gatekeeper of the Overworld. During battle, Hewdraw pounces around its lair, inflicting damage to anyone caught in its path. Its body is impervious to all attacks—only Hewdraw's head can be damaged.

World 3: Skyworld

	Name	Health	Attack	Heart Value	Point Value	Description
	Collin	1	3	10	500	This armored knight doesn't attack, but touching one causes Pit to lose a significant amount of Endurance.
	EelEye	1	2	1	0	These creatures circle Collin, protecting him from your attacks. They drop Hearts, but you receive no points for defeating an EelEye.
	Holer	1	1-2	5	300	Like the McGoos of the Underworld (and the Girins of the Overworld), this creature emerges from the ground, tosses a fireball, and vanishes from sight. However, Holers often appear on clouds, so it's rarely safe to duck under their attacks.
	Octos	4	3	10	500	These creatures behave similarly to the Commyloose of the Underworld. They always appear in groups, popping into view to attack from below.
	Pluton Fly	N/A	0	N/A	N/A	Like Plutons, Pluton Flies are capable of stealing enchanted Weapons. These creatures can't be defeated, but they're fairly easy to dodge. A Pluton Fly attacks by charging horizontally—just bait one into attacking and step out of its path.

	Name	Health	Attack	Heart Value	Point Value	Description
	Keepah	1	3	10	0	This flying Kobil utilizes a serpentine attack pattern. Keepahs aren't very durable, but they can do considerable damage—in some cases, these strange creatures even self-destruct. They drop Big Hearts, but you receive no points for defeating a Keepah.
	Komayto	3	2	5	300	These flying, jellyfish-like creatures always appear in groups. Shoot them out of the air when they get into range.
	Tros (Blue)	3	2	5	300	These enemies only appear in the Skyworld fortress. Tros always appear in large groups. Shoot them before they manage to fill the room.
	Tros (Red)	4	3	10	500	Red Tros are similar to blue Tros. They only appear in the Skyworld fortress, they always appear in groups, and they can quickly fill a room. However, red Tros are a bit stronger than their blue counterparts. Shoot each one as it appears.
	Uranos (Blue)	4	2	1	100	These enemies are only found in the Skyworld fortress. They move fairly slowly—just shoot them before they reach you.
	Uranos (Red)	10	3	5	300	A red Uranos is much stronger than a blue Uranos, but it moves just as slowly. Shoot these enemies before they can touch you.

	Name	Health	Attack	Heart Value	Point Value	Description
	Pandora	200	5	0	8,000	Pandora serves as the Gatekeeper of Skyworld. This strange, amorphous demon god is not only capable of summoning damage-dealing bubbles—it also seems to vanish and materialize at will.

World 1: Palace in the Sky

	Name	Health	Attack	Heart Value	Point Value	Description
	Totem	4	3	5	300	These creatures fall straight down from the top of the screen. Avoid flying high in Totem territory. Stay low and shoot them as they drop. These creatures often pass right through the stage, but sometimes a group of Totems land on solid ground, creating a makeshift pillar right in your path—clear them out before you reach them.
	Moila	2	3	5	300	These creatures approach from the left, move across the screen, then turn around and charge back to the right. When you reach Moila territory, move toward the screen's right edge to avoid being ambushed.
	Syren	2	3	5	300	Syrens fly in predictable formations, but that doesn't mean they're easy to handle. When you spot a flock of Syrens, try to take out at least two enemies with each attack.
	Erinus	1(×4)	1-4	1(×3)	500(×4)	In its starting form, this creature can't fly; it simply patrols its platform, launching projectiles as you approach. However, once you strike an Erinus, it splits into three floating parts that attempt to swarm you. Being struck by a projectile costs you a bit of Endurance—touching an Erinus costs significantly more. You can earn 500 points for splitting an Erinus, and 500 more points for each part you manage to destroy. Each Erinus part also drops a Heart when defeated. If you pass by an Erinus without splitting it, the enemy reappears on the path ahead of you.
	Daphne	2	2	5	300	These creatures jump up from below, spread their petals, and float back down at a much slower speed. Fly upward when you enter Daphne territory to avoid being ambushed.
	Zuree	1	2	1	100	These ghostlike creatures aren't particularly powerful, but they do appear in large groups. Move back and clear them out from a distance.
	Tanatos	1	3	0	100	This snake lives in Medusa's hair, leaping out to protect its mistress during battle. Tanatos can deal heavy damage, but it isn't particularly durable. Shoot this snake to momentarily remove it from the battle—Tanatos bounces at fairly predictable angles, so time your shots accordingly.

	Name	Health	Attack	Heart Value	Point Value	Description
	Medusa	150	5	0	100 (per hit)	Medusa has thrown Angel Land into chaos and taken control of the Palace in the Sky. With Tanatos by her side, she uses her magical gaze to subdue anyone who dares to challenge her.

COMPLETING *KID ICARUS*

GENERAL ADVICE

Kid Icarus can be a very challenging game, but there are a few things you can do to help ensure that you emerge victorious:

- Increase Pit's Endurance meter as quickly as you can. Before you complete Stage 1-1, battle McGoos to boost your overall score. Try to earn at least 50,000 points before you reach the first checkpoint. It might take some practice, but the extra Endurance makes it much easier to overcome some of the game's early challenges.

- Make an Angel's Feather your first purchase. As you continue to earn Hearts, keep a supply of at least two Angel's Feathers available at all times. Water of Life is also very helpful, so invest in a Water Barrel once you have sufficient funds.

- Items like Hearts and Water of Life Chalices vanish when you leave an area. Collect every available item before you pass through a door.

- Learn the properties of various platforms. Pit can jump or drop through some platforms, while others stop him cold. Icy platforms offer very little traction, and moving platforms often float past enemies or hazards. You're much more likely to conquer a stage once you understand the footholds it offers.

- In vertical stages, Pit can often move past the edge of the screen to emerge on the opposite side of the stage. This isn't just handy—it's an essential part of reaching some checkpoints.

- Pick your battles! Some enemies are bound to give you more trouble than others. If you're having trouble dealing with a specific enemy type, avoid fighting them until you've improved Pit's combat abilities.

- When it comes to selecting enchanted Weapons, consider picking the Protective Crystal first, followed by the Sacred Bow, and, finally, Fire (Flaming Arrows).

- Take your time. There aren't any time limits to worry about, and you don't receive any bonuses for completing stages quickly. Unless you're being hounded by troublesome enemies, there's no harm in assessing your options before you make a move.

UNDERWORLD

This is the underground world where Pit was held prisoner. It's a natural maze, so go forward carefully! It's full of lava pools and underground glaciers.

Stage 1-1

ENEMIES	
	Shemum
	Monoeye
	Specknose
	Reaper
	Reapette
	Nettler
	McGoo

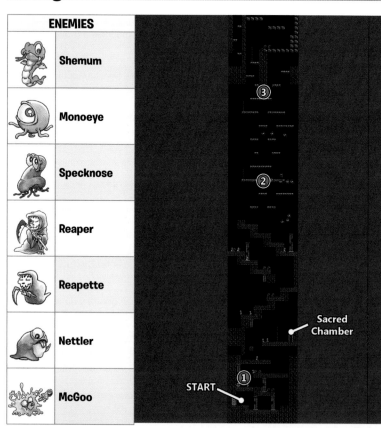

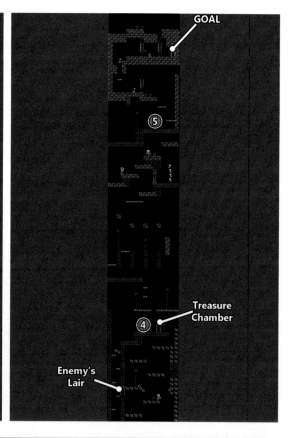

Sacred Chamber: Stage 1-1

This stage contains a Sacred Chamber, but you reach it before you've had much of a chance to impress the gods. Don't worry—you should be able to improve Pit's Strength rating soon enough. However, you might consider revisiting this chamber if you complete the game without reaching a Strength rating of five arrows.

The Shemums near the starting area aren't as tricky as the enemies you face later on. You can charge in to meet them head-on, but it's safer to let them come to you. Position yourself below a ledge and shoot each enemy as it lands in front of you.

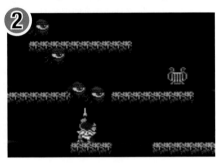

If swarming Monoeyes give you trouble, look for the Harp at Point 2. Grab the Harp to transform your attackers into collectible Mallets.

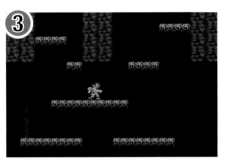

At Point 3, the area splits into two paths. If you want to test your skill in the available Enemy's Lair, take the path on the right.

Reapers are formidable enemies, and they can be quite a handful early in the game. Unless you're itching for a fight, consider slipping past patrolling Reapers until you've had a chance to improve Pit's Endurance and Strength.

There's an endless supply of McGoos at Point 5, and you can gain a big advantage by sticking around to battle them before you reach the checkpoint. Of course, you have to avoid taking too much damage! Watch the ground for signs of an emerging McGoo. When you see a McGoo forming, move to a safe position, face your target, and shoot the creature as it appears. Immediately after you attack, crouch down to avoid any incoming fireballs.

Battling McGoos can be a bit risky, but it's a great way to earn Hearts and boost your score. Remember—the faster you earn points, the sooner you improve Pit's Endurance!

Stage 1-2

ENEMIES	
	Shemum
	Monoeye
	Specknose
	Reaper
	Reapette
	McGoo
	Commyloose

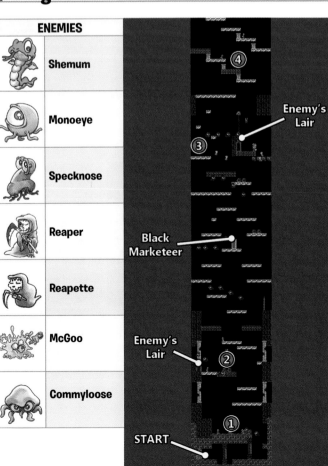

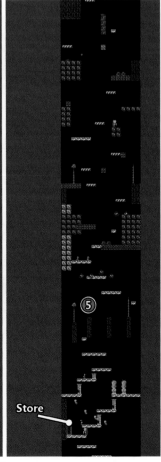

Sacred Chamber: Stage 1-2

This stage contains a Sacred Chamber. If you want to improve Pit's Strength rating, make sure you perform well. Defeat enemies, collect the Hearts they drop, and try your best to avoid taking damage or wasting too many arrows. A good performance here helps ensure that Pit is ready for the challenges ahead.

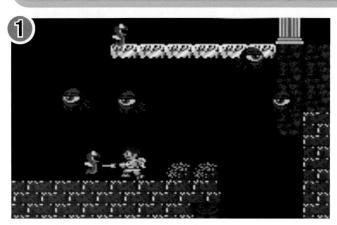

At Point 1, you face a combination of Monoeyes and Shemums. Deal with the Shemums first. Notice also that ice covers many of this stage's platforms. Icy platforms offer very little traction, making it fairly easy to slip off. Be careful!

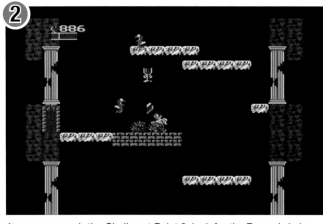

As you approach the Chalice at Point 2, look for the Enemy's Lair to the left. If you feel like testing your skill, grab the Chalice before heading inside.

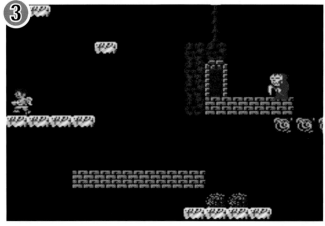

Remember that it's often necessary to move past the edge of the screen and emerge on the opposite side of the stage. As you near the Enemy's Lair at Point 3, time your approach to avoid being spotted by the patrolling Reaper. Again, if you choose to explore the Enemy's Lair, collect the nearby Chalice before you head inside.

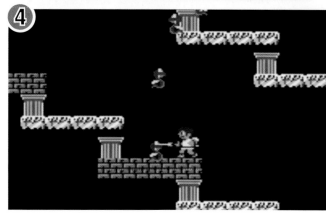

When you reach the Shemums at Point 4, pick a spot beneath the edge of a platform and let the enemies come to you. Moving around can cause the Shemums to scatter as they land—lure them in and pick them off one by one to earn some easy points.

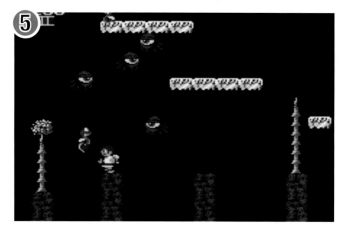

The narrow platforms at Point 5 can be tough to traverse— particularly when the area is swarming with enemies. Stand your ground and deal with nearby threats before you continue.

When you reach Point 6, stop climbing and wait for the nearby McGoos to emerge. Again, battling McGoos is a great way to earn Hearts as you boost your score—and because this stage contains a Sacred Chamber, it's also a great way to improve Pit's Strength rating. Once you're confident you've put on an impressive performance, continue up to the Sacred Chamber and claim your reward. As you do, watch out for the Commyloose that appear below you.

Stage 1-3

ENEMIES	
	Shemum
	Nettler
	Specknose
	Monoeye
	McGoo
	Commyloose
	Reaper
	Reapette

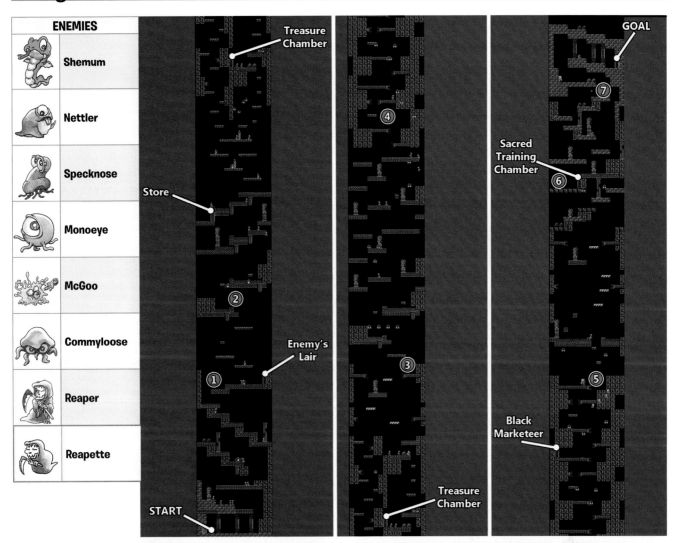

The terrain makes it difficult to attack a Nettler from a distance. Shoot these creatures as they drop down from ledges. Once a Nettler lands, it's more likely to duck under your arrows.

Touching a pool of lava costs Pit a bit of Endurance. Be careful, but don't linger near these hazards—enemies like Shemums, McGoos, and Commyloose often appear near the lava pools throughout this stage.

Stand on the platform at Point 3 to take out the incoming Shemums with ease. Get in position as quickly as possible, but take care to avoid touching the bramble sprouting from the edge of the platform.

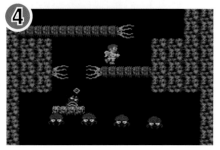

When you reach Point 4, you have to deal with Commyloose, McGoos, and hazardous brambles. It can be fairly daunting, but try not to rush. Deal with each threat as it appears, and continue climbing only when it's safe to do so.

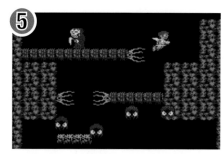

Keep an eye out for the Reaper at Point 5. Don't let the pursuing Commyloose force you into this enemy's line of sight. Whether you plan to attack the Reaper or slip past it, wait for this formidable enemy to turn its back before you make your move.

The Sacred Training Chamber at Point 6 offers your first opportunity to earn an enchanted Weapon. The test starts soon after you pass through the door, so be ready to defend yourself. When the trial starts, jump onto the interior doorway—stay close to the chamber's right wall to prevent Monoliths from appearing behind you.

Again, it's worth battling McGoos before you complete the stage. This is your last opportunity to boost Pit's Endurance before you face the first Gatekeeper, and you want plenty of Hearts to spend in the fortress's Stores.

Stage 1-4

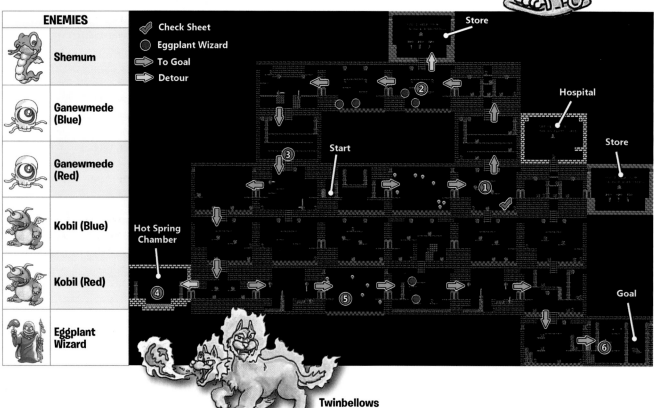

ENEMIES	
	Shemum
	Ganewmede (Blue)
	Ganewmede (Red)
	Kobil (Blue)
	Kobil (Red)
	Eggplant Wizard

Check Sheet
Eggplant Wizard
To Goal
Detour

Store
Hospital
Store
Start
Hot Spring Chamber
Goal

Twinbellows

Centurion Allies

Use the Mallets you've collected to free Centurions from their statues. Each Centurion you help joins the battle against the fortress's Gatekeeper.

The room at Point 1 contains the fortress's Check Sheet and two Centurion statues. It also features Shemum containers embedded in the ceiling. Look for these containers each time you enter a new room. Walking under one of these causes a group of Shemums to drop into the room—before you pass under a Shemum container, make preparations to deal with additional enemies.

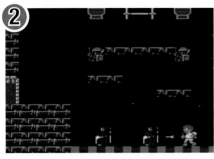

Once you've dealt with the Eggplant Wizards at Point 2, consider making a detour up to the nearby Store. Climb the ladder at the top of the room to pop in for a visit—just keep in mind that a new pair of Eggplant Wizards will be waiting for you when you exit the Store.

Beware of Eggplants

Due to their cursed eggplants, Eggplant Wizards rank among the most troublesome enemies in Angel Land. Whether you choose to fight them or charge past them, take care to avoid their projectiles. If Pit is transformed into an eggplant, head straight to the fortress Hospital to remove the curse.

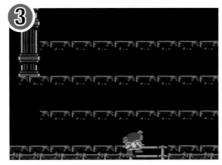

The ladder at Point 3 leads to a big drop, and where you land determines whether or not you can reach Twinbellows.

As you drop down from the ladder, press Left on the Directional Pad to land on the nearby platform. Be prepared to dodge the retracting spikes on your way to the next door.

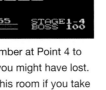

Visit the Hot Spring Chamber at Point 4 to replace any Endurance you might have lost. Don't hesitate to revisit this room if you take too much damage on your way to Twinbellows.

The room at Point 5 is a great place to earn Hearts and points. Defeat all the red Ganewmedes that appear, then exit and re-enter to find a fresh batch of enemies to battle. If Pit loses too much Endurance, simply revisit the nearby Hot Spring Chamber.

Twinbellows utilizes a sweeping fireball attack. Stay back and dodge the Gatekeeper's opening attack, then charge in and hit Twinbellows with a series of rapid shots. Each hit tends to knock the beast into the air, so most of Twinbellows's fireballs should pass right over you. If you need a bit of breathing room, use the available platforms to slip over Twinbellows and drag the fight back to the other side of the room. Depending on how many Centurions you managed to free, the battle with Twinbellows can end very quickly.

If you favor finesse over brute force, learn the timing of Twinbellows's fireballs. Jump over incoming projectiles, and shoot the beast as it prepares for its next attack.

OVERWORLD

Long, long ago, this world was inhabited by people of Angel Land. Now it's a den of creatures. The wide seas, glacier regions, and high mountain peaks lead to the fortress that stretches up to the heavens.

Stage 2-1

ENEMIES	
	Shemum
	Rokman
	Girin
	Specknose
	Minos
	Mick
	Keron

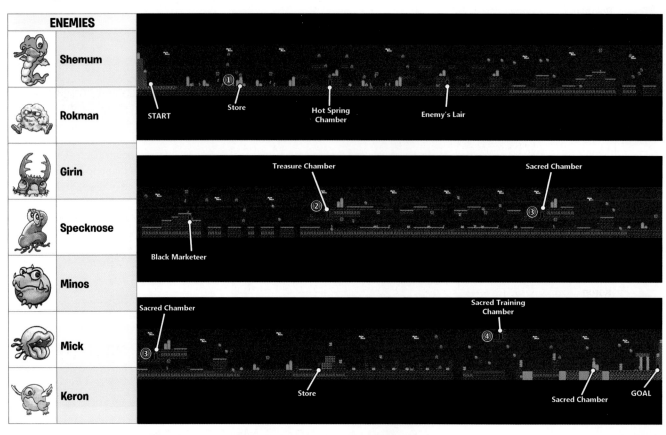

START   Store   Hot Spring Chamber   Enemy's Lair

Black Marketeer   Treasure Chamber   Sacred Chamber

Sacred Chamber   Sacred Training Chamber

Store   Sacred Chamber   GOAL

Sacred Chambers: Stage 2-1

This stage contains two Sacred Chambers, so you have two chances to add another arrow to Pit's Strength rating. If the first Sacred Chamber is empty, make sure you perform well on your way to the next one.

Remember that you receive no points for defeating a Specknose. Unless you're confident you can emerge unscathed, consider skipping the stage's Enemy's Lair—you find plenty of valuable, Heart-dropping foes out in the open.

Remember to visit the Sacred Chamber at Point 3. If you've performed well in this stage, Pit's Strength rating increases by one arrow—a boost in attack power makes it much easier to deal with troublesome Kerons. If the chamber is empty, do your best to impress the gods before you reach the stage's second Sacred Chamber. Defeat enemies, collect the Hearts they drop, conserve your arrows, and avoid taking damage.

Before you enter the Sacred Training Chamber at Point 4, know that you can't stand on the inner doorway. As soon as the training begins, jump down to the central platform and defend yourself from the incoming Monoliths. This ensures that you don't accidentally leave the chamber before the training is complete.

Grab the Harp at Point 1 while the Rokmen are still dropping. This should give you enough time to collect at least a few Mallets before they fall out of reach.

There's a Chalice near the Treasure Chamber at Point 2. If you want to collect it, drop down to the lower path before you move past the chamber entrance. Remember: the lower you are, the less time you have to spot incoming Minos.

Stage 2-2

ENEMIES	
	Specknose
	Rokman
	Minos
	Pluton
	Mick
	Snowman
	Keron

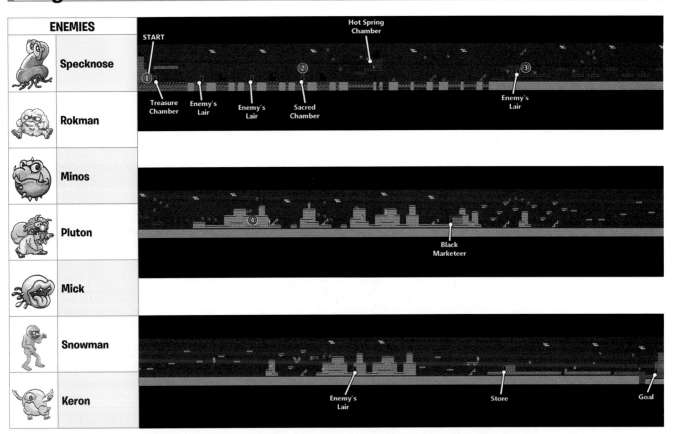

Sacred Chamber: Stage 2-2

This stage contains a Sacred Chamber, but it's located fairly close to the starting point. You don't have much time to impress the gods—don't waste an opportunity to prove your skill!

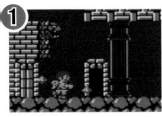

1 To impress the gods before you reach this stage's Sacred Chamber, you need to show great skill—but a little luck can be helpful too. Enter the Treasure Chamber at Point 1 and try to claim at least a few Big Hearts without revealing the God of Poverty.

After you exit the Treasure Chamber, visit the nearby Enemy's Lairs to battle for more Big Hearts. Collect as many as you can while avoiding damage.

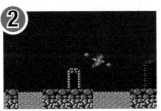

2 Before you enter the Sacred Chamber at Point 2, there's one more thing you can do to impress the gods. Jump over the chamber entrance and then hop across to the next island. Take care not to move too far from the door.

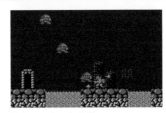

Rokmen begin falling as soon as you land. Shoot these enemies and collect the Big Hearts they drop. As you do, keep the Sacred Chamber entrance in sight. When you're ready, jump back to the Sacred Chamber and head inside. If you've performed well enough, you add another arrow to Pit's Strength rating.

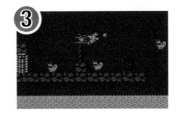

3 Several Plutons lurk past the Enemy's Lair at Point 3. These enemies can steal any enchanted Weapons you've earned, so keep your distance. Watch them as they pounce toward you, and jump over them one at a time.

4 Remember that crouching on some platforms causes Pit to drop through them. Avoid ducking under a Snowman's projectile unless you're certain it's safe to do so.

Stage 2-3

ENEMIES	
	Shemum
	Rokman
	Keron
	Minos
	Snowman
	Mick
	Specknose
	Girin
	Pluton

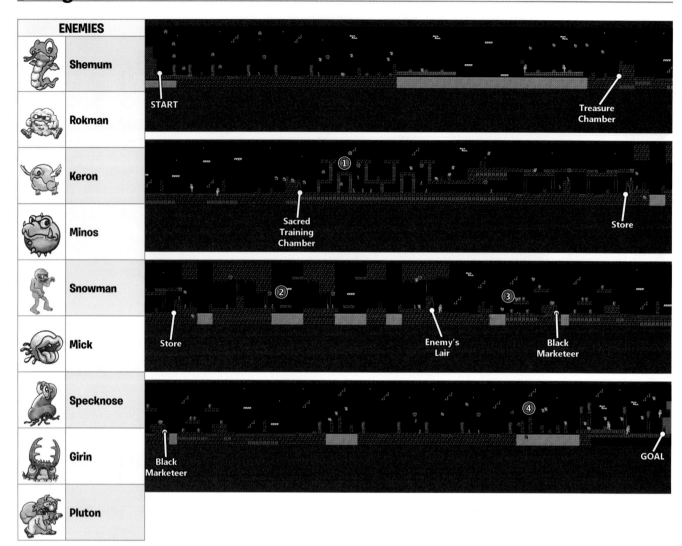

START

Treasure Chamber

① Sacred Training Chamber

Store

② Store

Enemy's Lair

③ Black Marketeer

④ Black Marketeer

GOAL

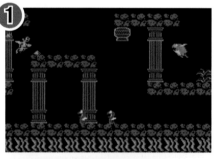

Consider using the platforms at Point 1 to follow the upper path. The lower path leads through some fairly tight spaces, making it difficult to dodge incoming enemies.

The platform at Point 2 passes through two thorn patches. Jump onto this platform when it rises up through the lower thorn patch, then keep running and leap to the next ledge. It takes some time for this platform to reach the ideal position—while you wait, take out any Shemums that drop out of the nearby container.

You find another gang of Plutons waiting at Point 3. If you plan to hang on to your enchanted Weapons, avoid touching these pouncing enemies.

Take your time crossing the narrow platforms at Point 4. It's much easier to focus on jumping after you've eliminated any approaching enemies.

Stage 2-4

ENEMIES	
	Shemum
	Tamambo (Blue)
	Tamambo (Red)
	Shulm (Blue)
	Shulm (Red)
	Eggplant Wizard

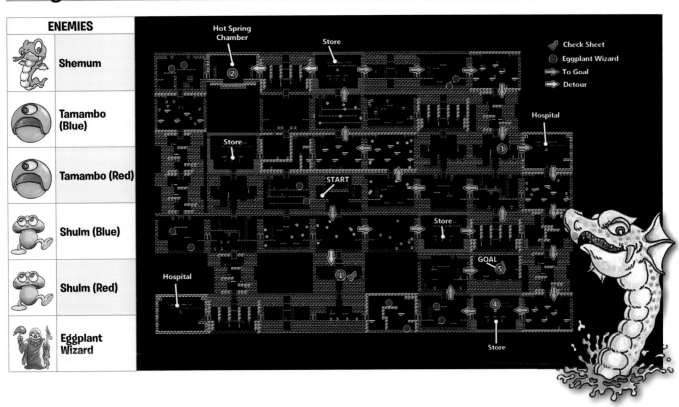

Hewdraw

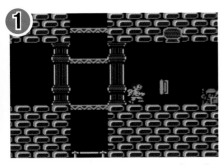

The Check Sheet is two rooms away from the stage's starting point. Drop down and collect it before you venture deeper into the fortress.

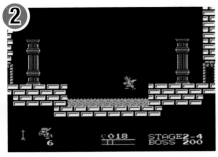

The Hot Spring Chamber is another essential detour. Stop in to top off Pit's Endurance.

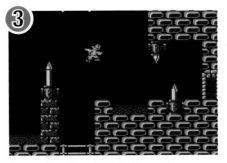

As you drop down to Point 3, use the Directional Pad to land on the small ledge near the lava. Slip past the spikes to the right and use the available door to enter one of the fortress's Hospitals. Even if you manage to slip past the Eggplant Wizards unscathed, visiting this Hospital allows you to avoid a few extra enemies on the way to Hewdraw.

The Store at Point 4 is a great place to stock up on Water of Life. If the items you want aren't in stock, leave and re-enter the Store to find a new selection of goods waiting for you.

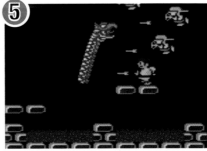

Hewdraw attacks by bouncing endlessly around the room. Its head is its only weak spot, but this serpent's entire body is a Weapon—touching any part of Hewdraw costs Pit a bit of Endurance. Centurion allies are particularly vulnerable to Hewdraw's touch, so stay well back if you hope to keep these allies in the fight for long.

Hewdraw can take a lot of punishment, even if you've managed to boost Pit's Strength rating at every opportunity. Pick your shots, and use the available platforms to avoid the serpent's pouncing attacks. Keep moving, stay out of the lava, and remember that only Hewdraw's head is vulnerable to Pit's arrows.

SKYWORLD

The skies are full of monsters. Flying through the air, Pit heads for the Palace in the Sky, where Medusa awaits him. Take care not to fall from the clouds!

Stage 3-1

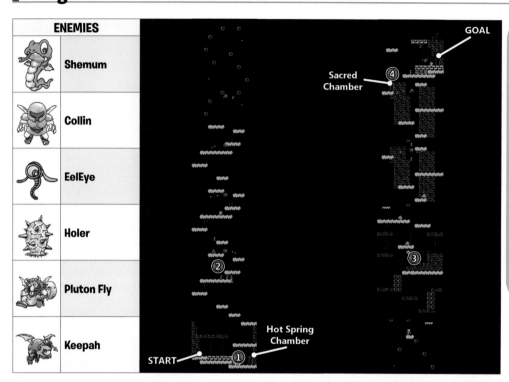

ENEMIES	
![Shemum]	Shemum
![Collin]	Collin
![EelEye]	EelEye
![Holer]	Holer
![Pluton Fly]	Pluton Fly
![Keepah]	Keepah

Sacred Chamber: Stage 3-1

This stage contains a Sacred Chamber, and it's conveniently located near the end of the stage. If you perform well enough, you shouldn't have much trouble impressing the gods by the time you arrive.

When the stage begins, take advantage of the Hot Spring Chamber at Point 1.

As you approach Point 2, keep an eye out for sprouting Holers. Crouching to avoid a Holer's projectile causes Pit to drop through these cloud platforms, so keep moving. It's much better to fight Holers on solid ground.

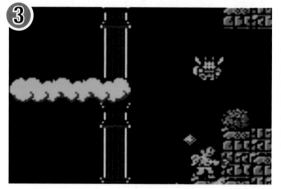

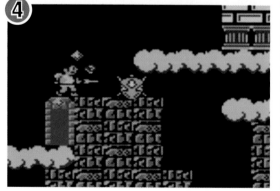

Whenever you encounter a Pluton Fly, jump up to bait the enemy into charging, then drop back down and wait as it flies off the screen. Like Plutons, Pluton Flies can steal enchanted Weapons, so keep your distance.

To make sure you impress the gods, consider doing a bit of Holer hunting before you enter the Sacred Chamber. Defeat these enemies and collect the Hearts they drop until you're confident you've done well—once your stage score reaches 20,000 points, you're virtually guaranteed to find a congratulatory arrow waiting for you.

Stage 3-2

ENEMIES

	Reaper
	Reapette
	Komayto
	Holer
	Shemum
	Octos

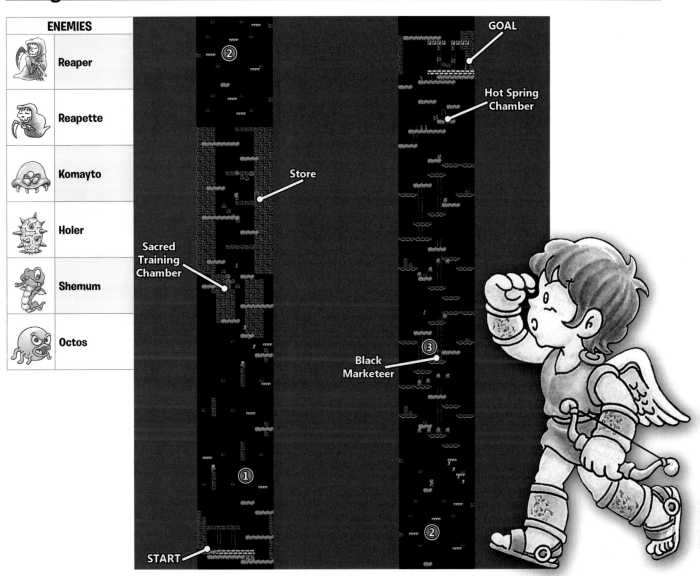

GOAL

Hot Spring Chamber

Store

Sacred Training Chamber

Black Marketeer

START

The Reapers in this stage patrol very narrow platforms. This means these creatures never face one direction for long. If you've managed to earn (and hang on to) all three enchanted Weapons, these Reapers shouldn't be much of a problem. However, if you're limited to short-range attacks, you might have to take a few risks to clear these enemies from essential footholds.

Take advantage of the stationary blocks scattered around Point 2. Stop to catch your breath and identify the best route along the moving platforms.

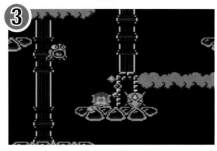

As you approach the Black Marketeer at Point 3, keep an eye out for lurking Holers. Remember that crouching on clouds causes Pit to drop through them—avoid battling Holers until you reach one of the more reliable footholds.

Stage 3-3

ENEMIES	
	Shemum
	Komayto
	Holer
	Octos
	Collin
	Eel Eye
	Reaper
	Reapette

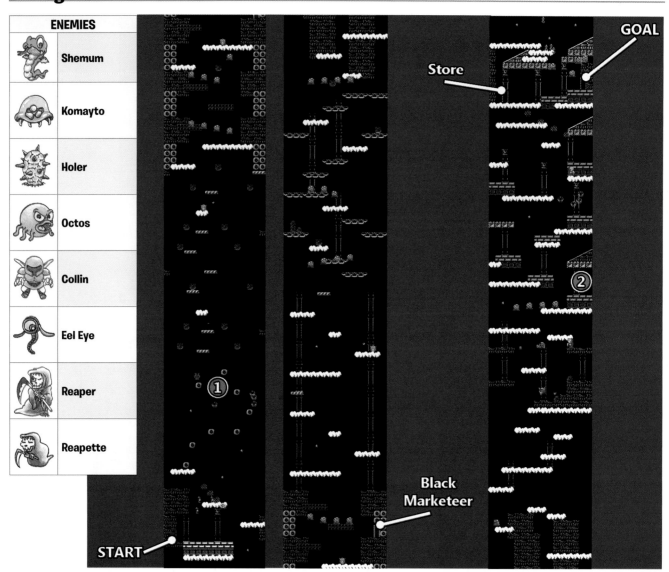

GOAL

Store

Black Marketeer

START

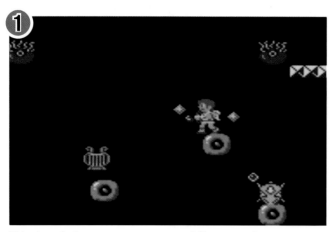

This stage features some very narrow platforms, so choose your path wisely. Just don't linger in one place for too long—you never know when a troublesome Holer might make an appearance.

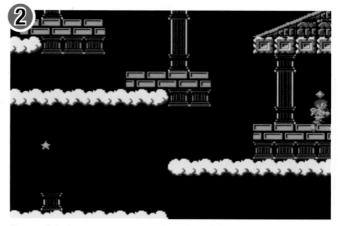

Be careful when you move past the edge of the screen in this stage—many of the platforms are staggered in such a way that you must jump as you transition from one side of the screen to the other.

Stage 3-4

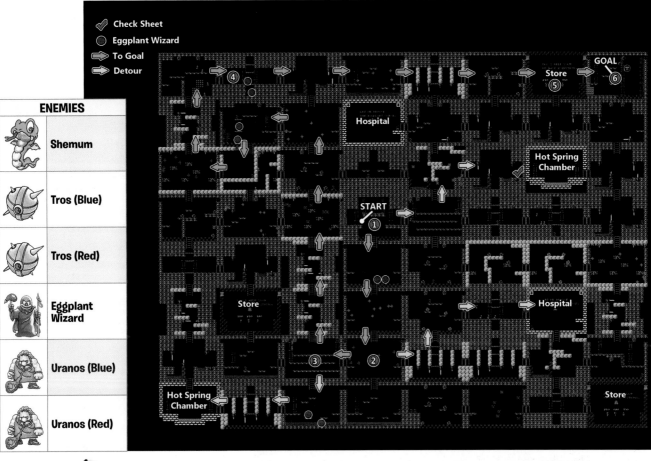

Check Sheet
Eggplant Wizard
To Goal
Detour

ENEMIES	
	Shemum
	Tros (Blue)
	Tros (Red)
	Eggplant Wizard
	Uranos (Blue)
	Uranos (Red)

Pandora

A Dangerous Drop!

The ladder at Point 1 leads to a room with two Eggplant Wizards. Avoid their attacks as you drop to the floor!

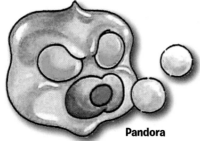

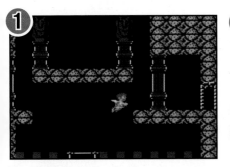

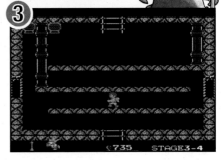

The Check Sheet is only a few rooms away from the stage's starting point. The ladder at Point 1 leads to a long drop—before you set out to face the final Gatekeeper, head through the door to the right. Make a quick detour to grab the fortress's Check Sheet, head back to Point 1, and climb down the ladder to begin the journey to Pandora's lair.

If you made it to Point 2 without being cursed, use the door to the left to continue toward Pandora. If you need some help from a nurse, head through the door to the right and make a quick detour—the nearest Hospital is only a few rooms away. Either way, remember how to get back to this room; you never know when an Eggplant Wizard will get the better of you.

When you reach Point 3, it's time to evaluate Pit's Endurance. If it could use a recharge, descend the ladder at the bottom of the room and make a detour to the nearest Hot Spring Chamber. You have to make it past another pair of Eggplant Wizards to reach the hot spring; if Pit's Endurance is relatively high, you might be better off continuing toward Pandora.

The Eggplant Wizards at Point 4 are particularly troublesome. The narrow corridor doesn't offer much room to move, and one of the wizards is located just below the only available path. At this point, a trip to the Hospital undoes virtually all the progress you've made. Approach with care, and don't be afraid to make a brief retreat if an incoming eggplant seems impossible to dodge.

Although it's possible to charge through the room unscathed, it takes precision timing and/or a significant amount of luck. Instead, consider allowing one of the available Shemums to strike—this small sacrifice grants a brief moment of invincibility. Defeat the first Eggplant Wizard while Pit is still flashing, then touch another Shemum and drop down to deal with the remaining wizard.

The Store at Point 5 offers one last chance to stock up on essential items. Once you defeat Pandora, you automatically enter the game's final stage. Even so, limit your spending—unless you have 999 Hearts by the time you defeat Medusa, you have no chance to receive the game's best ending.

This demon god serves as the Gatekeeper of Skyworld. When the battle starts, Pandora summons two hard-hitting bubbles that bounce around the room for the duration of the encounter. As you attack Pandora, keep a watchful eye on these bubbles—they bounce off walls, but they can also change direction without warning.

During the battle, Pandora often seems to vanish into thin air—this is an illusion. Just keep attacking the Gatekeeper's last known position; Pandora flashes into view each time an arrow lands. If you lose track of your target, look for the shadows that appear each time Pandora passes in front of a pillar or platform. Keep moving, avoid being touched, and continue shooting until Pandora surrenders the last of the Three Sacred Treasures.

PALACE IN THE SKY

If Pit has possession of the Three Sacred Treasures, he is ready to fight Medusa, who awaits him in the Palace in the Sky.

Stage 4-1

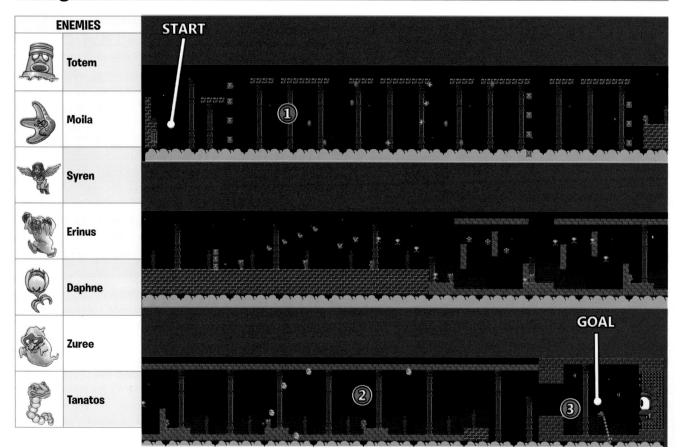

ENEMIES	
	Totem
	Moila
	Syren
	Erinus
	Daphne
	Zuree
	Tanatos

Medusa

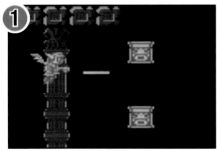

1 Pit enters the stage with the Three Sacred Treasures already equipped. The Wings of Pegasus grant the gift of flight, the Light Arrows allow him to pierce multiple enemies with a single bowshot, and the Mirror Shield deflects incoming projectiles.

The stage scrolls at a set speed, but you use the Directional Pad to adjust Pit's position on the screen. Attack the enemies as they appear. To use the Mirror Shield, simply stop attacking—Pit automatically raises it in front of his body. Just remember that the Mirror Shield doesn't protect Pit from collisions with enemies.

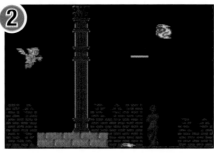

2 Soon after you reach Zuree territory, one of two things happens. If you've defeated at least 50 enemies, Pit arrives in Medusa's chamber; otherwise, the scenery loops back to the beginning of the stage. If this happens, the enemies you defeated during your first pass still count toward the minimum requirement. Continue defeating enemies—and avoid taking damage—until you reach Medusa.

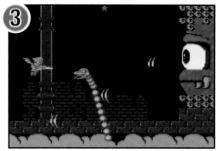

3 During the battle with Medusa, you have two basic options. If you like, you can fly around the chamber, dodging and deflecting Medusa's gaze. Remember, the Mirror Shield doesn't protect Pit from collisions with enemies—keep an eye on Tanatos throughout the battle. Dodge the serpent, or shoot it as it approaches to prevent it from reaching Pit.

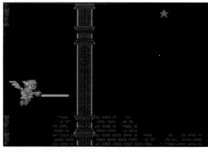

The safer option is to position Pit just below the center of the screen's left edge. This makes it impossible for Medusa's attacks to reach Pit—though you still need to keep an eye on Tanatos. More often than not, Tanatos gets struck by one of the arrows meant for Medusa. However, every so often, the snake manages to slip past your rapid-fire attacks. Hit Medusa with a steady stream of Light Arrows until Tanatos gets too close for comfort, then time your next shot to hit the serpent just before it strikes. Repeat the process until you defeat Medusa and complete the game.

METROID

Developers:
Nintendo R&D1, Intelligent System

Director:
Satoru Okada

Producer:
Gunpei Yokoi

Artists:
Hiroji Kiyotake, Hirofumi Matsuok
Yoshio Sakamoto

Writer:
Makoto Kano

Composer:
Hirokazu Tanaka

Original Release Date:
August 6, 1986 Famicom JP;
August 1987 NES US

THE METROID STORY

In the year 2000 of the history of the cosmos, representatives from the many different planets in the galaxy established a congress called the Galactic Federation, and an age of prosperity began. A successful exchange of cultures and civilization resulted, and thousands of interstellar spaceships ferried back and forth between planets. But space pirates also appeared to attack the spaceships.

The Federation Bureau created the Galactic Federation Police, but the pirates' attacks were powerful and it was not easy to catch them in the vastness of space. The Federation Bureau and the Federation Police called together warriors known for their great courage and sent them to do battle with the pirates. These great warriors were called "space hunters." They received large rewards when they captured pirates, and made their living as space bounty hunters.

It is now year 20X5 of the history of the cosmos, and something terrible has happened. Space pirates have attacked a deep-space research spaceship and seized a capsule containing an unknown life-form that had just been discovered on Planet SR388. This life-form is in a state of suspended animation, but can be reactivated and will multiply when exposed to beta rays for 24 hours. It is suspected that the entire civilization of Planet SR388 was destroyed by some unknown person or thing, and there is a strong possibility that the life-form just discovered was the cause of the planet's destruction. To carelessly let it multiply would be extremely dangerous. The Federation researchers had named it "Metroid" and were bringing it back to Earth—when it was stolen by space pirates!

If the Metroid is multiplied by the space pirates and then used as a weapon, the entire galactic civilization will be destroyed. After a desperate search, the Federation Police have at last found the pirates' headquarters, the fortress planet Zebes, and launched a general attack. But the pirates' resistance is strong, and the Police have been unable to take the planet. Meanwhile, in a room hidden deep within the center of the fortress, the preparations for multiplying the Metroid are progressing steadily.

As a last resort, the Federation Police have decided on this strategy: to send a space hunter to penetrate the center of the fortress and destroy Mother Brain. The space hunter chosen for this mission is Samus Aran. Samus is the greatest of all the space hunters and has successfully completed numerous missions that everybody thought were absolutely impossible. Samus uses a power suit that even the space pirates know and fear for its ability to absorb any enemy's power. But Samus's true form is shrouded in mystery.

Planet Zebes is a natural fortress. Its sides are covered with a special kind of stone, and its interior is a complicated maze. On top of that, the pirates have planted devices and booby traps in the maze, and the pirates' eerie followers lie in wait around every corner. Samus has now succeeded in penetrating Zebes, but time is running out! Will the space hunter be able to destroy the Metroid and save the galaxy?

SUMMARY

Your primary objective (and Samus's mission) is to destroy a giant mechanical organism known as Mother Brain. To do so, you need to explore a vast underground labyrinth filled with Mother Brain's minions. Luckily, this subterranean fortress also contains a variety of ability-enhancing Power Items; a meticulous search of each zone helps improve your chances of finding and defeating Mother Brain.

GETTING STARTED
Title Screen

From the Title screen, press the Start Button to activate the Main menu.

Main Menu

The Main menu offers two options:

Press the Select Button to choose either Start or Continue. If you chose Start, the game begins. If you choose Continue, the Password Screen appears.

Password Screen

Use the Directional Pad to select a letter or number. Press the A Button to confirm your choice. Use the B Button to backspace the register. When you finish the password, press the Start Button to continue your game.

HOW TO PLAY
Basic Controls

Move

Press Left and Right on the Directional Pad to move in the corresponding direction. During a jump, press Left or Right on the Directional Pad to steer Samus in midair.

Jump

Press the A Button to Jump. Tap the button for short jumps; press and hold it for longer jumps.

Curl Up

Press Down on the Directional Pad to curl Samus into a ball (requires Power Item: Maru Mari).

Aiming

By default, Samus aims her weapon in the direction she's facing. Press Up on the Directional Pad to aim Samus's active weapon upward.

Fire

Press the B Button to fire Samus's active weapon. Press the B Button while in ball form to set a bomb (requires Power Item: Bomb).

Switch Weapon

Use the Select Button to switch between Samus's beam weapon and missiles (requires Power Item: Missile Rocket).

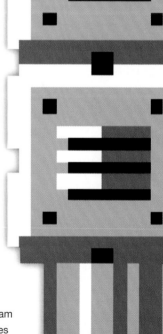

Game Over

As Samus takes damage from enemies or hazards, her energy reserves are depleted. When she runs out of energy, the game ends and a password appears. Press the Start Button to resume your last game right away, or use the password to continue your game at a later time.

Advanced Moves

Spinning Jump

Jump while moving to perform a spinning jump. The extra momentum allows Samus to jump farther, but also makes it harder to make midair adjustments.

Screw Attack

Once you collect the Screw Attack, Samus's spinning jumps automatically deal damage to enemies caught in her path (requires Power Item: Screw Attack).

Bomb Bounce

Samus can't jump while she's curled up, but you can use bombs to bounce her into the air. This technique is essential for accessing many of the secret passages hidden throughout Planet Zebes.

Bomb Climb

Some obstacles can't be overcome with a single bomb bounce. In these cases, use multiple bombs to perform a series of bounces. Proper placement is essential (and difficult!), but with the right timing, Samus can effectively climb up through narrow passages.

Screen Display

The status of Samus's power suit is displayed in the screen's upper-left corner. Early in the game, only Samus's energy reserve is shown.

As you collect specific Power Items, this readout expands to display the number of Energy Tanks you've collected, the energy remaining in the current tank, and the number of missiles Samus is currently carrying.

Advancing the Game

Your primary objective is to destroy Mother Brain, but there's a lot to do before you're ready (or able) to confront this powerful organism. In the simplest terms, you must:

- **Find and collect Power Items to improve Samus's abilities. Many Power Items are optional, but several of these items must be collected before you can access essential areas.**

- **Find and defeat two Mini-Bosses. Kraid's hideout is hidden below a corridor below Brinstar; Ridley's hideout is located below Norfair. You must conquer both of these powerful creatures before you can reach Mother Brain.**

- **Find and defeat Mother Brain. Your primary objective is located in Tourian, the fortress's central base.**

Of course, searching for Power Items and key enemies involves a great deal of exploration. Navigating this maze-like fortress can be a daunting task—most rooms contain a mix of hostile creatures and environmental hazards, and some of the game's most important areas are hidden beyond secret passages or seemingly insurmountable obstacles. Luckily, each Power Item you collect helps make exploration faster, easier, and safer.

Energy Management

When the game begins, Samus has 30 units of energy in her reserves. This energy depletes each time she takes damage from enemies or environmental hazards. If Samus runs out of energy, the game ends.

Defeated enemies sometimes leave behind energy balls. Collect available energy balls to replenish Samus's energy reserves. Move quickly! Once it appears, an energy ball remains in place for only a short time.

Initially, Samus can store up to 99 units of energy. Collect Energy Tanks to increase her storage capacity.

A Matter of Time

The time it takes you to defeat Mother Brain and escape the fortress determines which of the game's endings you receive. The faster you complete the game, the more your ending reveals about Samus's true identity. Of course, defeating Mother Brain as quickly as possible means forgoing many of the Power Items scattered throughout the fortress.

POWER ITEMS

When the game begins, Samus has only 30 units of energy and a short-range beam weapon. However, by finding and collecting Power Items, you can dramatically improve Samus's offensive and defensive capabilities.

	Power Item Statues	Some Power Items are concealed within ornate statues. When you encounter one of these statues, shoot its glowing orb to reveal the hidden Power Item.
	Long Beam	The Long Beam improves the range of any beam weapon, making it much easier to attack enemies from a safe distance.
	Ice Beam	The Ice Beam is capable of temporarily freezing enemies, rendering them harmless for a short time. Frozen enemies are not only easier to hit with missiles, they also serve as temporary platforms.
	Wave Beam	The Wave Beam is not only much stronger than Samus's standard beam, it also features a greatly improved spread—where a normal beam might fire over a smaller enemy's head, the Wave Beam's sweeping motion helps ensure that you land a successful hit. As an added benefit, the Wave Beam is capable of penetrating most obstacles.

The Right Beam for the Job

Samus can't carry the Ice Beam and the Wave Beam at the same time—collecting either of these Power Items instantly transforms her primary weapon. The only way to switch back is to reclaim the desired Power Item from its original location. Plan ahead!

	Screw Attack	The Screw Attack transforms Samus's spinning jump into a devastating weapon. Though not all creatures are vulnerable to Screw Attacks, this Power Item makes it easier (and much safer) to move through enemy-infested areas.
	High Jump	The High Jump significantly increases Samus's vertical leap. This not only makes it much easier to vault over enemies or climb vertical passages, it also allows you to reach zones and hidden rooms that would be otherwise inaccessible.
	Varia	The Varia doubles Samus's damage resistance. Once you collect this Power Item, suffering damage consumes only half as much energy.
	Maru Mari	The Maru Mari allows Samus to curl up into a compact ball. Use this Power Item to slip under obstacles or roll through narrow passages.
	Bomb	This Power Item allows Samus to set bombs while she's curled up. Use bombs to damage enemies, destroy barriers, and reach hidden areas. Bombs are also used to bounce Samus into the air while she's in ball form.
	Energy Tank	Collect Energy Tanks to increase the amount of energy Samus can store in her suit. The more energy she can store, the more damage she can absorb. Each tank you collect refills Samus's energy and adds 100 units to her maximum storage capacity.
	Missile Rocket	Collect Missile Rockets to enable Samus's missile attacks and increase missile storage. You can collect up to 21 Missile Rockets, each of which increases storage capacity by five missiles. Use missiles to open locked doors, and to deal heavy damage to particularly tough enemies. Defeated enemies sometimes drop replacement missiles; collect these items to replenish your supply.

Maximum Missiles

Collecting all 21 Missile Rockets allows Samus to carry 105 missiles. However, her missile storage also increases by 75 each time you defeat one of the game's Mini-Bosses. If you collect all available Missile Rockets and beat both Mini-Bosses, Samus can carry up to 255 missiles.

ENEMIES

Brinstar

	Mellow	Mellows usually appear in swarms, swooping down as their prey passes beneath them. These agile creatures also pass through walls. Luckily, they aren't particularly durable—a single hit from Samus's beam weapon is enough to deal with a fluttering Mellow.
	Zeb	Zebs often emerge from the air vents scattered throughout Brinstar. Once a Zeb appears, it moves in-line with Samus and flies straight ahead. A single blast from Samus's standard beam is enough to eliminate a pale Zeb; darker Zebs are twice as durable. When you see a Zeb exit an air vent, you can be sure more will follow. It's easy enough to blast your way through these enemies, but it's often faster to simply dodge them; jump up as a Zeb appears to bait it into flying higher, and then keep running as the enemy passes over your head.
	Zoomer	Zoomers secrete a sticky fluid that allows them to travel along virtually any surface. It's difficult to hit a floor-bound Zoomer with Samus's standard beam—until you collect the Wave Beam, it's usually best to hop over these scuttling creatures. If you're determined to take out a Zoomer, wait for it to reach a wall or ceiling before you attack. Pale Zoomers are less durable than darker Zoomers.
	Skree	These creatures can be found clinging to ceilings, ready to ambush Samus the moment she moves into range. Dash under a Skree and shoot up as it dives down, or simply keep running to avoid its attack. Soon after it lands, a Skree burrows into the ground, sending jagged shards of rock into the air. Defeat a Skree before it vanishes, or move quickly to escape the incoming shrapnel.
	Waver	These aptly named creatures fly in wave-like patterns. When a Waver collides with a wall or obstacle, it bounces off and reverses its course. Wavers are fairly durable, and their irregular flight patterns make them difficult to hit. Until you collect the Screw Attack Power Item, it's usually best to dodge patrolling Wavers.
	Ripper	These brainless creatures aren't capable of attacking, but touching one causes Samus to take damage. It's usually best to slip past these creatures as they move out of your way. Darker Rippers are extremely durable—you need a missile or the Screw Attack Power Item to finish one quickly. Pale Rippers are impervious to all damage. However, any Ripper can be temporarily frozen with the Ice Beam.
	Rio	These flying creatures swoop down to attack from above, but they can also scuttle along floors. Slip under a diving Rio and fire upward, or dash past it to avoid the attack. If you're being chased by a grounded Rio, jump to lure the creature back into the air. Pale Rios are fairly durable, but darker Rios are even tougher.

Norfair

	Mella	Like Mellows, Mellas move through rocks and walls. A single blast from any beam weapon is enough to defeat one of these enemies, and a properly executed Screw Attack can clear out an entire swarm at once.
	Squeept	These fast-moving creatures leap straight out of lava pools. Until you collect the Screw Attack Power Item, time your jumps to avoid these enemies, or freeze them with the Ice Beam.
	Polyp	These poisonous lumps of lava can be found streaming out of bright red vents. Polyps always appear in groups, and each group follows a predictable trajectory. Time your approach to slip past one group of Polyps before the next stream appears. Some of them can be destroyed.
	Nova	Novas behave similarly to the Zoomers found in Brinstar, but they're a bit more durable. Expect to find these pesky creatures circling platforms throughout Norfair.

	Gamet	These armored creatures sometimes emerge from the air vents throughout Norfair. A Gamet behaves just like the Zebs found in Brinstar. Once one appears, it flies upward until it's level with Samus, and then it charges straight ahead. Blast through these enemies, or jump up to bait them into flying too high.
	Ripper II	This jet-powered Ripper can't be destroyed, but it can be temporarily frozen with Samus's Ice Beam.
	Dragon	These lava-dwelling creatures attack by spitting balls of fire into the air. Their fiery projectiles not only deal damage, they also knock Samus off hard-to-reach platforms. Because Dragons only appear in lava pools, it's usually best to keep your distance. Dragon projectiles follow predictable trajectories, so time your jumps to avoid these attacks.
	Multiviola	These simple-structure organisms float through the air, changing directions as they bounce off walls and obstacles. Multiviolas are fairly durable. Until you collect the Screw Attack Power Item, it's usually best to blast a troublesome Multiviola with one of Samus's missiles.
	Geruta	Gerutas are among the most powerful enemies in Norfair. These jet-powered enemies repeatedly swoop toward their prey, dealing damage with each hit. If possible, use a Screw Attack to take out an approaching Geruta. If that's not an option, blast it with a missile, or freeze it with the Ice Beam.

Ridley's Hideout

	Zebbo	These creatures emerge from the air vents scattered throughout Ridley's hideout. Like most vent-dwelling creatures, a Zebbo flies upward before charging straight at Samus. Blast your way through them, or jump up to bait them into flying too high. Yellow Zebbos are twice as durable as green Zebbos.
	Holtz	While idle, these jet-powered creatures simply fly straight up and down. However, once a Holtz sets its sights on Samus, it usually swoops in for a more direct attack. These armored creatures are durable enough to survive multiple blasts from any beam weapon. To take out a Holtz with minimal fuss, use a missile or a Screw Attack.
	Viola	Much like Zoomers and Novas, these fiery creatures can be found circling various platforms. Yellow Violas are twice as durable as green Violas.
	Multiviola	The Multiviolas found in Ridley's hideout are faster and more powerful than the Multiviolas found in Norfair. Blast these enemies with missiles, or Screw Attack straight through them.
	Dessgeega	Dessgeegas utilize powerful leaping attacks to strike from both floors and ceilings. It takes several shots from a beam weapon to defeat a Dessgeega. It's generally better to utilize Screw Attacks or missiles when you encounter these enemies.
	Ridley	Ridley is one of two Mini-Bosses standing between you and Mother Brain. During combat, this monster spits out clusters of bouncing fireballs. These projectiles do serious damage to Samus, but they also provide the beast with a protective shield. Stock up on missiles and energy before you confront this formidable foe.

Kraid's Hideout

	Memu	These creatures tend to appear in groups and are capable of passing through rocks and walls. Shoot them, or use Screw Attacks to take out swooping Memus with ease.
	Geega	Geegas sometimes exit from the air vents in Kraid's hideout, but you also find them emerging from pools of acid. For the most part, Geegas behave just like other vent-dwelling creatures—after a Geega appears, it rises and attempts to fly straight toward Samus. Brown Geegas are twice as strong as yellow Geegas.
	Skree	The Skrees found in Kraid's hideout behave just like the Skrees scattered throughout Brinstar, but they're a bit more powerful. Screw Attack through them, or shoot them as they dive toward you.
	Zeela	You often find these boneless creatures scuttling around platforms. They aren't the toughest enemies you encounter, but blue Zeelas are noticeably stronger than green Zeelas.
	Ripper	The Rippers found in Kraid's hideout are just like those found throughout Brinstar. Darker Rippers are extremely durable; lighter Rippers are indestructible.
	Side Hopper	With their leaping attacks and impressive toughness, Side Hoppers are formidable enemies. These gravity-defying creatures use their powerful legs to jump down from ceilings before swooping back out of reach. Use a Screw Attack or a well-aimed missile to deal with one of these enemies.

Mini-Kraid

Depending on the route you take through Kraid's hideout, you might encounter Mini-Kraid. This imposter looks similar to the hideout's Mini-Boss, but don't be fooled. Hit Mini-Kraid with one missile (or a properly placed Screw Attack) to end the fight with ease.

	Kraid	As one of the game's Mini-Bosses, Kraid is a real threat. This beast attacks by hurling the spikes that jut out of his body. Kraid's projectiles do serious damage—you'd do well to collect at least a few Energy Tanks before you seek him out. The Wave Beam and a good supply of missiles also help to maximize your chances of defeating him.

Tourian

	Rinka	These troublesome enemies emerge from the rectangular nozzles found in the depths of Tourian. When a Rinka appears, it heads straight for Samus. Once a Rinka is in motion, it can't change direction. This makes it fairly easy to dodge a single Rinka—of course, dodging one Rinka can easily put you in the path of another. Rinkas aren't very powerful, but their attacks add up over time, and their persistence makes it difficult to focus on more serious threats. Try your best to dodge these enemies, and consider using the Ice Beam to freeze a Rinka or two when things get hectic.
	Metroid	Metroids are among the greatest threats you face anywhere in the fortress. When one of these creatures touches Samus, it latches on to her, draining her energy at an alarming rate. There's only one way to defeat a Metroid, and it's a two-step process. First, use the Ice Beam to freeze a Metroid solid. Once you've done that, blast the fiend with five missiles. These creatures are surprisingly swift, so keep the Ice Beam at the ready whenever you're in Metroid territory.

DESPERATE MEASURES

If a Metroid manages to latch on to you, you have two options. If you're near an open door, pass through it as quickly as possible—Metroids can't move between rooms.

In most cases, your best option is to curl up into a ball and set bombs until the creature releases you—it can take several explosions to shake off a Metroid, so freeze the creature as soon as you're free.

	Zeebetite	Zeebetites produce the energy needed to sustain Mother Brain. They aren't capable of attacking, but they are protected by indestructible turrets and an endless supply of Rinkas. Zeebetites are also extremely durable. They're only affected by missiles, and a weakened Zeebetite repairs itself in a few seconds. The only way to prevent a Zeebetite from regenerating is to keep hitting it with missiles until it's destroyed.
	Mother Brain	Located at the heart of Tourian, Mother Brain intends to cultivate a massive army of Metroids. To foil its plans, you need quick reflexes and a good supply of missiles. Mother Brain has no offensive capabilities, but it's very well-protected. Your only option is to fire missiles through the front of Mother Brain's tank as you dodge wave after wave of incoming Rinkas.

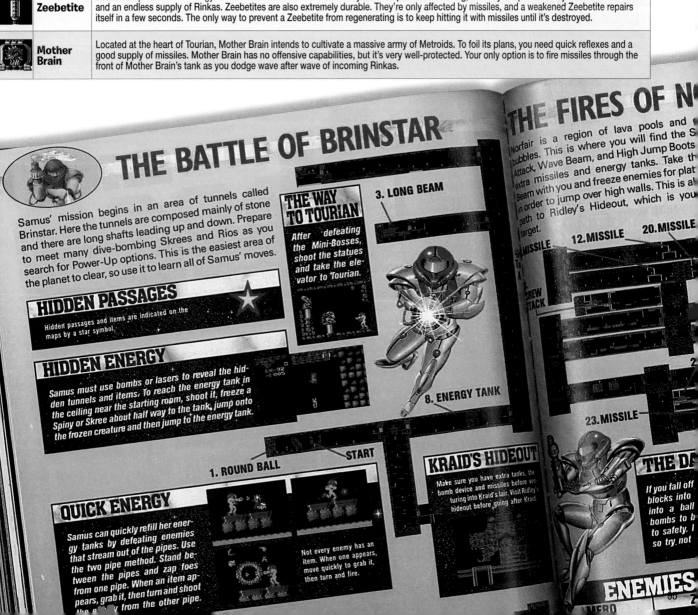

COMPLETING METROID
General Tips

A door's color indicates how it must be opened. To open a blue door, shoot it with any weapon. To open a red door, shoot it with five missiles. To open an orange door, shoot it with 10 missiles.

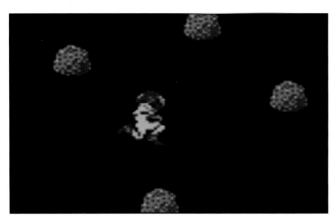

Standard jumps are much easier to control than spinning jumps or Screw Attacks. When you need to land on a narrow platform, jump from a standing position—the moment Samus leaves the ground, steer her toward the target platform.

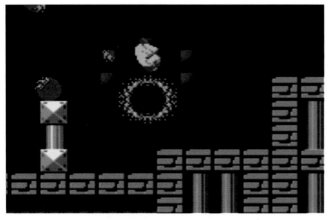

Unless you need to stock up on energy or missiles, it's usually best to avoid unnecessary combat. It can take a significant amount of time to clear a room full of enemies, and all your hard work is undone as soon as you leave the area.

If an enemy blocks your path or is likely to attack, take it out. Otherwise, use jumps and Screw Attacks to move through each area as quickly as possible.

When you do need to stock up on energy or missiles, keep an eye out for enemy-infested air vents. A single active air vent serves as an endless supply of enemies more than happy to fly into your line of fire. Better yet, find two active air vents to defeat enemies at an even faster rate. Stand on one vent and defeat the creatures that emerge from the other. When one of the creatures drops an item, slide over to collect it, then turn around and shoot at the enemies that emerge from the vent you just left. Repeat the process as needed.

The fortress is riddled with hidden passages. Many of these secret passages serve as shortcuts, but some lead to important areas that are otherwise inaccessible. When you suspect a hidden passage is nearby, check for weak spots in the surrounding terrain. Use your beam weapon to shoot walls and ceilings, and use bombs to test for hidden passages in floors.

Blocks of destructible terrain regenerate soon after they vanish. If Samus is in the way when a block reappears, she's knocked back and suffers a bit of damage. In many cases, a reappearing block serves as a vital foothold. Learn to anticipate exactly when a destroyed block will be replaced—it's a skill that serves you well in some of the fortress's more challenging corridors.

Recommended Route

The recommended route aims to provide new players with every possible advantage in the quest to defeat Mother Brain. Each numbered step specifies a Power Item to be collected or a powerful enemy that must be defeated, and the location of each step is marked on the related zone map.

If maximizing Samus's combat abilities is your priority, it's recommended that you complete each step in the order shown. Steps marked with asterisks (*) are considered optional. If speed is your priority, consider forgoing some (or all) optional steps as you work your way through the list.

Start in Brinstar

1. Maru Mari
2. Missile Rocket
3. Long Beam
4. Energy Tank
5. Bomb
6. Ice Beam

Enter Norfair

7. High Jump

Return to Brinstar

8. Energy Tank
9. Varia
10. Missile Rocket*
11. Energy Tank*

Return to Norfair

12. Missile Rocket*
13. Missile Rocket*
14. Missile Rocket*
15. Missile Rocket*
16. Missile Rocket*
17. Missile Rocket*
18. Missile Rocket*
19. Missile Rocket*
20. Missile Rocket*
21. Screw Attack
22. Energy Tank*
23. Missile Rocket*
24. Missile Rocket*
25. Wave Beam
26. Missile Rocket*

Enter Ridley's Hideout

27. Missile Rocket*
28. Energy Tank*
29. Missile Rocket*
30. Ridley (Mini-Boss)
31. Energy Tank
32. Missile Rocket*

Enter Kraid's Hideout

33. Missile Rocket*
34. Missile Rocket*
35. Energy Tank
36. Missile Rocket*
37. Kraid (Mini-Boss)
38. Energy Tank
39. Missile Rocket*

Return to Brinstar

40. Ice Beam

Enter Tourian

41. Mother Brain (Boss)

Brinstar

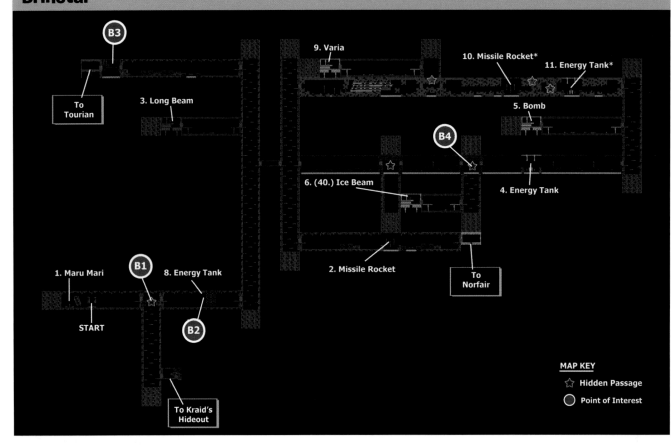

Points of Interest: Brinstar

B1

The entrance to Kraid's hideout is near the game's starting point. You can blast through the floor at Point B1 as soon as you collect the Bomb Power Item, but that doesn't necessarily mean you're ready to face Kraid. This powerful Mini-Boss is one of the fortress's most dangerous creatures. To maximize your chances of survival, collect as many Power Items as you can before heading into Kraid's hideout.

B2

The Energy Tank at Point B2 is hidden in the ceiling. To reach it, you need to collect the Ice Beam and the High Jump Power Items. Shoot at the ceiling to reveal the hidden Energy Tank, use the Ice Beam to freeze an enemy located about halfway between Samus and the tank, then jump onto the enemy and collect this elusive Power Item.

Depending on the available enemies, you can freeze a Skree as it dives toward you, or you can allow a Zoomer to climb across the ceiling until it reaches the wall to the right of the Energy Tank.

If there are no suitable enemies left in the area, leave the corridor and head back in to make another attempt.

B3

The entrance to Tourian is located beyond the statues at Point B3. After you've defeated Ridley and Kraid, shoot both of these statues to create a path across the room.

B4

The fortress contains two Ice Beam Power Items. The Ice Beam in Brinstar (Step 6 and Step 40 of the recommended path) is well-hidden, but it's also conveniently located. To reach it, use a bomb to reveal the hidden passage at Point B4.

After you collect the Ice Beam, exit this hidden area the same way you entered it. If you've already collected the High Jump, this shouldn't be a problem. To escape this passage without the High Jump, shoot the destructible block, and then jump up to the gap just as the block reappears. You lose a bit of energy in the process, but the impact knocks you back into the corridor.

Norfair

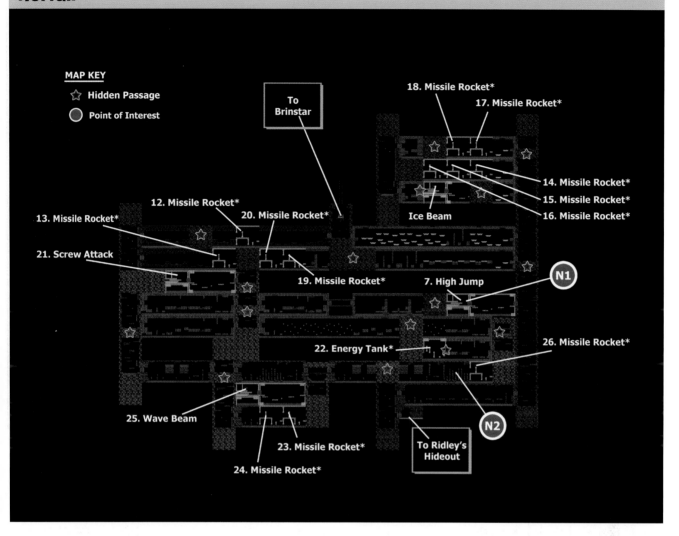

MAP KEY

☆ Hidden Passage

⬤ Point of Interest

To Brinstar

18. Missile Rocket*

17. Missile Rocket*

14. Missile Rocket*

15. Missile Rocket*

16. Missile Rocket*

Ice Beam

12. Missile Rocket*

20. Missile Rocket*

13. Missile Rocket*

21. Screw Attack

19. Missile Rocket*

7. High Jump

N1

22. Energy Tank*

26. Missile Rocket*

25. Wave Beam

23. Missile Rocket*

24. Missile Rocket*

To Ridley's Hideout

N2

Points of Interest: Norfair

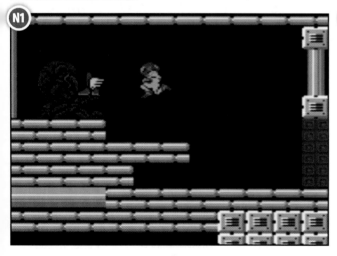

N1

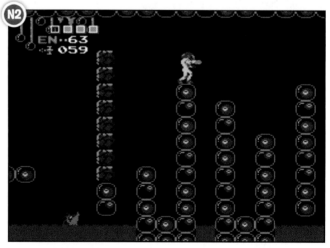

N2

EN··63
‡ 059

Once you collect the High Jump Power Item, you have everything you need to reach the Varia Power Item back in Brinstar. Norfair has some very challenging areas—you'd be well-advised to head back and collect the Varia before you head deeper into this fiery zone.

The pillars at Point N2 can be difficult to traverse—especially if an enemy baits you into using Screw Attacks. Be patient, and be careful. If you fall between two of the taller pillars, curl up and use bombs to climb back out of the lava. It's a difficult escape to pull off, so watch your step and stay in control.

Ridley's Hideout

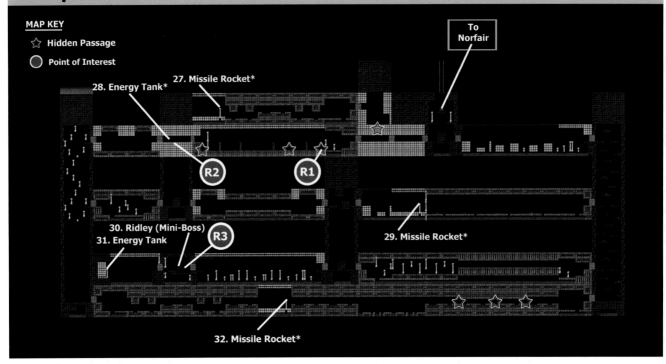

MAP KEY

☆ Hidden Passage

◯ Point of Interest

To Norfair

28. Energy Tank*
27. Missile Rocket*
R2
R1
30. Ridley (Mini-Boss)
31. Energy Tank
R3
29. Missile Rocket*
32. Missile Rocket*

Points of Interest: Ridley's Hideout

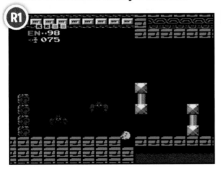

R1 Curl up and use a bomb to reveal the hidden passage at Point R1. Drop down into the opening and move left to follow the passage to the end of the corridor.

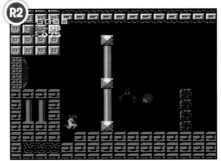

R2 This hidden passage not only allows you to bypass some tough enemies—it also lets you slip under a particularly tall pillar. When you reach the end of the passage, use a bomb to blast your way back into the corridor.

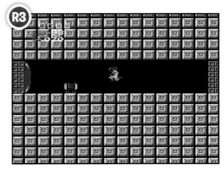

R3 There's a pitfall hidden at Point R2—the floor may look solid, but there are two rows of false blocks to the right of the Energy Tank. Running straight to this Power Item results in a costly fall. Instead, make a running leap onto the block just to the right of the Energy Tank.

Mini-Boss: Ridley

Ridley is a formidable foe, so bring plenty of missiles and energy into this battle. The most straightforward way to defeat Ridley is to fire a stream of missiles at point-blank range. Use Screw Attacks to force your way past each cluster of fireballs, then fire off as many missiles as possible until the next cluster appears. Repeat the process as many times as needed.

You can also use the Wave Beam to attack from the pool of lava below Ridley's platform. Stand below Ridley, fire upward, and keep jumping to minimize the damage you take from the lava.

Points of Interest: Kraid's Hideout

K1

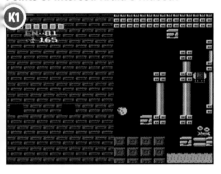

There's more than one hidden passage at Point K1. After you collect the Energy Tank from this room, curl up and use bombs to bounce to the upper passage—the lower passage is blocked by a platform in the adjoining room.

K2

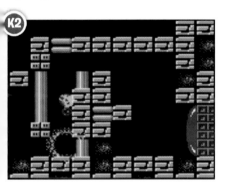

To get past the pipes at Point K2, curl up and use a series of bombs to climb up through the space between them. As you approach the top of the gap, press Right on the Directional Pad to avoid falling back down. The timing is difficult to pull off, but overcoming this obstacle allows you to reach the hidden passage above Kraid's room.

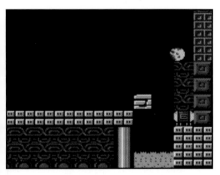

After you defeat Kraid, collect the hidden Energy Tank from his room. Grabbing this Power Item is a two-part process. First, you must reveal the tank—drop down into the lava below the door, and shoot the blocks to the right as you fall. While the Energy Tank is exposed, jump up to the blocks near the door, curl up, and drop back into the lava. As you fall, press Right on the Directional Pad to collect the Power Item.

Kraid's Hideout

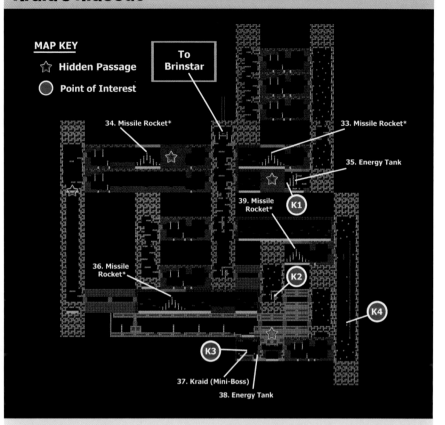

MAP KEY

☆ Hidden Passage

⬤ Point of Interest

To Brinstar

34. Missile Rocket*

33. Missile Rocket*

35. Energy Tank

39. Missile Rocket*

36. Missile Rocket*

K1

K2

K4

K3

37. Kraid (Mini-Boss)

38. Energy Tank

Mini-Boss: Kraid

K3

Kraid's a tough opponent, and his spikes do considerable damage—enter this battle with a full supply of energy and plenty of missiles. To end the encounter quickly, it's usually best to keep the fight on Kraid's platform. Dodge his spikes, and fire a missile every time you have an opening.

You can also use the Wave Beam to attack Kraid from the pools of lava on either side of his platform. Keep jumping to minimize the damage you take, and fire off a few shots from the Wave Beam each time Kraid is in your sights.

K4

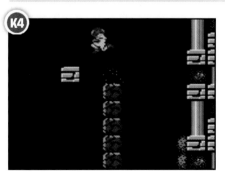

Once you've dealt with Kraid, use the column of destructible blocks at Point K4 to reach the doors at the top of the shaft. Use your beam to clear out several blocks at a time, and then jump up to land on the blocks as they reappear. As you make your way up the column, look for the scattered footholds floating off to the left—if a reappearing block is likely to knock you out of position, reach one of these footholds as quickly as possible.

Tourian

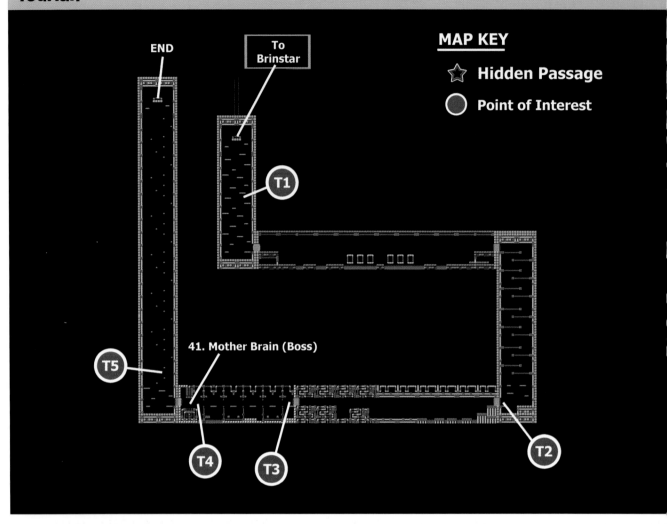

MAP KEY

⭐ **Hidden Passage**

⬤ **Point of Interest**

END

To Brinstar

T1

T5

41. Mother Brain (Boss)

T4

T3

T2

Points of Interest: Tourian

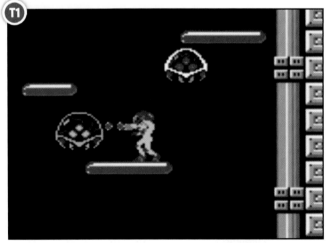

Remember that defeating a Metroid is a two-step process. First, use the Ice Beam to freeze a Metroid; then hit it with five missiles. If multiple Metroids attack at once, freeze all of them before you switch weapons. If a Metroid manages to latch on to you, curl up and set bombs until you break free.

Like most enemies, Metroids can be used to restock your missiles or replenish your energy. If you need to fill up your reserves before you confront Mother Brain, take advantage of the Metroids at Point T2. Use the Ice Beam and missiles to dispatch these enemies, gather any items they drop, and head through the nearby door. Turn around and head back through the door to find new Metroids waiting for you. Repeat the process as many times as needed.

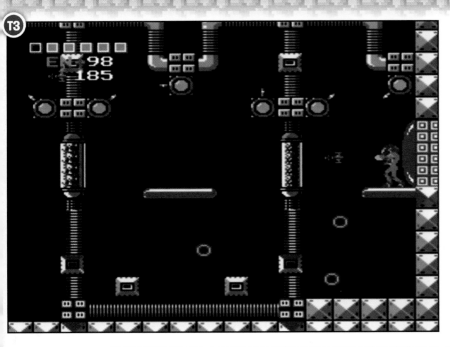

The Zeebetites not only provide Mother Brain with power, they also serve as effective barriers. To destroy a Zeebetite, hit it with a barrage of missiles. Dodge incoming Rinkas and turret fire, but don't let these threats distract you for long—it only takes a few seconds for a weakened Zeebetite to regenerate. Keep attacking a Zeebetite until it's completely destroyed, then jump through the resulting gap and begin attacking the next Zeebetite. A total of five Zeebetites sustain Mother Brain, and you need to destroy them all before you can reach your main objective.

Final Objective: Mother Brain

Mother Brain can only be damaged by missiles, so have plenty of them on hand when you begin this encounter. Jump onto the small platform left by the final Zeebetite, and then fire a stream of missiles straight into Mother Brain's tank.

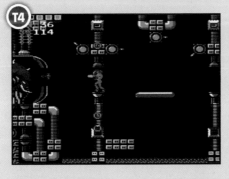 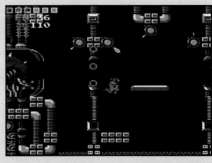

As you attack Mother Brain, keep an eye on the Rinkas that emerge from the nearby nozzles. Just before the Rinkas reach you, drop down to the right. Wait on the lower platform until the Rinkas clear the gap, then jump back up and resume your attack. Repeat the process until Mother Brain is destroyed.

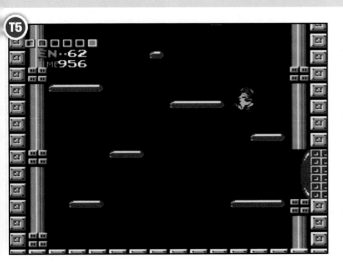 

Once you've defeated Mother Brain, a countdown begins. Head through the door past Mother Brain, and use the available platforms to escape the fortress.

You have a limited amount of time to escape the fortress, but try not to rush. Some of the available platforms are extremely small, so avoid performing any spinning jumps or Screw Attacks; stick to standard jumps to help ensure precision landings. When you reach the top of the shaft, use the elevator to leave the fortress and complete the game.

CLASSIFIED INFORMATION

We've got eyes and ears on the field to find tips and tricks that you never even thought possible for your favorite games. Our Agents sent us the following Classified Information for your eyes only. The secrets are yours to keep and the tricks are yours to use. Master your favorite games, and you may even be able to join our Agents someday. Now get out there!

DR. MARIO
Quick Reset

Sometimes the Vitamin Capsules stack up so high that it seems hopeless to continue with the same screen. If you can't bear to see the bitter end and you're sitting far away from the Reset Button, press the Select, Start, A, and B Buttons simultaneously. The game will automatically Reset and give you a chance to choose a different level and speed!

Press Select, Start, A, and B all at once to Reset.

PUNCH-OUT!!
The End Is Near

The rumor is true! There is a code that sends you directly to the Dream Fight against Mr. Dream! He is, by far, the best boxer in the game, and you'll really wish you had cut your teeth on the other opponents first. You'll see what we mean by entering 007 373 5963 as your Pass Key.

Type in 005 737 5423 to face Don Flamenco. Give Don Flamenco the ol' "one-two" after he lets loose his uppercut.

Type in 777 807 3454 to face off against Piston Honda. Guard against his powerful Piston Punch.

You can also take a different, more challenging route through the game. Enter 135 792 4680 and leave the last digit 0, then press and hold the Select Button and A and B at the same time. Can Little Mac take this level of punishment?

SUPER MARIO BROS.
Super Mario Super Code

When the game is over, hold A and press Start. You begin again in the same World in which you left off.

Bonus Points

You can see Fireworks when you reach a Flag Pole by simply studying the remaining time in the stage. Try to hit the Flag Pole when the last digit of the time is a 1, 3, or 6. If you make it, you receive 1, 3, or 6 Firework bursts, each worth 500 points. If you jump very high and hit the top of the Flag Pole, you earn an additional 5000 points.

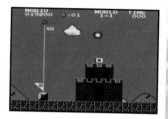

First Warp Zone

At the end of World 1-2, take the lift to the top of the bricks and walk over them to find your first Warp Zone. Two other Warp Zones are yours to find in World 4-2.

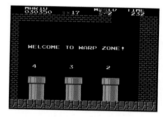

Turtle Tip

There are a few places where you can try this challenging but valuable trick. The best place to give it a shot is on the stairs near the end of World 3-1. Jump on the second Koopa Troopa so all that is left is a shell, then jump down to the next lower step. Now leap and hit the left edge of the shell to knock it into the step, and it will bounce back. If your timing is perfect, Mario will hit the shell into the step again and a chain reaction will begin. You'll start by earning extra points and then 1-Ups.

Let the first Koopa Troopa pass and knock the second Troopa out of his shell with a jump.

Jump onto the left edge, and a chain reaction will begin.

Don't collect more than 100 1-Ups or your game could be over quickly.

SUPER MARIO BROS. 3
Fire-Free Bowser

The Castle of Koopa in World 8 is full of dangerous traps. You'll find it much easier to get through the Castle by using a P-Wing and flying high above the many hazards. With a P-Wing, you can also perform an odd maneuver that takes the flame from Bowser's attack. On your way to Bowser, you fly through an open room of Podoboos and Donut Lifts. In that room, far to the right, you come across four possible passages. Enter the second passage from the top and follow the path until you reach Bowser's chamber. In Bowser's chamber, fly straight up against the wall to the left until you see the other side of the wall, then turn around and return to Bowser's chamber. When Bowser appears, he tries to spit fire but his flame is extinguished! After Mario has been stomped by Bowser, he shrinks to his smallest size and the P-Wing is no longer activated. If you keep Mario on the ground, though, he'll be invincible from other attacks. Once the floor breaks under the pressure of Bowser's incredible jumps, move out of the way and let Bowser fall through!

Enter the second passage from the top of this room.

Normally, Bowser has a dangerous flame attack.

With this trick, Bowser's just a lot of hot air.

Remember to crouch!

You'll be invincible as long as you stay on the ground.

STARTROPICS
Extra Hearts

One of the most challenging sections of StarTropics is the second underground battle in the Lost Ruins of Chapter 6. Not only is the passage long, but the enemies inside are strong and numerous. It helps to have as many Hearts as possible before you go into battle, and our Agents have found a way to accumulate two full rows of Hearts.

In the area outside the underground passage, you find a simple maze that leads to a Big Heart. Usually, if you collect a Big Heart, it disappears, never to be found in the same place twice. This particular Big Heart, though, comes back to be collected again and again. Once you collect the Heart, go to the beginning of the battle scene, then exit and retrace your steps. Continue on this path until you have accumulated the maximum of 22 Hearts, then fight to the end of Chapter 6 with extra endurance.

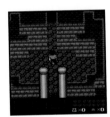
Collect the Big Heart in the Lost Ruins of Chapter 6, then enter the second underground passage. Leave and collect the Heart again. Continue with this loop until you have two full rows of Hearts.

THE LEGEND OF ZELDA
One at a Time

There's a way to avoid ambushes in the Overworld. When you get to a new section, defeat all but one of the enemies in the screen. Every time you return to this screen, only one enemy will be there! It will be super simple to avoid and move on.

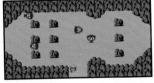
Enemies inhabit almost every section of the Overworld.

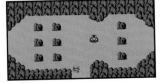
Leave one enemy in each screen, and no others will appear.

ZELDA II: THE ADVENTURE OF LINK
Magic and Experience

In your adventure through Hyrule, you can attack the Ironknuckle statue located at the outside of Palace Two and beyond to gain Magic and Experience Points. When you hit Ironknuckle, it will either come to life or produce a Red Magic Potion. If the Potion appears, use the Life Spell to replenish your magic. If the statue comes to life, defeat Ironknuckle for 100 Experience Points, leave, then come back and repeat the process.

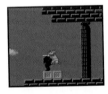
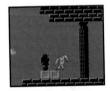

Walk Through Walls

The last Palace that Link must conquer to free the princess from her sleep has many mysterious elements. Investigations in this Palace have led to the discovery of a number of hidden rooms where valuable Magic Potions can be found. On his way to meet the challenges in the deepest parts of the Palace, Link can fill his Magic completely in these few important locations.

The Palace includes a number of elevator shafts that take more than one screen to complete. After Link has descended or ascended an entire screen length and he appears at another full screen of the elevator shaft, he may find a hidden passage in the wall here. In the center of the screen, he can work against the wall to the left or right to go through the wall and into a hidden room. Here, Link finds a statue that either comes to life or produces a Magic Potion when hit with the sword. If the statue comes to life, Link can defeat it, leave the room, and come back for another try.

Agents have also found that if Link moves to the left after coming down from the last elevator, he invariably finds a Magic Potion in one of the blocks in the wall.

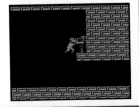

THE LEGEND OF ZELDA

Developer:
Nintendo R&D4

Director:
Shigeru Miyamoto,
Takashi Tezuka

Producer:
Shigeru Miyamoto

Programmers:
Toshihiko Nakago,
Yasunari Soejima,
I. Marui

Writers:
Takashi Tezuka,
Keiji Terui

Composer:
Koji Kondo

**Original Release
Date:**
February 21, 1986
Famicom JP;
August 22, 1987
NES US

The legend of
ZELDA®

*Includes invaluable maps
and strategic playing tips.*

(Nintendo) ENTERTAINMENT SYSTEM®

THE LEGEND OF HYRULE

A long, long time ago, the world was once in an age of chaos. In the midst of this chaos, in a little kingdom in the land of Hyrule, a legend was being handed down from generation to generation: the legend of the "Triforce," golden triangles possessing mystical powers.

One day, an evil army attacked this peaceful little kingdom and stole the Triforce of Power. This army was led by Ganon, the powerful Prince of Darkness who sought to plunge the world into fear and darkness under his rule. Fearing his wicked rule, Zelda, the princess of this kingdom, split up the Triforce of Wisdowm into eight fragments and hid them throughout the realm to save the last remaining Triforce from the clutches of the evil Ganon. At the same time, she commanded her most trustworthy nursemaid, Impa, to secretly escape into the land and go find a man with enough courage to destroy the evil Ganon.

Upon hearing this, Ganon grew angry, imprisoned the princess, and sent out a party in search of Impa. Braving forests and mountains, Impa fled for her life from her pursuers. As she reached the very limit of her energy, she found herself surrounded by Ganon's evil henchmen. Cornered! What could she do? Hope was restored when a young lad appeared. He skillfully drove off Ganon's henchmen, and saved Impa from a fate worse than death.

The young man's name was Link. He had discovered Impa and Ganon's henchmen while traveling. Impa told Link the whole story of Princess Zelda and the evil Ganon. Burning with a sense of justice, Link resolved to save Zelda. The quest would not be easy; Ganon was a powerful opponent who held the Triforce of Power. In order to fight off Ganon, Link had to bring the scattered eight fragments of the Triforce of Wisdom together to rebuild the mystical triangle. If he couldn't do this, there would be no chance Link could fight his way into Death Mountain where Ganon lived.

HERO TRAINING

There are tons of items, enemies, and mechanics to find and overcome in *The Legend of Zelda*. Use this section to prepare for all the challenges to come.

Main Screen and Subscreen

There are two screens in this game: the Main Screen and a Subscreen. Usually the Main Screen is on display. When you press the Start Button, the Subscreen appears.

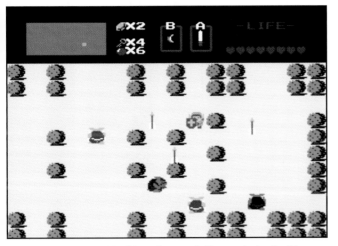

The Main Screen: Displays Link's fights and movements. The game is played on this screen.

Subscreen: Displays Link's Possessions. Use the D-Pad to choose the item you want to use.

Overworld and Underworld

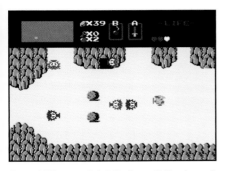

Overworld: The game starts in the Overworld. Enemies await you everywhere you go.

The stages of this game consist of the vast Overworld and the nine Underworld labyrinths.

The Overworld consists of 128 screens. It is composed of forests, lakes, mountains, and deserts. You must face these challenges and descend into the Underworld to obtain the Triforce pieces.

Underworld: The Underworld is a complicated maze. The enemies are strong, and there are many traps. Advance with care. The Triforce pieces are hidden somewhere in the Underworld.

Be Aware of Link's Life Hearts

The red Hearts in the upper-left corner of the Main Screen indicate the young hero's life force. As he sustains damage, the red Hearts turn white. When all of them become white, it's "Game Over." Link starts his adventure with only three Hearts. As he proceeds, he can gain additional Heart Containers.

These Hearts show Link's life force.

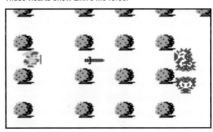

When all the Hearts are red, you can shoot beams from the tip of the Sword.

Fight with a Sword and a Shield

Link's main weapon is a Sword. There are three kinds of Swords: the Regular Sword, the White Sword with double strength, and the Magical Sword, which is the strongest. Operate the Swords with the A Button. There are two Shields that Link can obtain as well: a Regular Shield and the Magical Shield.

When enemies appear, fight with a Sword.

Gather the Triforce

To battle against Ganon's Triforce of Power, you need the Triforce of Wisdom. However, the Triforce of Wisdom is divided into eight pieces, and they are hidden in each of the first eight Underworld labyrinths. When you obtain a piece of the Triforce, all your Heart Containers refill and you are transported back to the entrance of the labyrinth.

The Triforce pieces are hidden in the depths of the Underworld labyrinths.

ITEMS

As Link continues his adventure, he obtains various items. Your effectiveness in advancing through the game depends on how well you use them. Read on for a complete list of all the items in the game.

Rupees

Rupees are the currency of Hyrule. When you collect them, you can buy items from merchants. There are yellow and blue Rupees. Yellow Rupees are the base denomination, worth one unit. One blue Rupee is equal to five yellow Rupees. You can hold up to a total of 255 Rupees; after that, picking up Rupees won't have any effect on your wallet until you spend some of them.

Heart

Link's health descreases when he is attacked. When you obtain a Heart, you recover one full Heart Container. In other words, this gives you more life. A Heart appears sometimes after destroying an enemy.

Heart Container

When you obtain this Heart Container, your total life capacity increases by one. You gain up to 16 Heart Containers during the course of the game.

If you hope to survive Ganon's minions and the King of Evil himself, you'll want as many Heart Containers as you can get your hands on.

Fairies

During the game, if Link defeats an enemy and rescues a Fairy from its devilish hands, she'll thank him by refilling all his Heart Containers.

Life Potion

Drink this to refill all of Link's Heart Containers. Second Potion turns to Life Potion after Link sips it. Drink the Life Potion and you'll be fresh out of water!

Boomerangs

 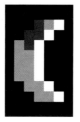

Use the Boomerang to stun enemies temporarily. There are two types of Boomerang: the Wooden Boomerang and the Magical Boomerang. The only difference between the two is that the Magical Boomerang can travel longer distances.

Bow and Arrows

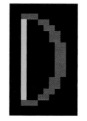 

The Bow, like the Boomerangs, can hit enemies at a distance. However, unlike the Boomerangs, the Bow destroys enemies at a distance with little effort. There are two types of Arrows for the Bow: Wooden Arrows and Silver Arrows. The Silver Arrows are stronger than their wooden counterparts. These will consume a single rupee for each arrow fired.

Bombs

Bombs do massive damage to any enemies their explosions hit. They also have the unique ability to blow apart weakened walls to reveal secrets. Whenever you pick up a Bomb item from a defeated enemy, your Bombs stock refills by four. Keep in mind that you only have eight Bombs at the start, so use them wisely!

Keys

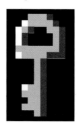 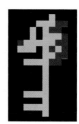

Link needs these to open the locked doors in the Underworld labyrinths. The Magical Key, in particular, is very useful, because Link can use it over and over again. Other Keys are single-use.

Swords

Link's survival depends not only on his courage, but his sword. Use this to damage most enemies. The White Sword deals double damage, and the Magical Sword will deal double that damage.

Candles

Link will need to acquire both of these candles throughout his travels in Hyrule if he is to uncover the secrets hidden throughout the land. The Candles will burn bushes in the Overworld to reveal hidden staircases and provide light within dark rooms in a dungeon or cave. The Blue Candle can only be used once per screen however so be careful!

Stepladder

You can cross a river or a hole with this item if it is no wider than Link. You can escape from bad situations by crossing rivers and holes, so keep that in mind after picking it up.

Raft

You encounter plenty of rivers, lakes, and the sea itself during your journeys in the Overworld. If you have the Raft, these bodies of water will be your playthings. There is a catch, however: the Raft only works if you set sail from a dock.

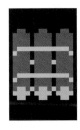

Recorder

The Recorder is a mysterious instrument said to hold magical powers. They say that those who master its secrets are able to control the waters and winds themselves.

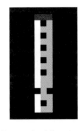

Underworld Map and Compass

Link can uncover the entire layout of an Underworld labyrinth if he finds that labyrinth's Map, located inside the labyrinth itself. If he finds a Compass, he can discover where the Triforce fragment is hidden within a specific labyrinth. Together, these items make Link the master of the Underworld.

Letter

When you choose this Letter at the Subscreen and press the B Button, Link can show the Letter to the Old Woman who lives inside one of the many caves in the Overworld.

Rings

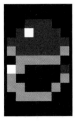 

The Blue Ring reduces enemy-inflicted damage by half, and the Red Ring reduces damage to one-quarter.

Power Bracelet

This bracelet grants Link amazing strength. With this Power Bracelet in hand, Link can push giant rocks and massive statues with little effort.

Magical Clock

The Magical Clock sometimes appears after defeating an enemy. Pick it up to freeze all enemies on the screen in place.

Food

Link can use this bait to lure an enemy to an area and then attack while the enemy eats it. Use this item with care! It doesn't work on every enemy.

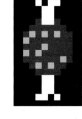

Magical Rod and Book of Magic

This is the wand the Wizzrobe uses. Wave it to let loose magic spells. What's more, if Link picks up the Book of Magic and learns some new spells, he can chant to send out flames!

CHARACTERS

You find many characters and enemies during your time in Hyrule. We cover all of them in this section, so you know who's a friend and who's a foe.

Link

You are Link, the hero of the game. Your job is to find all the Triforce fragments and save Princess Zelda.

Old Man

He lives in a cave. He gives Link weapons and information.

Old Woman

She lives in a cave and sells Link the Water of Life, but only if she is shown a certain item.

Merchant

He, too, is in a cave. He sells Link the Magical Shield, Arrows, and other valuable items.

Fairies

If you save a Fairy from an enemy, it refills your Heart Containers.

OVERWORLD ENEMIES

These are the enemies you see while exploring the Overworld.

Armos

Boulder

Leever

Octorok

Peahat

Tektite

Moblin

Ghini

Lynel

Zora

UNDERWORLD ENEMIES

Below are all the enemies you can expect to find while exploring the Underworld.

Blade Trap

Bubble

Darknut

Gel

Gibdo

Goriya

Keese

Lanmola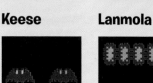

Pols Voice

Rope

Stalfos

Vire

Wallmaster

Wizzrobe

Zol

BOSSES

This is where you find all the bosses in the game.

Aquamentus

Dodongo

Manhandla

Gleeok

Digdogger

Gohma

Ganon

Patra

Moldorm

THE OVERWORLD

Here is a complete map of the Overworld. It is made up of a total of 128 screens. You have to climb mountains, brave monster-filled forests, cross rivers and lakes, and even survive a haunted cemetary in order to find all the Triforce fragments and save Princess Zelda.

THE UNDERWORLD

This section covers all the Underworld labyrinths in the game. Find full maps of every labyrinth here.

LABYRINTH 1: EAGLE

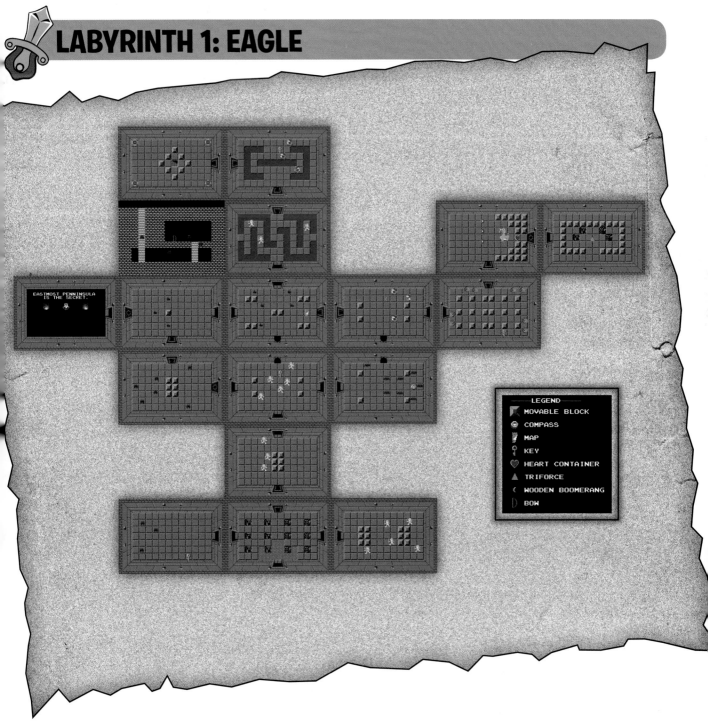

EASTMOST PENNINSULA
IS THE SECRET.

LEGEND
- MOVABLE BLOCK
- COMPASS
- MAP
- KEY
- HEART CONTAINER
- TRIFORCE
- WOODEN BOOMERANG
- BOW

The Easiest Underworld Labyrinth

Level 1 is the easiest of all nine Underworld labyrinths. This is the perfect place to learn how *The Legend of Zelda* works.

Pay Attention to the Wall Master

A Wall Master appears in the room just before Aquamentus. If a Wall Master lands its grabby mitt on you, it takes you back to the entrance of Level 1. Talk about a worst-case scenario!

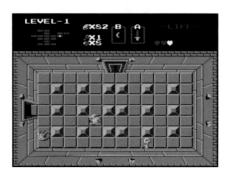

But this won't happen unless you touch the wall; Wall Masters only appear when the wall is touched—they are fiercely territorial! If a Wall Master does appear, get away from it as soon as possible and carefully wear it out with your Sword. You can do it!

Go for the Triforce!

The Triforce of Level 1 is in the far-east room of the dungeon, but a strong enemy named Aquamentus is guarding it. In short, unless you beat Aquamentus, you won't obtain the Triforce.

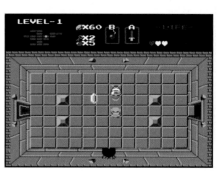

Get Your Wooden Boomerang!

The Wooden Boomerang is one of the treasures that you can get in Level 1. It appears after you defeat all the Goriyas in the room before the Wall Master's lair. Be carefully, though! The Goriyas have boomerangs of their own that they'll use to attack Link. Dodge their attacks and defeat them one by one.

Getting a Map and a Compass

There may be nothing as helpful to traversing the Underworld as the Map and Compass are together. Every Underworld labyrinth has this pair of explorer's tool, but before you can use them, you have to find them. You can find the Compass in the room two rooms north and one room east of the labyrinth entrance. The Map is three rooms north of the entrance, requiring you to work your way around to reach it.

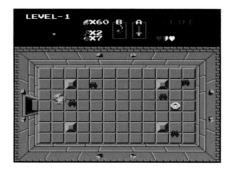

Obtain a Key to Open the Door

There are many rooms with keyholes in the Underworld. You can't open these rooms without Keys. One way to get a Key is to find

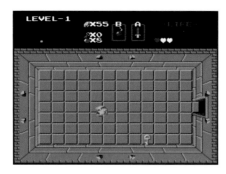

one on the floor in the labyrinth; another way is to get the Keys that appear when you beat all the enemies in a room. Although you can buy Keys from the merchant, the Keys from the Underworld labyrinth are sufficient. Buying Keys unnecessarily from the merchant merely wastes your Rupees.

Take the Key from the Stalfos

There are some enemies in Underworld labyrinths who possess Keys; the Stalfos in the room directly east of the

entrance and the one second from the top of the Map are proof of this. Defeat them and claim the Keys for yourself!

Defeat Your Enemies and Open the Door

There are several doors that don't open no matter how many Keys you have. If you walk into a room where the door closes behind you, stay calm! The only way to open these doors is to defeat all the enemies in the room, and panicking just makes this more difficult. Stay levelheaded and careful, and you'll get those doors open once again!

CLEAR YOUR WAY WITH A BOMB

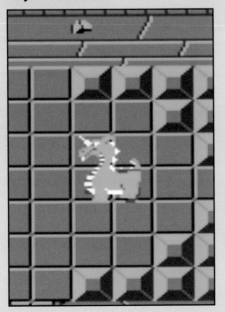

Sometimes there's more to a wall than immediately meets the eye. If your adventurer's instinct is going off about a potentially suspicious wall, go ahead and plant a Bomb right in the center of it! You can find all sorts of surprises with a well-placed Bomb.

AQUAMENTUS

Get the Bow!

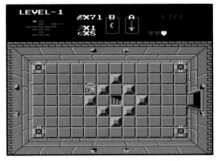

The Boomerang isn't the only special item in Level 1; the Bow can also be picked up down here. Find the Bow by heading to the room at the top-left corner of the labyrinth.

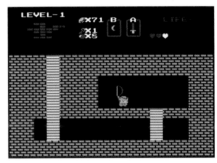

Once you're there, move one of the blocks barricading the stairway in the center of the room—which one is for you to discover.

Once you've made your way down the stairway, the Bow is yours! Remember, you still need to find some arrows in order to use it!

Since Aquamentus shoots beams in three directions, aim at his head with the Sword beam as you try to avoid his projectiles. When the Sword beam doesn't work anymore, aim at his head with a hit-and-run strategy during the breaks between his attacks.

Your reward for defeating the giant beast Aquamentus is a permanent increase to your maximum Heart Containers and a piece of the Triforce!

LABYRINTH 2: MOON

Level 2 Is a Piece of Cake!

Level 2 has a crescent shape like a moon. Even if it's a little tougher that Level 1, it's still very straightforward. With the Boomerang and Bow in hand, this should be no problem at all!

Boomerang Gels and Keese

Gels and Keese are the weakest of all the enemies in the Underworld labyrinth. They don't have much offensive power, nor do they move quickly.

You can make short work of these enemies with a simple throw of your Boomerang. A single hit with the Boomerang instantly defeats either enemy and allows you to keep your distance from the baddies. Just don't underestimate either of them. Both enemies have erratic movements, and Keese are speedy, making them hard to hit and avoid.

LEGEND

🔲	MOVABLE BLOCK
◎	COMPASS
📜	MAP
🗝	KEY
❤	HEART CONTAINER
▲	TRIFORCE
(	WOODEN BOOMERANG
)	BOW

DODONGO DISLIKES SMOKE.

Looking for the Map and Compass

You can find the Compass in the bottom-right corner of the labyrinth, and the Map a room just above that. Approach both rooms from the west, so from the entrance, head east one room, then north one room. From here, go east to reach the Compass; go one more room north, then east, and the Map is yours.

Blade Traps! Look Out!

The Underworld is a deadly, dangerous place full of monsters and traps. One such trap is the fast-moving Blade Trap, found in the third room from the top of the right row of rooms in your Map. These traps sit completely

still in a room until you pass them either horizontally or vertically. As soon as you enter their line of sight, these bladed baddies swiftly slide toward you in an attempt to smash Link into Swiss cheese! Stay out of their line of sight at all costs to make it out in one piece.

114

Pull the Ropes

Ropes are the snake enemies encountered in this labyrinth. They usually move slowly, but once they vertically or horizontally align with Link, they make a mad dash toward him.

Use their predictable movements against them for an easy victory. If you're at full health, align with the Ropes and unload Sword beams at them as they charge toward you. The key here is to not let them get close, so if you lack a Sword beam, shoot them with the Bow or stun them with the Boomerang and go to work!

Desert Fire Worm, Moldorm

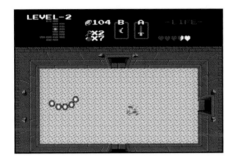

The intimidating worm enemies called Moldorms inhabit the fifth room in the center column of the Map. They aren't particularly hard if you know what to look for.

The trick is to fight them calmly and to make sure your attacks land. They don't move particularly fast and they usually gravitate toward your location, so just stand still and wait them out. As they approach, give them a good stabbing. If you go hunting for them, you're almost certain to take damage when they jump out of the ground, so turtling is definitely the best strategy here.

Challenging Treasure: The Magical Boomerang

You can get a new Boomerang in the third room from the bottom of the right column of rooms (it's the room above the Map and Compass rooms). The Magical Boomerang appears after you clear out all the Goriyas in the room, but that's much easier said than done.

Arm Yourself with Knowledge

While in this room, you must defeat Goriyas while avoiding not only their boomerangs, but also fireballs spit from the statues in the four corners of the room. If you grabbed the Magic Shield before entering Level 2, you can block the incoming fireballs without too much issue. Otherwise, stay nimble, move quickly, and dodge those attacks! You can do it!

An Old Man is in the room at the top of the right column of rooms. A quick visit to him gives you information on how to defeat the indestructible Dodongo, boss of this labyrinth! Not a bad deal for a quick visit with a friend, huh?

BOSS

DODONGO

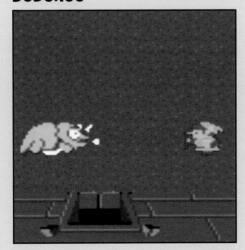

Dodongo's lair is the room at the very top of the middle column of rooms. When you begin the fight, one thing becomes painfully obvious: you can't damage Dodongo! Don't panic! While Dodongo's hide is too thick to take damage, he is a notorious glutton who eats anything left in front of him. Take advantage of this and plant a Bomb directly in front of his mouth, and he'll scoop it up swiftly.

Repeat this twice to take Dondongo down for the count, leaving the Triforce piece unguarded and a shiny new Heart Container yours for the taking.

LABYRINTH 3: MANJI

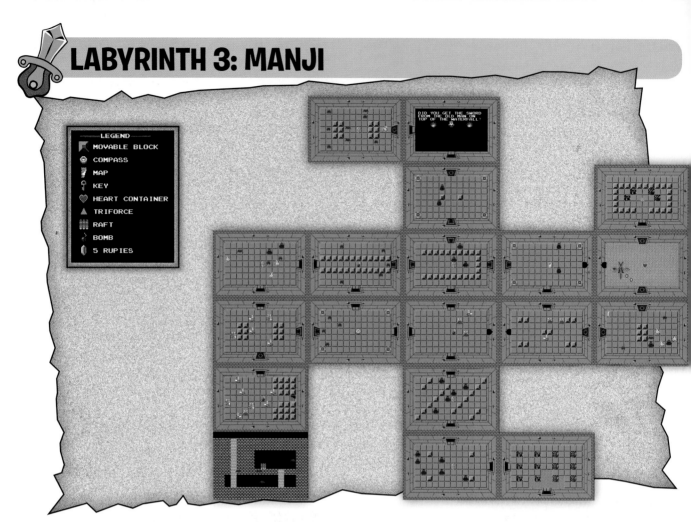

It's Time for the Real Fight

Level 3 is a real challenge, especially in comparison to the two previous levels. For starters, you encounter one of the most difficult enemies in the game here: the Darknut.

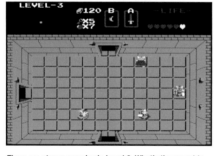

There are strong enemies in Level 3. What's the secret to beating them?

Darknuts block your attacks if you attack them from the front, and they hit like trucks.

On top of Darknuts, you also have to battle Manhandla in order to reach the Triforce piece. This enemy is no slouch, so expect a tough battle if you want to complete this labyrinth!

Get a Map and a Compass

Find the Map to this labyrinth in the top room of the second-to-the-right row; the Compass is in the first room in the second-to-the-left row.

Link gets the Map in this room.

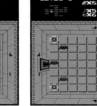

And the Compass in this room.

Trapped! Defeat the Enemies to Proceed!

Several of the rooms in this labyrinth lock down as soon as you enter them. The only way

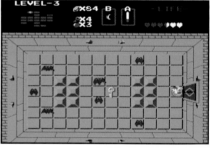

Calm down and beat all the enemies in the room.

out? Defeating all the enemies in the room. Once the enemies are cleared out, the doors spring back open and you're free to leave. When the shutters close, don't panic. Keep a cool head and carefully take out each enemy, and you'll be just fine.

Get the Raft!

The Raft is the treasure of Level 3. The treasure room concealing it is in the basement of the far-bottom-left corner of the Map. The entrance to the treasure room

Avoid the Darknut barrage and head straight for the stairs.

is visible, so you can go in with no problem. There are, however, a great number of Darknuts. The secret is to run into the treasure room as quickly as possible without fighting the Darknuts. Once the Raft is yours, race back out of the room, avoiding every Darknut along the way.

Battling the Dastardly Darknuts

A forward attack is totally ineffective against the Darknuts. For this reason, you must attack them either from the side or from behind. As soon as a Darknut senses your attack, he turns and faces you, so be ready to escape from him fast! It will be easier later if you blow up a few Darknuts now. Throw Bombs at Darknuts that are gathered close together.

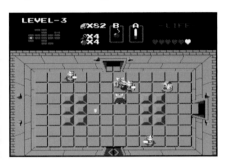

It's easier to beat a Darknut if you have the White Sword—especially if you soften them up with a bomb or two first!

Don't Get Caught by the Bubbles

Touching the Bubbles does no damage to Link; however, it does steal his ability to draw his Sword for a while, so be on alert! Dodge the Bubbles as much as you can, although doing so is not always possible, because other enemies demand your attention as well. It's wise to switch to ranged weapons, such as the Boomerang or Bow, before you enter a room where Bubbles are waiting. That way, you can continue your attack against your enemies even without the Sword.

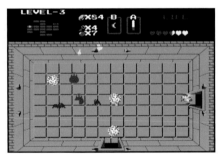

Get ready to use flying weapons in the rooms where Bubbles lurk.

Attacking Your Enemies from Cover

When there are obstacles in the room, use them to fight even more fiercely. Link's Sword can't reach through the side or bottom, but it can reach up through obstacles above. This allows you to take advantage of the obstacles. To attack your enemies without worrying about taking damage, hide under the obstacle and thrust your Sword upward swiftly as soon as an enemy crosses your path. This is an especially effective technique against enemies that don't use ranged weapons.

Take Your Time and Investigate

Before you fully advance into the next room as the screen changes, wait in the doorway and investigate the room. From this position, your enemies can't attack you. Take your time to come up with a good countermeasure as you confirm what kinds of enemies are in the room and whether traps await you. This way you won't be attacked as soon as you enter a room. You should know, however, that this method won't work in rooms where the doors close as Link enters.

Proper Boomerang Usage

What would you do if Rupees or Hearts appeared in the middle of battle? It's too difficult and dangerous to reach them with all those enemies around, right? In this kind of situation, the Boomerang really shines.

Did you know that you can pick up Rupees or Hearts by throwing the Boomerang at them? That's right! The Boomerang allows you to pick up items while facing down foes. It's a sophisticated technique, but it's certainly helpful to know. Rupees and Hearts don't stay long, so grab them before they disappear. The Boomerang can do just that!

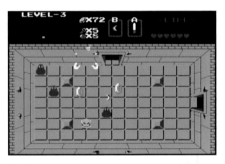

The Boomerang is a great weapon; it can be used in several ways.

Make Sure to Meet the Old Man

Our old friend is in the room at the top of the middle row of this labyrinth. He asks whether Link got a Sword from someone somewhere. This is very important, because you won't find the White Sword unless you listen to his message. Once you meet him, get out of Level 3 and get the White Sword right away. It's much easier to clear Level 3 with it.

Defeat the Zol with a Single Strike

You come face-to-face with an enemy named Zol in Level 3. If you cut a Zol with a Regular Sword, it becomes two Gels, effectively doubling your number of enemies. Take care not to hit a Zol while it's near a wall. If a Zol splits near a wall, it can cause one of the Gels to bounce off the wall toward you to hit you. Your best bet is to fight a Zol in the center of a room, or with your back to a wall. However, you can beat a Zol with a single swing of the White Sword—another reason why you should get the White Sword immediately.

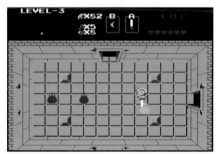

Beat the Zol with the White Sword to prevent it from splitting into Gels.

BOSS

MANHANDLA

The Triforce is in the top-right corner of the Map, and the boss of this labyrinth, Manhandla, is in the room just before that.

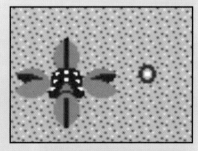

Your goal is to beat Manhandla with a single Bomb.

Manhandla is a plant-like monster with four biting, chomping heads. In order to beat it, you must remove all four heads. You can use your Sword as a portable weedwhacker, but Bombs are definitely more efficient. Place a Bomb in the middle of Manhandla to defeat it right away.

As Manhandla loses its heads one by one, it moves more quickly, making it much more difficult to hit. It reaches its maximum speed when it only has a single head left.

LABYRINTH 4: SNAKE

Level 4's Tricks and Traps

The main feature of this labyrinth is a new enemy type, known as the Vire. Vires come in droves. If you pay close attention to their movements, they're not too difficult, but underestimate them and you'll see a "Game Over" screen faster than you can blink.

Manhandla, the boss of Level 3, makes its reappearance here for a rematch, but not as the boss of the stage. After going through all that, you have to deal with Gleeok, the two-headed dragon, if you want to grab the Triforce piece.

An advanced player can get through this labyrinth without the Water of Life, but all other players should definitely consider picking some up to make it without dying.

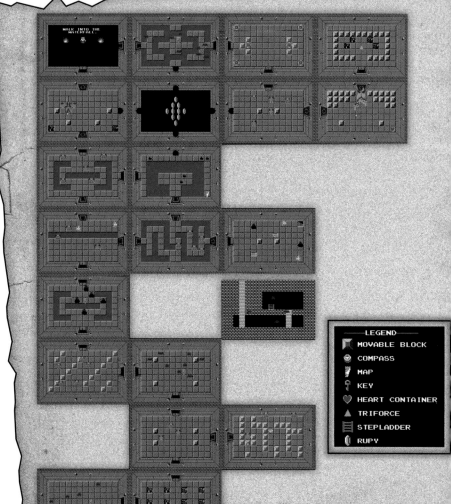

Be ready for these tricky, mobile enemies.

Buy a Blue Candle for Later

You traverse some dark rooms while in Level 4. Without a light, these rooms are really dangerous. Fortunately, you can buy a Candle before entering the labyrinth to light your way.

With the Blue Candle in hand, wait in the doorway of a room until the Candle takes effect. You'll be safe in the doorway while waiting for the room to light up, which is why patience is key.

On top of lighting up a room, the Candle can also shoot out a flame directly in front of Link to burn enemies and bushes in the Overworld. Not a bad deal!

Getting through dark rooms is a real challenge...

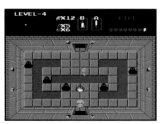

Unless you have a Blue Candle to light the way.

Getting the Map and Compass

Find the Compass for this labyrinth by going one screen north and one screen east. To get the Map, head to the room four rooms north of the entrance (not counting the empty space in the middle of the labyrinth). Grab the Ladder from this level to reach the Map— we'll tell you where to find that first.

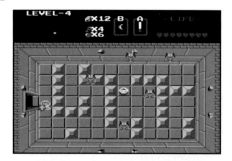

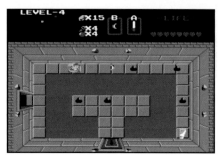

LEGEND

▮ MOVABLE BLOCK
◉ COMPASS
▯ MAP
♀ KEY
♡ HEART CONTAINER
▲ TRIFORCE
▤ STEPLADDER
◊ RUPY

Finding the Ladder

The Ladder is the treasure of Level 4. It allows you

to cross a single uncrossable space at a time. For example, if you attempt to walk across a single square of water, your Ladder automatically comes out and you cross unimpeded.

To find the Ladder, go to the second room in the

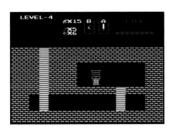

second-to-the-right row of rooms. The Ladder is hidden in the basement of that room, but finding the entrance to the basement requires some investigating. Defeat all the enemies in the room and investigate the two blocks. One of them holds the secret to unlocking the basement.

Advancing with the Ladder

The Ladder you just found can be put to use immediately. For example, the fourth room in the leftmost row of rooms has a small moat near its top that prevents you from progressing through its northern door. With the Ladder's aid, walk right over the moat and into the northern door.

There are a couple of other rooms in this labyrinth that have similar obstacles, so get plenty of use out of the Ladder now that you have it.

The Ladder is a very useful tool aboveground as well as in the Underworld labyrinth.

Attack Your Enemies Using the Ladder

The Ladder allows Link to cross a single uncrossable square if it's the same width as Link, but the Ladder can also be used as an offensive tool. If Link is on the Ladder, certain enemies, such as Zols, can't attack him, but he can attack them no problem.

This method doesn't work on flying and jumping enemies like Vires or Keese, unfortunately. They have little issue crossing over the obstacles in any room.

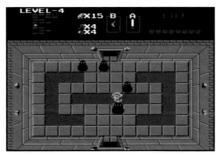

If Link is on the Ladder, he can avoid attacks from many of his enemies.

Tricky Doors

Some of the doors in this labyrinth slam shut when you enter, just like in other labyrinths before this. Unlike in those previous labyrinths, however, they won't reopen after you defeat all the enemies.

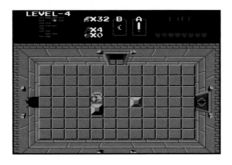

When this happens, inspect the blocks in the room and give them a push from all sides. That almost always unlocks any doors that don't unlock after you defeat a room's enemies.

Finding Hidden Rooms

The hidden rooms start to appear in Level 4. For example, Level 4 as a whole has the shape of a snake, and a hidden room can be found at the eyes of the snake. Find the passage to this hidden room by Bombing the walls. You don't want to miss this hidden room, because there is a nice collection of Rupees here.

Most likely, you'll find hidden rooms in empty spaces on the Map, like the eyes of the snake or in a labyrinth's corners.

Go to the hidden room to find a lot of Rupees.

Seeking Information from the Old Man

The Old Man can be found in the top-left corner of the Map. Go to him for information, and he tells you to seek out a certain place. After you've found the Triforce piece in Level 4, go to the place he indicated. The person you meet there gives you a hint about reaching Level 5. Since the people living in the Underworld labyrinths can help Link, you'd better listen to their suggestions.

Keep in mind what he says. It will help a lot later.

How to Fight Vires and Keese

The Vires, which appeared for the first time in Level 4, attack Link as they jump. The Vires and the Keese are similar to Zols and Gels in that a Vire becomes two Keese when the Vire is cut in half. Split the Vire into two Keese first with your Sword, then beat the Keese with the Boomerang. This is a very effective strategy, because you can attack the Vires and Keese at the same time.

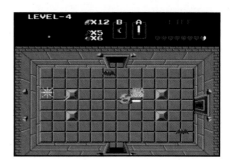

Use your Sword and the Boomerang at full capacity to beat all the Vires and Keese.

Manhandling Manhandla

The boss of Level 3 is back for a rematch. Manhandla fights exactly the same as before, but this time with the assistance of two stone faces in the corners of the room that gladly spit fireballs at Link during the fight. Use your experiences from your first Manhandla fight and try to defeat Manhandla with a single Bomb to end this fight as quickly as possible.

You can find Manhandla in the second room from the top in the top-left corner of the Map.

Unless you go through here, you won't be able to progress.

GLEEOK

You should buy the Water of Life before fighting with Gleeok.

The Triforce is in the top-right corner of the Map, and its guardian, Gleeok, is in the room just below that. This two-headed dragon shoots fireballs at Link while its heads move around uncontrollably. The secret to beating Gleeok is to stab its neck area with your Sword in between its fireball shots. The heads separate from Gleeok's body and continue to attack Link. Ignore them and keep attacking! If you brought the Water of Life into this labyrinth, you can manage the damage that Gleeok's heads send your way. Strike, strike, and strike again to bring this wannabe Hydra to an untimely end!

LABYRINTH 5: LIZARD

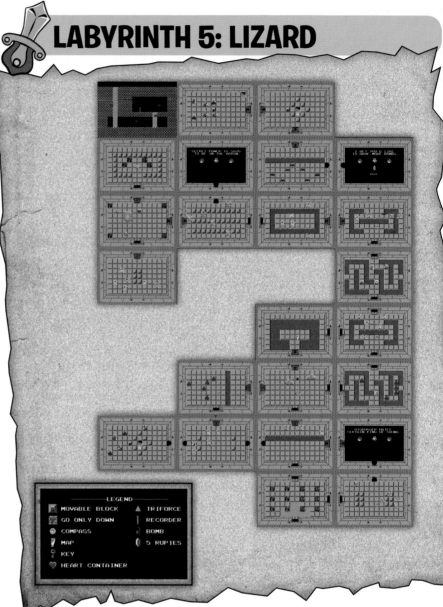

Struggling with the Darknuts

Darknuts are the enemies that give you the hardest time in Level 5 of the Underworld labyrinths. Darknuts inhabit only two rooms here, but these two rooms are the toughest of all the rooms in Level 5. It's almost impossible to get through these two rooms, even for an advanced player, without the Water of Life. Enemies that have unique weaknesses, like Digdogger and Pols Voice, appear in this level. Some people in Level 5, including the Old Man, tell you about the weaknesses of these enemies. Don't miss them.

Let's Find a Map and a Compass

The Map and the Compass become more important as the labyrinths get more complicated. Get the Map two rooms north of the entrance. The Compass can be found in the third room from the top of the far-right row of rooms.

After you get the Map, check the rooms with it one by one as you advance. If you skip this check, you may get lost. The secret is to take your time and not rush through the labyrinth.

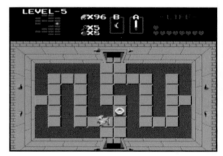

The Map and the Compass help you not get lost in the labyrinth.

You may find it helpful to use some of your own ideas in making a map.

Find the Entrance to the Shortcut

There are four rooms located in the upper part of Level 5, but you must go through the room in the bottom-left corner of the labyrinth. This grants you access to the upper rooms. As soon as you enter this room, find the set of stairs surrounded by eight blocks. Push one of them in order to gain access to the stairs. You'll need to contend with a small platoon of Darknuts before you can even think of investigating the blocks. Use Bombs to take them out quickly, then get to that staircase!

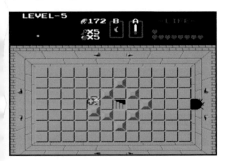

Reach the upper levels of the Map by going through these stairs.

Look for the Entrance to the Treasure Room

The entrance to the treasure room is hidden in the top-left corner of the Map, where again, several Darknuts await you. They are nasty enemies because they always block the rooms you must go through. You have no choice: defeat all the Darknuts. Put aside the task of finding the entrance to the treasure room until later. Don't give up!

After you've beaten all the Darknuts, look for the entrance. To open the entrance, investigate the block in the middle of the room.

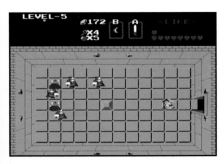

The Whistle is the treasure of Level 5. It will be useful somewhere in this labyrinth.

Gibdos Hit Hard!

The Gibdos make their first appearance in this level. They are slow enemies, but if they touch Link, he takes massive damage. Underestimating them because of their speed gets you into trouble.

Their slowness, however, is still an advantage for Link. Since they don't attack suddenly, Link has plenty of time to avoid their attacks. Expect to see them a lot in Level 5 and the later labyrinths.

Gibdos Don't Hide Items Well

Some Gibdos hold things like Keys, just as some of the Stalfos did in previous labyrinths. For example, one Gibdo walks around with a Key in his hand in the room just above the entrance, and another one holds a Bomb in the room just west of that.

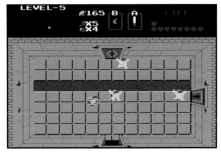

It's almost yours as soon as you see which Gibdo has what. Beat them quickly!

How to Deal with Pols Voice

There are many Pols Voice in Level 5. Their movement patterns are pretty simple—jumping up to the top of the room, then back down to the bottom.

Avoid fighting Pols Voice from the front, because they can jump into you with little effort or notice. Place yourself at the side of the screen until the Pols Voice come toward you, then attack them with your Sword just as they jump up. If only there was a quicker way to beat them…

Cash in on More Bombs

Link receives 12 Bombs if he pays the Old Man in the top-right room of the labyrinth 100 Rupees. Consider this a warning of things to come and save up your Bombs. You need a Bomb in order to enter this room in the first place, so don't burn through them all while fighting tougher enemies, like the Darknuts found in this labyrinth.

Pay the money and get your 12 Bombs. Onward!

The Secret of Digdogger's Weakness

Link can learn about the weakness of Digdogger, the boss of this labyrinth, from the Old Man one room north and one room east of the starting room. According to him, the Digdogger hates certain sounds, but this information is a little too vague to use. At least you know Digdogger's weakness has something to do with sound.

If you find something that produces a certain kind of sound, you might be able to take advantage of the weakness.

Getting Helpful Info in a Hidden Room

Open your Map and give it a gander. Level 5 is shaped like a lizard, and one of the empty spaces on the Map represents the lizard's eye. But that space is more than an aesthetic element; it conceals a hidden room. Find another Old Man in this hidden room, and he'll divulge important information on how to defeat Pols Voice. These floppy-eared creatures are surprisingly resilient—perhaps Link's sword isn't his best option.

Wondering what secret power might be in the arrow? Fire one at a Pols Voice to find out!

DIGDOGGER

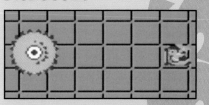

Attack the Digdogger after shrinking him, using his weakness.

The Triforce is in the top-left corner of Level 5, which means Digdogger, the boss of this labyrinth, must be in the room just below that. This huge monster is entirely too big for Link to battle, but there is a way to even the playing field. Digdogger shrinks if it hears a certain noise, but what noise could that be? Maybe it has something to do with the item hidden in the treasure room.

LABYRINTH 6: DRAGON

Level 6 Is Ultra-Difficult

The enemies you have to be careful about in Level 6 are the Like Likes and the Wizzrobes. Both are very tough opponents individualally and even tougher when they appear together in some rooms. Bubbles are also thrown into the mix, making these fights even harder. Whether or not you clear Level 6 depends on how well you get through the combined attacks of the Like Likes and Wizzrobes. It's a double challenge!

The Like Like, the Wizzrobe, and Bubble attack you at the same time. Get ready for a real challenge!

Getting the Map and the Compass

The first thing to do is get the Map and the Compass when you enter Underworld Labyrinth Level 6. Find the Compass one room west and one room north of the starting location. To find the Map, head to the room second from the top of the second row of rooms. Until you have both the Map and Compass, always verify the rooms you come through by using the Subscreen. That way you avoid getting lost or confused. Always stay calm and take careful steps.

If you have the Map and the Compass, you're halfway to conquering Level 6.

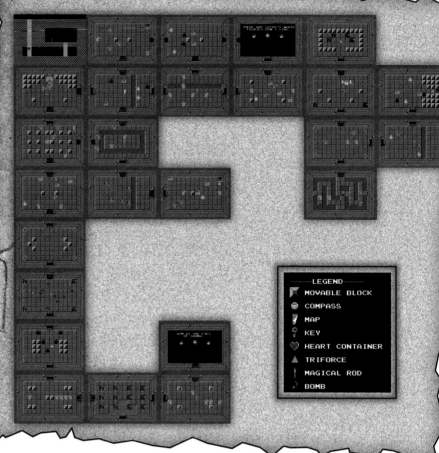

LEGEND
- ▯ MOVABLE BLOCK
- ◉ COMPASS
- ▯ MAP
- ⚷ KEY
- ♥ HEART CONTAINER
- ▲ TRIFORCE
- ▮ MAGICAL ROD
- ◈ BOMB

Escaping the Locked Rooms

The room one room east and four rooms north of the starting area locks as soon as you enter it. You have gone through many rooms similar to this one. Do something with one of the two blocks in the room to unlock the doors. However, you must beat the enemies in this room first—the Like Like and the Wizzrobe. Concentrate all your energy and get ready to do battle!

The enemies here pose bigger problems than finding the trick to unlocking the room.

Attack the Like Like from a Distance

The trick to beating a Like Like is to get him before he gets too close to you. For this, the Bow and Arrow, Blue Candle, and Bombs are all effective weapons. However, you can't use the same treasure forever, so when one wears out, quickly switch to a different one.

If a Like Like happens to grab you, don't panic. Quickly pull out your Sword and stab him before he can eat your Magic Shied. You might be able to beat him in time!

There Are Two Kinds of Wizzrobes

The Yellow Wizzrobes always appear in either the line running horizontally or vertically from Link, and can shoot magic spells only toward Link's current position. When you first see one appear, quickly jump out of its path. It is safest to attack a Wizzrobe from the side.

The Blue Wizzrobe is a lot tougher than the Yellow Wizzrobe to battle, because its pattern of movement is harder to predict. You have to really be on your toes, because the Blue Wizzrobe can also teleport into you, causing Link to lose health. Your best bet is to focus on a hit-and-run strategy. Keep moving; the worst thing you can do when you battle a Wizzrobe is panic.

Even when you're in the safety of the entrance to a room, the Blue Wizzrobe can get you. Watch out!

Gleeok Is in the Central Room

Gleeok, the boss you beat in Level 4, is back, in the room in the top-left corner of the labyrinth, only now it has three heads and is a lot more powerful! Be careful! Just like you did in Level 4, go up to Gleeok's side and plunge your Sword into the base of its neck; that's the way to beat it.

This three-necked Gleeok is harder to defeat than the previous one, as are the enemies you meet as you progress to higher levels. Don't let them sap Link's Hearts!

Dodge the beam and stab Gleeok in the neck!

Discover the Door to the Shortcut

The shortcut leading to the top-right corner of the labyrinth is somewhere in the third room of the third row of rooms. In fact, the only way for you to get into that top-right room and the rooms surrounding it is to find the shortcut. If you fail to find the entrance to the shortcut, you could end up walking all over the labyrinth.

In order to find this entrance, you must do something to the block in the center of this room. It's really quite a simple device, and since it's used repeatedly, you've most likely figured it out by now.

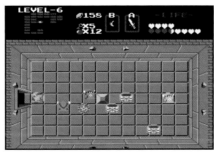

The shortcut is in here somewhere!

Where to Find the Magic Wand

You find Level 6's treasure, the Magic Wand, in the room at the top of the second row of rooms. There are two blocks in this room, and if you do something to one of them, the door to the treasure chamber opens.

The Magic Wand can be used in place of the Bow and Arrow and is quite a useful item. By all means, try to get it!

On the Underworld Map, the treasure room is usually hidden in the corner. This is true with the Triforce as well. Important things are in the corners of the labyrinths.

Get that Wand! It'll really help Link fight!

Destroy the Like Like with a Wand

Your Bow and Arrow and Bombs are good weapons for attacking Like Likes, but eventually they will run out. You can use a Blue Candle too, but since you can only burn it once within each screen, it's not the best weapon either. The Wand, however, can cast an endless supply of magic spells. It's a lot easier to destroy the Like Like if you get your hands on the Wand.

The good old Wand gives Link a big boost in fighting power.

Listen to the Old Man's Story

The Old Man who lives in the room at the top of the fourth row of rooms gives you a hint about where to find the Level 7 labyrinth.

So, after you clear Level 6, search out that place where no Fairies live. But what in the world did he mean by "secret"? It's you who must discover it. Use your imagination to find a way into Level 7.

GOHMA

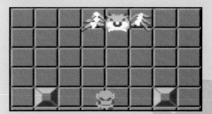

Timing is essential to catch Gohma between blinks in order to get him right in the eye.

To get to the Triforce piece in the top room of the fifth row of rooms, fight Gohma in the room just below that. Unfortunately, Gohma is a terrible enemy, because he has a hard shell that can repel any attack.

Now's the time to use the secret of Gohma's weakness the Old Man in the room one east and one north of the entrance told you about. "Aim for the eye" were his words. The eye is Gohma's weakness, but which weapon should you use on it? Try different weapons and aim at Gohma's weak point.

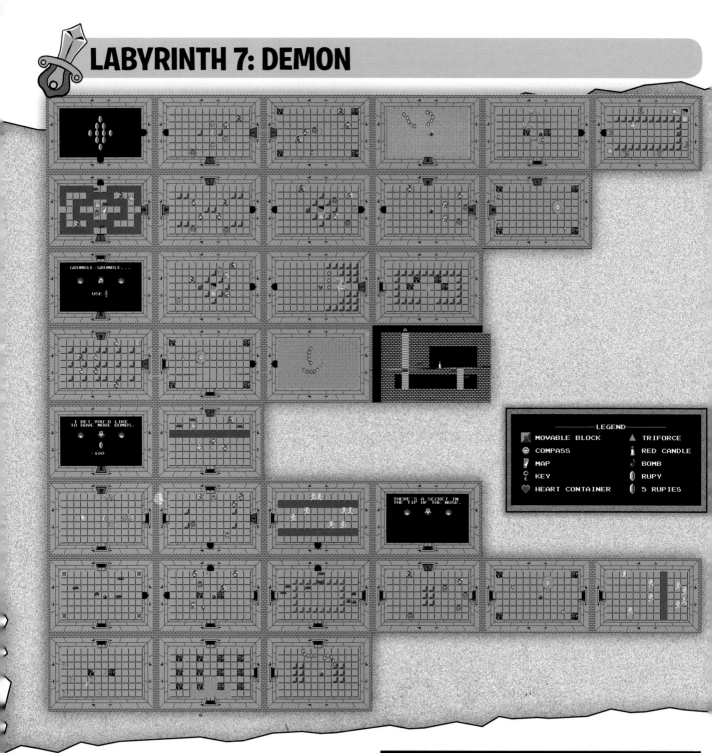

LEGEND

MOVABLE BLOCK		▲	TRIFORCE
COMPASS			RED CANDLE
MAP			BOMB
KEY			RUPY
HEART CONTAINER			5 RUPIES

Level 7: A Nest of Goriyas

One thing to note about Level 7 is that there are an awful lot of boomerang-wielding Goriyas. They aren't very strong enemies, and they can be beaten easily. Aquamentus, who guards the Triforce chamber, isn't particularly powerful either; defeating him is a breeze.

As you can see, Level 7 isn't all that difficult, relatively speaking. You might say it's of medium-range difficulty.

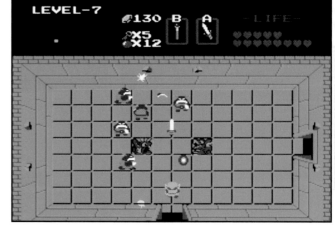

Getting the Map and Compass

Level 7 is a very large labyrinth, meaning a Compass and Map are even more useful here than in other labyrinths. Find the Compass two rooms north and one room east of the starting area; the Map can be found in the room second from the top of the first row of rooms.

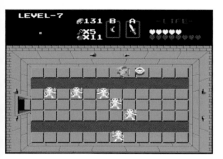

The Compass can be found here.

Holy Hidden Rupees!

While you're off to get the Map for this level, also look for a hidden treasure trove of Rupees. Make sure you have a Bomb or two handy to get them, and you're ready to go!

In the top-left corner of the labyrinth is a hidden room. Blowing up the wall in the Map room opens the passage to this secret treasury.

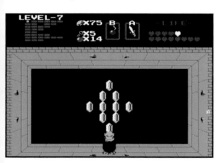

The Secret Treasure of Level 7

The secret treasure for Level 7 is the Red Candle—an updated version of the Blue Candle that can be used as many times per room as you want! That means you can use it in fights nonstop!

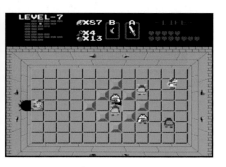

To find the Red Candle, head to the room second from the top of the third row of rooms. Experiment with the blocks in the center of the room to gain access to the treasure room. One of the blocks gives you access, but first, defeat all the enemies in the room!

Increase Your Bombs

One of the Old Men hiding in this labyrinth offers a very special service to Link. That is, if you can find him. If you pay this Old Man 100 Rupees, he increases your Bomb-holding capacity, which means you run out of Bombs less frequently.

To find this Old Man, head to the room fourth from the bottom of the first row of rooms. You need a Key to get in.

Digdogger's Revenge!

Digdogger's back for another chance to defeat Link. You find him lurking throughout this maze! And don't be surprised if he's picked up a new trick. Both Digdoggers are located in the fifth row of rooms, one in the bottom room and one in the second room. Remember: you can't damage Digdogger while he's big, so produce the sound he hates in order to shrink him down to size. Once he's on your level, take him on in earnest.

Triple Strike: Dodongo's Motley Crew!

After you defeat Digdogger in the room second from the top of the fifth row, a Dodongo fight immediately follows. Easy enough, right? We beat Dodongo labyrinths ago! Well, it would be, but Dodongo refuses to go quietly this time and has brought along some friends—two of them, to be precise!

You face off with three Dodongos in this room, but the strategy remains the same: place a Bomb in front of his mouth, and he eats it like a greedy pig. Repeat this method until each of the three Dodongos has been blown back to the Cretaceous period.

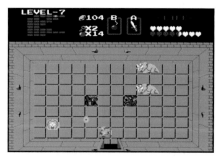

On the Tip of the Nose

You'll never find Aquamentus, the guardian of the labyrinth, without first finding the hidden passage to his lair. The entrance to this secret passage is in the room at the top-right corner of the labyrinth, but simply getting there won't be enough! Avoid Bubbles and defeat Wall Masters while inspecting each of the blocks.

We'll give you a hint: the block you're looking for is on the right side of the room. Once you open the passage, you gain access to Aquamentus and the Triforce piece.

AQUAMENTUS

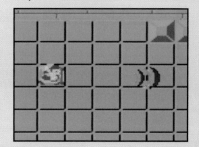

Aquamentus is just as you remember him, so you don't have to worry about a big, dramatic fight—maybe Ganon was feeling guilty for putting so many other bosses in this labyrinth and decided to go easy on you for the actual labyrinth boss.

Do what you did last time and strike in between Aquamentus's beam attacks. Move between his projectiles, strike, and jump back. Repeat this until Aquamentus is no more and the Triforce piece is yours!

One more to go!

LABYRINTH 8: LION

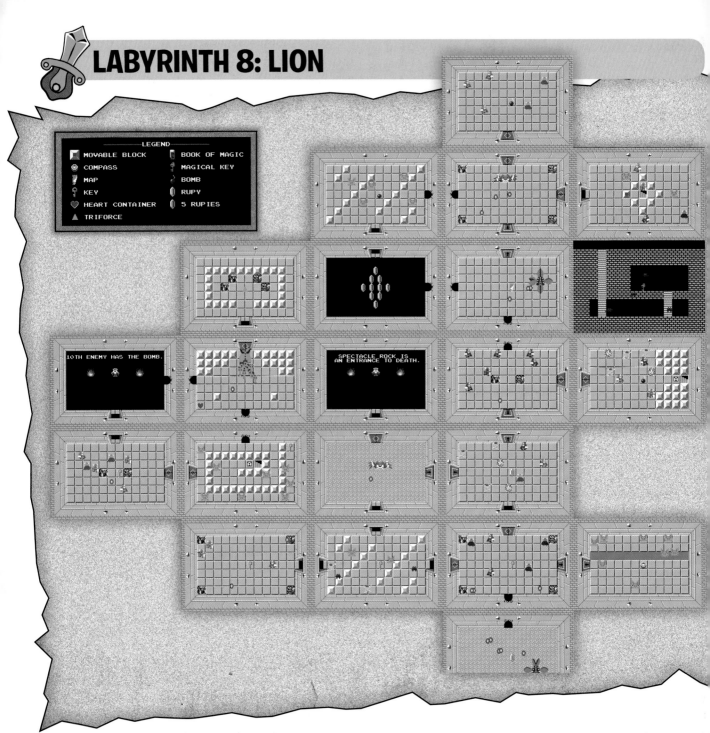

LEGEND
- ▨ MOVABLE BLOCK
- ◎ COMPASS
- ⚑ MAP
- ♀ KEY
- ♥ HEART CONTAINER
- ▲ TRIFORCE
- ▮ BOOK OF MAGIC
- ▮ MAGICAL KEY
- ◔ BOMB
- ◊ RUPY
- ◊ 5 RUPIES

10TH ENEMY HAS THE BOMB.

SPECTACLE ROCK IS AN ENTRANCE TO DEATH.

Attack of the Stone Statues!

The eighth Underworld labyrinth has a simple layout, so there's no need to worry about getting lost. Its overall shape is similar to the profile of a lion's head.

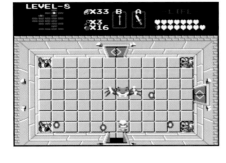

Though the level may appear straightforward, beware, as there are a lot of rooms with beam-shooting stone statues. You should already have the Magic Shield with you, but remember, while you fight your enemy, you must also dodge the statue's beams. It could get tough, but overall Level 8 is of medium difficulty.

The Darknut Labyrinth

This labyrinth is absolutely packed with peril, but one of the most common sights here is the groups of Darknuts littering several of

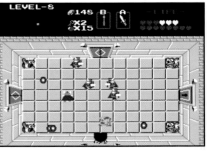

the rooms. Taking these foes on can really drain your health and Bombs, so play it smart and use your resources carefully. There are a ton of foes who used to be bosses in this labyrinth as well, and the last thing you need is to drain all your health and items trying to take out Darknuts.

A Boss Bonanza

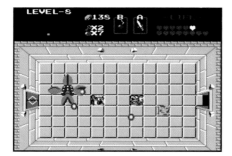

This labyrinth contains five total boss enemies, including the guardian of the Triforce piece, Gleeok. You must

face three Manhandlas and Gohma while traversing the dungeon. One Manhandla inhabits one room west of the starting room, and another one room north of the starting area. There's another Manhandla five rooms north of the starting zone, and a Gohma can be found one room north of that; one more Gohma is in the third room in the second row of rooms. Needless to say, you've got a lot of boss-busting to do in this Underworld labyrinth.

Remember that Gohma can only be wounded when you hit it with its weakness while its eye is open. For Manhandla, racing up and planting a Bomb as near to its center as possible can make for a one-hit KO. Keep these tips in mind while dealing with these foes, and you'll get through just fine.

Obtaining the Map and Compass

As always, the Map and Compass are incredibly useful to exploring the Underworld labyrinths, so make a point to get your hands on them as early as possible.

The Compass can be found two rooms north and one room west of the starting area, while the Map is located five rooms north of the starting area. Go in expecting a battle! Defeat Manhandla in that room to obtain the Map.

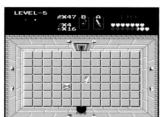

The Secret of Death Mountain

An Old Man hides in the fourth room in the second row of rooms in this labyrinth, and he's got some pretty important

information to share with a brave adventurer. That brave adventurer just happens to be Link in this case, and the information relates to the location of Level 9. The final labyrinth of the game can be a real challenge to find without assistance, so speak with the Old Man to make your search that much shorter.

The Magic Book

The treasure for this labyrinth is the Magic Book. This item combines with the Magic Wand to make a magical set with flame-throwing power—you can use them as a Candle too.

Find the Magic Book in the bottom-left corner of the labyrinth. Clear the room of enemies, then investigate the blocks to access the entrance to the treasure room. You must also fight Manhandla before gaining access to the room, so expect some trouble on your way to the treasure.

Reaching the Triforce Piece

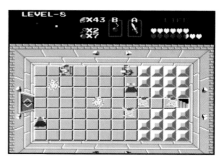

Like the labyrinths before this one, in order to reach the Triforce piece and its guardian, you need to find a shortcut. The boss's room is tucked

away on the left side of the labyrinth, but reaching it requires you to find a secret passage on the right side of the Map. The secret passage is in the third room in the rightmost row of rooms.

Once you head through the passage and reach the other side of the labyrinth, Bomb the north wall to open a passage to Gleeok's lair.

The Key to End All Keys

There's actually one more treasure item you can find in Level 8: the Magic Key. This Key is hidden in a treasure room inside the room in the top-right corner of the labyrinth. The Magic Key has the ability to unlock all locked doors without the need for multiple Keys. This extremely useful item makes the rest of the game much easier.

GLEEOK

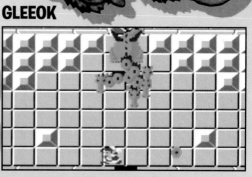

This Gleeok is four-headed, so you can expect a tougher fight than you got in Level 4. The same strategies still apply here: stab its neck between fireball shots and avoid the heads that move around of their own will. Defeat this beast, and you're ready for the final level: Death Mountain.

LABYRINTH 9: DEATH MOUNTAIN

The Final Showdown

You've finally reached the last maze. The second room from the entrance of Level 9 contains an Old Man. If you haven't assembled all the parts of the Triforce, he won't let you pass. This maze is the largest one yet, and it's extremely intricate. Some rooms lead to shortcuts, others lead nowhere. To keep from getting lost, plan your route carefully, and make sure to keep a close eye on your Map in the Subscreen. One wrong turn and Death Mountain becomes a much more difficult place.

Use what you learned in earlier mazes to overcome the challenges of Death Mountain. Use bombs to reveal secret passages between rooms. Defeat enemies to claim the items they hold. Push blocks to reveal secret passages and hidden shortcuts. Everything you've experienced has prepared you for this moment.

Prepare Yourself

The Compass, the Map, and the Red Ring are all fairly close together. Your first order of business should be to plot a simple route that allows you to collect all of them. None of these items is mandatory, but gathering them makes your time in Death Mountain much easier.

---LEGEND---

MOVABLE BLOCK   TRIFORCE
GO ONLY UP   RED RING
COMPASS   SILVER ARROW
MAP   BOMB
KEY   5 RUPIES

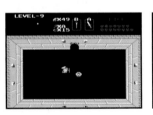

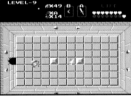

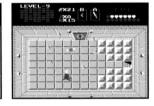

Fighting Patra

You encounter a new kind of enemy in this Level. Patra, a flying eyeball with a ring of smaller, similar-looking minions, appears in rooms around the labyrinth. Your Sword is the only thing you can use against them. You must finish off the little ones first, or you'll never be able to beat the bigger ones. They are persistent!

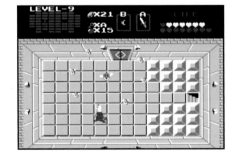

Remember the Way Out

No matter how confident you are, it pays to know the way back to Death Mountain's entrance. Water of Life certainly comes in handy, but you also need to maintain a supply of bombs and Rupees. If you find yourself running low on vital items, consider making a temporary retreat—particularly if you've already claimed some of the important items scattered around Death Mountain. You can always come back when you're restocked and refreshed.

Claim the Silver Arrows

Without the Silver Arrows, you won't stand a chance against Ganon. Remember to track them down before you enter his chamber. The power of the Triforce makes Ganon impervious to most forms of damage, but a single Silver Arrow can take him right out of the fight.

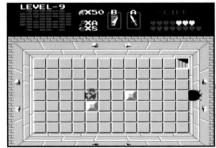

The Final Battle

You've come this far, conquering many mazes and overcoming dangerous challenges. Now it's time to finish Link's quest. Soon after you enter Ganon's chamber, he vanishes into the shadows. You didn't think it would be that easy, did you?

DEFEATING GANON

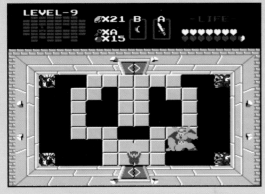

You've come this far, conquering many labyrinths and overcoming dangerous challenges. The rest is up to you. Just remember that the key to beating the King of Evil lies in one of the items you found here in Death Mountain. You can do it!

Dodge his fiery projectiles, but note each attack's point of origin. Before long, you should start to notice a pattern. Ganon tends to follow a somewhat circular path. Sometimes he moves clockwise between his attacks; other times he moves counter-clockwise. Try to predict where he'll be next, and then slash that spot with your sword. You have only a split second to hit him before he dashes to his next location, so keep at it. Don't let a few near-misses discourage you.

You'll know you've landed a blow when Ganon flashes into view. This is a good start, but it's just the beginning. You need to land a few more hits on Ganon before he's vulnerable to a Silver Arrow. Wait for him to vanish, then continue to pursue him around the room.

Each time your sword strikes Ganon, he reappears. If he's blue, he's still immune to the power of the Silver Arrow. After a few hits, though, Ganon should change color. When you see this, shoot him with a Silver Arrow to finish him off.

Free Zelda

Once you've defeated Ganon, it's time to free Zelda. Head through the doors at the top of Ganon's chamber, and extinguish the wall of flames, then approach Zelda to complete Link's quest.

THE SECOND QUEST

When you've succeeded in overthrowing Ganon, you have the opportunity to start a second quest: the Master Quest! If you're impatient and want to start the new adventure right away, just enter "ZELDA" as your filename when starting a new file. The second adventure is much tougher than the first. Expect more enemies to try and stop Link this time around!

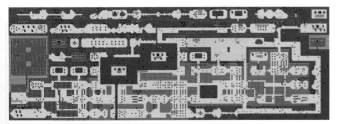

What's Different from the First Quest?

The structure of the Second Quest is almost the same as the First Quest, except for three geographical features. But you still have to think over your strategy, because things like hidden caves in the Second Quest are located in different

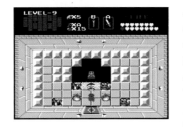

places. To discover location details, check out the map in this section of the guide.

STORY

Were you brave enough to beat all of Ganon's henchmen in the First Quest? Were you crafty enough to find your way through the many hazards to Ganon's lair? Were you mighty enough to take on Ganon, the ultimate villain, and win? If your answer to all of these questions is YES, then get ready for another super challenge: the Second Quest of The Legend of Zelda. The land of Hyrule isn't safe yet. You beat Ganon once, but now you must do it again to truly save the land from his evil clutches. Can you be victorious the second time around? Sharpen your Sword and your wits!

CONQUERING THE UNDERWORLD

There are two big differences between the First and Second Quests of The Legend of Zelda. You'll discover in the course of the Second Quest that the lay of the land in the Underworld is vastly different. Can you find your way in these labyrinths? The second big difference is the placement of items in the Underworld. Where are they? The challenge is definitely more complex than it is in the First Quest. To make matters worse, the enemies guarding the labyrinths have become much tougher, too! It's more difficult to get to Ganon in the Second Quest.

PUNCH-OUT!!
FEATURING MR. DREAM

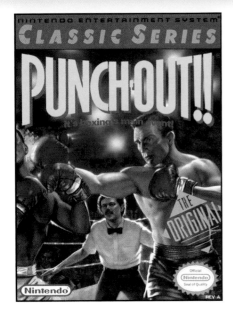

Developer:
Nintendo R&D3

Director:
Genyo Takeda

Producer:
Minoru Arakawa

Designers:
Kazuo Yoneyama, Mayumi Hirota

Artist:
Makoto Wada

Composers:
Yukio Kanooka, Akito Nakatsuka, Kenji Yamamoto

Original Release Date:
1983 Famicom JP; October 1987 NES US

STORY

Little Mac: A 17-year-old fighter from the Bronx in New York. He loves nothing more than a tough challenge.

Doc Louis: An ex-heavyweight who was a famous hard hitter in the U.S. around 1954.

It all began one day when Little Mac and Doc Louis met by chance. Doc became Mac's trainer, teaching him everything there is to know about boxing. Doc and Mac's story continues over a seemingly endless path to reach the World Heavyweight Championship.

ROADWORK

Becoming the World Heavyweight Champion will require hard work, patience, and perseverance. You'll find all the tools and tips you need to work your way to the top right here!

Starting the Game

Press the Start Button and you're ushered to the Main menu. Use Up or Down on the D-Pad to select either NEW or CONTINUE. Selecting NEW will, of course, start a new game. Selecting CONTINUE sends you to the Pass Key input screen.

PASS KEYS

Pass Keys are displayed whenever Little Mac becomes the champ of a circuit. Make sure to write down the Pass Key when it's displayed to continue your progress when you decide to take a break.

As an additional note, Little Mac's match record and circuit level are saved with the Pass Key.

WVBA Rules

A match in Punch-Out!! consists of three rounds, and each round is three minutes long. If a boxer is knocked down and doesn't get up by the count of 10 seconds, the match ends in a KO. If a boxer is knocked down a total of three times in a single round, that boxer loses and the match ends in a TKO. If a match goes through all three rounds without a KO or TKO, the winner is determined by whichever boxer has the highest points, which is decided by the referee. In matches against title holders, the decision will always be ruled in favor of the defending champ.

The Main Event

There's a lot more going on in a fight than just throwing punches while wearing boxing gloves. You've gotta learn to dodge! You've gotta learn to block! And you've gotta have Heart (and Stars)! Read on to learn how to keep Mac performing at his best!

Hearts (Mac's Stamina)

Little Mac can punch as much as he wants, so long as he still has Hearts. He loses a Heart each time his opponent blocks or dodges one of his punches, and Little Mac loses three Hearts if he is punched by his opponent. If he loses all of his Hearts, he enters a fatigue state, and is temporarily unable to throw any more punches or block, meaning he must dodge and duck to avoid damage.

Stars

When Little Mac has a Star in the box next to the Hearts box, he can throw his patented move, "the Knock-Out Punch!"—a devastating uppercut that can bring most opponents to the mat if used properly. In order to get Stars, Mac needs to hit his opponent at the time when they are at their most vulnerable. This changes for each opponent Mac faces, but it's usually just before they strike. Learn when to steal a Star from each opponent you face and you'll be champ in no time!

131

Stamina Meters

POINTS: 50

The white bars at the top of the screen are Mac and his opponent's Stamina Meters. Your goal is to deplete your opponent's Stamina Meter while keeping yours from being depleted. Every hit received is a loss to the Stamina Meter; the harder the hit, the larger the depletion. When a fighter's meter is fully depleted, they hit the mat and the ref begins his count. If the fighter gets back up, their Stamina Meter refills based on what count they got back up on, what round it is, and how many times the fighter went down in that match.

When a round ends, while both fighters are in their corners, if you hold the Select Button, Mac will listen to Doc's advice and refill his Stamina Meter as a result. You can do this only once per match, so make sure you pick the right time to use it.

Scoring

If a match is taken to a decision, the score will be based on the performance of the fighters. Little Mac will score points for every hit landed on his opponent; Knock-Out Punches and Star-producing punches score the most points.

Rounds and Round Time

0:25 Round 2

The time for each round and round number can be found in the top-right corner of the screen. When the timer reaches three minutes, the round ends. When the timer reaches that time on the third round, the fight will go to a decision. The victor is determined by points (if it's not a title fight).

MINOR CIRCUIT

This circuit is perfect for those new to the ring. You're a little fish in a little pond, but if you make your mark here, you'll be fighting the sharks in no time!

GLASS JOE – 1 WIN, 99 LOSSES, 1 KO

Ranking: W.V.B.A. Minor Circuit 2nd Place

Nickname: France's Glass Jaw

Condition for a winning decision: over 5,000 points

From: Paris, France

Age: 38

Weight: 110 lbs.

Glass Joe is at his most vulnerable just after he taunts Little Mac. When Joe steps back to begin his taunt, stop punching. As soon as Joe starts to move forward, hit him to score an instant knockdown. The sooner you punch him, the more likely he is to stay on the mat.

If Mac knocks Joe down in less than one minute without any mistakes, he gets up on the first count. This is your KO chance! When Joe gets up, quickly

throw an uppercut. He probably won't be able to get up a second time. If you're trying for a minimum KO time, don't miss the second punch.

VON KAISER – 23 WINS, 13 LOSSES, 10 KOS

Ranking: W.V.B.A. Minor Circuit 1st Place

Nickname: The German Steel Machine

Condition for a winning decision: 8,000 Points

From: Berlin, Germany

Age: 28

Weight: 144 lbs.

In order to beat Von, try to avoid his punches. Even if you block his punches, you'll still be injured. The most reliable way to earn a Star is to throw body-shot when Von Kaiser crouches down for a power punch. Otherwise, your best tactic is to stay away from his punches, then stun him with a quick blow to the face. Once he's stunned, you can knock him down with a single uppercut. Be sure to hit him with an uppercut as soon as he's stunned!

THE WINNING TECHNIQUE

Dodge your opponent's punches and counter-punch immediately. You'll startle your opponent (his face will show it). This is your chance! Punch furiously to rack up damage!

If your opponent gets up on a 1 count after hitting the mat, go for a Knock-Out Punch for a sure knockdown!

During a round break, use the advice of Mac's trainer Doc Louis to your advantage. If you've taken significant damage, make sure to hold the Select Button during this time to refill as much of your Stamina Meter as possible.

Minor Circuit Champion:
Piston Honda – 26 wins, 1 loss, 18 KOs

Ranking: W.V.B.A Minor Circuit Champion

Nickname: Kamikaze

Condition for a winning decision: there is no winning by decision

From: Tokyo, Japan

Age: 28

Weight: 174 lbs.

Honda telegraphs his fastest punches by twitching his eyebrows. If you manage to land a punch before he attacks, you usually earn a Star for your trouble. Otherwise, slip his punch and catch him off-guard with a quick jab. Beware of Honda's lethal Piston Punches! When Honda jumps back and hops around the mat, make sure you're ready to block the impending flurry of jabs. This combination ends with a right uppercut—make sure you sway to the left!

Don't Back Down!
Title fights can only be won with a KO or TKO; decisions are always ruled in favor of the champ. Give it your all if you want to claim the title and don't let your opponent keep you on the ropes!

Winning Strategy for the Piston Punch

In order to KO Piston Honda, you must block his deadly Piston Punches. These five straight punches come at a steady rhythm, so make sure you time your blocks to stop each and every one of them. At the end of the Piston Punches, he throws a right uppercut; sway to the left, and then throw a counter-jab to his face. After stunning Honda with this blow, follow with a Star-powered uppercut. However, even without this uppercut, you can put him down using the "one-two" punch pattern. Avoid Honda's punch and use your "one-two" punch again.

If you're feeling bold, you can also try to counter Honda's Piston Punches. Wait for him to finish his quickstep, then hit him just before he throws his first punch. It isn't easy to pull off, but a properly-timed counter will knock him to the mat.

MAJOR CIRCUIT

You're the Minor Circuit Champion now, so expect things to get much tougher from here on out. Give it your all and fight to your last and you'll take the Major Circuit title!

Don Flamenco – 22 wins, 3 losses, 9 Kos

Ranking: W.V.B.A. Major Circuit 3rd Place

Nickname: Red Rose of Madrid

Condition for a winning decision: over 10,000 points

From: Madrid, Spain

Age: 23

Weight: 152 lbs.

Don Flamenco refuses to throw a punch until Mac incites him. As soon as Mac punches, Flamenco fights back, throwing an effective uppercut. After three uppercuts, Mac will be sent flying, so be careful! Throw a jab and let him block it. When he winds back for his uppercut, sway to the left and repeat your "one-two" jab combo until Flamenco is knocked down. Each time Don Flamenco recovers from a knockdown, he attempts to throw his uppercut—as soon as he returns to the fight, hit him in the ribs with a left hook to earn a Star. Sway left to dodge his uppercut, stun him with a jab, and then hit him with an uppercut of your own.

EMERGENCY EVASION

Because Don Flamenco can block most punches, being too aggressive can cost you a lot of Hearts. If Mac runs out of Hearts, Don Flamenco attacks by throwing a series of right hooks. Sway to the left to dodge each of these punches until Mac recovers.

King Hippo – 18 wins, 9 losses, 18 KOs

Ranking: W.V.B.A. Major Circuit 2nd Place

Nickname: Tropical Chief

Condition for a winning decision: there is no winning by decision

From: Hippo Island

Age: Undisclosed

Weight: Undisclosed

King Hippo's guard is very tight, so expect it to be difficult to land a hit on him. But he does have one weakness—his navel! You have only one chance to drop him. Just before throwing a punch, King Hippo sometimes opens his mouth. If you throw a jab to his mouth, he will try to guard it. With his navel unguarded it's yours to attack, so let 'er rip! Once you put him down, he won't get up again.

Great Tiger – 24 wins, 5 losses, 3 KOs

Ranking: W.V.B.A. Major Circuit 1st Place

Nickname: Great Magician of India

Condition for a winning decision: over 10,000 points

From: Bombay, India

Age: 29

Weight: 132 lbs.

The ruby in Tiger's turban always glimmers just before he jabs. When you see the ruby flash, sway to dodge the incoming attack, and then counter with a single jab. Keep dodging and countering until Tiger crouches down to begin a series of uppercuts. When Tiger leans to his right (Mac's left) hit him with a left body blow. When he leans to his left, hit him with a right body blow. By the time you counter three of Tiger's uppercuts, you'll have three Stars. Keep it up until he steps back to begin his Magic Punches. Block each of his five whirling strikes, then hit him with a jab (or an uppercut!) to the face to knock him down with a single blow. Stick with this strategy, and Tiger won't last for long.

Winning Strategy for Tiger's Magic Punches

The winning strategy is all about defending against Tiger's Magic Punches. The Magic Punches, which come in five successive blows, are not threatening if you block all of them. You can then knock Tiger down with a direct blow to the face.

You'll know that Tiger's about to start his Magic Punches when he backs away and crouches down. Just after he vanishes, block to protect yourself from the first punch of his combo. He throws four more punches before he's done, so make sure you block them all. After five whirling punches, Tiger becomes dizzy. Hit him in the face to knock him down with a single punch.

Major Circuit Champion:
Bald Bull – 34 wins, 4 losses, 29 KOs

Ranking: W.V.B.A. Major Circuit Champion

Nickname: The Reckless Bald Bull

Condition for winning decision: there is no winning by decision

From: Istanbul, Turkey

Age: 36

Weight: 298 lbs.

Bald Bull spins his fists just before each jab. When you see him do this, slip the punch and counter with a quick jab to his face. If you immediately follow up with a second jab, you might just catch him before his next strike. A successful follow-up earns you a Star, but it can be risky.

Bull raises and lowers his gloves just before he throws a hook, and he bends low before he throws an uppercut. In either case, sway to avoid Bull's attack, then stun him with a jab to the face. When it comes to strikes, it's just a matter of dodging and countering. When it comes to the famous Bull Charge, however—well, that's another matter. If you dodge his charge, Bull just heads back for another attempt. If you want to shut him down, you must hit him just as he hops into range. It can be difficult to time, but a successful counter sends Bald Bull tumbling to the mat.

Winning Strategy for Bull Charge

The Bull Charge is a devastating move, but one well-timed punch stops it cold. When Bull prepares to charge, he hops to the back of the ring. After a brief pause, he hops toward you to deliver an extremely powerful uppercut. As he does this, hit him with a body blow—throw your punch just after Bull finishes his third hop. It might take a bit of practice, but you must master this counter if you hope to win this fight.

Countering Bull's signature move will knock him down, but it may not finish him off. Don't let your guard down until the ref counts him out.

WORLD CIRCUIT

You'll face a lot of old opponents with renewed vigor in this circuit. They all bring new moves to the table, so don't expect the same old fights!

Piston Honda Rematch –
26 wins, 2 losses, 18 KOs

Ranking: W.V.B.A. World
Circuit 5th Place

Nickname: Honda Turbo

**Condition for a winning
decision:** over 3,000 points

From: Tokyo, Japan

Age: 28

Weight: 174 lbs.

Piston Honda's back for round two. He's largely the same Piston you've already fought, but with a few new tricks. When he wiggles his eyebrows, expect three consecutive jabs, followed by a couple of uppercuts. Duck each of the jabs, then sway left and counter-jab each time he attempts to uppercut. Honda's also updated his Piston Punch. Instead of quickstepping around the ring, he simply hops back and dashes in to deliver four consecutive jabs, followed by some uppercuts. Block each jab, then sway and counter-jab each time he uppercuts. Hit him with a few more jabs while he's stunned.

Watch out for Honda's feint—occasionally he ducks down and turns his hips back and forth before throwing an uppercut. Before you dodge, wait until he's turned back and forth two times. If you can land a solid hit on him just before he throws a punch, you're bound to earn a Star—but there's always a chance he'll block your strike. The safest bet is to counter each of his uppercuts and chip away at his Stamina until he stays down.

Soda Popinski – **33 wins, 2 losses, 24 KOs**

Ranking: W.V.B.A. World
Circuit 4th Place

Nicknames: The Fizzy Fighter,
the Bubbly Beast, The Carbonated
Cannonball

**Condition for a winning
decision:** over 10,000 points

From: Moscow, U.S.S.R.

Age: 35

Weight: 237 lbs.

This is a test of footwork more than any other fight. Popinski doesn't have any particularly fancy tricks up his sleeve; he's just quick and powerful. One hit can lead to several more pretty easily. His quick jabs are tough to predict, but Popinski shuffles his feet right before he does a three-jab combo.

Be ready to dodge left or right at a moment's notice. You don't have many Hearts in this match, so don't waste them on punches that are sure to be blocked.

Each time you dodge one of Popinski strikes, hit him with a jab to the face. Successfully countering one of his hooks or uppercuts will leave him stunned—hit him with flurry of punches until he recovers. Don't hesitate to throw a punch the instant he reels back for a hook or squats down for an uppercut—hitting him just before he swings will most likely land you a Star, so be quick and confident!

Bald Bull Rematch –
34 wins, 5 losses, 29 KOs

Ranking: W.V.B.A. World
Circuit 3rd Place

Nickname: Crazy Bucking Bull

Condition for winning decision: over 7,000 points

From: Istanbul, Turkey

Age: 36

Weight: 298 lbs.

Bull is back and he's fiercer than ever. He's largely the same Bull you remember, but tougher, meaner, and out for revenge. Many of the same tricks work here, but with slightly different timing. To knock him down, you must land a Star-fueled uppercut or counter his Bull Charge. Otherwise, Bald Bull simply regains his Stamina before he goes down.

Bald Bull still raises and lowers his hands just before he throws a hook, but he also uses a slower version of the same motion as

a taunt—whenever you see this taunt, hit Bull with a punch to earn a Star. Counter one of his power punches to momentarily stun him, then immediately throw your uppercut for serious damage. If Bull's Stamina is low enough, he'll drop to the mat—if not, you've still managed to inflict some serious damage.

His Bull Charge is largely the same, and you can still knock him down by hitting him with a body blow just after his third hop. However, there's another option this time around. If you dodge Bull's charge, he doesn't return to the ropes for another pass—instead, he hops back twice, pauses, and then hops forward for shorter charge. If you prefer, you can dodge the first charge and counter just after he hops in for the shorter charge—just throw a body blow once he starts hopping toward you again. Either way, countering his charge is still the key to besting Bald Bull.

Don Flamenco Rematch –
22 wins, 4 losses, 9 KOs

Ranking: W.V.B.A. World
Circuit 2nd Place

Nickname: The Rose's Thorn

Condition for a winning decision: over 5,000 points

From: Madrid, Spain

Age: 23

Weight: 152 lbs.

Don Flamenco is another returning fighter who's learned a few new tricks. He was a cautious fighter before, but this time he plays a more offensive game. Since he's new to the aggression game he provides a few clues when he's about to strike— namely his bad habit of putting his gloves to his

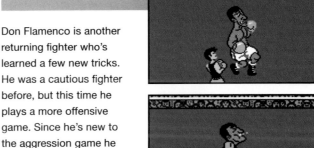

face before throwing a left jab. If you see those gloves go to his face, dodge and throw some counter punches to his head. Of course, you should also counter after each of Don's right hooks and Flamenco Punches.

Flamenco still enjoys taunting—and once he starts, he won't stop until you attack—but he won't always throw his Flamenco punch when you take the bait. After blocking your punch, there's a good chance Flamenco will simply continue to taunt you. You must hit him each time he taunts. Each time you do, he blocks your punch. This virtually guarantees that you'll run out of Hearts at some point during the match. Make sure you dodge his punches until you're back in the fight.

Mr. Sandman – 27 wins, 2 losses, 21 KOs

Ranking: W.V.B.A. World Circuit
1st Place

Nickname: Mr. Lights Out

**Condition for a winning
decision:** over 10,000 points

From: Philadelphia, Pennsylvania

Age: 31

Weight: 284 lbs.

One of the best
fighters in the sport
of boxing, Mr.
Sandman fights
like an even more
vicious Bald Bull.
He comes out of the
gate throwing jabs
like Zeus throws
thunderbolts. Each
hit that connects will
cost you three Hearts
and a significant
amount of Stamina;
if you have trouble
dodging these jabs,
try blocking them
instead—it's not
ideal, but it should
let you hold out long
enough to retaliate.
Otherwise, sway to
dodge each hit of his
opening combo—
just know that Mr.
Sandman tends to
mix up his rhythm every so often.

When he's done jabbing, that's your chance to strike! Dodge one
of his hooks, hit him with a jab to the face, then go for the gut as
fast and hard as you can! Don't hit his head more than once or he'll
retaliate with another jab. Repeat this strategy until he unleashes his
triple-uppercuts.

Before he uses his signature attack, Mr. Sandman stops fighting
and shuffles his feet. Be ready to dodge when his feet stop moving.
Slip all three uppercuts, and then retaliate with a jab to the head,
followed by more body shots. Mr. Sandman is one tough opponent,
but if you can dodge his strikes, your counters should put him on the
mat before the match ends.

World Circuit Champ:
Super Macho Man – 35 wins, 0 losses, 29 KOs

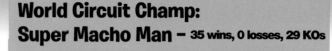

Ranking: W.V.B.A. World Circuit
Champion

Nickname: Hollywood Muscle Man

**Condition for a winning
decision:** there is no winning by
decision

From: Hollywood, California

Age: 27

Weight: 242 lbs.

Right from the start
of the fight, Super
Macho Man starts
throwing uppercuts.
If you're quick at the
start of the fight you
can get a gut punch
off of him. Expect
immediate and
furious retaliation in
the form of a flurry
of uppercuts. Show
him your footwork
by dodging all of the
uppercuts, and then
give him a hailstorm
of face hits. Use the
same tactic when
he throws hooks
into the mix. Of
course, beating the
champ won't be that
simple—watch for
Super Macho Man's
signature punches!

If you want to take
the title, you must overcome Super Macho Man's spinning punch.
If he suddenly stops attacking, beware! After a brief pause, the
champ unleashes one of two spinning attacks. If he vibrates, it
means he's about to perform a spinning punch. Dodge this attack
and counter with a jab to his face. If, instead of vibrating, Super
Macho Man steps back, it means he's about to perform a series
of spinning punches. When this happens, dodge each and every
spinning punch he throws. When the onslaught ends, throw a punch
to his head to begin your counterattack.

THE DREAM FIGHT

Everything's come down to this! Fight after fight, champ after champ has all led to fighting the world's greatest in his own ring. Get ready to give it your all, because your opponent is known for his quick, brutal KOs and he's not about to go easy on the current World Circuit Champ! You've got this, kid! Give him your best and don't take any of his!

Mr. Dream

Ranking: W.V.B.A. World Heavyweight Champion

Nickname: The Legendary

Condition for a winning decision: there is no winning by decision

From: Dreamland

Age: ??

Weight: 235 lbs.

The other fights can be won with trained, tempered skill, but Mr. Dream will decide if you should win or lose every time you fight him. Some fights he throws you a bone, but others he's as merciless as they come.

Right as the fight begins, he releases a barrage of uppercuts. He keeps up the pressure for the first minute and a half of the fight. A single uppercut and you're on the ground, so perfect dodging is a must! As soon as he throws an uppercut, dodge, grab a couple of headshots, then get ready for the counterattack. You're not going to get too much damage on him in this first half of the round, but every bit of damage goes a long way toward taking down the champ.

Once the first minute and a half passes, he changes up his strategy and starts throwing jabs. Watch his eyes; the eye that blinks indicates where his next punch is going to come from. If he blinks both eyes, give him a clean face hit to earn a Star. Dodge the jabs, counter, repeat.

You're taking this fight all the way to round 3, without a doubt, and each round is a little different than the one before it. The second round is a much more technical affair. He mixes in uppercuts with his jabs. Punish his uppercuts with counterpunches. If he raises his gloves to his face and blinks his eyes, immediately throw a gut punch to net a Star. He rushes you down after you hit him in this state, so get ready for a barrage of heavy hits!

The third round follows a similar pattern to round 2, so keep up the dodge-counterpunch strategy and he'll be down for the count. This is it, kid! Send him back to Dreamland!

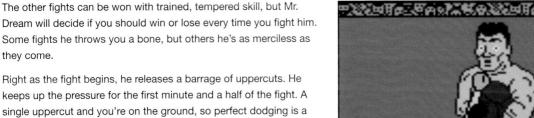

SUPER MARIO BROS. 2

Developer:
Nintendo R&D4

Director:
Kensuke Tanabe

Producer:
Shigeru Miyamoto

Composer:
Koji Kondo

Original Release Date:
October 9, 1988 NES NA;
September 14, 1992 Famicom JP

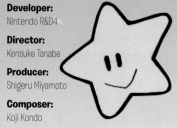

STORY

One evening, Mario had a strange dream. He dreamed of a long, long stairway leading up to a door. As soon as the door opened, he was confronted with a world he had never seen before, spreading out as far as his eyes could see. When he strained his ears to listen, he heard a faint voice saying, "Welcome to Subcon, the land of dreams. We have been cursed by Wart and are completely under his evil spell. We have been awaiting your arrival. Please defeat Wart and return Subcon to its natural state. The curse Wart has put on you in the real world will not have any effect on you here. Remember, Wart hates Vegetables. Please help us!" At the same time this was heard, a bolt of lightning flashed before Mario's eyes. Stunned, Mario lost his footing and tumbled upside down.

He awoke with a start to find himself sitting up in his bed. To clear his head, Mario talked to Luigi, Toad, and Princess about the strange dream he had. They decided to go to a nearby mountain for a picnic. After arriving at the picnic area and looking at the scenery, they saw a small cave nearby. When they entered this cave, to their great surprise, they discovered a stairway leading up, up, and up. It was exactly like the one Mario saw in his dream. They all walked together up the stairs and, at the top, found a door just like the one in Mario's dream. When Mario and his friends, in fear, opened the door, the world he'd seen in his dream spread out before them!

CHARACTERS

As a major change in the *Mario* series, *Super Mario Bros. 2* allows you to choose from four characters, each with his or her own advantages and disadvantages.

Mario

Mario's got solid jumping power and speed, but his jumping power takes a small hit whenever he's carrying an item.

Luigi

Luigi has the best jump ability, but he loses the most jumping power out of anyone whenever carrying an item.

Toad

Toad has the least jumping power, but the highest speed in the game. On top of that, items do not hinder his jumping power at all.

Princess Toadstool

In terms of speed and jumping power, Princess Toadstool is on the low end of the spectrum. But her ability to float in the air more than makes up for these shortcomings.

Luigi   **Mario**   **Toad**   **Princess Toadstool**

WELCOME TO SUBCON

Mario, Luigi, Toad, and Princess Toadstool have found the strange dreamworld of Subcon, where they jump, run, and use Vegetables to defeat enemies. To make it through the seven worlds of Subcon, you must learn many special techniques. To play well, you must practice, practice, and practice some more. Good luck with your new adventures!

The Dynamics of Jumping

You played *Super Mario Bros.*, so you know how to jump with the best of them, right? Wrong! *Super Mario Bros. 2* changes things up with the Power Squat Jump. Let's go over each jump here to get you up to speed.

   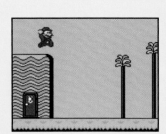

A Jump on the Spot

While Mario and friends are motionless, press the A Button. They jump up and down in one spot, and not very high. This can be helpful at times, but it's best to learn a few other tricks.

Running Jump

Press A while running, and you get a higher jump than when Mario and the others simply stand still. It's a good way to escape enemies and get over obstacles.

Power Squat Jump

This is the game changer. A Power Squat Jump takes Mario and friends to new heights. Hold Down on the Control Pad until your character begins to flash. If you press the A Button at this point, you make the highest jump yet!

Master the Basics

Mario's got a new repertoire of moves this time around. Jumping on enemies no longer defeats them; you've gotta use what's lying around to take down these mysterious Subcon foes. Read on to learn the tricks of the trade.

Run and Jump

Control your character's movements by using a combination of A, B, and the Control Pad. To jump, press the A Button. To increase your speed and hightail it away from danger, hold the B Button to run. It takes a bit of practice, but you'll get the moves down eventually.

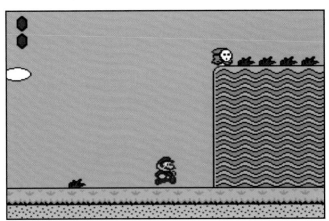 

Without items, all the characters move at the same speed. When carrying items, each character assumes a different speed.

Overcome difficulties by using the three techniques. Mario's motto: When it doubt, jump!

Pick Up Items and Throw Them

Mario and his friends may be in a strange land, but they are quick to find lots of handy survival tactics. This group of heroes is tough, and they are at their toughest when you use the B Button. With the B Button, they pull up the red grass to reveal Vegetables, or pick up enemies. Throw either at another enemy to take it out.

You can use the majority of items you pick up along the way as weapons with which to attack enemies.

Stay right on the target and Press B. Practice, and you'll be pulling trick shots in no time!

Defeating Wart's Entourage

The World of Dreams consists of seven worlds. Each world has three areas, except for the seventh. Most areas feature a Little Boss at the end. When a Little Boss is defeated, you can collect the crystal ball and proceed through the gate to the next area. You have three chances to continue from the first area of the world you were last on.

Earth Shakes

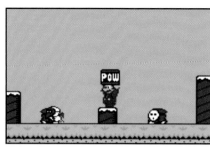

The most powerful weapon in your Subcon arsenal is the POW Block, which blasts away enemies with its pow-pow-pow-power!

Lift Enemies

Defeat enemies by throwing them into other enemies. First, jump on top of the enemy and lift it with ease.

Vegetables

Fight your enemies with Vegetables. Simply pull them up from the ground and throw them at the bad guys.

Slide and Hit

Defeat as many enemies as possible while you are in hot pursuit of a Turtle Shell.

Explode!

Bombs can be found to destroy walls and attack enemies. Learn the timing of these explosive goodies and use it to your advantage.

Items That Help Mario and His Friends

As you work your way through the dangers of the World of Dreams, you discover 16 items. Some of them help you get the best of your enemies. Others are handy for restoring your character's life or moving the characters to more advantageous places. The appearance of items might change in each world, but the effectiveness is the same. Check out any unfamiliar item you come across in the course of your adventures. Give it a test run to see what it can do for you.

Sprout

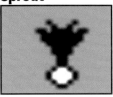

This vegetable is not completely ripe yet, which means you can only use it to attack the enemy. But, to that end, it works wonders!

Vegetables

Ah, a ripe Vegetable. You can use it to attack. After pulling out a fifth Vegetable, a Stopwatch appears.

Stopwatch

Stopwatch stops all enemy movements for a brief amount of time.

Mushroom Block

Throw it to attack enemies, use it as a lid, or stack them to reach high locations!

Bomb

It will flash and explode within a few seconds after you pick it up. Use it mainly to destroy walls. Careful handling is a must!

Shells

When you throw a shell, it glides on the surface of the ground and crashes into enemies.

Cherries

Starman appears when you find enough Cherries, which are scattered randomly around an area.

Starman

Collect five Cherries to cause a Starman to appear. Touch it to become temporarily invincible.

Heart

It appears when you defeat multiple enemies. When you get one, you can refill your Life Meter by one.

Mushroom

It appears only when you enter a "Sub-Space" at a particular spot. Can you find it?

1-Up

This is especially helpful. Reach out and catch or pick it up, and it gives you a new life.

Magic Potion

Throw the Magic Potion to create a door to the subspace.

Key

A Key, of course, unlocks a door. You can also throw Keys to attack enemies.

POW Block

Throwing a POW Block creates an earthquake, which eliminates all the enemies on the ground.

Coin

All grass you pull up in Sub-Space turns into Coins. Use these Coins at the Bonus Chance stage.

Rocket

Pulling up grass in certain spots reveals Rockets, which are capable of taking your character to different places.

KNOW YOUR ENEMIES

In Subcon, the world of dreams, you find many different and strange creatures lurking at every turn. Lackeys of Wart, they try in every way conceivable to interfere with the brave Mario, Luigi, Princess Toadstool, and Toad, the Mushroom Retainer.

The key to victory lies in your ability to study and learn the different strengths and weaknesses of each lackey. You must plan the best ways to tackle them. After you learn how to beat every one of them, head for World 7, where Wart awaits you.

Pokey

Porcupo

Shy Guy

LITTLE BOSSES

These are the big bads of *Super Mario Bros. 2*. Each one has its own way of giving our heroes trouble, so take care when you face them to come out unscathed.

Birdo

Clawgrip

Mouser

Mask Gate

Tryclyde

Wart
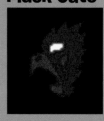

Fryguy
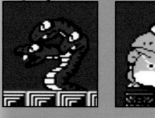

Albatoss

Cobrat

Ostro

Snifit

Autobomb

Flurry

Panser

Spark

Beezo

Hoopster

Phanto

Trouter
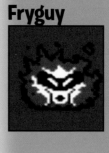

Bob-omb

Ninji

Pidgit

Tweeter

WORLD 1

We give you some important pointers on how to tackle each area in *Super Mario Bros. 2.* To be on the safe side, try out each character and get to know their movements at the beginning of the game. Once you pass through the door below, the real fast-action fun starts. The first area is an easy win.

Choose Wisely

You can't switch your character until you complete the current area. Make your selection carefully at the beginning of each world. Some characters work better in certain worlds than in others. Get to know which character plays the best for you in each of the seven worlds.

World 1-1

At two places in this stage, your jumping techniques are tested. Watch out! It's all over if you fall into the waterfall—even if your Life Meter is full.

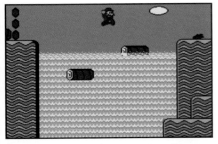

As you approach this waterfall, two logs fall at different intervals. Timing is critical. Watch your footing as you cross over to the other side.

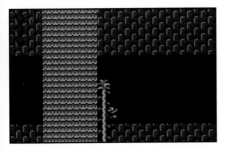

All characters can jump across this waterfall, but you may need a running start. (Hold the B Button to build up speed!) After you land, look for the shortcut to get to the Little Boss quickly. Don't waste the nearby bombs—you'll need them to clear the path to the door!

Entering Sub-Space

Watch out for looming Shy Guys before you enter Sub-Space. Get a Mushroom here.

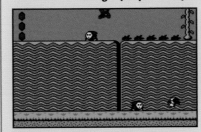 

A Treasure Trove

There is a lot of grass in Sub-Space near the vine at the end of the first area of this level. Find a Mushroom in the same area.

Take a Shortcut

With enough speed (or a powerful jump), you can leap over the waterfall and take a shortcut to the Little Boss. Use a Bomb to destroy the wall and open the door—make sure you throw the Bomb just before it detonates.

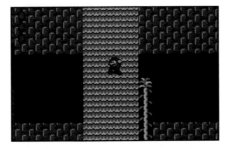 

How to Defeat the Little Boss

The first Little Boss you encounter is Birdo. Her main method of attack involves spitting eggs out of her mouth. When you have a chance, hop on top of her flying eggs.

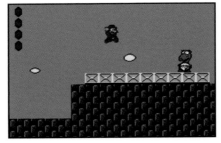 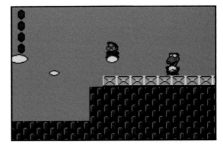

Pick up the flying egg by quickly pressing the B Button. Aim and throw the eggs back at Birdo. She goes down once you hit her three times.

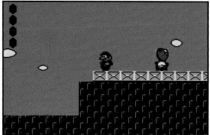

World 1-2

Right after you start your adventure in this level, you find yourself soaring across the sky. Take the magic carpet away from Pidgit to get to the other side of the chasm. Later, when the going gets rough, use Bombs. That makes a big difference.

Ride on a Flying Carpet

Be patient and wait for Pidgit floating in the air to make its way to you. Moving carelessly can cause you to fall off the cliff. You will be okay if you get on top of Pidgit's head. You don't have to land on the middle. Control the carpet with the Control Pad after you toss Pidgit out of the way.

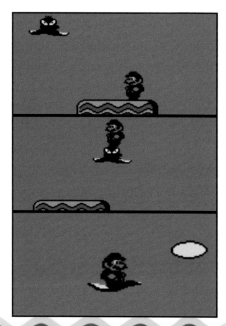

Entering Sub-Space

Aim and throw the Magic Potion between the two jars right after you fly over the chasm. Once you enter Sub-Space, you find the first Mushroom hidden in this stage.

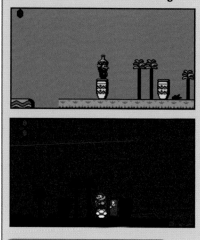

Pots Instead of Pipes

Press Down on the Control Pad while standing on top of a jar to slide down into it. Find a 1-Up in the first jar. What luck!

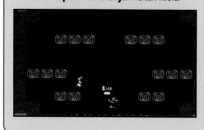

Escape from Phanto

Pressing Down while standing on the second pot sends you to an area with a Key at the end of it. If you take the Key, a malicious mask named Phanto comes after you in hot pursuit. Tenacious as he is, he continues his chase after you get out of the jar—what a nasty bad guy! Don't worry: if you put the Key down on the ground, Phanto goes away. Don't press your luck in a tight situation. If need be, drop the Key for a moment to catch your breath.

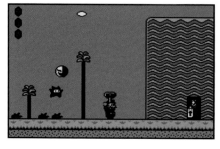

Using Bombs Effectively

The majority of the items you find in the caves of this area are Bombs. Use them wisely.

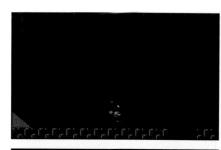

Perfect Bomb Placement

Destroy the wall near the top of the ladder using two Bombs (you'll find the Bombs under the nearest clumps of grass). This is the simplest way to ensure that you can reach the cave's hidden Mushroom. Just throw down the Magic Potion and drop through the newly created hole!

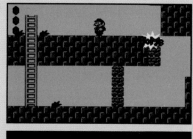

Do the Little Boss Toss

The Little Boss in this area is none other than Birdo herself. You know how to handle her. It's a sure win!

World 1-3

This is the last stage of World 1. The level begins with a horizontal scroll, changes to a vertical scroll, and then goes back to the horizontal scroll. While in the vertical scroll, you can't open the door far below unless you get the Key from the top room. Remember this while you move; without this step, you can't succeed.

Cross the River

Are you ready for consecutive log rides and lots of waterfalls in a row to keep you hopping? This is the toughest log jumping you've faced yet. And each one is more difficult than the last, so get rolling!

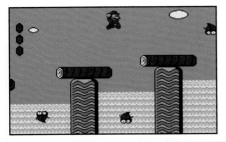 

Choices

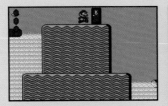 

You should encounter two Magic Potions before you head underground. There are two ways to use the second Potion, so you've got an important choice to make. If you want to find another Mushroom, head back across the river to the left, climb up to the top of the large hill, and enter Sub-Space to collect your prize.

If you'd rather use the Potion to access a handy shortcut, keep moving right and toss it near the jar at the end of the area. If you enter Sub-Space and head down into the jar, you'll be warped straight to World 4!

Finding the Key

When you make it to the long, vertical corridor, climb up instead of heading down. At the top of the corridor is a door that leads to a Key room. Grab the Key and dodge the Phanto attacks while heading to the bottom of the corridor. Unlock the door and step through.

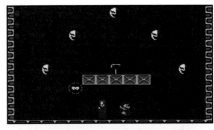

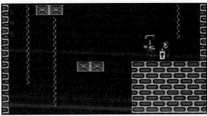

Final Battle to Clear World 1

It takes three Bombs to put Mouser in his place. Throw or place the Bombs so Mouser is nearby when they explode!

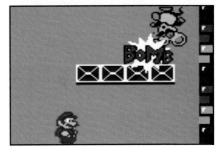

WORLD 2

New dangers lurk here: quicksand that pulls you down if you stand still, and stacked bricks that block your path. Don't sweat it! Keep going. You'll make it if you're fast, smart, and a little lucky.

World 2-1

Are you ready for quicksand? How about deep pits? Digging your way out through the sand isn't so easy. These are just a couple of the multitude of hair-raising challenges you face. Here's a clue to remember: don't stop unless you have a good foothold.

Time for a Character Change?

Watch out for the many traps of the world of deserts. You're bound to run into the snaggle-toothed Cobrat. Also, beware of Panser's fire attacks. Maybe you should switch to a better jumper? Luigi fits the bill!

Wrong Jar?

You can jump into the first jar you see in the level. But what's this? There's nothing inside but a Snifit and a buried Shell! Don't worry: Shells make for useful weapons outside.

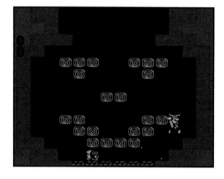

Sub-Space

See the four patches of grass just past the second jar? The one on the left is a Potion. Use it here, enter Sub-Space, and take the Mushroom and Coins. Your meter can never be too high!

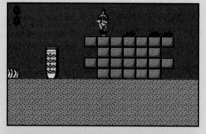

Heave a Shy Guy at Panser

Panser is spitting flames at the top of the pyramid shown in our screenshot. Be careful! Look for a Shy Guy below, pick him up, and throw him at Panser. Now you can get by safely.

Leave the Hole Digging to Luigi

This room is full of sand that's perfect for digging through. Dig holes with the B Button to reach the ladder on the bottom-left side of the room, under the sand. But watch out for Shy Guys. They come at you from all sides. This is the time for Luigi to show you how fast he can dig a hole.

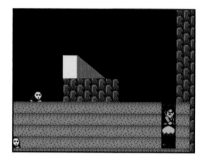

Take a Cherry and Keep Going

There are Cherries hidden in the sand. If you picked up some earlier in this level in addition to the ones in the sand, Starman appears. Grab him, and you can dig your holes with no trouble at all—piece of cake!

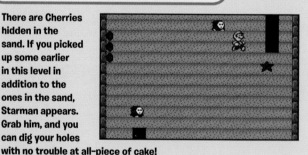

Birdo's Back!

You'll never guess who's the Little Boss of World 2-1—Birdo. Long time, no see! Throw three eggs at her again. But be careful that you don't drop into the pits scattered around the area.

World 2-2

This stage seems extremely difficult at first. The quicksand is faster, and you have a smaller area to move around in. If you haven't selected Toad as your character yet, now might be a good time.

Sub-Space

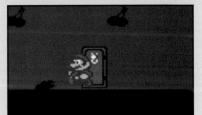

The Magic Potion lies in the first patch of grass you see in World 2-2. Don't wait! Use it and get the Mushrooms and Coins in Sub-Space.

Sub-Space Has Its Limits

You know by now that the Magic Potion makes a door to subspace appear, which gives Mario and friends a chance to find Coins, Mushrooms, and warps. But don't drop them willy-nilly! There are a limited number of Magic Potions in each stage and lots of Coins and Mushrooms to collect. After two Magic Potions, subspace plants will no longer give Coins.

Bounce Off the Bones

This quicksand is definitely quick. No matter how much you press the A Button, you're still in trouble. But all is not lost. Leap on the sinking bones and quickly jump to the other side. That's easy enough, isn't it? But watch out for Cobrat's attacks once you get there.

A Mysterious Cave

Did you notice that opening just past the falling bones? Head inside—you'll be glad you did.

Take a 1-Up

As soon as you enter the next room, head right and pull at the grass at the very bottom to get a 1-Up.

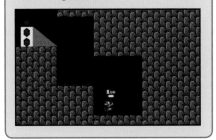

Three bombs: That's what you have at your disposal to break through the wall near the cave entrance. As soon as you pull one of them, Squat Jump back up to the entrance and use the Bomb to clear away the wall to the left.

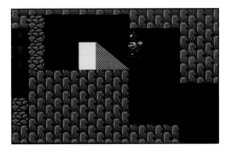

Sub-Space

Where's the Magic Potion? Try the second clump of grass from the right. Throw the Potion on the ground near where you found it for Coins and a Mushroom.

Beware of Pokey

Steer clear of Pokey; he does a lot of damage. If you decide to mess with him, go for his weak spot—he's kind of softheaded.

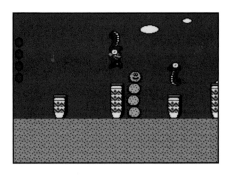

Speed Off to Safety

Don't relax yet. There's trouble ahead at the top of those stone steps—double trouble! Two Pansers are waiting to give you a flaming-hot welcome.

Unless you find something at the bottom of the stone steps to cool their jets, your best bet is to hotfoot it to safety.

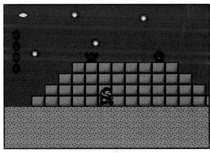

Get Starman's Help!

Remember in World 2-1, where you had to grab Cherries while digging your way down into the sand to find Starman? Do the same thing here to make this whole area a lot easier.

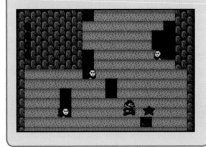

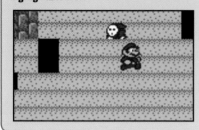
Right Is the Right Way

The end of this area splits into two passages. Take the right path; the left leads down to a dead end, and you get stuck climbing up again. The right path leads to the door with no problems. Just remember: right is right... right?

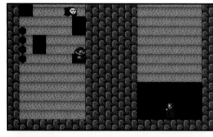

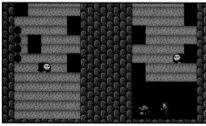

Use the Mushroom Block

There she is again: Birdo. She does her thing—namely, spitting fireballs and eggs at you. Carry three Mushroom Blocks up and hit her from above. Now you've got her beat!

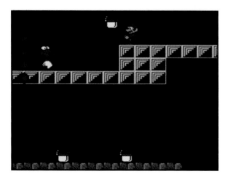

World 2-3

The last stage of World 2 is a desert, of course. Expect to do some digging to reach the end of the level, which is guarded by the three-headed serpent, Tryclyde—you won't have it easy.

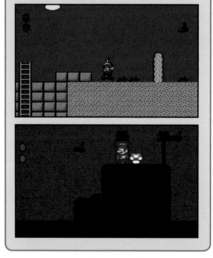
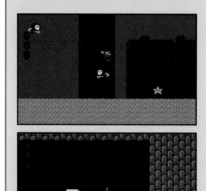
Take a Key

In the middle of the area inside the pyramid, you come to a locked door. That's your destination, but you need a Key first. To get in, go through the door at the very bottom of this area, take the Key, and come back. Just watch out! Phanto's guarding the Key, and he has a number of nasty ways of getting exactly what he wants.

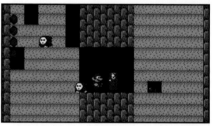

Defeat Tryclyde

Once you unlock the door, you begin your battle against the three-headed serpent, Tryclyde.

You can avoid Tryclyde's attack easily enough; just build a wall with your Mushroom Blocks. From the top of the wall, clobber him with the three Mushroom Blocks you have left.

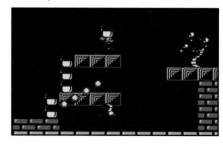

WORLD 3

Welcome to the World in the Sky. Clouds replace the ground, and there's not much below you except a long, hard drop to the earth. Time your jumps well, and be patient to avoid dropping to your doom.

World 3-1
To Climb or Not to Climb?

As soon as you pass through the door in the first area, you come to a massive waterfall. For a direct route through the level, immediately start climbing the cloud platforms.

If you're feeling more adventurous, drop down the waterfall and aim for the center of the map to find a secret room with a Magic Potion and a potential warp to World 5.

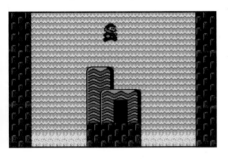

Choices

Inside the secret room at the bottom of the waterfall, there's a Potion hidden in the grass. Use it for warping or for taking Coins. The question is, can you find it?

Use your Potion right after picking it up to collect Coins.

If you want to warp to World 5, enter Sub-Space and go into the jar.

Taking Flight Again

Defeat the rascally Pidgit near the top of the waterfall and fly up on its carpet. Fly straight up and grab the vine to reach the next area.

Shortcut for the Princess

If you're playing the game with the Princess, you can take a shortcut to the end of World 3-1. Clear out the Shy Guy wandering near the top of the vine, then make a running leap from the left edge of the cloud and glide to find a secret door. It's a long jump, even for the Princess. Remember to hold the B Button as you dash toward the gap—you'll need the extra speed!

Sub-Space 1 and 2

Ready? This Potion is hard to get; so are the Mushrooms in this Sub-Space.

Descend the ladder near the end of this area. In the patch of grass on your right lies the Potion. Take special care, because the Mushroom is on the edge of the cliff.

Birdo Again!

Birdo has gotten really sneaky. She spits eggs in quick, tricky motions—and don't be surprised by the occasional fireball! Mario moves fast and dodges with skillful squats and jumps to avoid disaster.

World 3-2

Welcome to World 3-2. Here, the only way to progress is by going up and down the ladders that bridge the individual areas. Watch out for sneak attacks, and make plenty of headway by blasting off your Bombs where necessary.

Don't Take This POW

You run into many enemies in this first area, and you're probably tempted to use the POW Blocks at the latter half of the level. Hold it! If you drop to the underground, you'll never make it to Sub-Space on the right.

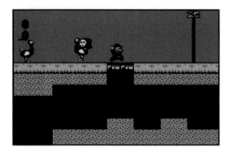

Look out for Snifit

Use Bombs to get to the underground, instead of picking up the POW Blocks. There are some cracked bricks you can blow up with Bombs, but take care of Snifit first. He shoots at you as you approach.

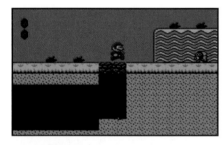

Sub-Space 1

Find a Magic Potion at the far-right end of the first area. Use it to locate a Mushroom. Take the two Coins too, but watch out for Snifit. He attacks you from below when you return from Sub-Space.

Make Headway with a Bomb

Once you reach the underground, climb down the first ladder to the second area of the level. Use the Bombs above you to destroy the first and second walls. Use the ones below to destroy the third and fourth walls. Watch out when the Bombs explode. After all, you don't want your trick to backfire.

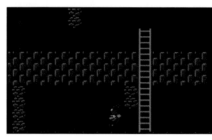

If you didn't make it this time, go back to the first map and try again.

Don't Get Hurt

This wall crumbles if you know how to use your Bombs. It isn't easy, though, because this is one tough wall. Someone in the World of Dreams used a lot of cement to build it. Time your throw carefully.

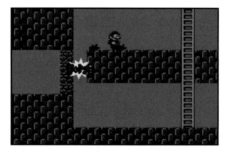

Sub-Space 2

You've finally cleared the underground. Good! Before you enter Sub-Space, destroy the floor on the right with a Bomb—if you want the Mushroom, that is.

Defeat Birdo

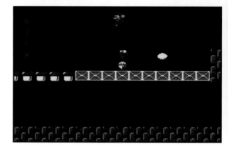

It's a cinch to defeat Birdo here. You already know how. Throw the eggs she spits back at her, or use the Mushroom Block on your left. Goodbye, Birdo!

World 3-3

Here you find a whole bunch of rectangular rooms. Go up and then travel down to get inside, but stay sharp. You meet up with a whole lot of Sparks. Watch your step at the very end, because Mouser is waiting for you.

Sub-Space 1 and Double

Here in World 3-3, you discover something really weird. If you have a POW inside Sub-Space, and Sub-Space disappears, you get two POWs.

Take the Mushroom, then lift the POW up high.

In World 3-3, you're in for a double surprise: two POWs!

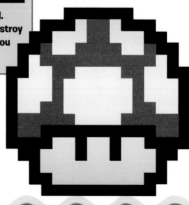

Sub-Space 2

There's a Mushroom hidden above the locked door at the end of the area. To get it, use the Potion between the locked door and the one before it. But look out for Ninji and Spark. They do everything they can to give you a bad time.

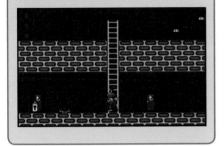

Grab that Key!

Before you can start climbing the tower, you'll need to unlock that door. Climb up the ladder and jump across the platforms to the right—when you reach the door, head inside.

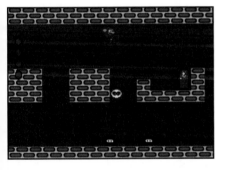

Dodge the emerging Shy Guys as you make your way to the top of the room. The Key is waiting for you behind another door. The trip up is fairly easy, but the trip down can be very difficult. It's much more challenging to dodge Shy Guys when an angry Phanto is on your trail.

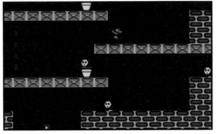

A Challenging Climb

This is one tough tower! The jumps are tricky enough on their own, but enemies like Sparks and Pansers can make your climb much more challenging. Take your time! Observe troublesome enemies from a safe spot to determine when and how you can slip past them.

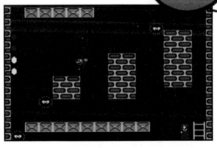

Defeat Mouser

Mouser's back for a rematch. He's a bit tougher this time—it takes five bomb-blasts to beat him—but the tactics you used last time around will work just as well here. Each time you manage to catch one of Mouser's bombs, place it on the right half of his platform. So long, Mouser!

WORLD 4

This is the World of Ice: a place covered in slick, slippery platforms that slide you into enemies or off into the frigid ocean. Get some practice on the ice to progress safely.

World 4-1

The fourth world Mario enters is encased with ice. Watch your step! It's slippery here. To make matters worse, enemies like Flurry, Autobomb, and your old pal Shy Guy are on your heels. Have any ice skates?

Which Character to Choose?

Before you pick your character, think smart. Choosing the right character for you is super important in World 4. If you are good at avoiding enemies with smaller jumps, take Mario or the faithful Toad. If you are not so hot at that, make big jumps with Luigi or the Princess. Whatever you do, choose the character that helps you most at your skill level.

Sub-Space 1

It requires skill, know-how, and nerve to get from here to Sub-Space. Take Potions, because you need them here as never before. Here's another hint: create a door whenever Flurry is not around.

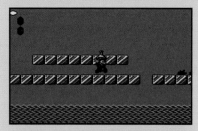

Sub-Space 2

You're finally out of Area 1. Good going! How about taking a breather to build up your strength? These rocks aren't slippery, so you don't have to worry. Relax!

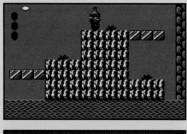

Get the Best of Autobomb

Autobomb follows you everywhere and shoots flames at you. Here's a hint: get rid of Shy Guy and get above Autobomb. And look: Autobomb gives you a lift!

Where's the Boss?

At the end of World 4-1, you probably expect to find a Little Boss waiting for you. Nope! Don't be disappointed; it was hard enough getting here. Enjoy the breather.

World 4-2

World 4-2 is as challenging as taming and riding a whale. At the start of the level, you encounter troublesome Beezos flying about. The best strategy is to make small jumps and keep moving. In the second area of this level, you walk across the backs of whales.

Get Flurry

Take care of these pesky Flurries now, or they keep after you. Even worse, the Flurries and Beezo attack you at the same time.

Sub-Space 1 and 2

When you reach the second area, move left to find three grass patches on a whale's back. Pluck the leftmost patch to reveal a Potion, then throw it down and enter Sub-Space to find a Mushroom on the whale's tail.

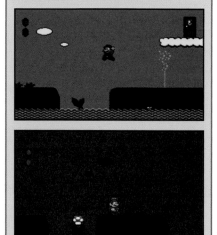

There's another Potion on the craggy cliffs to the right. If it's Coins you're after, enter Sub-Space near the patches of grass and pluck away! Before you do, though, you should know there's another use for this particular Potion.

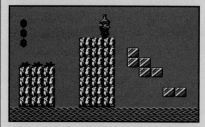

There's a jar beyond the whales to the right. If you enter Sub-Space there, you can enter the jar and warp right to World 6! Be warned: It's easier said than done–it takes quite a leap to reach the jar, and you'll encounter several enemies along the way.

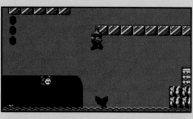

Ride Across the Water on the Whale Spout

The whale spout carries you up to the Cherries. But be extremely careful. If you blow it, you've got big problems.

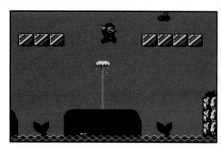

Autobomb and Cherry!

You can't walk on this floor, because it's covered with spikes! Why not hitch a ride on the Autobomb! If you collect the available Cherries, Starman shows up and can defeat the waiting Porcupo—if you move fast enough, you might even be able to use Starman's power on whatever's waiting in the next room!

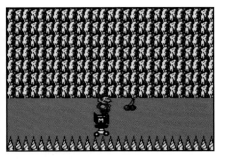

Sub-Space 3

Care to find another Mushroom? There's one more Potion in this area, which means there's one more chance to enter Sub-Space. It takes a bit of planning to put it to use, though! First, throw Shy Guy off of his Autobomb—try to toss him away from the spikes. If you move quickly, you can pluck the Potion and jump onto Autobomb. Otherwise, hitch a ride with Shy Guy as he drops down from the ledge.

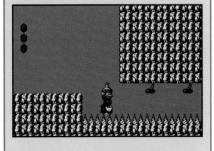

Once you've safely crossed the spikes, enter Sub-space to find another Mushroom!

Oh, No! Birdo Again

You already know this Little Boss: Birdo. When you throw eggs at her this time, beware of the slippery floor.

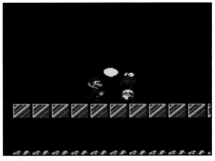

World 4-3

Once you climb up the ladder and get above ground, you run into Birdo again. This time get on her egg and ride it across the ocean. Next, move toward the two towers. Guess what's waiting for Mario there: Fry Guy.

Sub-Space 1: Mushroom or Coins?

Before you hop onto Birdo's egg, grab the nearby potion and use it near the icy spires to the left. Enter Sub-Space here to find a Mushroom! It's way up there, so you may have to Squat Jump to reach it.

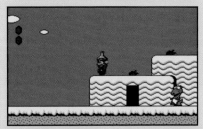

If you're more interested in Coins than Mushrooms, grab the Potion and hop onto Birdo's egg. When you land, enter Sub-Space and pluck away!

Get on the Egg and Get Moving

Wait! Don't defeat this Birdo—as much as you surely want to. You need to hitch a ride on one of her eggs to get across the ocean. Just stand to the right of Birdo, wait for her to launch an egg, and hop on.

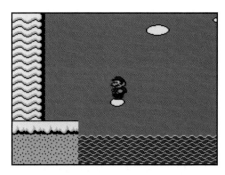

Another Shortcut for the Princess!

If you're playing as the Princess, you can take a shortcut straight to Fry Guy's tower. Instead of entering the first tower, dash past the door (hold the B Button!), leap from the end of the ledge, and glide over to the second tower. Then follow the bridge to the third tower and head inside!

Spinning Spikes Are Bad News

These icy platforms don't offer much traction, and one slip-up can send you plummeting to certain doom. Stay in control, and stay off of those spikes!

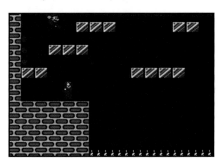

Beware of Flurry

Heads up! As you make your climb, be on the lookout for falling Flurries. These enemies try their best to head straight toward you. Use this to your advantage. You can usually bait a Flurry into charging right off of a platform. When that's not an option, be patient. Wait for a Flurry to come to you, then hop right over and keep moving—in most cases, you'll be out of reach before a charging Flurry has time to change course.

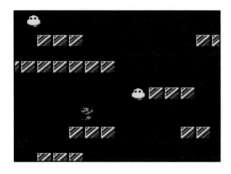

Sub-Space 2

When you exit the first tower, look for the two patches of grass to the right. There's a Potion hidden under the nearest patch. Grab it and move to the left edge of the bridge. Use the nearby clouds to reach the top of the left tower, and then head back to the right. Enter Sub-Space near the right edge of the right tower to find a Mushroom.

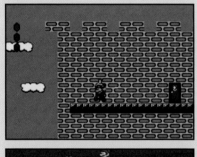

Step on Shy Guy

More spikes! Looks like it's time for the hard-headed approach. Jump onto the red Shy Guy's head and let him carry you toward the next door.

Look for the Cherries floating near the drop-off. Once Shy Guy carries you into range, jump over and grab them. You'll find more Cherries on the way down—try to grab them all. A little help from Starman can make it much easier to reach the tower's exit.

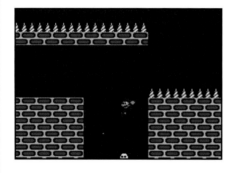

Grab the Key!

Enter this door and you'll be in a room with a Key. You need this Key to open the locked door at the bottom of the tower. Remember, the Key can also be used as a weapon. If a persistent Flurry gives you trouble along the way, hit him with the Key and he's a goner.

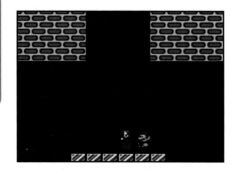

Unlock the Door and Scram!

Once you've carried the Key to the bottom of the second tower, you're almost there. Unlock the door, step outside, and follow the bridge to the third tower.

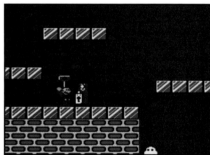

Is This the Calm Before the Storm?

There are two Flurries and a crystal ball in this room. Quick! Get to the Mask Gate and into the room with the Little Boss. Prepare yourself: this is Fry Guy's territory! And he's practically boiling over with ideas for keeping you out.

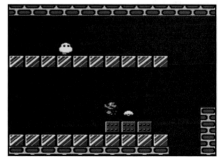

Fry Guy Is One Tough Customer

World 4 might be a frozen world, but Fry Guy is a ball of fire. He's the strongest Little Boss you've met yet. When he spits flames from his mouth, attack with Mushroom Blocks from the upper stairs. Once three Mushroom Blocks strike him, he splits himself into four pieces and keeps coming at you. Use the Mushroom Blocks skillfully for attack and defense.

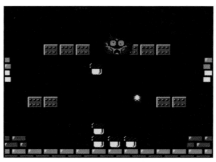
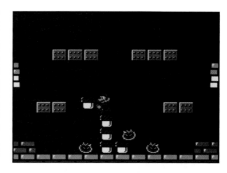

WORLD 5

The World of Night is a challenging gauntlet of obstacles and enemies that put your skills to the test. Be ready for anything!

World 5-1

This may very well be the most difficult stage in *Super Mario Bros. 2*. You must cross a waterfall that seems endless. Accomplish this by stepping on the logs and Trouters. One false move and you're gone. Concentrate, or you're in the drink!

Sub-Space 1

You can get a Potion later with no trouble, but if you are looking for the glitter of gold Coins, enter Sub-Space here. To increase Mario's Life Meter by two, cross the falls and go to the very end.

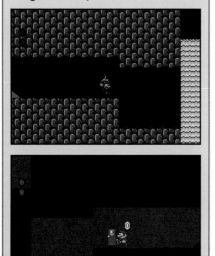

Jump on Trouter Again and Again

You can't get over to the other side without jumping on the Trouters' heads three times in a row. This is the toughest part. Practice until you learn the best timing. And don't give up! You can do it!

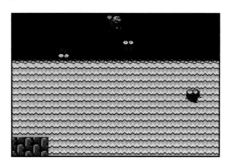

Sub-Space 2

The clump of grass on the left is a 1-Up. The one on the right is a Potion. Enter Sub-Space here to find a Mushroom on the lower rock on the right. Hey, you've cleared half of stage already!

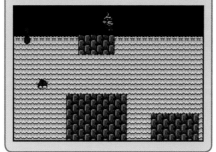

Take the High Road!

There's another Mushroom to find, but reaching it takes a bit of planning. Once you've made it past the Trouters, dash toward the last two logs (hold the B Button!), jump across them, and make a big leap onto the rocks near the top of the screen. You'll find two Mushroom Blocks there. Grab the Mushroom Block on the right to clear it from the gap as you drop down to the ground. Now you're ready to enter Sub-Space!

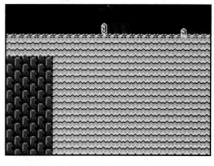

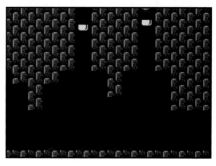

Sub-Space 3

Before you head in to face the Little Boss, pluck the last Potion and toss it down. If you moved the correct Mushroom Block on your way into the area, the second Mushroom should drop straight to the ground!

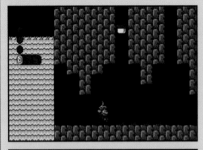

Fight with a Mushroom Block!

Here's Birdo again, and now she's only spitting fire! Looks like you have to rely on the nearby Mushroom Block. Fight cautiously— it's more important now than ever.

World 5-2

World 5 is a night world. You see clouds, but no moon or stars. In the first half of World 5-2, you have to cross the vines with Hoopsters. Good luck! It's not easy. After that, there's a drop to the bottom of a deep valley.

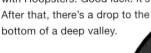

Sub-Space

There's no Potion hiding in the grass you see above ground. Unfortunately, getting Mushrooms is much trickier in this world. First, get inside the jar, then blast the floor with a Bomb to discover another room below. There's the Potion! Grab it and use It outside the jar.

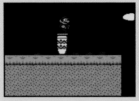  

Get Past the Hoopsters!

Those are hostile Hoopsters moving up and down the trees. Use these enemies to your advantage! When a jump is too high to make on your own, hop on a Hoopster and take a quick ride.

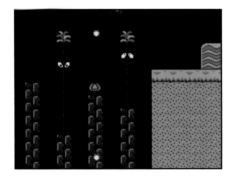

Climb Up the Right Side of the Vine!

At the end of Area 1, you must climb up the vine. But look out! On your way, you're attacked from the sides by two Snifits, and you have to dodge some bothersome Beezos. Stick to the right vine as long as possible. Move quickly to get above the first Hoopster, and then hop over to the left vine to avoid the next enemy.

Battle on the Bridge!

You've made it to the top of the vines, but all you find is a POW in the middle of dead-end bridge. Well, you might as well take the POW, but what's going on? You're falling all the way down! You're on the right path, though. Try to relax and enjoy the ride down. Things will look up soon.

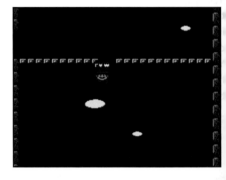

It's Dangerous Here–Watch Out!

If you drop straight down, you land right on some spikes. You can avoid that by controlling your fall. Once you grab that POW Block, move left and right to steer clear of scattered spikes. You won't run into many enemies while descending, but you can get hurt if you're not careful.

Goal!

So you thought you'd finally made it to the ground after the long fall, right? Wrong. You've come to a river with Trouters jumping around. Move right to land by the river. But be careful—there's one more set of spikes to avoid, and you definitely don't want to land in the water!

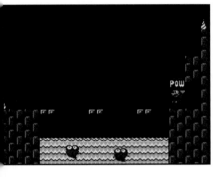

Battle on the Bridge!

You can't miss the Little Boss at the end of the stage. Birdo, with her eggs and flames, is waiting for you. She plans to knock you off the bridge into the water, so get ready. You can defeat her the same way you have before, but don't let Trouter take you by surprise!

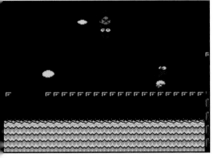

Grab the Trouter below and throw it at Birdo. That should help even the odds!

World 5-3

World 5-3 is a long one. First of all, Bob-ombs attack you one after another, so climb up inside the big tree and ride on Pidgit's carpet. Brace yourself! Clawgrip, the big crab, awaits you at the end of the stage; he's all too eager to pummel you with rocks. Be prepared for a challenging fight.

Luigi's Warp Zone

At the beginning of Area 1, you see a jar above you when you climb the ladder. That's a Warp Zone—but you need Luigi's jumping skills to reach it. If you want to warp straight to World 7, make sure you pick Luigi before you enter the stage. Squat Jump onto the hill, use the nearby Potion to enter Sub-Space, and then head down into the jar to take this handy shortcut.

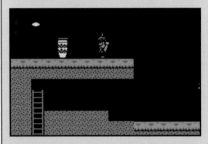

Enter Sub-Space with the Potion and go into the jar— you're off to World 7!

There are several Cherries in the first area— grab them all! Starman's power makes it much easier to deal with falling Bob-ombs.

Sub-Space 1

Look for the low hill near the beginning of the stage. If you enter Sub-Space near the hill's left edge, you'll find a Mushroom! Of course, Albatoss will be dropping Bob-ombs at you from above. Hopefully you grabbed those Cherries!

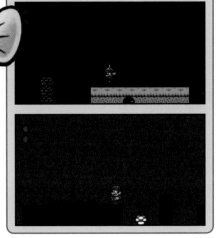

Here Come the Bob-ombs!

Remember: Bob-ombs can hurt you by touching you, but they can also explode on their own. Use small jumps to hop over Bob-ombs as quickly as possible— big jumps are bound to send you sailing right into more Bob-ombs!

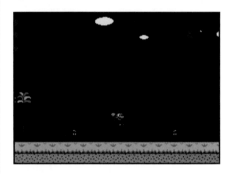

Sub-Space 2

There's a Potion on the hill at the end of Area 1. Before you grab it, use the wandering Bob-ombs to destroy the first wall. Jump onto the hill and grab the Potion, then drop down and enter Sub-Space on the ground to find a Mushroom!

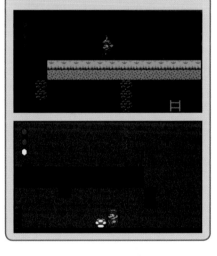

Don't Take That Block!

If you take this Mushroom Block, Bob-ombs begin pouring out of the jar. This is handy if you want to destroy the nearby rocks, but if you're done entering Sub-Space, it's best to leave that Mushroom Block alone!

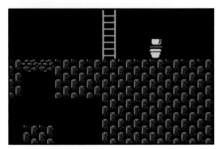

Sub-Space 3

Remember: Once you've entered Sub-Space twice, you can't collect any more Coins until you reach the next stage. However, if you skipped one (or both) of the Mushrooms near the beginning, you can collect plenty of Coins here! Use a Bob-omb to destroy clear a path to the grass patches, then drop down, pluck the rightmost patch of grass to find a Potion. Enter Sub-Space near the remaining grass patches and pluck away!

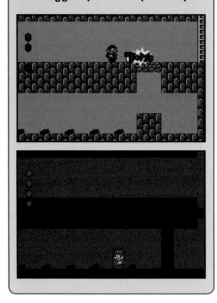

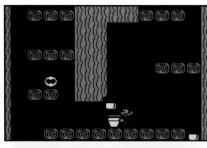

Use Mushroom Blocks!

You're right in the middle of a gigantic tree. Go down to the bottom and around to the left, then climb all the way to the top branches. On your way, you find two jars with Shy Guys bursting out of them. This is not as bad as it looks. Just cover them with the Mushroom Blocks. You can also use Mushroom Blocks to deal with any troublesome enemies you encounter during your climb.

Fight or Flee?

Panser comes down the stairs spitting flames. If you have a Mushroom Block, you can try to throw it at him—but it's usually easier to simply stay out of his way. If Panser approaches you from the left, run to the right and you appear on the left. Lucky for you, the sides of the screens are connected!

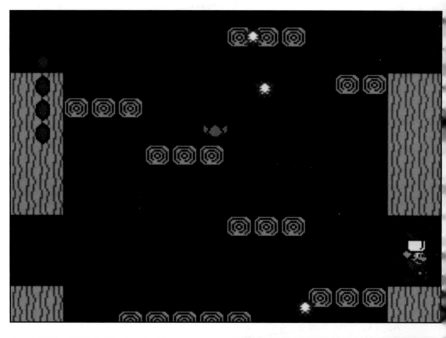

A Thrilling Mid-Air Flight!

Ride Pidgit's flying carpet all the way to the edge of the cliff on the right. But take care of Snifit first, then wait for Pidgit to fly your way. Once you've seized his carpet, move quickly to the right. You'll encounter another Pidget during your flight—you're free to switch carpets, but your first carpet should last long enough to get you across the gap. When you come to the log with the grass, you're safe.

Can She Stop Mario?

Two Little Bosses show up in this level. One of them is your old enemy Birdo. You've beaten her many times before; she's a piece of cake by now, right? Don't be too confident! This egghead is smart!

Fight Rocks with Rocks!

The second Little Boss is Clawgrip, one of the most powerful of all the Little Bosses. He throws a steady stream of triangle-shaped rocks at you. Don't let him hit you! Move fast, and when you see an opening, pick up the rocks that fall and throw them back.

WORLD 6

Welcome back to the World of Deserts. Things are much tougher in these stages than your first tour of the desert, so don't let your guard down! Hang in there! You're almost to the end!

World 6-1

World 6-1 looks a lot like the World of Deserts in World 2, but you run into more quicksand here. Look hard to find the Key hidden in the second area of this stage.

Sub-Space 1

The first jar you reach contains a Potion. Toss Cobrat out of the jar, head inside, and pluck the Potion–but don't use it yet! Take the Potion back outside and enter Sub-Space on the bones just to the right of the jar. When you do, a Mushroom drops down onto the quicksand. Hop over and grab that Mushroom before it sinks!

Clear the Cobrats!

Cobrats can be a real pain! Remember that even if you make it safely past a Cobrat, it can still attack you. It's best to clear out these persistent pests as you move through the area.

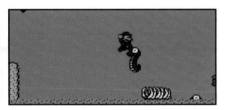

Sub-Space 2

You'll find a Potion buried between two cactus plants. If you take it and enter Sub-Space on the hill to the right, you find a Mushroom–but it won't be easy. You must carry the Potion past two Pokeys and a Panser! It can be tough to deal with these enemies while your hands are full. Be careful!

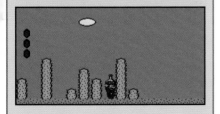

Where's the Key?

There are a whopping 21 jars in this stage! Don't bother searching all of them. There's a 1-Up hidden in the third jar from the left—make sure you grab that first. The Key is stashed in the fifth jar from the right. Head down and collect it when you're ready to leave the area. You have to dig through sand to reach these items, but you shouldn't have any trouble finding them.

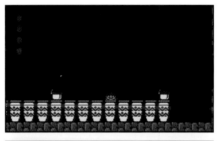

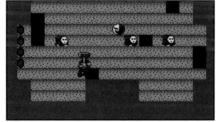

Fire-Breathing Birdo!

Birdo shows up again, but in this world she only blows fire. And she's not so hot at that! Destroy her with three Mushroom Blocks.

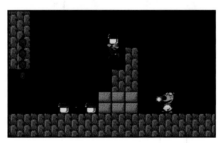

World 6-2

In World 6-2, get on the back of your enemy Albatoss and start on your looooooooong night journey. If you fall off, you're done for. But you can move ahead so much easier this way, compared to leaping across waterfalls on Trouters.

Make it Across with Squat Jump

Now head into World 6-2. Uh-oh, can't get over the wall? They sure build them high around here. But there is a way. A running leap (or a Squat Jump) should get you up there, no problem!

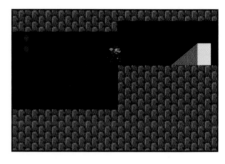

Albatoss Airlines

Once you make it outside, you find yourself on the edge of a steep cliff. There's only one clump of grass at your feet. And an army of angry Albatosses is coming for you! You have to hitch a ride on an eastbound Albatoss! Look for the Albatoss that's flying to the right, and let it carry you to the goal. Don't think this will be a relaxing flight, though. You run into plenty of baddies along the way. Pluck that grass before you go; you never know when a fresh Vegetable might come in handy. And always be ready to perform an emergency Squat Jump!

Sub-Space

When you reach the cliff with two clumps of grass, get off Albatoss. The Potion lies in the patch of grass on the left. Enter Sub-Space here and you can get a Mushroom. There won't be any more Albatosses flying to the right, so when you come out of Sub-Space, hitch a ride back to the left until you find an Albatoss once again flying to the right.

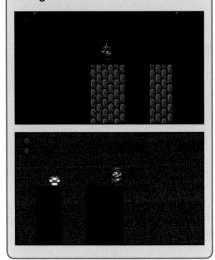

Nasty Little Birdo

The Little Boss of World 6-2 is Birdo again. This nasty character doesn't give up easily! She really goes looking for trouble. Meet her flaming throws with the Mushroom Blocks! You don't have much room to dodge, so stay on your toes!

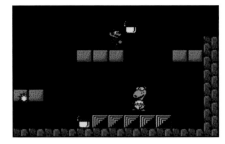

World 6-3

Get through this world and you finally advance to World 7, where your ultimate enemy—Wart—is waiting for you! Birdo and Tryclyde, the Little Bosses of the pyramid, are guarding the finish. It's not over! The worst is yet to come.

A Hidden Shortcut!

After you climb the ladder, start sinking into the quicksand while holding left against the wall to the left. You eventually drop into the sand and under the wall.

Keep moving left, and continue jumping to avoid sinking too low into the quicksand. Eventually, you reach a hidden door. Enter it and you can go straight to the end of the stage—just follow the clouds to the Little Boss' pyramid.

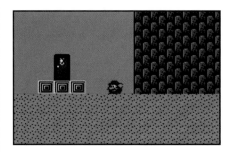

Sub-Space 1

If you avoid taking the shortcut, you can find a Mushroom near the beginning of the stage. When you reach the top of the ladder, pluck the grass to the right to find a Potion. Take it, jump across the quicksand to the right, and enter Sub-Space on the second set of bones. There's a Mushroom on a nearby cactus!

Avoid Bob-ombs with a Ladder!

After entering the cave, Bob-ombs come out of the jar one after another. You don't need to run away, though. Just climb up the ladder and wait. The Bob-ombs explode by themselves and destroy the jar.

Call Starman!

Have you been collecting those Cherries? Let's hope so, because there are a lot of Ninjis here! Instead of destroying the upper wall, dig a path to the lower wall. Then pluck a Bomb and drop it into the hole to clear a path to that fifth cherry. Head down, grab Starman, and use his power to charge right through those nasty Ninjis!

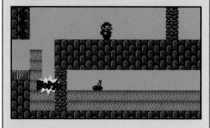

Sub-Space 2

See that pit containing a single block of rocks? There's a Potion buried just to the left of it! Before you grab it, though, destroy a few of the walls to the right. Most of the other grass patches contain bombs, so that shouldn't be a problem. Blast a hole in the wall to the right, and then destroy both of the blocks in the next pit. Drop one more Bomb down through the opening, and you're good to go.

Head back and grab the Potion, and then drop down through the path you made. Enter Sub-Space somewhere near your landing spot to find a Mushroom! If you destroyed that last wall, you should also have plenty of Coins to pluck.

Scaling the Walls of Vines

After exiting the cave, climb the vines from the bottom all the way to the top. The only things that help Mario here are the Mushroom Blocks. You may not see many enemies, but beware! If you fall down, you must start all over again from the very beginning.

Step 1

If you're not good at travelling sideways, you can go up by holding onto the vines on your right. But you have to go over three Hoopsters. It's up to you! Which is the worse evil?

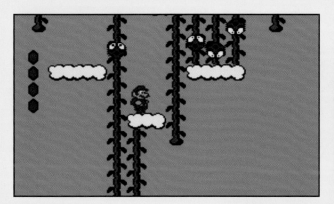

Step 2

Move sideways from vine to vine. Don't hesitate! You won't fall off if you're fast. You can make it by pressing Up and Right or Up and Left on the Directional Pad.

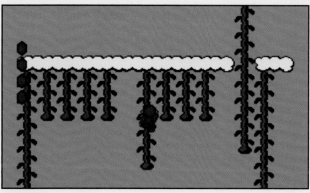

Step 3

You encounter pesky Snifits along the way. Be patient. Watch each Snifit until you can predict his attacks. Get close, and then slip past the Snifit when you know it's safe.

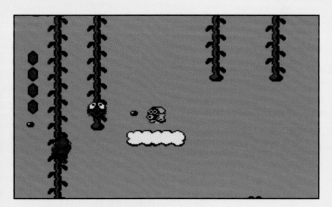

Step 4

Climb up the vines on your left. If you go to the right where you see the three vines, you find three Hoopsters above you. So if you want to play it safe, go to the left.

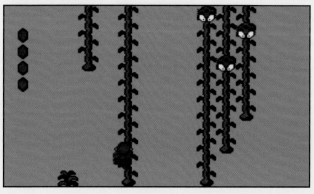

Fight Without Using Blocks

Birdo is the first Little Boss. There's a Mushroom Block below her, but it's probably more useful as a stepping stool. Use Birdo's eggs to attack her—just make sure you avoid her flames!

Who's Afraid of Tryclyde?

Tryclyde is the second Little Boss. Check out those seven Mushroom Blocks on the floor. Remember the stunt you pulled against Tryclyde in World 2-3? Build a wall by stacking three of them in a row. This way you can stay cool even though he's spitting flames. Now fling the Blocks you have left at him. You need to bonk him three times.

You've arrived at the final world: Wart's Castle. There are only two stages left between you and Wart, Subcon's greatest foe! You can do it!

World 7-1

Mario's long quest is almost over. Only one adventure left: you must go through 7-1 to get to Wart's castle in the sky. Now is the time to use the skills you've been building up all along, like riding Albatosses and climbing ladders.

Move Ahead Right Away!

This is one rocky road you're travelling. Ninji and Bob-omb come at you, but don't be afraid. Just keep going; otherwise, Bob-omb explodes and you lose all the ground you've gained. Albatoss carries Bob-ombs from above, so get to the other side as fast as you can. Don't forget that POW Block—it's sure to come in handy!

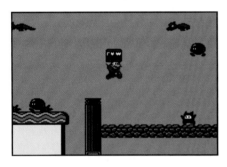

Sub-Space 1

See the tuft of grass on the top of the pole? There's another Potion under there. Grab the Potion, back up a little, and use it on the structure to the left. Get moving! If you take too long, Bob-ombs destroy the rock bridge and you'll be trapped.

Sub-Space 2

There's a small house at the end of the path. Head inside, climb to the upper level, and pluck the third patch of grass from the right. It's a Potion! Enter Sub-Space to find a Mushroom and plenty of Coins to collect.

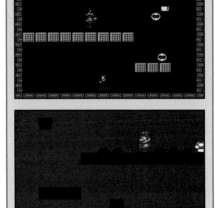

Go Back on Albatoss

Well, you've reached the end of the path. What now? Jump on top of the house and hitch a ride on Albatoss! You need to fly left—clear past the starting point. Watch out! You must get past a few particularly tall columns, so be ready to jump. There's a single patch of grass near the left edge of the area. Hop off of the Albatoss and pluck this grass to head up to the next part of the stage.

Maze of Clouds

Go all the way down the stair-like clouds and jump to the cloud on your right. From there, you can jump up to a ladder that leads to the next area. Of course, Shy Guys, Snifit, and Ninji won't make it easy for you.

Luckily, there are five Cherries in this area. Collect them all, grab Starman, and charge through these enemies until Starman's power wears off.

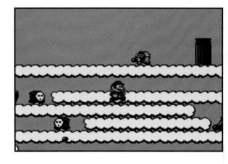

Pile Up Blocks and Jump!

Pile up Mushroom Blocks and perform a Squat Jump. This is the only way to reach the ladders near the top of the area—but two Sparks are going to give you trouble. Before you stack the Mushroom Blocks, use them to take care of those pests!

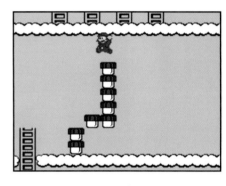

Say Goodbye to Birdo!

You've fought Birdo many times. This battle in Area 3 is your last with the egg-spitting troublemaker. The narrow path makes it tough and Birdo isn't going to stop spitting flames now. But do your best! Use that Mushroom Block to hit her three times. She'll be sorry!

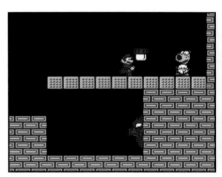

World 7-2

Finally, you've come to Wart's twisting castle, the source of all the evil in the World of Dreams. Now is the time to show your strength! Many different traps await you, but if you've come this far, you should be able to defeat Wart.

A Moving Floor!

Aside from a few pesky Snifits, there's not much going on in the first area—head right until you enter the castle. When you step inside, the floor starts moving like crazy. You've got to keep your footing, and, worse yet, battle bad guys. Is it too tough? Take your time and keep moving. Shy Guy? Ninji? Bob-omb? You know how to handle these guys.

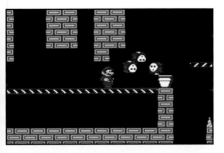

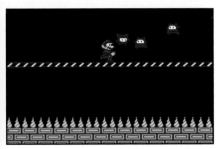

Two Ways to Wart

Wart's Castle has a multitude of branching paths. Once you're inside, you can go up or down. It doesn't really matter which path you take—you can enter Sub-Space on either path to obtain an all-important Mushroom. You can even explore both paths to get both Mushrooms.

If you want to take the upper path, use the ladder beyond the moving floors. If you prefer the lower path, climb down the chain below the moving floors. To find both Mushrooms, it's easier to explore the upper path first—just turn back and take the lower path once you collect the first Mushroom.

We cover each path individually, so you can be informed on what to expect, no matter your choice.

The Upper Path

Let's start with the upper path. To reach it, just ride the moving floors to the end of the room. Climb the chain, and you're on your way!

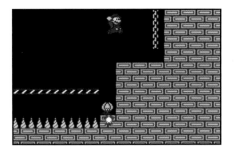

Everything Depends On Your Timing!

It takes precision timing to slip past some of these Sparks. Stand in front of a chain until you're ready to make your move. When you see an opening, go for it!

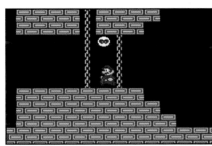

Be Sure to Go Left!

Chains are hanging on both sides, but take the one on the left and climb up. If you take the one on the right, you won't be able to get to the door that leads to the bonus area—and if you want to find a Mushroom, that's where you need to go.

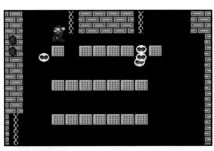

Take the left chain...

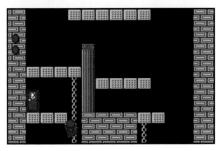

Now head through that door!

Avoid Panser!

Think a bit of a break from that castle sounds nice? Think again! As you follow the ladders down to the bonus area, keep an eye out for Panser's flames—wait for an opening, then drop to the ground. There are a couple of Tweeters hopping around the area, so be ready to move as soon as you land. Get to that last ladder!

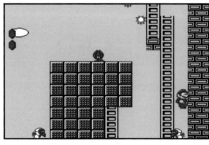

Upper Path Side Room

The ladder below the Panser leads to a door—head through the door to find a bonus room! The grass on the right holds a Potion. Enter Sub-Space and take a Mushroom right away. You can take the Coins, too, but you don't need them anymore, do you?

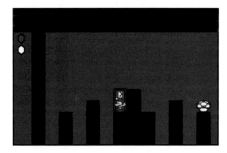

The Most Difficult Place!

Once you're done in the bonus room, climb back up the ladders and return to the castle. Don't bother sliding back down the chain—once you're inside, just jump through the platform above and keep heading upward.

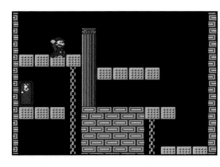

These jumps are challenging enough, but the circling Sparks can make it pretty tough to reach the top of the tower. Timing is the key—when you see an opening, take it. Once you make your move, commit to it!

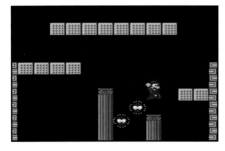

Find That Key!

Once you reach the top of tower, head through the door and climb up to the moving floor to the right. Once you're in place, duck down to dodge incoming Sparks. Climb down the chain on the far side of the room to find the Key.

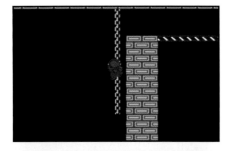

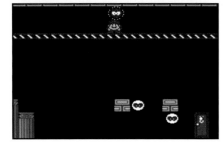

Birdo's Back!

Yikes! Birdo's back, and this time she's guarding a Key. Use Birdo's eggs to defeat her, grab the Key, and head through the nearby door—you emerge in the previous room, under the moving floor. Avoid Phanto and move left until you reach the locked door. Then use the Key to open it.

The Lower Path

Would you rather take the lower path? Then after you first enter the castle, look for the chain at the bottom of the room. It appears just after the Bob-ombs, but you might have to slip past a Panser to reach it.

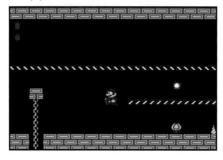

A Mushroom Block Floor!

Pull out the Mushroom Blocks at your feet and keep going down. Protect yourself from those nasty Sparks by throwing the Blocks and remember to always keep moving. If you pick up the Cherries on your way, Starman makes an appearance.

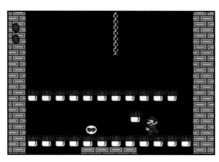

Lower Path Bonus Room

As you make your way through the Spark-infested corridor, look for the door near the center of the area. That leads to the lower path's bonus room, so stop in to investigate. The room contains two patches of grass. Pluck the patch on the left to reveal a Potion, then use it to enter Sub-Space. There's your Mushroom!

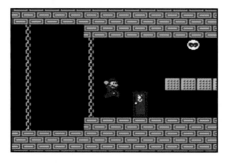

Stay in the Center!

Once you leave the bonus room, continue to the right to find another door. Pass through it, then start climbing the nearby chain. This place is crawling with Sparks, but they're pretty easy to avoid if you stick to the chains in the center of the area. The nearby Cherries might tempt you, but you should probably ignore them and keep going—that is, unless you're very, very sure of yourself!

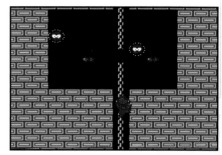

Slip Through by a Hair's Breadth!

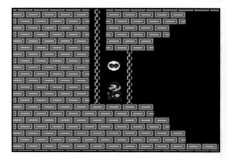

So many Sparks! Since you don't have a block to use as a weapon, you must avoid these enemies. Watch what the Sparks do and run whenever you have enough space to slip past them.

Another Tough Climb!

You're in another tough spot here. You have to climb up the moving floor and avoid attacks from Shy Guys, Snifits, and Sparks. For the most part, you can move up carefully by using short, steady jumps. Every so often, you'll need to make a running leap. Stick those landings!

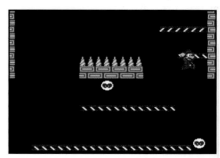

What Are You Doing, Birdo?

Climb up the chain to find Birdo guarding the way. Didn't you defeat her in World 6-3? If you see an opening to slip past her, go for it! Otherwise, use Birdo's eggs to knock this nuisance out of your path. Climb up the chain to reach the next area.

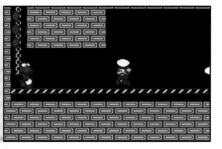

When you reach the top of the chain, you have two options. You can head through the unlocked door to the right, or you can Squat Jump up to the moving floor above you. The door takes you straight to the Key, but you must get past some troublesome Sparks along the way. The conveyer belt takes you to a chain at the edge of the room. The Sparks up here are much easier to dodge—just duck down! Either way, you need that Key. Head through the unlocked door, or make your way to the chain and slide down to the next room.

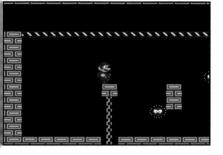

Birdo Again!?

Back so soon, and now Birdo has the Key! Use her eggs to take her out, then grab the Key and scram through the nearby door. Move left and use the Key to open the locked door. Remember to dodge Phanto, and don't be afraid to toss the Key into any Sparks that block your path.

The Paths Converge

No matter which path you took at the start of the level, you reach this point. You're almost there! Head through that locked door!

Mask Gate Attack!

Here's a room with only two Mushroom Blocks, a crystal ball, and the Mask Gate. Take the crystal as usual, but look out! The Mask Gate is coming toward you. Is this more of Wart's evil magic? Land three hits with the Mushroom Blocks to subdue the gate, and then climb into its mouth to reach Wart.

Finally, Wart!

Wart, creator of all the monsters in the World of Dreams and the source of all its evil! You've come this far, so you can't back down now. This takes all the strength and courage you've got. This guy is sly, wily, strong, and full of ways to stop your progress. But you have a few tricks of your own to achieve victory and bring peace to the Subcon!

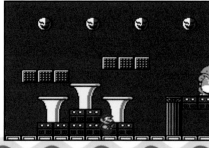

Defeat Wart!

Here you are, face to face with the big, ugly Wart! The time has come for you to fight against the evil ruler of Subcon. He approaches you spitting foam from his mouth. The Dream Machine is shooting the Vegetables he hates so much. Catch them and throw them at Wart!

Here they come! You need these Vegetables to beat Wart. And make sure you dodge those bubbles!

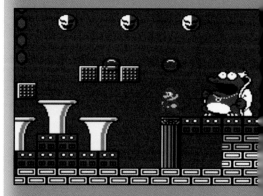

You can get Wart only when his mouth is open. Keep going! Feed him those veggies until he can't take any more!

Congratulations! You've beaten Wart! Your skill and courage have led you to victory!

Behind the Scenes with

SHIGERU MIYAMOTO

THE MAKING OF SUPER MARIO BROS. 3

A LOOK INSIDE NINTENDO R&D, BACK IN THE DAY!

This article originally appeared in the Jan/Feb 1990 issue of *Nintendo Power Magazine*.

Video games combine the best aspects of cartoon animation and computer programming to create a magical world of entertainment. As the result of a mix of two rather diverse fields, it requires the talents of many people to produce a video game.

A Behind-the-Scenes Look

Based on the number of letters and game ideas Nintendo receives regularly, we know that many fans are interested in knowing about how video games are created. So we decided to find out a little more about what is involved in designing a game ourselves. *Super Mario Bros. 3* was the obvious choice, and to find something out about the stories behind the characters and the kinds of things that were done during the design process, we went right to the source, Nintendo Company Ltd. (NCL) in Kyoto, Japan.

Where It All Began

Design work and programming on almost all games developed by Nintendo are done by the staff of NCL's Research and Development Departments (some is also done by independent software companies). Each of Nintendo's R & D "teams" competes to come up with the best ideas. And each team member works hard to make sure his or her own contributions find their way into the final program.

J A P A N

TOKYO

KYOTO

We interviewed Mr. Shigeru Miyamoto, project head in charge of development on *SMB 3*. He was intensely involved with the game at the very beginning idea stages and then at the end in the final polishing of the concept. Throughout he offered the other programmers advice, ideas, and guidance. He was happy to take time out of his busy schedule to give us some inside information on *SMB 3*.

A New Look for Mario

Designing a game in the *Super Mario Bros.* series is certainly different from creating one based on all new characters, but it is just as challenging. The difficult task is to make familiar characters seem fresh.

In each of the previous *SMB* games, Mario gained new power-ups, so in *SMB 3*, Mr. Miyamoto and the other designers wanted to invent yet another new and interesting way for Mario to power-up. Their initial ideas tended toward having Mario turn into some sort of creature. One of the rejected concepts had Mario power-up as a centaur (half man, half horse). The idea that they finally settled on was to give Mario a tail and the ability of flight. Their first tail concept, that of a Raccoon, was the one that finally stuck.

"I'm sorry to say there isn't a funny story behind why we chose the Raccoon tail," Miyamoto remarked. "We thought the Raccoon tail worked best from a practical point of view and it fit right in with Mario's style. It also created some great new gameplay possibilities."

New Enemies!

The most important new enemies created for *SMB 3* were Bowser's children. Each was given a unique look and personality. Another new creature that is one of Miyamoto's personal favorites is the chained "dog" (Chain Chomp) that first appears in the Sky World. "This is a strange enemy, because it is chained and can't get at Mario, which probably accounts for its vicious behavior," Miyamoto said. As for the inspiration behind this mean character, Miyamoto mentions that he did have a "bad experience" with a dog when he was young.

Some of the familiar enemy characters from the previous *SMB* games were also included, but some were changed slightly. Winged Goombas, Giant Koopas, new species of Piranha Flowers, and additional members of the Hammer Brother family were all created to add spice to old familiar stand-bys.

Mr. Miyamoto has hundreds of partial game ideas in his head at all times. "Chatting with the other designers on a casual basis helps me bring my ideas together," he commented. "Also, ideas can come together at any time, even in the middle of a hot bath!" (That must be the inspiration for the difficult water worlds in *SMB 3*—they really put Mario in hot water!)

Planning Gameplay

Once a collection of ideas has been assembled, the game must be plotted out in its entirety. According to Mr. Miyamoto, "The general plan for *SMB 3* was to make it a game that players of all skill levels could enjoy."

To do this, the planners put plenty of bonus coins and 1-Ups in the early Worlds of the game to help beginners. The later Worlds, however, contain some of the toughest gameplay challenges of any video game. In the two-player mode, turns are taken from World to World, making for an equal amount of playing time for both players.

After a general plan has been made, each scene must be laid out in minute detail. Even the simplest action by Mario may set into motion many reactions. For example, when Mario hits a breakable brick, the exact movement of all the pieces of the brick must be mapped out. Points gained and sound effects must also be considered.

Programming

Translating all the diagrams and drawings into computer graphics is a long and complicated process. A tool that makes this procedure easier is the Character Generator Computer Aided Design (CGCAD) machine. Using this computer, designers can create "character banks" that contain the graphic shapes used to draw images during gameplay. Each shape is given a number that the NES can use to access the shape and combine it into a complete image. An NES game program consists entirely of numerical data strings for creating the graphics of a game. Since the look and feel of the game are determined by the shapes in the "character banks," they must be designed and used very carefully.

Conclusion

Even this short look behind the scenes shows the enormous amount of work it takes to produce a video game. The team that produced *Super Mario Bros. 3* consisted of over 10 people, and they worked on the game over a two-year span. In all, though, the time and effort were well worth it and the final product is something they are all happy with. "We are especially proud of the magical wonderland we created in *SMB 3*, and the dastardly, fascinating, and repulsive enemy characters that live in it," Mr. Miyamoto said. We can't wait to see what he has in store for the NES in the future!

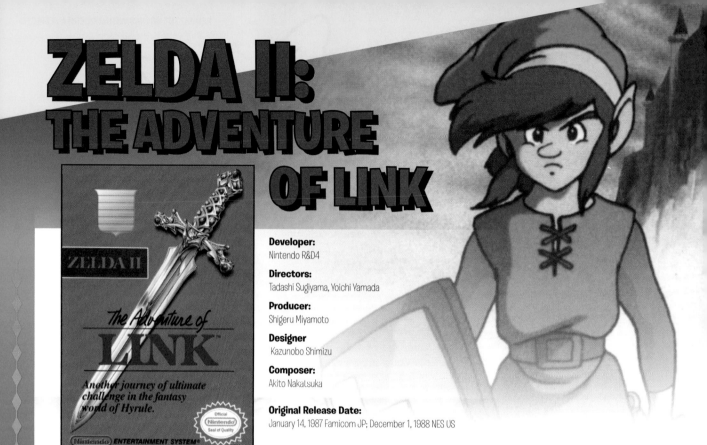

ZELDA II: THE ADVENTURE OF LINK

Developer:
Nintendo R&D4

Directors:
Tadashi Sugiyama, Yoichi Yamada

Producer:
Shigeru Miyamoto

Designer
Kazunobo Shimizu

Composer:
Akito Nakatsuka

Original Release Date:
January 14, 1987 Famicom JP; December 1, 1988 NES US

THE STORY OF THE ADVENTURE OF LINK

At the end of a fierce fight, Link overthrew Ganon, took back the Triforce, and rescued Princess Zelda. But is it all really finished?

Many seasons have passed since then…

Hyrule was on the road to ruin. The power that the vile Ganon left behind was causing chaos and disorder in Hyrule. What's more, even after the fall of Ganon, some of his underlings remained, waiting for Ganon's return. The key to Ganon's return was the blood of Link—the valiant lad who overthrew the King of Evil. Ganon would be revived if Link's blood was mixed with Ganon's ashes.

Meanwhile, Link remained in the little kingdom of Hyrule and lent his hand to its restoration. But circumstances did not look very good.

One day, a strange mark, exactly like the crest of the kingdom, appeared on the back of Link's hand as he approached his sixteenth birthday. The worried Link went to Impa, Princess Zelda's nursemaid, who was shocked and frightened when she saw the mark. When she regained her composure, she took Link to the North Castle.

There was a door in the North Castle called "the door that does not open." Only the descendants of the Impa family who served the king knew how to open the door. Impa took Link's left hand and pressed the back of it again the door. There was a sound of a lock falling open. The door slowly creaked open, and there, on an altar in the middle of the room, lay a beautiful woman.

"Here lies Princess Zelda," Impa began to speak calmly. "Link, the time has come when I must tell you the legend of Zelda handed down in Hyrule. It is said that long ago, when Hyrule was one country, a great ruler maintained peace in Hyrule using the Triforce. However, the king too was a child of man and he died. The prince of the kingdom should have become king and inherited everything, but he could not inherit but a part of the Triforce.

"The prince searched everwhere for the missing parts, but could not find them.

"Then, a magician close to the king brought him some unexpected news. Before he died, the king had said something about the Triforce to only the younger sister of the prince, Princess Zelda. The prince immediately questioned the princess, but she wouldn't tell him anything. After the prince questioned the princess, the magician threatened to put the princess into an eternal sleep if she did not talk, but still, she said nothing."

Hyrule Has Changed

Unlike *The Legend of Zelda*, this game consists of two viewpoints. In the Overhead View, Link can hike along the roads or venture into the wilderness. If he meets an enemy off the road, he is thrown suddenly into the Side View action screen, where he must do battle. The interiors of many palaces and towns Link encounters during his travels also utilize Side View. Other changes include the many people who talk to Link and help him with clues. He also has the ability to use magic.

Study Well the Map of Hyrule

Do not be deceived! The distances of Hyrule are greater than they at first appear. Long is the road Link will travel, and fraught with many dangers. Yet he will find help in the most unexpected of places.

Setting out from North Castle where lies the sleeping princess, Link explores the roads open to him, putting them to memory and learning secret ways through hill and desert and treacherous swampland.

Action Scene

Off the beaten path, Link encounters enemy creatures and servants of Ganon. The scene switches to Side View and scrolls either left or right as Link fights toward freedom from the center. Each action scene consists of three screens where Link must prove himself to be the Champion of Hyrule.

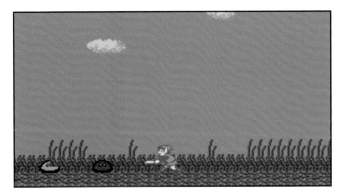

Items

As Link searches out clues and battles the minions of Ganon, he must uncover powerful items in secret places. He finds many more tools than just these, but none quite so important as the ones listed here.

Magic Jar

The potion within restores Link's magic. Red potions fill the meter all the way while blue potions refill a single measure.

Boots

The way ahead lies sometimes across the seas in places where no man may venture, save he who has the Boots.

Doll

A small doll that looks like Link. Acquiring one will grant Link an extra life.

Handy Glove

Where a fall of stones blocks the way, the Glove proves to be Link's salvation.

Magic Container

An increase in one measure of magic will Link gain from this vessel, and his magic meter fills up!

Cross

With its secret power, Link will be able to spot enemies normally hidden to him.

Hammer

Many roads in the Overworld screen are blocked by boulders. Only the Hammer can shatter them.

Flute

Long has it been told that the music of this ancient Flute has powers both myserious and strong.

Magical Key

A magical key that can open any locked door inside a palace.

Raft

Divided by a great sea, the vastness of Hyrule can be explored fully only if Link wins the Raft.

Candle

A flame to brighten the dark caves through which Link must pass. Once lit, it cannot be extinguished by any foe or force.

Heart Container

Adds one measure to the staunchness of Link's heart and restores his life to its fullest.

Treasure Bag

A wealth of points (worth 50, 100, or 200 points) awaits Link if he is quick, brave, and lucky.

Magic

During his travels, Link learned eight spells of Hyrulian magic, which helped him overcome Ganon's evil. Will you find them as well?

Shield

Strengthens Link's defenses. Within one screen, an enemy's blow falls with only half the force.

Jump

Once earned, the magic of the High Jump allows Link passage over walls and other barriers along his way.

Fire

This magic will allow Link to shoot fireballs from the tip of his blade, giving him an added edge in battle.

Spell

Casting this spell on particular enemies can cause odd things to happen to them. Use it to uncover hidden secrets as well.

Life

Dark moments come when Link is nearly spent. Using Life regains him three measures of vitality.

Fairy

In narrow places, impassable even to Link, he may choose the magical transformation into a flying pixie.

Reflect

With this powerful magic, Link can block projectiles he normally cannot and reflect magic back at sorcerers.

Thunder

When all seems lost, the magic of Thunder brings hope, for its power affects all enemies present.

The Servants of Ganon Have Invaded!

As Link searched the six palaces of Hyrule, many servants of Ganon did he encounter. These are but a few of the creatures bent on Ganon's return.

Color shows strength.

Weak

Normal

Strong

Bot

This jumping jelly drop is found everywhere.

Deeler
Like a giant spider, the Deeler drops on a thread from trees.

Lowder

A crawling beetle that gobbles up life energy.

Bago-Bago

Vicious flying fish that spit rocks at Link as he crosses bridges.

Geldarm
A centipede that stands upright; only its head is vulnerable.

Moa

A graveyard ghost.

Goriya

A boomerang master, the Goriya lurks in caves. Link must use his Shield to deflect this creature's attacks.

Daira

Against the Daira's axe, Link's Shield is useless.

Megmat

Tough-skinned, the Megmat is a dangerous pest.

Octorok

This land-octopus leaps and then spits rocks to defend itself.

Ache

They swoop down from the shadows of deep caverns.

Boon

This giant fly persistently drops stones.

Acheman

A batlike monster that breathes fire and changes shape.

Myu

Small, thorny, and hard, the Myu is weak on top.

The Palace Guardians

In the depths of each of the six palaces of Hyrule, a mighty guardian challenges Link. Long ago, the king who broke the Triforce and hid the fragment of Courage set these guardians to the task of protecting six mystical statues that are the key to regaining peace in the land.

Barba

This monstrous being will be Link's final challenge before he can proceed to the Grand Palace. Can he prove his skill as a hero?

Jermafenser

A knight armored in shining blue steel, his haunted helms make him more dangerous with every one that falls off. How can Link hope to defeat an enemy such as this?

Carock

A dastardly wizard who fires off spells with deadly accuracy and speed. What will Link do to stop his wicked magic?

Mazura

This strange beast has upheld its duty of guarding the statue of Parapa Palace since times long past. Will Link be able to contend with his fighting prowess?

LINK SETS OFF TO MEET HIS DESTINY

Not all paths are open to the hero when he first ventures forth from North Castle. The map that follows reveals the limits of his wandering, from Ruto in the mountains of the northwest to Rauru in the east. Parapa Palace is within reach if he travels to the northeast. And yet in this region of Hyrule, buried in the hills and deserts, hidden away in forests and caves, can be found items essential to Link's quest. It is but for him to find them.

Gooma

This giant troll, as mighty as he is fierce, will make quick work of Link with his spiked ball and chain. Link must find a way to dodge his swings and fight back.

Rebonack

A proud knight atop his abnormal steed lies in wait, lance and wits at the ready. Can Link best him in this battle of skill?

HYRULE

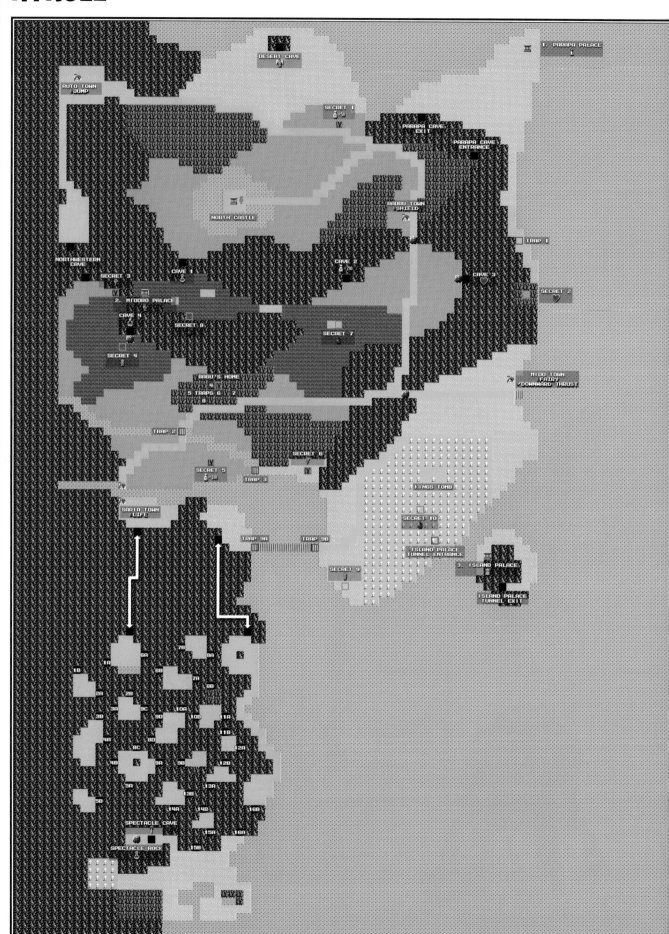

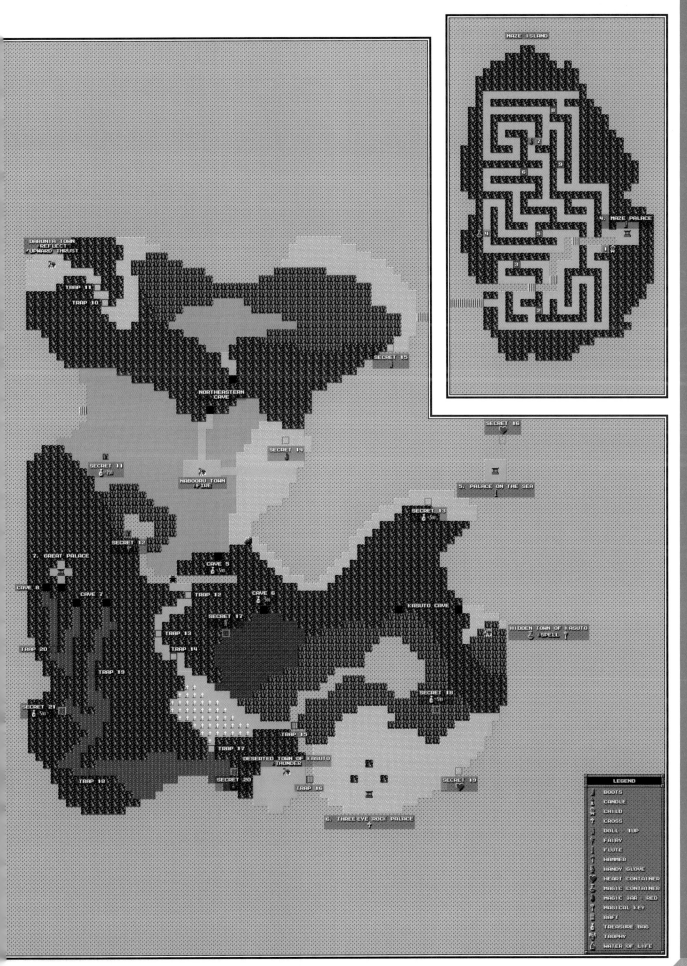

MAZE ISLAND

8

7
6
9
4. MAZE PALACE
4
5
3
2

DARUNIA TOWN
REFLECT
/UPWARD THRUST

TRAP 11
TRAP 10

SECRET 15

NORTHEASTERN
CAVE

SECRET 16

SECRET 14

SECRET 11

NABOORU TOWN
FIRE

5. PALACE ON THE SEA

SECRET 13

SECRET 12

7. GREAT PALACE

CAVE 5

CAVE 8

CAVE 7

TRAP 12

CAVE 6

KASUTO CAVE

SECRET 17

HIDDEN TOWN OF KASUTO
/SPELL

TRAP 13

TRAP 14

TRAP 20

TRAP 19

SECRET 18

SECRET 21

TRAP 15

TRAP 17

DESERTED TOWN OF KASUTO
THUNDER

TRAP 18

SECRET 20

SECRET 19

TRAP 16

6. THREE-EYE ROCK PALACE

LEGEND

BOOTS
CANDLE
CHILD
CROSS
DOLL 1UP
FAIRY
FLUTE
HAMMER
HANDY GLOVE
HEART CONTAINER
MAGIC CONTAINER
MAGIC JAR / RED
MAGICAL KEY
RAFT
TREASURE BAG
TROPHY
WATER OF LIFE

From North Castle

Always will Link's journey begin here where Zelda sleeps. Should he fall during his journey, he reawakens at this location to start his adventure anew. Only while Link retains a life does he continue at the place where he falls.

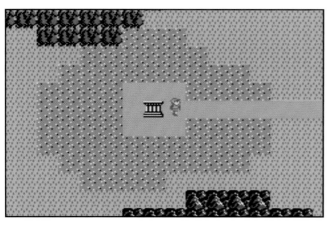

Desert Cave

Far across the burning sands of Tantari Desert lies a deep cave in which it is rumored there rests the statue of a Goddess and a great prize to he who wins it. But the prize must indeed be won, for the quest is never easy.

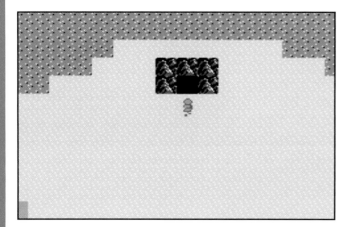

Parapa Palace

To the north and east, beyond mountains and deserts, is set Parapa Palace. Only columns of marble rise above the lonely sands. But below, in the great halls and passages, it is said that a candle awaits.

Ruto

Nestled between northern peaks, the village offers rest and aid to weary adventurers.

From Ruto came the statue of the Goddess. Return it for a rich reward.

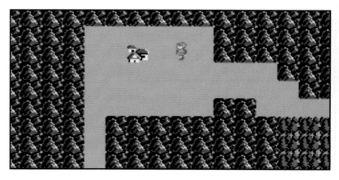

Rauru

Near the forest east of North Castle, Rauru offers lessons in magic!

Here dwell folk with powers to restore spent life and magic.

Secret 1

Under the eaves of this isolated forest, look for a Treasure Bag worth 50 points.

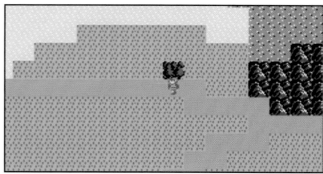

Parapa Cave

This dark passage leads to the desert, but beware: a lone Lowder lurks within.

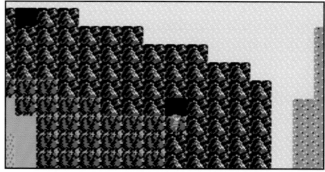

Link First Visits Rauru

In the quiet town of Rauru, Link approaches and speaks with many people (get close and press B). Some know nothing but town gossip, while others help with guidance and words of wisdom. Here, too, Link may restore both his life and magic.

From a wise man in the town, he may learn a secret of magic power. Here, in Rauru, Link need only discover the whereabouts of this sage old man. But in all other towns, secret lessons are offered only to those who have proved their valor and good nature. By finding treasure objects lost, and by doing valiant deeds, Link gains the trust of the townsfolk, who then reveal the home of their local magician. Much evil has come to pass due to Ganon's henchmen, and many wrongs must be righted in Hyrule. So this, too, is Link's fateful task.

Those who step from their homes give the best clues.

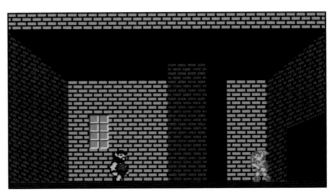

Link can enter freely those houses with open doors.

Cautiously Link Takes the Dark Path

Carved from the roots of the mountains, the tunnel to the desert remains the only way open to Link. There darkness hangs like a cloak, and so too lurks a Lowder that Link must pass. Although in the blackness, he still catches glimpses of the creature's feet.

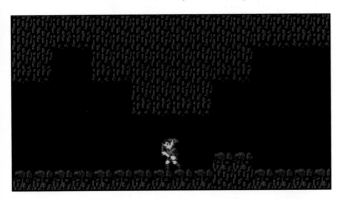

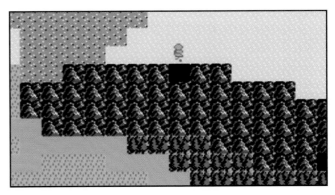

Parapa Palace

The screen switches to Side View as Link reaches the palace in the desert. Cautiously he passes a silent guardian of stone and moves swiftly to the lift, which takes him below. There, in the ancient hallways, the servants of Ganon roam, ever searching for the key to revive their dark master. Long has it been since adventurers dared to enter this shadowy ruin, and few know to fear heroes such as Link. Branching tunnels, stairways, and deep shafts all are there to be explored. Treasure, too, lies buried in the vaults, but with each step Link takes, new terrors may awaken seeking his end.

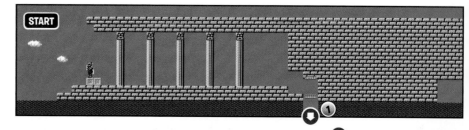

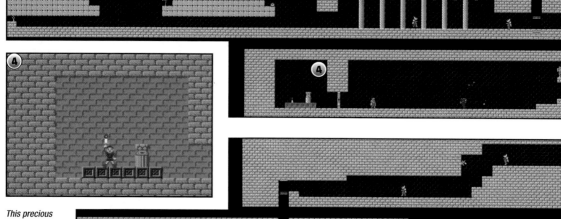

This precious gift of light is worth more than gold or jewels to Link.

Mazura: The First Guardian

In a time long forgotten in Hyrule, Mazura was given the task of guarding the statue in the back of Parapa Palace. Suddenly coming face-to-face with the monster, Link stops short. He cannot proceed until he defeats Horsehead, and only an attack to the creature's huge head can succeed. After a moment, he knows he must use a Jump attack to defeat his towering foe.

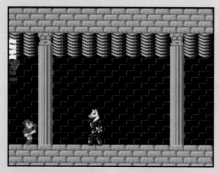

The guardian has the head of a horse and attacks by whirling a giant club.

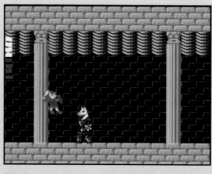

Mazura wears no helmet. Link need only leap high and strike hard!

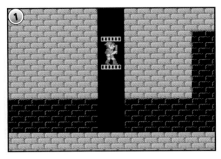

An elevator gives Link access to the many palace levels.

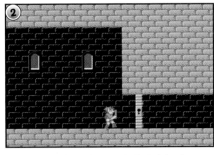

Link must seek hidden Keys to enter locked chambers.

Bridge stones crumble with each step as Link runs across.

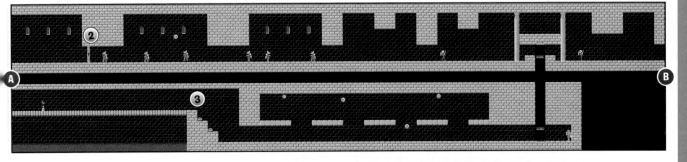

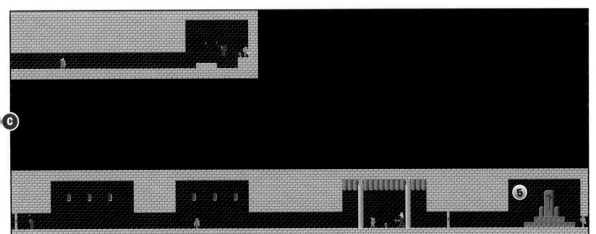

To the Statue Link Returns the Crystal

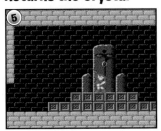

Each palace holds a statue that resembles a face of mystic origins. Together they create a binding force that locks the Great Palace. The crystals destroy the statues, palaces, and the force.

Only after Mazura is defeated can Link place a crystal in the statue.

The Desert Cave

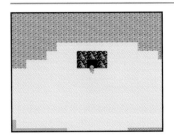

In a cave in the Tantari Desert, north of North Castle, a statue of a Goddess awaits the hero. It is more perilous than the other caves Link has visited, for invisible holes pit its floor, and dreadful creatures rush and swoop at Link. With the Candle from Parapa Palace, the way is made easier.

Whispers in Ruto Tell Link Much

GORIYA OF TANTARI STOLE OUR TROPHY.

Link listens well to all those he meets in this village. Some speak of a mysterious stolen statue that can be traded for magic.

Southwest of North Castle is the cave to which Link must now go. With the Candle in hand, Link can navigate the cave safely.

Midoro: The Swamp Palace

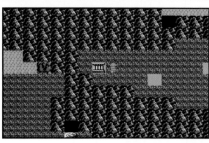

With the Candle and a greater sense of confidence, Link now seeks the second palace. Through a cave he must pass and there defeat a fierce, boomerang-wielding Goriya. He must also have earned the magic of the High Jump to escape. Once outside, he finds himself on the south side of the mountains in a new land. Here the Midoro Marsh stretches wide before him. First south, then east and north, finally turning back to the west he must travel. Through a narrow gap in the mountains, he struggles on through the swamp until there ahead he sees the palace. When he has increased all his levels at least to three, Link enters this new maze. He has heard that a Handy Glove is somewhere hidden in the second underground level to the far left and that one cannot proceed far without it.

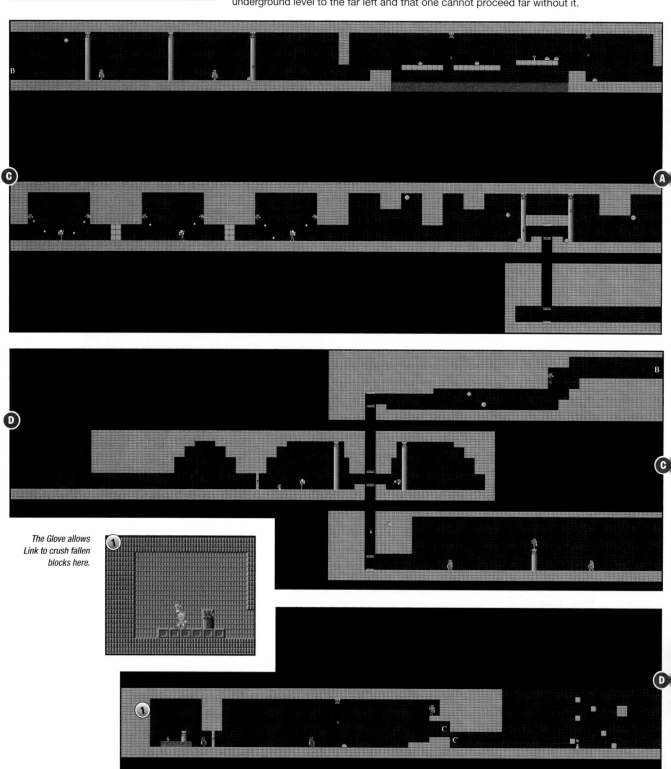

The Glove allows Link to crush fallen blocks here.

Palace Secrets

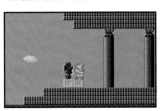

On the steps, stone statues guard the palaces. If Link strikes one with his Sword, he may receive something valuable.

The prize in this case is a jar of magic potion.

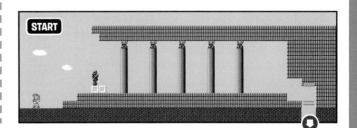

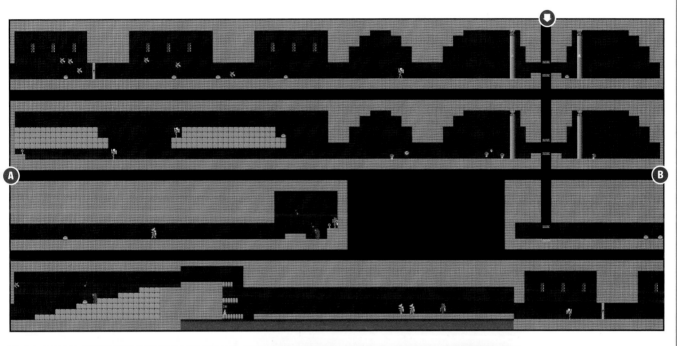

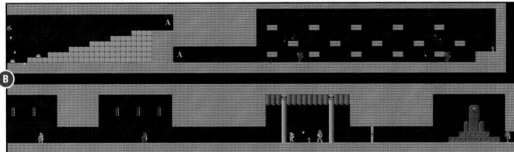

Jermafenser: The Second Guardian

Link comes upon another of the guardians in the most remote corner of the palace. A knight armored in blue steel bars his way. With his Shield, Link foils its attacks, but his counterblows merely ring off the guardian's hard head. Here, to succeed, he must learn the art of the Downward Thrust.

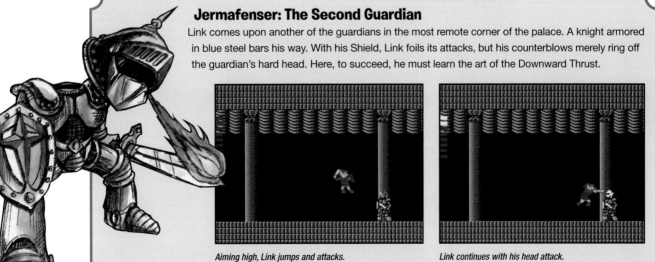

Aiming high, Link jumps and attacks.

Link continues with his head attack.

Island Palace

Off the shore of Hyrule, protected by mist and sea, a rocky island is home to the third palace. Neither boat nor bridge avails Link as he attempts to cross the channel. Instead, he must take another, darker path. One day, he wanders directly south from the King's Tomb, and suddenly he is falling through the earth!

He has stumbled upon an ancient tunnel linking the mainland to the palace. Picking himself up, he makes toward the right and the Island Palace.

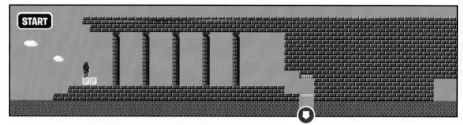

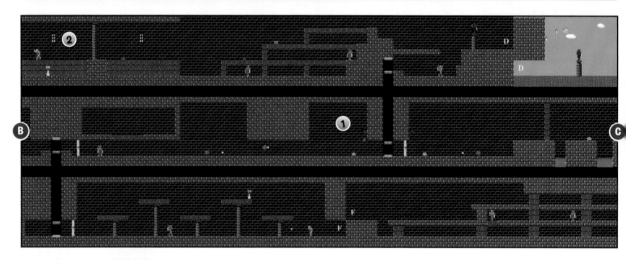

The Island Palace was built with fewer twists and turns, but a powerful enemy waits within. Link shrewdly uses Jump and Shield magic to work his way through.

Link Uses Down Thrusts to Reach the Key

Having learned the Down Thrust attack from a swordsman in the Harbor Town of Mido, Link uses it on these fragile blocks. Digging away, he eventually reaches a Key.

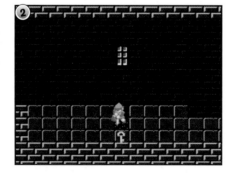

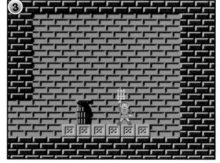

Discovering the Raft will open new horizons to Link, if he ever gets out.

Link sets to memory the path he must take from the King's Tomb. "Eight steps in a line straight to the south." Later, he would draw a map of all his travels, for he knows the importance of this.

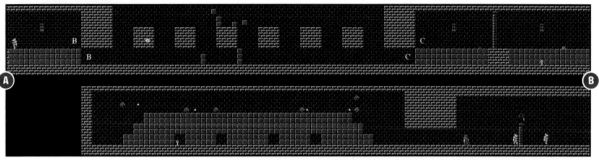

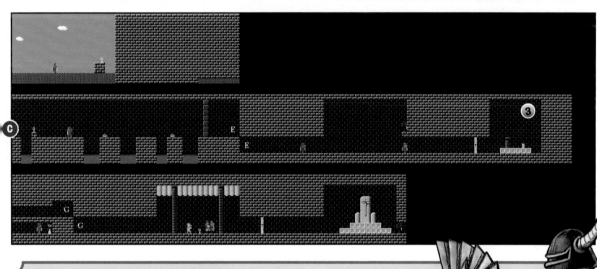

Rebonack: The Third Guardian

Astride an unearthly horse, Rebonack charges into the final chamber of the palace. Link jumps at his foe, swings his Sword, and discovers that this technique may be the key. Many times the knight thunders toward him, but eventually he dismounts and fights hand-to-hand.

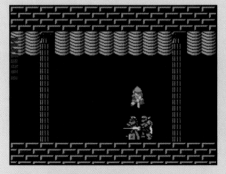

Link's Jumps and the Down Thrusts of his Sword begin to take their toll on the still-mounted knight.

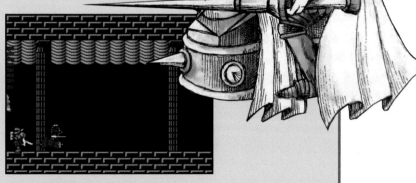

When the knight dismounts, Link leaps in close to the attack, sensing victory.

Palace of Maze Island

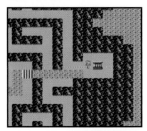

Sailing east across the sea, Link comes to the second continent of Hyrule. Here he encounters more of Ganon's servants, new villages, and puzzles to solve. One of the most intriguing is the puzzle of Maze Island. Connected by a bridge to the mainland, the island is the home of the fourth palace, wherein live a host of Wizards and other beings. For a time Link wanders through the maze. In a few places he uncovers secrets, and with luck and patience he eventually arrives at the entrance to the palace. But that is only the beginning. The maze outside is nothing compared to that which awaits Link within the palace walls; it is his greatest challenge yet. Hidden pits drop into fiery pools, and no path, it seems, is free of the Wizards.

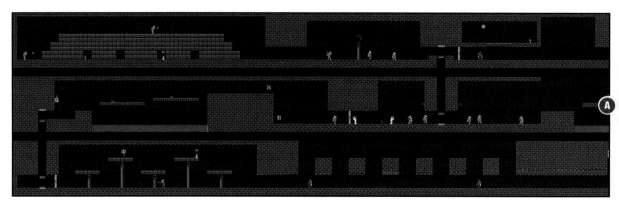

To Defeat Doomknocker

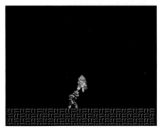

An attack from above frustrates the giant.

Link must face many who have the strength and cunning of Ganon. Doomknocker is one such enemy. Alone the Shield is not enough. Link must use Reflect magic.

Reflect's Effect

While traversing Maze Island, Link stumbles across a kidnapped child. After rescuing the child from his captors, Link escorts the young one back to the town of Darunia, where he is rewarded for his good deed with the Reflect spell.

With the magic of Reflect, Link's Shield now repels the spells cast by Wizards and shoots them back. With Reflect on, Link can close the distance between himself and his opponent.

Carock: The Fourth Guardian

Quickly Link learns that the power of the Wizards is not only in their spells, but also in their quickness, and the fact that they vanish without warning. Only with Reflect can he fight them. He waits, crouching at the left of the screen.

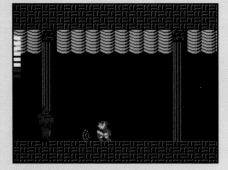

Link activates Reflect and crouches, ready for any attacks that come his way.

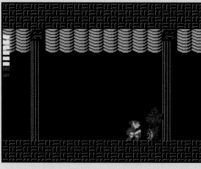

Link must be patient and alert for this method to work.

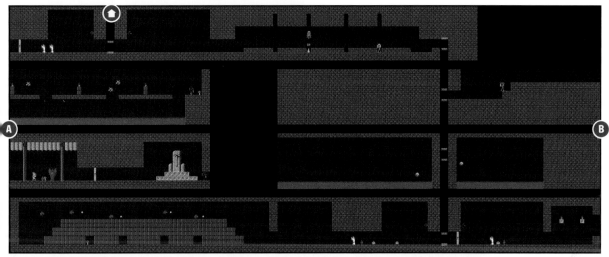

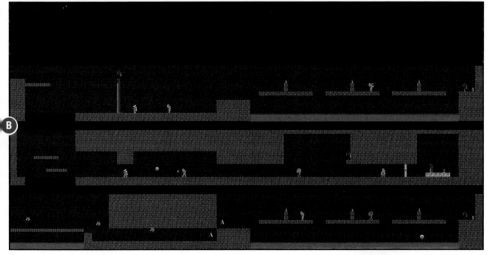

Preparations

Link now makes his way to the fifth palace, located on a storm-battered island off the coast of Hyrule. Already his thoughts have turned to the hidden sixth palace, but an item of great importance must first be found if he hopes to unlock the palace's secret location.

As he continues, enemies become meaner and the palaces more puzzling. Link must make preparations before heading any farther.

He looks at his trusty map, taking account of all the places he has visited and the secrets he has found. He takes this time to visit any areas he left untouched that may have treasures hidden within them.

The Ocean Palace

Off the coast of East Hyrule lies the island of the fifth palace. Inside Link encounters the Fiery Moa, and though later he does battle with this creature, for now he decides to leave it alone. Somewhere ahead he also walks through a wall as in *The Legend of Zelda*.

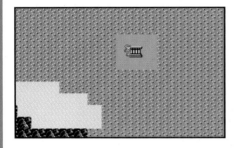

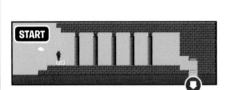

Ready Yourself for Battle

Before challenging the palace, Link builds up his Attack and Magic to seven and adds Life by taking the path over the sea, going north, then east, and finding a hidden Heart Container.

Experience Wanted!!

In the room where blocks rain down, Link can greatly increase his Experience Points. With each shot he can earn 50 or 200 points.

Link waits for all the blocks to fall.

Makes a stairway up to the center of the stack.

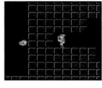

Opens a tunnel all the way through.

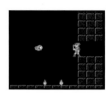

Then stands back and attacks the Moas over and over as they approach for maximum points.

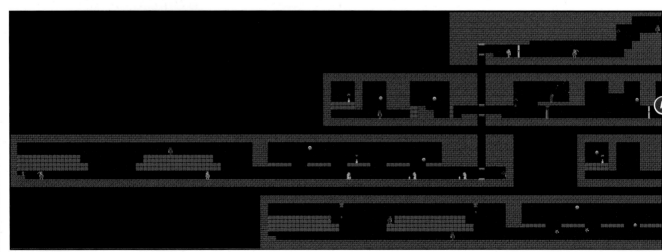

Strategy Change

Back in the fourth palace, Link learned to use Reflect against Wizards. Here it might be a waste of time…

It Looks Like a Dead End, but It Isn't

Ironknuckle seems to be guarding a blank wall, but Link presses on undeterred.

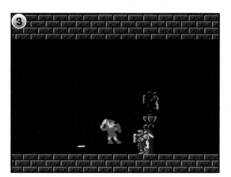

When battling Ironknuckle, Link keeps close, using his Shield magic for defense against the swords Ironknuckle throws.

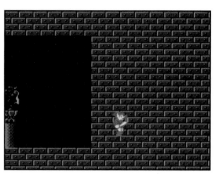

Once Ironknuckle is defeated, Link can pass through the solid wall at the back of the room.

Beyond Ironknuckle and the walkthrough wall, Link finds Keys and an ancient Flute, the latter of which is the prize of this Island Palace. With the Flute, Link can reach southeast Hyrule and Old Kasuto.

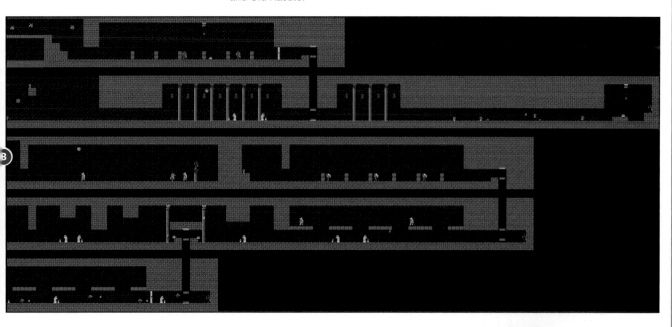

Gooma: The Fifth Guardian

Gooma, the giant troll who swings an iron, spiked mace, protects the statue in which Link must place the fifth crystal. Avoiding his mace by jumping and dodging, Link then leaps in close and uses his Sword when Gooma tires.

Link prepares for battle by using Shield and Jump magic, then stays well back when Gooma swings the heavy mace.

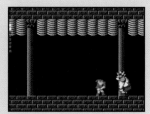

Even Gooma cannot forever swing his weapon. When he rests, Link ducks in quickly and attacks low!

Link's advice: take the opportunities as they come; be patient; dart in and dodge back.

Three-Eye Rock Palace

The home of Barba the dragon extends seven levels deep, with many secrets and pits to trap the unwary. In places, Link must use Fairy magic to continue, and throughout the maze he must battle enemies with his other magical options. It is vital that he keeps his magic levels filled, as he must be ready at every moment to use Reflect, Jump, or Shield. Studying the map, he plans a route to Barba. He also makes notes as he passes through the maze on where the pits are located, because a hole may turn out to be bottomless if he is not careful. Since Link built up his Attack, Life, and Magic back in the fifth palace, he is ready to begin.

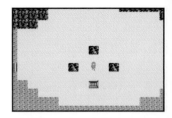

Get the Magic Key!

Since he cannot find any Keys in this palace, Link must first get the Magic Key. Search for it in Kasuto. With the Magic Key, Link can proceed to the sixth palace and open its secrets.

Kasuto is very well hidden in a secret forest on the east side of the east continent. In order to uncover it, use your Hammer on the trees by pressing the A button while on the Overworld screen.

Barba: The Final Guardian

In Barba's chamber, Link comes to three fiery pools from which the dragon rises in flame-breathing horror. He prepares for the battle by using Jump, Shield, and Reflect, then stands on the middle column. As soon as Barba appears, Link attacks, then dodges his flames and attacks again when the dragon dives back into the pool.

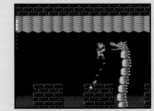

By standing on the middle column, Link is positioned perfectly to attack Barba when he first appears.

With the help of Jump magic, Link can dodge Barba's blistering breath and counterattack. Timing is critical!

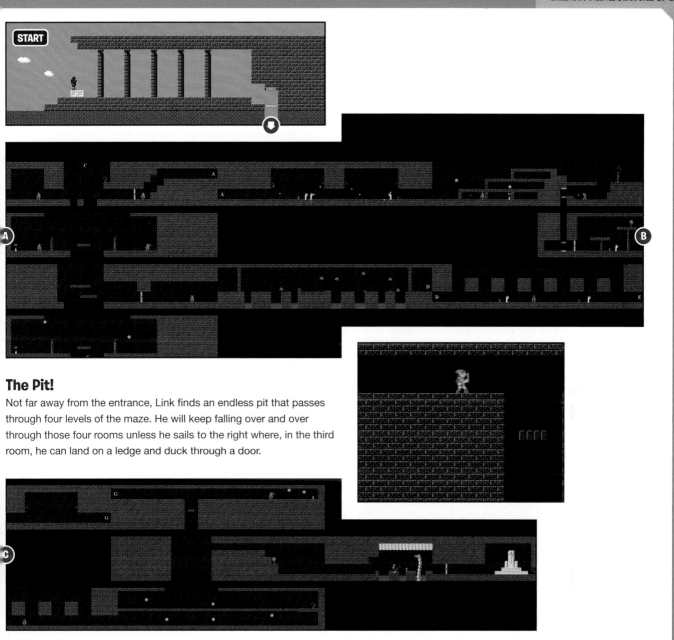

The Pit!

Not far away from the entrance, Link finds an endless pit that passes through four levels of the maze. He will keep falling over and over through those four rooms unless he sails to the right where, in the third room, he can land on a ledge and duck through a door.

On to the Great Palace

Link can sense the end of his journey nearing, but even with victory in sight, he faces a great many more challenges. He uses his map to find his way along the path to reach the Great Palace.

Trap 17

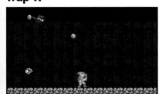

The path to Ganon's lair is guarded by many determined foes. Getting through this section can be a trial.

Trap 18

Here on the path Link meets enemies who attack him. He must take care not to tumble into the lake.

Trap 19

With the powerful Spell magic, Link transforms a Moa into a Bot, making it all the easier to finish off.

Cave 7

Coming to a cave, Link encounters many challenging foes, such as Arurodas and Achemen, creatures he defeats using his Sword and Fire magic.

Trap 20

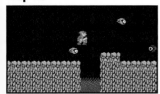

Link encounters another narrow corridor guarded by fierce foes. Quick thinking leads Link to use magic spells to defeat those who bar his path.

Cave 8

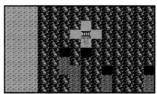

After overcoming many obstacles and powerful foes, Link arrives at his destination: the Great Palace.

The Great Palace

Link has arrived; the massive Great Palace stands before him. His journey has been long and arduous, but through perseverance and unparalleled skill, he has conquered all the obstacles in his path and was led here, to his final destination. He doesn't know what to expect, but he knows that after everything he's faced, he is ready for anything.

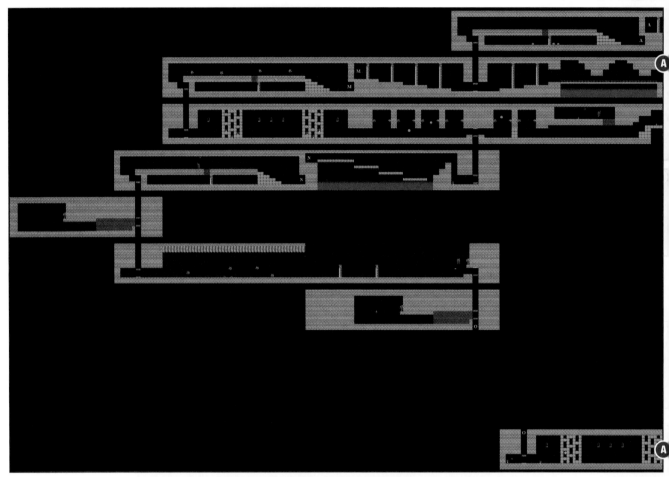

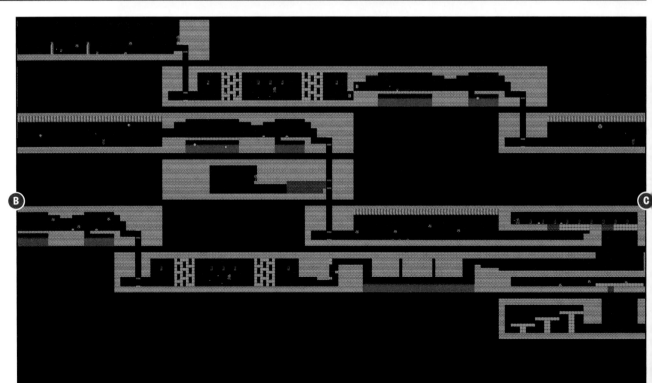

Thunderbird: The Final Guardian?

A massive creature known as Thunderbird guards the Triforce Chamber. Link tries his best to wound the foe, but none of his attacks work. Even worse, he has no way to reach the creature when it flies high up into the room.

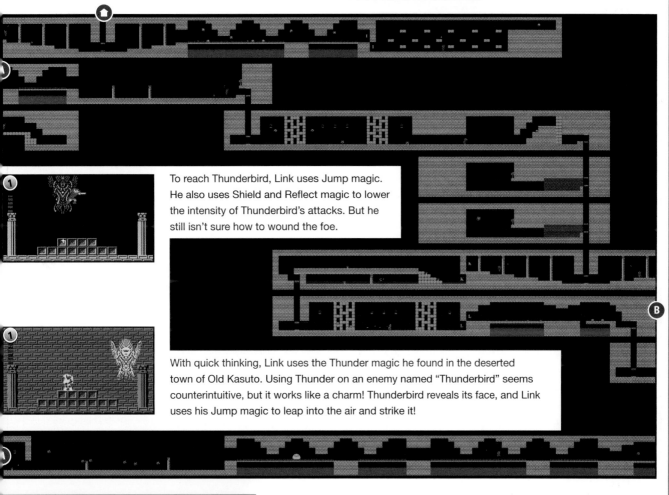

To reach Thunderbird, Link uses Jump magic. He also uses Shield and Reflect magic to lower the intensity of Thunderbird's attacks. But he still isn't sure how to wound the foe.

With quick thinking, Link uses the Thunder magic he found in the deserted town of Old Kasuto. Using Thunder on an enemy named "Thunderbird" seems counterintuitive, but it works like a charm! Thunderbird reveals its face, and Link uses his Jump magic to leap into the air and strike it!

The End?

Having defeated Thunderbird, Link enters the Triforce Chamber, but what happens next is uncertain; the rest of the pages of this story are blank.

It's up to *you* to determine Link's fate. There is one more challenge Link must face to prove his worthiness to possess the Triforce.

Use all your skills and cunning to overcome this final challenge and finish the book titled *The Adventures of Link*. You can do this!

THE LATE PERIOD (1990-94)

By the start of this period, Nintendo had shown North America that video games were here to stay. Other companies arose to directly compete with the NES in hopes of taking a piece of the market that Nintendo rebuilt. Nintendo originally had plans to support only the NES for the foreseeable future, but with their competitors finding a foothold with games with a higher graphical fidelity, Nintendo realized they had to respond with a console that went beyond the NES. Enter the Super Nintendo.

With the launch of the Super Nintendo Entertainment System in the North American market in 1991, Nintendo began to put its efforts into producing content for their new console experience. Nintendo's production of first-party titles slowed down during this period, but the third-party developers only increased their bounty of classic NES hits.

Even with Nintendo focusing more on the Super Nintendo's development, they still managed to release classics like *Dr. Mario, Kirby's Adventure, StarTropics 1 & 2,* and one of the most beloved NES titles of all time, *Super Mario Bros. 3.*

The production of NES titles began to slow down in 1992, with several titles being released cross-platform for both the NES and SNES. In 1994, the NES saw its final licensed release in the form of *Wario's Woods*, a cross-platform puzzle title that featured Mario's rival, Wario.

The Nintendo Entertainment System reached the official end of its life in North America on August 14, 1995, but would continue to be produced for nearly a decade more in Japan—all the way into 2003!

Super Mario Bros. 3
February 1990

"New, different worlds!

New, exciting levels!

New challenges galore!

Fight monsters and mini-bosses, avoid ghosts and the burning sun. Make your way through water and quick sand. Dodge cannon balls and bullets and rescue the King's wand!

In *Super Mario Bros. 3* there are more warps, more chances at extra lives, and new special suits! The raccoon suit lets you fly and knock out blocks. The frog suit helps you out-swim deadly fish. There are suits for every occasion!

Store up flowers and mushrooms to use later on. Play game-show-type bonus rounds! Go back to that last screen and get a mushroom! Pause to take a break, then continue where you left off!

Super Mario Bros. 3 is fun to play alone, or team up with a buddy to prolong the adventure!"

Super Spike V'Ball
February 1990

"Bump, Set, Spike, Kabooom!!

Warm up with a few exercise games, then face contenders in the American Circuit. For the ultimate challenge, play against the best in the World Cup.

Jump and block opponents' spikes, dive to dig a cross court spike, or set up for a smash that only the best player can return. Kabooom!! Your Super Spike blasts your opponent off his feet! "X" marks the spot so you can track the ball.

Pick players with speed, strong defense, or killer offense. Your quick reflexes and competitive spirit complete the team.

Play against the computer, by yourself, or challenge a friend. With the NES Satellite or the NES Four Score, any combination of one to four can play—even two vs. two!

Now you can play on sand courts from Daytona to Los Angeles. Face off international teams in Hawaii, or challenge the hot Navy team aboard an aircraft carrier.

Watch the sand fly! Hear the applause! Soak up the rays! It's *Super Spike V'Ball* for World Class fun!"

Pin*Bot
April 1990

"Dares you to survive.

If you think arcade pinball is fun, wait 'til you try video *Pin Bot.* The outerworld sound effects and fast-as-light action will blow you away.

Live-action flippers move with lightning speed. Bumpers and chutes jet your ball across the galaxy. Pin Bot himself growls out messages of doom, daring you into battle, flashing light and color in a menacing attempt to stun you into confusion.

And just when you think you have it down, here comes another ball—a chance to earn bonus points, sure, but an extra challenge, too! Master that, and Pin Bot tosses another evil shock—an unpredictable, ball-gobbling monster that wants to end your turn NOW.

It's the best of pinball action! It's *Pin Bot!* Live action pinball for one to four players.

It's live-action pinball with video excitement!"

Snake Rattle 'n' Roll
July 1990

"Brilliant 3-D graphics and a colorful new duo—Rattle and Roll!

It's a race to the moon! But first you must travel through 11 levels of adventure. Hurtling anvils, exploding Nibbley Pibbleys, flying carpets, ferocious 3-D terrain, plus BIGFOOT and more!

The action is non-stop. The challenge is terrific. Help Rattle and Roll, the two snakes, make their way up the perilous mountain.

Gobble up Nibbley Pibbleys to gain enough weight to advance to the next level. Defeat enemies while you gather points, food, and extra lives along the way.

Play alone or with a friend, and get ready to *Snake Rattle N Roll*."

Barker Bill's Trick Shooting
August 1990

"Barker Bill is your host. Join him and assistant Tricksie for arcade-style Trick Shooting!

Get out your Zapper video gun. Blast floating balloons before they drift away. But don't hit the friendly dog—he'll get mad!

Rack up points by shooting spinning plates tossed by Barker Bill and Tricksie. They are happy when you make a shot, but scold you when you miss!

Shoot around window panes to knock falling targets out of the picture!

Take aim at tomatoes, eggs, and watermelons before they land on poor Tricksie's head!

So, set your sights for a day at the carnival with Tricksie and Barker Bill!"

NES Play Action Football
September 1990

"Real pro action in the NES Power Bowl.

Choose from eight powerful teams packed with real pro players. Pick your play or defense, then knuckle down for head-banging action. Miss a key block and risk a sack. Pick the right play for a big gain.

But watch out for that tightening defense. Zone coverage can eliminate the long ball.

It's realistic, hard-core football, and you make the decisions. Your backfield is tired. Do you substitute?

That last pass was complete, and they're measuring it. It's fourth and inches, with seconds to go! Do you go for it?

It's a fourth down showdown at the NES Power Bowl."

StarTropics
December 1990

"Tropical adventure of epic dimensions!

A teenager's dream vacation on a tranquil south sea island… A shooting star!? It's an omen of disaster! Mike's archaeologist uncle has been kidnapped. Mike alone can rescue him. Thus begins the test of island courage.

Happy villagers eagerly assist, but endless enemies threaten every step. Mike's search leads him through the lush wilderness of the StarTropics. As he travels on foot, or by submarine through this sunny land of dark secrets and deadly peril, Mike is a tireless fighter.

Using common sense, an island yo-yo, magic potions, and mysterious new weapons and skills, Mike must defend himself. Restore his strength with coconut milk. Help him defeat strange creatures, sea monsters, and hidden attackers.

Join Mike in his adventure. Journey to the StarTropics.

Modern-day adventure in an island paradise!"

Dr. Mario
October 1990

"Dr. Mario—the prescription is fun.

It's Dr. Mario for an intense new challenge! Mario throws multi-colored vitamin capsules into a bottle that contains an ugly variety of nasty viruses. You can move, shift, or spin capsules as they fall. Arrange them to align with other capsules on top of the virus. If you can get four or more of the same color in a row, POOF! They disappear! Destroy all of the viruses in the bottle and you progress to the next round where things get even more difficult.

Play alone or enjoy simultaneous two-player action.

Dr. Mario, with germs that are fun to catch."

Super Mario Bros. & Duck Hunt & World Class Track Meet
December 1990

"**Super Mario Bros.**

You'll have to think fast and move even faster to complete this quest! The Mushroom Princess is being held captive by the evil Koopa tribe of turtles. It's up to you to rescue her from the clutches of the Koopa King before time runs out. But it won't be easy. To get to the Princess, you'll have to climb mountains, cross seas, avoid bottomless pits, fight off turtle soldiers and a host of black magic traps that only a Koopa King can devise. It's another non-stop adventure from the SUPER MARIO BROS.!

Duck Hunt

Your trusty hunting dog wades into the marshes to flush out your prey. Your fingers tighten around your Zapper light gun. Suddenly, there's a duck, and if you miss, even your dog laughs at you! But become a sharp-shooter and you'll progress to the next round where two ducks fly up at the same time. And then you're on to the ultimate challenge: Clay Shooting, where you'll compete in a wild clay-pigeon shooting contest! Play *DUCK HUNT* and discover you can have lots of laughs and be challenged at the same time.

World Class Track Meet

This action-packed game turns your home into an exciting stadium! With the performance of the Power Pad, this will dare you to increase your physical ability and surpass your athletic goals. Compete in four different events against a computer or friends for an ultimate challenge that could reward you the gold!"

1992

Yoshi
June 1992

"**An airborne puzzle invasion!**

It's raining Goombas, Bloopers, and Boo Buddies! You have to help Mario cope with the airborne invasion! As the critters fall, catch them on trays. Switch and shuffle to save the day! Stack two of a kind and they both disappear. Or, capture the whole bunch in-between egg shells. When the egg shells match, out hatches Yoshi and up goes your score!

The action heats up as the characters fall faster and faster. If your piles get too high, the game is over. Choose your difficulty level and play for a high score, or challenge a friend in a head-to-head hatch-off!

If you like *Dr. Mario*, but you're ready for a whole new kind of challenge, you'll love this quick-shuffle action puzzle game!"

1991

NES Open Tournament Golf
September 1991

"**How can sand traps and water be this much fun?**

Whether you're an aspiring amateur or a professional-class golfer, *NES Open Tournament Golf* puts you right in the thick of a world-class golf tournament. Select your club, check the wind and the lay of the turf, and then drive your ball toward winnings worth over one million dollars!

Pick from three tough courses: one in the US, one in Japan, and one in the UK. Practice your strokes, then compete against a friend. For the ultimate challenge, tee off against 36 computerized golfers and compete for top ranking. It's all here in *NES Open Tournament Golf*!

So warm up on 18 holes and move up to tournament play. The better the golf, the bigger the prize. Give it your best shot and go for the big money!"

1993

Yoshi's Cookie
April 1993

"**Cookie chaos for Mario and Yoshi!**

Mario and Yoshi are filling in at the Cookie Factory, and they need your help! Fresh baked cookies roll out of the ovens. It's up to Mario to sort and stack 'em before they pile too high!

Line up a row of the same kind of cookies either vertically or horizontally, and they vanish! Clear the screen to move on to a new level of cookie chaos. Yoshi appears from time to time to stir things up. Play for a high score, or head-to-head against a friend. The mouth-watering madness doesn't let up!

And be sure to keep some cookies close by, 'cause you'll get the munchies during this lip-smacking good time!"

Kirby's Adventure
May 1993

"Kirby's back in power-puffing action!

What would Dream Land be without dreams? A Nightmare! The Dream Spring, source of all dreams, has dried up, taking with it all the blissful dreams of Dream Land. It's up to Kirby, the bombastic blimp, to return happy naps to the inhabitants of Dream Land!

Kirby's appetite for adventure is big as ever as he eats his way through a feast of all new enemies! In this adventure, he can also steal the abilities of the bad guys he scarfs down! With this new power, Kirby can perform 20 new tricks that will help him make his way through the nightmare-infested Dream Land!

Kirby's Adventure features brand new worlds to explore with the same fun, action-packed feel that made *Kirby's Dream Land* for Game Boy a hit!"

Tetris 2
October 1993

"Be a puzzle prodigy!

The mesmerizing fun of *Tetris* returns—and the challenge escalates to new heights! Test your dexterity, tease your brain, and rack up points with *Tetris 2*. Your split-second decisions lead you to a new dimension in puzzle-solving action!

Play alone or challenge a friend in simultaneous, split-screen action.

Line up three blocks of the same color and vroosh!—they explode.

Get rid of special Flash Blocks and wipe out matching color pieces in one move.

A tougher *Tetris* with more shapes, more components, 30 levels—and unlimited solutions!

If you loved the international game sensation *Tetris*, you'll be wild for the newest dimension in puzzle fun: *Tetris 2*!"

1994

Zoda's Revenge: StarTropics II
March 1994

"Stop Zoda's revenge and break the code!

Intrepid adventurer Mike Jones, just back from the South Pacific, is off on a new journey through time and space. Mike's mission: to save the seven mystic Tetrads while he faces the avengers of his foiled foe, the evil Zoda! Now three alien clones are hot on his trail through time!

Unfold nine new chapters of adventures to decipher codes, solve mysteries, and battle dragons with heroes of days gone by. Mike won't stop until the Tetrads are found and the Zodas are history!

Wind your way through more than a dozen action-packed stages in eight settings!

Save your progress and continue your time travels with the battery-backed memory!"

Wario's Woods
December 1994

"It's up to Toad to keep the woods safe in this new puzzle action game!

Toad is back in his very own big adventure in this game with the challenge of *Tetris*. It's up to you and Toad to keep peace in the Mushroom Kingdom—and that means outfoxing the wicked Wario!

Monsters, goblins, and bombs fall from the sky faster and faster as Wario fires them into the woods. Toad must scramble to catch and line up the falling puzzle pieces to eliminate Wario's evil hold. If you love *Tetris*, this puzzle action game is for you!

Choose one- or two-player action!

Run the field to line up puzzle pieces and bombs!

Many levels, from challenging to gut-busting!"

SUPER MARIO BROS. 3

Developer:
Nintendo R&D4

Directors:
Shigeru Miyamoto,
Takashi Tezuka

Producer:
Shigeru Miyamoto

Composer
Koji Kondo

Original Release Date:
October 23, 1988 Famicom JP; February 9, 1990 NES NA

A MESSAGE FROM MARIO

"It's me, Mario! It's been such a long time since we've seen each other.
Bowser is up to his old tricks again, so Luigi and I are going on another adventure. You're welcome to come along."

"This time it's *Super Mario Bros. 3*, the latest in the Super Mario Brothers series. You'll experience lots of excitement as your journey unfolds. For beginners and seasoned veterans of our previous games, this one is going to be a lot of fun! Let's look at *Super Mario Bros. 3* in a bit more detail."

STORY

The Mushroom Kingdom has been a peaceful place, thanks to the brave deeds of Mario and Luigi. It forms an entrance to the Mushroom World, where all is not well. Bowser has sent his seven children to make mischief as they please in the normally placid Mushroom World. They stole the royal magic wands from each country in the Mushroom World and used them to turn their kings into animals. Mario and Luigi must recover the royal magic wands from Bowser's seven kids to return the kings to their true forms. "Goodbye and good luck!" said the Princess and Toad as Mario and Luigi set off on their journey deep into the Mushroom World.

BEING MARIO

There are plenty of features in *Super Mario Bros. 3* that you need to know before getting started. This section covers them all.

Mario's Basic Moves

Super Mario Bros. 3 gives Mario more moves to use than all of his past adventures put together! Some you may know already, some are brand new, but all will help you conquer Bowser and his Koopalings and save the Mushroom Worlds.

Walk

You might walk when you first enter a world and are unfamiliar with the terrain, but once you gain knowledge of your surroundings, it's easier to run!

Running and Flying

By holding down the B Button and running, Mario can build up a lot of steam. Not only can he jump farther, but when his P-Meter is charged, he can take-off as Raccoon Mario!

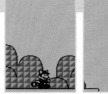

Jump

The A Button controls Mario's famed leaping abilities. If you tap A, Mario makes a short jump; if you press and hold it, Mario will make a higher jump.

Super Jump

Jump on an enemy and hold down the A Button after you stomp him. Your momentum will carry you extra high. This is useful for reaching out-of-the-way places.

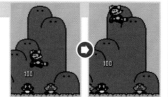

Jump Out Of The Water

When you're at the water's surface, jump and press Up on the Control Pad to leap out of the water. This move is great for getting on top of floating Blocks.

Float

Whether you're falling from the clouds or coming down from a jump off an enemy, by wagging your tail as Raccoon or Tanooki Mario, you can slow your descent to the ground.

Squat

Press Down on the Control Pad to duck. You can get through tight gaps using this technique, or collect items from low "?" Blocks.

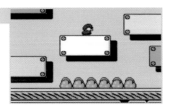

Sliding

Press Down on the Control Pad when you're on a slope to slide down and wipe out enemies in the way.

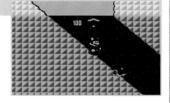

Stomp

This offensive technique is Mario's trademark. Jumping and landing squarely on top of an enemy will usually defeat it, but be careful: some enemies can't be stomped.

Pick Up And Kick

Approach a stomped Koopa from the side while holding down the B Button to pick him up and carry him wherever you like. Release B to kick him away.

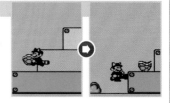

Tail Attack

Mario's Raccoon Tail is stylish and functional. To attack an enemy or hit a "?" Block with your tail, face your target and press the B Button.

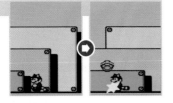

Swim

Rapidly press the A Button to swim, using the Control Pad to change direction. Frog Mario can swim using the Control Pad alone; pressing the A Button gives him extra speed.

Smash It Up

Hitting a Block where an enemy is standing defeats him. Hitting Blocks from below also reveals items they contain.

Pipes

You probably already know how to get into normal pipes—just press Down on the Control Pad. To get into upside down pipes, jump directly under them and press Up.

Climbing the Vines

Some "?" Blocks contain magic vines that Mario can climb to reach bonus stages or secret rooms in the clouds. In difficult stages, these vines also become important safe spots. Just jump and hold Up on the Directional Pad to climb up a vine.

Doors

Press Up on the Control Pad when you're in the doorway to open the various doors you encounter. Some doors are always visible; others are revealed by P-Switch.

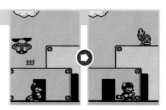

Mario's Advanced Moves

Learn these advanced moves to explore new areas of the Mushroom Kingdom's Worlds and survive in dangerous situations.

Diagonal Jumping

Some Blocks are in difficult-to-reach places. Invisible Blocks that are diagonal to a visible Block appear only if you stand on the corner of the visible Block and jump up.

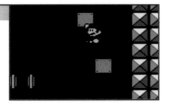

Slide Under

While running, press diagonally down and Left or Right (depending on the direction you're moving) on the Control Pad to slide through small gaps. In the Ice World, you need only press Down.

Jump Around Corners

To get on top of a Block from one that's directly below, stand on the corner of the lower Block, then jump up and bend your jump around (using the Control Pad), so you come out on top.

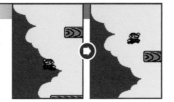

Jet Coaster Jump

On slopes with small ramps at the bottom, you can slide down and make a last-second leap at the bottom for an extra high jump.

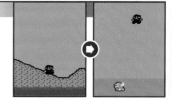

Jump And Squat

To get into narrow passages, get a running start and then press Down at the last second before you jump. You'll squat and jump into the passage. You can also fly while squatting if you time it right.

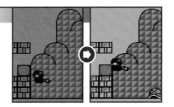

Dash Over Small Gaps

If you accelerate (run while holding the B Button) over small pits and holes, you can make it over them without jumping. This can sometimes be faster and safer than jumping.

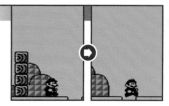

Free Fall Jump

When you're on an overhang and need to get under, jump up and then use the Control Pad to change your trajectory mid-fall.

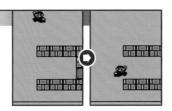

Koopas Can Clear Blocks

When you have a lot of Blocks that need to be cleared quickly, sometimes a well-placed Koopa will do the trick. In any event, kicked Koopas make excellent Block removers.

Mario's Power-Ups!

What would a Mario adventure be without Power-Up items? Doubly difficult and half as fun! Not only do the Power-Up items in *Super Mario Bros. 3* make some super gameplay moves possible, they also give Mario some cool looks! Items in action scenes must be used right away, but those obtained in Toad's House can be saved for later use.

Mario
Also known as Small or Regular Mario, this is how you start.

Tanooki Mario

This fuzzy brown suit gives Mario all the powers of Raccoon Mario—plus the ability to turn into Statue Mario!

Super Mario

Collect a Super Mushroom to become Super Mario!

Hammer Mario

The Hammer Bros. Suit is a crafty outfit; the hammers he throws are powerful, and the shell is fireproof!

Raccoon Mario

The Tail Attack and the ability to fly are new powers you can gain by collecting a Super Leaf and becoming Raccoon Mario!

Frog Mario

Get ready for aquatic action with the Frog Suit. This allows Mario to swim like a frog—and leap like one, too!

Fiery Mario

There's nothing like good old firepower to get the enemies sizzlin'. This attack affects almost every foe.

Mario's Magical Items

Unlike Power-Ups, which can be obtained in many different places, some of these items can be found only in White Mushroom Houses or other secret locations!

Starman

Grants temporary invincibility, and is usually found in "?" Blocks.

P-Wing

This high-powered Raccoon Suit lets Mario fly at will for an entire stage, or until he gets hit.

Jugem's Cloud

Allows Mario to skip one stage of a world; it's useful for passing problem levels.

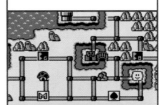

Magic Whistle

The three Magic Whistles take Mario to World 9, the Warp Zone. They are well hidden, but we'll point out each one during your adventures.

Hammer

Use this to break boulders on the Map Screen and travel to remote stages of a world.

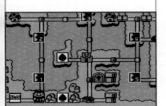

Music Box

The beautiful music of this magic tune box puts wandering Hammer Bros. to sleep.

Anchor

Using the Anchor, Mario can keep the Koopaling Airships from escaping.

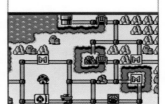

1-Up Mushroom

The key to success in *Super Mario Bros. 3* is collecting these valuable Mushrooms. And they are everywhere!

The Enemies

Some are new and some are old, but all the bad guys in this game spell trouble for Mario. Fortunately, there are usually multiple ways to defeat each enemy, but some are totally invulnerable or susceptible to only a few attacks. Enemies are worth various numbers of points—the tougher the enemy, the more points you get.

Green Koopa Troopas

Single-minded reptiles that charge forward, even into a pit.

Red Koopa Troopas

These red Koopas have a bit more self-preservation than their green counterparts. They walk forward until reaching a pit or an obstacle, then reverse and repeat.

Green Koopa Paratroopas

Similar to their wingless cousins, these Paratroopas charge directly at Mario.

Red Koopa Paratroopas

Like Red Troopas, these winged Koopas go back and forth in a given area.

Green Gargantua Koopa Troopas

Bigger Heads don't mean bigger brains for the giant Koopas. They're still easy to defeat.

Red Giant Koopa Troopas

Identical in action to normal Red Koopas, this variety can be dealt with in a similar fashion.

Colossal Koopa Paratroopas

Creatures this big shouldn't be able to fly, but anything goes in the Mushroom Kingdom!

Dry Bones

A mummified zombie Koopa that comes back to life after you stomp it.

Buzzy Beetle

This fireproof beetle from the original *Super Mario Bros.* returns with some new tricks.

Para-Beetles

Flying members of the Beetle family, these aviators can be used as stepping stones.

Buster Beetle

He's not fireproof—he likes the cold and attacks by tossing Ice Blocks.

Blooper

Another familiar foe from the past, Blooper is a squid that appears underwater.

Blooper Nanny

Talk about adventures in babysitting! Watch out for this Blooper's stinging kids!

Spiny

Lakitu's pet is a familiar sight to Mario veterans. Don't try to stomp him!

Piranha Plant

Those dangerous carn ivorous plants are really making comeback! They're everywhere!

Venus Fire Trap

A hot tempered variety of the visually laid-back Piranha Plants.

Hanging Piranha Plant

Piranha Plants have truly overgrown some areas in *Super Mario Bros. 3*, including upside-down pipes!

Piranhacus Giganticus

In the Land of the Giants, giant Piranhas grow to their own beat, and ignore Mario.

Ptooie

A mobile species of Piranha Plant, it juggles a deadly spiked ball with its over-sized lips.

Nipper Plant

This walking Piranha bulb is hungry for Mario, and will even jump to get at him!

Fire Nipper Plant

A fire-juggling Nipper that loves burning unsuspecting trespassers.

Munchers

Indestructible Piranha Plants that are often found in huge clusters. Starman, help!

Goomba

The traitorous mushroom tribe from Mario's original adventure comes back for more!

Para-Goomba

Bowser's magic has given these rascals wings. Watch the skies!

Para-Goomba With Micro-Goombas

Look out for this flying pest. Avoid him and his kid brothers entirely.

Mugger Micro-Goomba

If one of these gets close, you won't be able to jump high or run fast. Jump repeatedly to get away.

Pile Driver Micro-Goomba

These tiny terrors try to trounce you with a Block. Get the jump on them!

Grand Goomba

Larger than life and twice as ugly, Grand Goombas are otherwise like regular Goombas.

Kuribo's Goomba

Found only in stage 5-3, he wears Kuribo's Shoe—a high-stepping item that Mario can use.

Cheep-Cheeps

Flying fish that make the aquatic adventures more than just a day at the beach.

Boss Bass

Even if Mario is Super, Boss Bass, the terror of the high seas, can swallow him whole.

Spiny Cheep

Swift swimming and spiny, look out for these in later water worlds!

Big Bertha

This giant fish is a mouth breeder, so it spits babies at Mario.

Baby Cheep

They may be small, but their touch is as deadly as that of their giant mother!

Hammer Bros.

These roving bandits from the original *Super Mario Bros.* game have brought along the family!

Boomerang Bros.

G'day Mario! It's the Hammer Bros. from "Down Under," the Boomerang Bros.!

Fire Bros.

These Twin Toasters want to start a Mario inferno. Give them a taste of their own medicine.

Sledge Bros.

Tubby turtles that really throw around their weight. Heavy stuff, man!

Spiny Egg

Lakitu tosses these around, trying to hit Mario. They turn into Spinies.

Lakitu

Mario's high flying antagonist from the original *Super Mario Bros.* returns for more fun!

Thwomp

A nasty Block of blue stone that will try to mash Mario in the Fortresses.

Podoboo

Living bubbles of magma that leap out of lava lakes and drop off the ceilings.

Jelectro

Avoid a shocking encounter with this unmoving and unbeatable aquatic enemy!

Fire Snake

This flaming serpent inhabits desert locales. A tail attack or Koopa will defeat it.

Fire Chomp

Floating in the sky above the Mushroom Worlds, these fire-spitting orbs attack at inopportune moments.

Chain Chomp

One of the most frustrated villains in video games, this foe bites if you get too close.

Bob-omb

The only enemy from *Super Mario Bros. 2* to appear in the adventure, Bob-omb explodes after being stomped.

Spike

Spike attacks by throwing a magical spiked ball at Mario. Duck and cover!

Roto-Disc

Unbreakable whirling traps that often Block the direct path through Fortresses.

Rocky Wrench

These turtles often serve as crew of Koopaling Airships and military vehicles.

Lava Lotus

An aquatic relative of the Piranha Plants, the Lotus spits fiery lava bits.

Angry Sun

It's quite a shock when the Sun comes down in the Desert World. Don't get sunburned!

Tweester

The tornadoes that will gladly either help or hinder Mario's progress.

Boo Diddly

Don't turn your back on this ghost. Face up to him until you're ready to run away!

Hot Foot

Hot Foot haunts Fortresses and behaves like Boo Diddly, chasing you if you turn away.

Stretch

Another spooky inhabitant of Fortresses, Stretch lives inside weird white Blocks.

Bullet Bill

Turtle Cannons relentlessly fire this living, deadly projectile at Mario.

Missile Bill

Bullet Bills with a red hue travel back and forth in search of their target.

Rocket Engine

The flames from these powerful rockets propel the Airships and burn intruders.

Boom-Boom

This Koopa boss controls the Fortresses in each Mushroom World.

Larry Koopa

Bowser's youngest Koopaling, Larry has taken over the Grass Land.

Morton O. Koopa

Grouchy old Morton waits for Mario in his Airship over the Desert Land.

Wendy O. Koopa

The only girl Koopaling, Wendy has conquered the Island World. She's tough!

Iggy Koopa

Iggy's fast, but not too tough. He now controls the Land of the Giants.

Roy Koopa

Big and burly, Roy is the master of the Sky World. He's a big boy!

Lemmy Koopa

Also known as the Clown Prince of Koopas, Lemmy would rather join the circus.

Ludwig von Koopa

Bowser's oldest Koopaling and second-in-command, he's a real monster!

Bowser

Bowser is back and at the bottom of Mario's troubles. Can Mario defeat him again?

Mario's Matching Game

The Match Game Panel appears on the Map Screen every time you score 80,000 points. If you clear the board, you get lots of items and coins! Turn over two cards. If they match, you get the item. If not, they turn back over. Miss again and you're out!

Use these charts to determine the location of each item. To use them, pick a card in the Match Game and match it to the charts on this page.

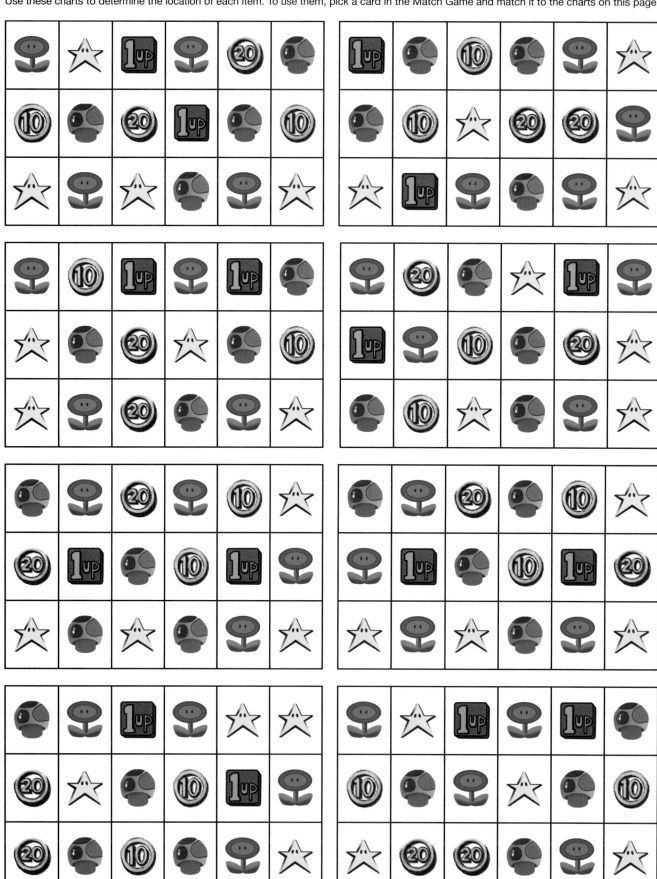

World Data Box

A				C			
B	★						

White Mushroom House: 1-4:44 coins

World 1-1

A great refresher course for veteran Mario players and a great practice course for those of you who are new.

Kick this Crazy Koopa

Boot this Koopa so it hits the Block, then get the item. If you're still Super Mario, you'll find a Super Leaf inside this box.

Up, Up and Away

After you defeat the Goombas, get a running start as Raccoon Mario so you can fly, then follow the coins in the sky.

This Sky Pipe Leads to a Secret Coin Room!

Use the P-Switch to turn the Blocks into coins. Collect all the coins and you'll have runway room to fly to the sky pipe.

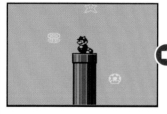

The Physics of Falling Mushrooms...

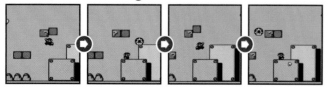

A Mushroom may appear if you hit a "?" Block from below. If you hit it on the bottom-left side, the Mushroom will move to the right, and vice versa. This helps in tricky stages where a Mushroom could mean the difference between success and defeat.

World 1-2

Your first chance to get 99 lives!

Score Points and 1-Ups if You Stomp Without Landing!

Squash nine Goombas without touching the ground between stomps to earn more and more points for each one until the ninth, when you'll get a 1-Up. Then, for each Goomba after the ninth, you get another 1-Up. Use the endless spill of Goombas here to score unlimited 1-Ups!

1-Up Mushroom

Above and slightly to the side of the pipe shown in these screenshots is a 1-Up Mushroom! Score it!

Going Down Pipes Resets "?" Blocks!

If you collect a Power-Up item from a "?" Block and then go down a pipe into a secret room, the item will be back in the "?" Block when you come back out. Get it again!

How to Make Treasure Ships Appear

Collect a number of coins in a multiple of 11. Make the tens digit in your score (the second number from the right) match the multiple of 11. Stop the timer at the end of the stage on an even number. One possible combination is: 11 coins, score of 9,310, timer at 104. Doing this turns one of the Hammer Bros. on the map into a Treasure Ship. (This only works in Worlds 1, 3, 5 and 6.)

World 1-3

This stage hides the first magic Warp Whistle! Each of the well-hidden Whistles takes Mario to World 9, the Warp Zone. The first is found in World 1-3, and it's difficult to discover by chance. You must take advantage of the background scenery.

Send Mario to Coin Heaven!

Kick the Koopa (shown in these screenshots) to the left so he clears some of the Blocks. Then jump straight up while standing against the right side of the left set of Blocks to reveal a Magic Note Block. Jump on it and press Up to get to Coin Heaven. Once there, run back and forth to get the speed you need to fly. There's a 1-Up in the sky, at the middle of the stage.

How to Find the First Whistle!

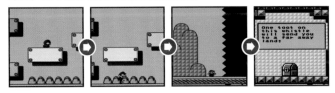

If you get on top of the Block shown in these screenshots and squat for five seconds, you fall "behind" the background scenery. Once there, proceed to the end of the stage and visit a secret Toad House where the first Whistle is kept!

Anchors and P-Wings

With some fancy footwork and quick coin collecting, you can cause Toad's White Mushroom House to appear and earn two different kinds of items in the first seven Worlds. In odd numbered Worlds, you earn P-Wings. In the even numbered Worlds, you earn Anchors. P-Wings allow unlimited flight through an entire stage, while Anchors stop Airships from moving if you lose a life on one.

WORLD	COINS	REWARD
1-4	44	P-Wing
2-2	30	Anchor
3-8	44	P-Wing
4-2	22	Anchor
5-5	28	P-Wing
6-7	78	Anchor
7-2	46	P-Wing

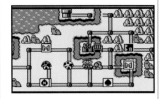

The following table shows the number of coins that you must collect and the Worlds where you must collect them to receive these valuable items.

World 1-4

Automatic scrolling makes for a frantic stage! In this world, you have no choice but to move fast, so be sure to look before you leap! It requires skill!

Remember Your Physics

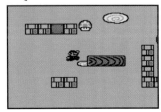

You can collect this 1-Up only if it falls toward the right, so hit the Block the bottom-left.

Frenzied Hopping Pays Off!

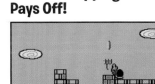

The only way to get all 10 coins here is by jumping fast and furiously!

World 1 Fortress

The second Whistle is found here! Boom-Boom, a big Koopa bully, guards a danger filled fortress in the middle this world.

A Well-Hidden Room Hold the Whistle

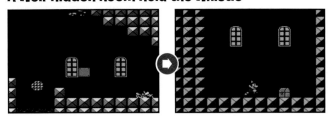

There's enough room in the area shown in the first screenshot above to fly after you knock out the Dry Bones. Fly left and up off the screen, then fly right. The screen will scroll right. When you can't go any further, stop flying and press Up! You'll find the second Whistle inside this room and the stage is completed without you having to fight Boom-Boom. Pretty sweet deal!

World 1-5

This odd, grayish world offers another chance to go to Coin Heaven. It also gives you an opportunity to practice your Slide Attack.

Slide Attack!

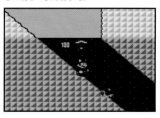

Press Down while on a slope to eliminate nearby enemies.

Find a Magic Note Block

Jump around in this tunnel to reveal the Magic Note Block. It takes you to Coin Heaven.

Use a Koopa!

Wilt this Piranha Plant with a well-timed Koopa or a few fire balls.

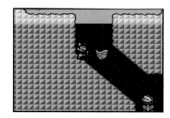

World 1-6

This stage is full of perilous platforms. Rail Lifts with motors are safe to stay on, but those without them will fall off the screen upon reaching the end of the line.

This Rail Lift is Safe

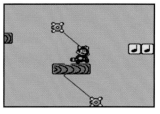

You can stand on the Rail Lift shown in this screenshot and wait until the time is right before jumping.

A Tricky 1-Up

Stomp the Koopa and then toss him out of the way before you go for this 1-Up.

World 1 Airship

Bowser's seven bratty kids, also known as the Koopalings, have each taken the magic wand from a King of a Mushroom World. Larry, the youngest Koopaling, turned the King of Grasslands into a dog. It's Mario to the rescue!

Cannon Ball Capers!

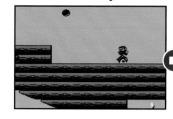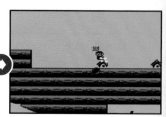

If you stand on top of a cannon, the cannon balls will harmlessly hit your feet and give you 100 points a pop!

Point-Blank Range is Safe!

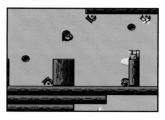

As long as you're right next to Bullet Bill, he won't fire at you. But watch out if you step away!

A Lone Power-Up Item!

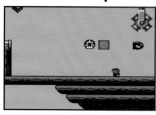

The only "?" Block in the stage contains the only Power-Up. This is your solitary chance to Power-Up on the Airship, so be sure to grab it!

"Yo, Mario—you made it dis far! Well, I'm gonna make sure you don't get past me! (Mario'll never think dat he has to stomp me on da head three times ta knock me out! With my quick jumping skills, he won't have any room to leap himself! And the easiest way to avoid me is running underneath when I jump! (He'll never figure dat out!)

If At First You Don't Succeed, Try Again!

If you don't beat Larry the first time, you can try again. However, the airship flees to another spot on the Map Screen. It tries to take a position beyond unfinished sections of the world, but the Anchor item can prevent it from getting away.

You won't have access to an Anchor in this world, but keep this in mind for World 2!

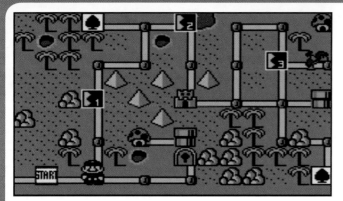

World 2-1

Mario plays archaeologist in these ancient ruins, leaving no stone unturned in search of coins and Power-Ups!

Micro-Goomba

Look carefully at the Blocks around this level. Some conceal Micro-Goomba's who are just waiting to pounce on unsuspecting

adventurers. A good way to spot them is by looking for gold Blocks that don't shine or shimmer. You can also see the Micro-Goomba's feet right before he leaps at you. Try to get the jump on them!

Kick a Koopa Here!

Pick up the Koopa at the beginning of the world and hit the Block in this screenshot with it for an item.

A Sky Pipe Surrounded By Blocks!

As Raccoon Mario, fly straight up above the two Magic Note Blocks to find a Pipe surrounded by Blocks. Hit the P-Switch inside to reveal coins.

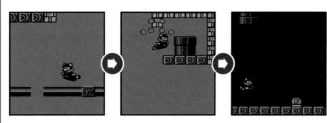

Tail Attack Tactics!

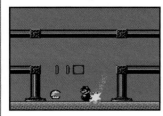

Although the tail won't defeat every enemy, it does work on Fire Snakes.

Another Secret Bonus Stage

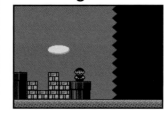

The last pipe in the world leads to a room with a P-Switch. Hit it, then leave quickly and collect the coins outside.

World 2-2

Collect 30 or more coins in this level, and the White Mushroom House appears on the Map Screen. It's a tough feat and takes practice!

How to Collect 30 Coins

Avoid touching the wooden, floating platform and swim to the right, collecting all of the coins while being careful not to destroy the gold Blocks. Next, swim back to the left and hop on the wooden platform. The rightmost of the first two gold Blocks you encounter hides a P-Switch. Hit it and get all of the coins that were Blocks. Make a running, Koopa assisted leap off the platform to get the last four!

Your reward is the Anchor! Use it to keep the Airship from moving.

World 2 Fortress

As Raccoon Mario, you can use a similar technique to the one you used with the Goombas in World 1-2 to get unlimited 1-Ups, but this time it's with Dry Bones.

Dry Bones Comes Back After Being Stomped!

If you group the three Dry Bones at the start of the level together, you can stomp them as Raccoon Mario. Hold the Jump button every time you land on a Dry Bones, then frantically flap your tail to stay airborne. Keep stomping the Dry Bones without touching the ground to earn 1-Ups.

Trick the Thwomp Traps!

Trigger the Thwomp and run under it as it goes back up.

Mario Knows Diddly!

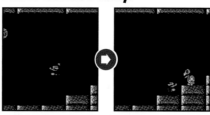

If you turn your back on Boo Diddly, he chases you, but he stays put if you face him.

Sticky Ceiling Spikes

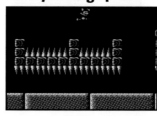

Take the high road or the low one, it's up to you—just watch out for Boo Diddly!

Beat Another Boom-Boom

Another Boom-Boom waits for you here. He's pretty similar to the last one, so stomp him quickly and you won't have any problems.

World 2-3

The pyramids of the Mushroom Pharaohs loom ahead. Although filled with coins, they are daunting obstacles.

Get These Power-Ups!

Once again, use a Koopa to get the items in the Blocks at the top of the first two pyramids if you're not Super.

Neat Stuff in the Sky!

When you reach the Magic Note Blocks in this stage, jump on the first one, then jump up and slightly to the left to reveal a hidden Block. Keep jumping up and slightly to the left to uncover more hidden Blocks. This path of Blocks eventually leads to a set of gold Blocks; the leftmost of the higher pair conceals a P-Switch. Hit it and immediately drop down to find all the smaller, Block-based pyramids have been turned to coins.

An Imposing Obstacle

To clear the Blocks away from the exit Pipe, stomp on one of the Koopas and kick it into the hole above the Pipe. This takes care of the rest.

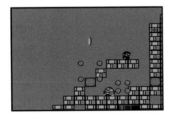

World 2 Desert

Natural forces work to halt Mario's progress through this world—a sinister sun and a terrible tornado.

Capture the Koopa Troopa!

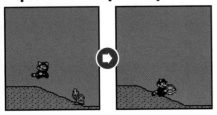

Don't kick this character after you stomp him, but pick him up and take him with you. You'll need him later, trust us.

Ride the Whirlwind to Danger

Run toward the right with your captured Koopa, and when you get to the tornado, jump directly into its center. If you time your jump correctly, it carries you a long way.

When you land, the sun tries to set on your head. Let him have it with the Koopa!

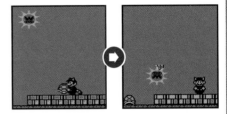

World 2-4

You have a choice of ways to go here, but we definitely recommend the upper path, because it's guarded by fewer enemies and offers a chance at many more coins!

Get the Power-Up in the Floating Block!

Grab a Koopa, get on the ground to the left of the floating Block and let the Koopa go. Now jump for the item!

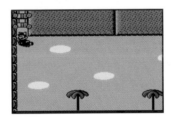

Take Mario to a Higher Ground!

As Raccoon Mario, fly up to the upper-left corner, breaking bricks as you go.

World 2-5

Just like in the original *Super Mario Bros.*, some Blocks have vines inside of them. The vine in this world leads to a path of clouds that takes Mario to a sky pipe and a bonus coin room.

Poor Chain Chomps...

Talk about getting no respect! Because of their chain, these Chain Chomps can't get at Mario—or can they? If you stand there and

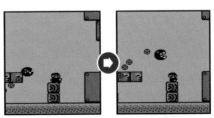

watch one for 160 timer seconds, his chain breaks and he has a chance to get you.

The Case of the Helpful Koopa

A Koopa Troopa can unwittingly help Mario retrieve a Power-Up item by clearing away the Blocks around the Wood Block where it is hidden.

Mario and Beanstalk

Kick a Koopa into one of the small pits shown in these screenshots and it will break the bottom-most Block. What's inside the bottom Block, you ask? A vine, of

course! Climb the vine and follow the clouds to the left to find a Coin Room.

Break just enough Blocks to clear your way to the P-Switch, then activate it and collect!

World 2 Pyramid

Walls seal off portions of the pyramid. You must either use Buzzy Beetles to break these down, or your Raccoon Tail. Since you can reset the "?" Blocks near the entrance door, you should be able to fully Power-Up.

Reset the "?" Blocks

Collect the Power-Up item just ahead of Mario's starting location, then leave the pyramid and come back. It will be there for you to collect again.

Navigating the Pyramid

There are only two sets of Blocks you need to pass in this mini-maze. First, head through the middle path. When you reach the short Pipe, jump up to the platform to the left, follow it until it dead ends, then head right. You

encounter a second set of Blocks. It isn't the toughest maze, but this path will definitely save you some time.

Use a Hidden Block to Enter the Secret Room

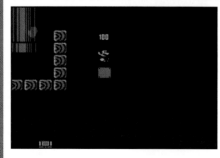

Right after you pass through the second set of Blocks, you'll see a Pipe surrounded by wood Blocks directly above you. To reach it, just step three Blocks to the right of the wooden

Blocks and jump. This reveals a hidden Block, allowing you to reach the Pipe.

Buzzy's on the Ceiling!

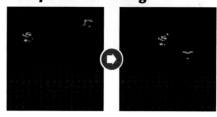

That tricky beetle, Buzzy, has a new tactic to ambush Mario. He falls off the ceiling when you get close. Be ready to jump over him as he spins toward you.

Beyond the Sand Dunes

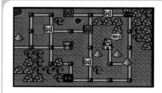

Bring the Hammer!

In a later world, a letter from the Princess informs you that bandits have taken a Whistle beyond the Sand Dunes. Well, to get beyond the sand dunes and bring those bandits to justice, you must get the Hammer from the wandering Hammer Bros. Break the rock in the upper-right corner of the Map Screen to reveal the path.

World 2 Airship

Mean old Morton has turned the King of the Koopahari Desert into a spider. Being one of the older Koopalings, Morton's ship is more advanced than Larry's—and more dangerous! There's a couple of places to use extra caution.

A Single Chance to Power-Up!

The first "?" Block you encounter is also the only one you'll encounter. Don't miss the opportunity to get Mario in fighting form to conquer this Airship and its captain.

Rocky Wrench, Ninja Turtle

He's not a mutant or a teenager, but Rocky is a turtle and he does toss ninja throwing wrenches! He's also a major nuisance in World 8.

Morton Koopa Jr. is a Real Grouch!

"Grrr... Mario, I ain't feelin' too good today. My hair looks terrible and I can't be bothered wit' you. So come over here where I can blast you wit' dis here wand. We'll just see if you can stomp me on the head three times."

World Data Box

			E			
			F			
			G			

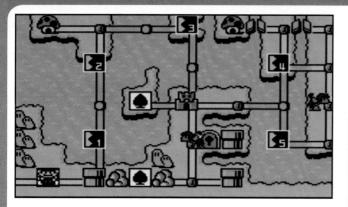

World 3-1

These critters are lean, mean, and hungry! Since water is the primary element in this stage, we recommend the Frog Suit or Fire Flower as the gear of choice.

A Power-Up in the Deep

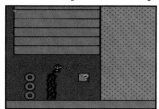

Go straight down at the beginning of the world to find a Power-Up. You should always collect Power-Ups, because they're worth 1,000 points.

Don't Lose Control

A strong current flows out of many of the underwater pipes. Don't let the flow make you lose control, but swim through it as quickly as possible.

Blooper Alert!

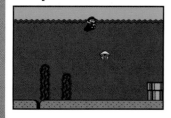

Bloopers are a constant underwater hazard. Swim with care when you see one.

Go Over the Top for a Power-Up

By jumping at the water's surface, you can get on top of the island in these screenshots. Once there, you'll find a Power-Up.

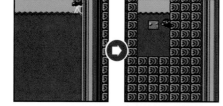

A Tricky 1-Up to Collect

The 1-Up in the "?" Block shown in this screenshot drops into the pit below if you're not careful. A current boost carries you past.

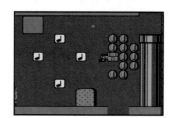

World 3-2

Those pesky flying fish, the Cheep-Cheeps, are back and more bothersome than ever! It's best to use firepower to fry them, but you can also stomp them.

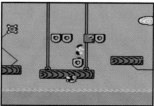

Dropping Donut Lifts

Donut Lifts flicker and fall if you stand on them for a few seconds. Look out below!

Get Three Starmen in a Row

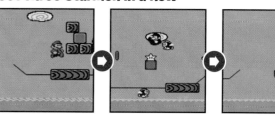

If you get the first Starman and then hit the two indicated "?" Blocks while you're invincible, there will be Starmen inside instead of coins! It's a trick maneuver, but worth the effort for triple invincibility!

A P-Switch Makes a 1-Up Accessible

Hit the P-Switch. While its magic is in effect, it's easy to get the 1-Up in the Invisible Block.

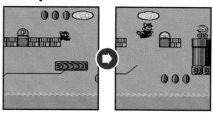

Go Raccoon Mario!

As Raccoon Mario, you can fly up to this area and score a few extra coins!

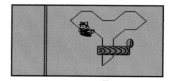

World 3-3

Boss Bass: He's big, he's bad, and he's hungry! We also think you'll dislike him. He can swallow you whole even if you're fully powered-up! Plus, the land in this world rises and sinks, putting you right within his reach!

Use the Koopa to Hit the P-Switch

Once you hit this P-Switch, you can collect some extra coins, and try for the Power-Up in the Note Block. Just keep an eye on Boss Bass!

Another Helpful P-Switch

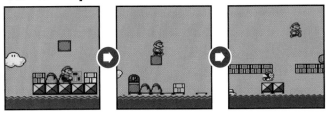

Use an Ice Block to make the P-Switch appear. Activate it and the coins turn into a bridge to the goal. Boogie across the bridge (holding the B Button as you run) and Boss Bass won't be able to catch you.

Not for the Faint at Heart

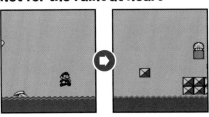

If you're feeling brave, you can go for a hidden 1-Up on the far right side of the stage. But first, get rid of the Boss Bass with a fireball if you can.

World 3 Fortress

The doors in the fortress lead to a flooded "back" stage. Most of the doors just waste your time if you take them, so follow our directions carefully.

Boo Diddly Sandwich!?

Be sure to give both ghosts a look as you wait for the Thwomp to reset, or one of them will get you.

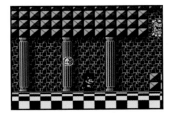

Take This Door to Boom-Boom

If you're in a hurry to get through the Fortress, head through the sixth door (fourth from the last) to get to Boom-Boom's room.

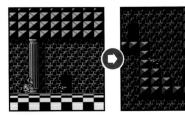

Alternatively, if you head to the third door and enter it while mashing Up on the Control Pad, you have a chance to enter a door suspended above the water in the next room. If you're lucky, you'll end up in Boom-Boom's room.

The Last Door Leads to a Secret Coin Room

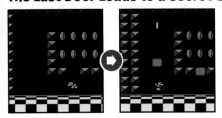

An Invisible Block directly above the door in this room allows you to collect all of the coins here.

Repeated Item Collection

Going back and forth between the main hall and the water hall of this stage resets Power-Up items. That means you can repeatedly collect the Power-Up at the start of the water hall.

Boo Diddly Sandwich!?

Be sure to give both ghosts a look as you wait for the Thwomp to reset, or one of them will get you.

This Boom-Boom Can Fly

You'd better stomp this guy three times as fast as you can; otherwise, he sprouts wings and flies about the room. Then he's really tough to defeat!

World 3-4

Most methods for getting unlimited 1-Ups involve skill and practice. In this world, the technique works automatically.

The Jet Coaster Jump

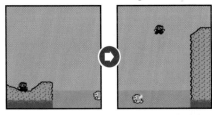

Slide down the hill and wipe out the Goombas. At the last second, jump and you should make it over the pond.

A 1-Up Factory, Courtesy of Lakitu!

Get rid of the two Para-Goombas near the pipe that's hanging from the ceiling. Go right until Lakitu appears, then backtrack left. Capture a Koopa and kick him while standing on the golden Blocks under the hanging pipe. The shell begins to oscillate back and forth, defeating any of the Spinies that Lakitu throws out. Eventually, the Koopa shell begins scoring 1-Ups for you. Easy peasy!

World 3-5

By now, you know that the Frog Suit makes it much easier to swim in the water worlds. Also, certain underwater pipes can be entered only if you're wearing the Frog Suit. The secret rooms you reach usually have valuable things inside, like 1-Ups.

Big Bertha and Her Babies

Big Bertha won't try to eat you, but she does send her baby Cheep-Cheeps after you.

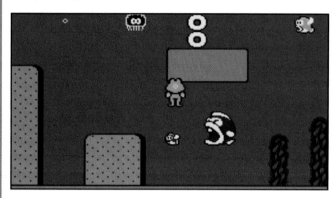

A Frog Suit Exclusive!

You can get into this pipe while wearing the Frog Suit. Hold Right as you enter to reach the giant "?" Block.

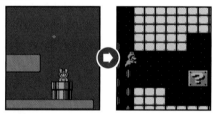

Go Against the Flow for a 1-Up

Swim against the current coming out of the final hanging pipe in the stage to reveal a 1-Up in an Invisible Block.

World 3-6

This is an autoscroller with some precarious platforming. Don't stay on the Donut Lifts for too long!

Don't Just Stand There! Jump!

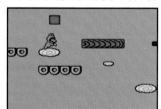

Whenever on Donut Lifts, always jump up as fast as you can. This prevents them from falling and buys you some time while you wait for the screen to move forward.

Use the Koopa to Collect the Coins

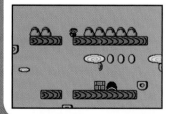

Kick the first Koopa you meet to the right to score 10 coins.

An Icy Situation

Kick one of the Ice Blocks into the first Block on the right to reveal a P-Switch. Hit the P-Block, then jump to grab the first coin on the left above you. This is actually a secret Block containing a 1-Up. Race right and grab it as it falls.

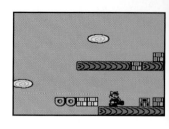

Look Out for the Rotary Lift

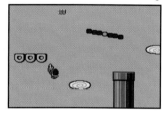

Time your jump to the lift so that you land on the Rotary Lift as it stops spinning. Immediately jump off the Lift and into the pipe to avoid being knocked off of it.

World 3-7

A spacious stage with big, grassy Blocks, this area is the home of a new enemy named Spike.

Meet Spike!

Spike attacks by pulling spiked balls from his gullet and throwing them at you. If you're in his line of sight, he throws them with reckless abandon, so try to stay above him and jump on his head as soon as you get the chance.

Vine Time!

Use the screenshot above to find a hidden vine Block. Climb it and head to the left to grab coins and a P-Switch.

Off to Coin Heaven!

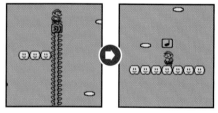

Before you drop back down, stand on the Block on the top of the vine and jump to the right. You should land on another cloud platform. Stand in the middle of the platform and jump to reveal a red Magic Note Block. You can jump off this Block to shoot up to another Coin Heaven.

Bouncing Wood Blocks?!

You can jump against the Wood Blocks at the end of this stage to bounce them into the enemies in front of them; the second Wood Block also contains a Power-Up.

World 3 Fortress

This water-filled Fortress is the home of another new enemy: Stretch—a ghost who hides in white platforms scattered all over the stage. He can't be defeated, so you must sneak by him to make it through this level.

Your Only Power-Up Item

The first "?" Block in this level contains the only Power-Up you have access to here. If you're already Super Mario, the Power-Up will be a Fire Flower, which helps you deal with all the Cheep-Cheeps.

Heeeeeeeeeeeere's Stretch!

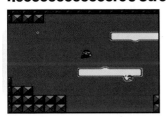

If you're a powered-up Mario, make sure to stay below all of the Stretches scattered throughout the stage. If you're small, however, you're free to take any path you see fit.

Boom-Boom is Flighty

A flying Boom-Boom controls this Fortress and his dwelling has Blocks suspended in mid-air. These can be a bit bothersome, so try to fight him in the center of the room.

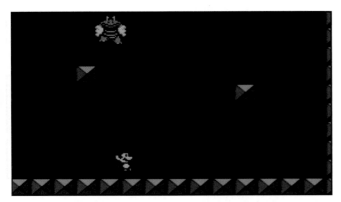

World 3-8

This is one of the toughest stages in the game. Boss Bass is back and the tides go deeper, leaving you with nothing to stand on. Use the vines in this stage and climb to safety!

Life Saving Vines

Hit the first Block you see with a Koopa, an Ice Block, or your Raccoon tail to make a vine grow. Climb to the top and wait for the tide to drop before moving ahead!

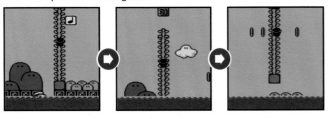

There are three other Blocks concealing vines. Check out our screen shots to find the other two.

All the Help You Can Get!

Use an Ice Block on the Block pictured in this screen shot to reveal a 1-Up. Grab it quickly! You'll need it.

More P-Switch Magic

There's an alcove that dips into the water just before the pipe leading to the end of the level. Look there to find a P-Switch, then hit

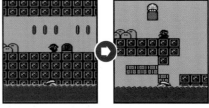

it and race up to the platform above. The top of the tower of coins holds a hidden Block with a 1-Up.

World 3-9

Another chance to gain unlimited lives!

A Regular 1-Up Farm!

At the start of the stage, grab the Koopa hopping around just ahead of you. Race to the right while holding it until you pass the second cannon, then quickly kick the Koopa over the cannon and hop onto the platform above it. Race over and stand directly above the pillar of gold Blocks and wait. The Koopa shell will bounce between two cannons, defeating the Bullet Bills that come out of them. You can just stand there while the Koopa shell racks up all the 1-Ups you could ever need.

How to Make Mario Invisible!

When you kicked the Koopa to do the unlimited lives trick, it actually opened up a path to a pipe that leads to the second half of the level. Stand on the tall, white platform directly in front of the second cannon that you kicked the Koopa over and hold Down to fall into the background of the level. If you head to the right and go down the aforementioned pipe into the second half of the level, Mario becomes invisible! Well, really he'll just be behind the background, but it's still neat!

A Free Frog Suit -- What a Bargain!

Once you're in the underwater second half of the level, swim all the way to the left to find a pipe. Go down the pipe and immediately

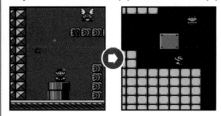

hold Right to land on a platform with a giant "?" Block on it. Punch that Block and a Frog Suit comes out!

Mario's Ocean Adventure!

To completely explore this world, Mario must get a Hammer from a wandering Hammer Brother and use it to open the path to the Canoe. He can then set sail to islands with Mushroom Houses and Bonus Games on them.

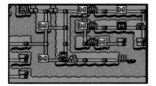 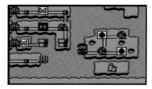

If you sail just past the first bonus island, you'll find a second island with a lone Mushroom House on it.

World 3 Airship

You can jump over some of the walls in this warship, even though the gap you go through is off the top of the screen. This can save you lots of time and effort.

You Can Do It!

Although the automatic scroll of the Airship makes it tough, you can collect this Power-Up if you're quick!

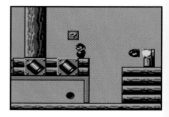

Use Your Momentum

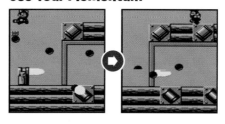

If you jump on top of an enemy or cannon ball and hold the A Button, your momentum will give extra height to your jump.

A Kooky Mode of Transportation

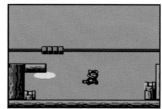

Jump repeatedly on the Bolt Lift and it will take you across the gap. In this case, though, it might be easier to take the low road and just avoid the flame jets.

Through an Unseen Gap!

Hold down the B Button and jump at this wall to reach the other side!

Wendy O. Koopa's Candy Rings Ain't Sweet!

"Hey Mario! Try some of my candy rings, I think you'll be surprised how they taste! (I hope Mario falls for this trick... He doesn't know that these sweets are deadly—yet!)"

World Data Box

ꕤ	ꕥ	ꕦ		E	ꙮ	
ꕧ				F	ꕨ	
ꕩ				G	ꕪ	ꕫ	ꕬ
ꕭ	ꕮ	ꕯ				

White Mushroom House: 4—2:22 coins

Final Thwomp

B Button run and jump over this one: it's easy if you know he's there.

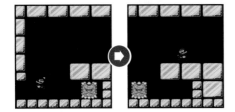

Boom-Boom's Cold

It must be because of the cold, but the Boom-Boom here doesn't jump much. He just stays on the floor and moves back and forth, so you can almost get him by just jumping straight up and down on him. Don't get trapped under the ice ledge in the right corner.

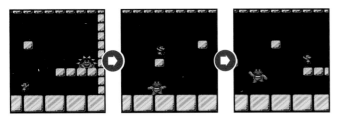

World 6-8

Use a P-Wing here to collect 88 coins and perform a neat trick!

Wipe Out the Walking Piranhas!

Capture the Koopa here and kick him so he goes right. Run after him, holding the B Button, and he'll wipe out the White Piranhas!

Use the Ice Blocks

Use on Ice Block here to knock out all the Walking Piranhas on this little hill.

Oh, Boy! 88 Coins!

Activate the P-Switch and fly up quickly, because these Blocks turn into coins. You can get all of them if you have a P-Wing.

Mole Mario?

There's a tunnel under the entire world that you can fly through with the P-Wing. The entrance is right here! It's not especially useful, but it's a fun trick!

World 6-9

Either the P-Wing or the Frog Suit gives you a bonus in this world.

Only a 1-Up for a P-Wing

Don't use a P-Wing to get a single 1-Up unless you have a ton of them in reserve. This is a shortcut to the end of the stage, though, and that's a bonus!

Small Mario Can Make It

Although it takes perfect timing and not everyone can do it, Small Mario can make it up this wall.

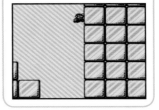

Way to go Frog Mario!

You can enter this pipe only if you're wearing the Frog Suit. Inside, you'll find 35 coins and three 1-Ups.

Exchange Munchers for Money!

The P-Switch in this area turns all the indestructible Munchers into coins! Collect as many as you can!

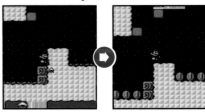

World 6-10

It looks like some of Bowser's Munchers and the treasure they were guarding were frozen in a sudden cold snap. That's just too bad.

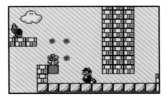

Find the Vine Block

Get rid of Buster Beetle to the right, then hit the Vine Block with an Ice Block. Climb up, hit the P-Switch, and collect the loot!

Don't Slip!

Once you've hit the P-Switch, get on top of the Blocks at the vine's top, and jump into the coins!

Fiery Mario Can Get a Hammer Bros. Suit!

Hit the P-Switch and head right. At this pipe, melt the ice and the Munchers turn into coins. Collect and go down the pipe. There's a Hammer Bros. Suit inside.

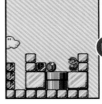

World 6 Fortress 3

The Ice World is well fortified indeed! There are three Fortresses, and this one is the worst! All the enemies here (Roto Discs, Stretch, and Thwomp) are invincible.

Boo Diddly's Back!

To safely jump here, you must draw the ghost close by turning your back on him. Once he's near, jump over him and run!

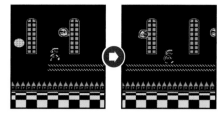

Fly For a 1-Up

Take off running right from the start and you can avoid the Roto Disc and fly to this 1-Up, passing some conveyor belts.

Hold Your Position

Make several small jumps on the conveyor belt to hold you place until it's safe to run under Thwomp.

Jump Over Stretch

As soon as Stretch is all the way to the left, hold down the B Button, jump over him, and run like heck!

It's a Boo Diddly Trap!

The door to Boom-Boom is accessible for only a second as the floor rises and falls. Go right when you hit the floor to hold off the ghosts.

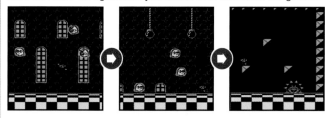

World 6 Airship

Lemmy's Airship has a couple of places where it appears that Bolt Lifts are the only way to go, but in both instances you can make it by holding down the B Button when you jump. This can be tricky.

Ignore the Bolt Lift

You can easily make this jump without using the Bolt Lift.

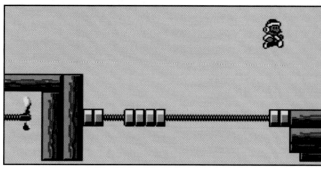

A Daring B Button Dash!

Although it looks like you might not be able to make it without using the Bolt Lifts, this is actually an easy jump to make unassisted.

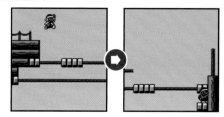

Be Patient

It's wise to stand between the fire jets here. You need to take your time, though. If you just run through, you'll get burned.

Score a Power-Up

If you take the higher path through the ship, this Power-Up is easy to collect. You must act more quickly to get it from the lower route.

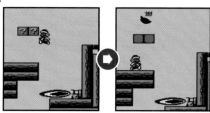

Hurry On Through

Immediately after the flame fires, run and jump through here. It's tough to make it without getting singed.

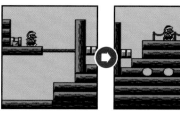

Clown Around With Lemmy

"Welcome to Lemmy's Magical Circus, Mario! Would you like to have some fun with these magical balls? See if you can balance yourself on top of them like I can. Hahaha!"

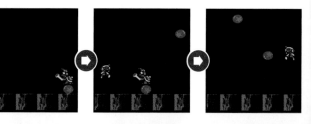

World Data Box

A			
B			
C			

White Mushroom House: 7-2:46 coins

World 7-1

A couple of the stages in Tube City scroll upwards and involve difficult climbs through a maze of pipes.

The Might of Mario's Hammer!

Mario is invulnerable to Piranha Plant fire when he kneels while wearing the Hammer Bros. Suit. Plus, his Hammers can defeat foes like Boo Diddly and Thwomp.

Eager Eaters!

You must get into this pipe quickly, because Piranha stay in its pipe for only a second. You might want to take them out with a tail attack or fire ball first.

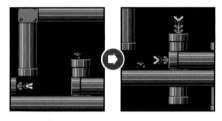

Nab a 1-Up

"Bend" your jump around the three "?" Blocks to get this 1-Up.

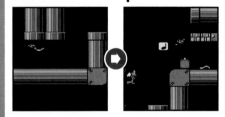

Collect a Power-Up

Stomp the Koopa, pick him up, and get on top of the left "?" Block. Kick him so he goes between the Blocks and he'll hit the Block you're standing on!

Follow That 1-Up

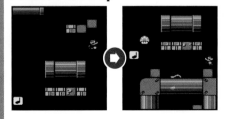

Once you make this 1-Up appear, it will probably fall to the right. Follow it and you should land on a pipe and not lose any height. Continue climbing!

Now Departing to the Coin Room

Kick the Koopa on this pipe so he falls down the narrow gap. You can then use this area as a runway to fly up to the coin room as Raccoon or Tanooki Mario.

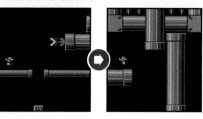

Get a Boost from a Koopa

Jump straight up off the back of this Paratroopa to reveal a 1-Up.

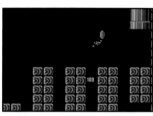

World 7-2

Pipes in this desert join upper and lower areas. Piranha Plants infest the upper; the lower is loaded with Power-Ups and coins! Only Frog Mario can collect more than 46 coins and get a White Mushroom House to appear.

You Need the Frog Suit's Speed

After you hit the P-Switch, you have mere seconds to collect the coins that it created to the right. Only the Frog Suit allows you to swim through the water fast enough to get them all.

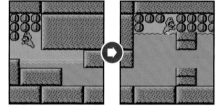

Is This a Trap?

Don't panic when the Note Blocks seal you in here with the Koopa. To get over the gap between the pipes, you must make all of the Note Blocks appear. Once you've done that, leave via the lower area and go across easily. Don't forget the 1-Up.

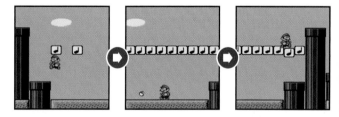

An Underground Power-Up

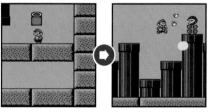

Firepower is probably the best weapon to have in this world. If you want to be Fiery Mario, grab this out-of-the-way item.

World 7-3

You can be invincible through this entire stage if you hurry! As we've seen before, some Blocks have Starmen inside if you hit them while you're invincible; that's the case here.

Get the First Starman!

To start the process, get the first Starman and then use the B Button run to make it to the other "?" Blocks before your invincibility wears off. If you're not invincible when you hit them, they will contain only coins.

Skip the P-Switch

Don't stop for this P-Switch, but focus on staying invincible. If your invincibility wears off now, you'll have to face Lakitu.

Dash Over These Gaps!

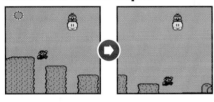

By holding down the B Button as you run, you can make it over all of these pits, even the large one at the end.

World 7-4

You've seen some troubling water stages on this adventure, but this is probably the most difficult one of all. It features an automatic scroll that pushes you through a mine field of Jelectros! Put on a Frog Suit! Quick!

Fly Over the Wall For 2-Up

As Raccoon Mario, you can fly over the wall and collect two 1-Ups. But don't think you've found a shortcut—this is as far as you go. Don't be a chicken—go back and take on the world!

A Squid with Kids

This Blooper attacks you with its babies just as you enter and exit the Jelectro mine field. Don't panic! Just swim precisely.

Boogie On By Big Bertha

It's easiest to make it past Big Bertha when her back is turned.

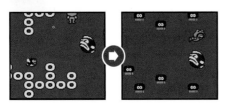

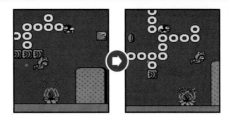

Lava Lotus

Swim past the Lava Lotus as fast as you can, but be watchful for the Cheep-Cheeps in your path.

World 7-5

To get through this maze, you must make invisible Blocks appear and create walkways over gaps that you can't jump over. Some back-tracking is also required.

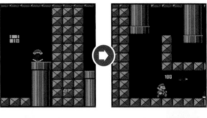

Bring Along Koopa

Clear out the Bob-ombs in this stretch by using a Koopa from the room above.

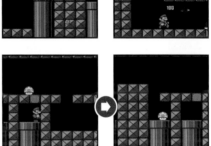

1-Up in Waiting

Make the 1-Up appear so it falls to the left. Go back down the pipe and up the next one to the left. The 1-Up is waiting there for you.

Bob-omb Dead End!

If you go down to the right of this pipe, you'll be trapped there by Invisible Blocks with a Bob-omb coming down the corridor! It's tough to escape without being hit.

Create a Bridge

Make all the Invisible Blocks here appear, then use them as a bridge and proceed to the right.

And Another!

Although you can fly over the other gap as Raccoon Mario, the only way to get through here is to make the bridge appear and backtrack so you can go over it.

World 7 Giant Piranha Plant

The Piranha Plant on the Map Screen represents a mini-world that's infested with different types of Piranhas. Use Starman from your inventory at the start of the stage.

Jump Far, Jump Fast

Cover as much ground as possible with each jump by holding the B Button as you leap. If you leap toward a Muncher when it's out of the pipe, as you land, it should be going back in.

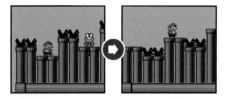

A Valuable P-Wing

You earn a P-Wing for getting through this world. Not bad for a hard minute's work!

World 7 Giant Piranha Plant #2

This Piranha Plant mini-world looks intimidating, but it's actually pretty easy. Try to make it past the first field of Munchers in just one leap.

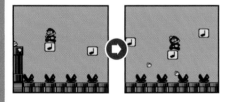

Get Starman If You Can

There's a Starman in the first Block here that makes this area less hazardous. If you miss him, don't panic.

A Big Reward

Besides being able to advance to the Koopaling's Airship, your only reward here is a Power-Up Mushroom.

World 7 Fortress

The only inhabitant of this Fortress is Boom-Boom. The pipe to his room is in the ceiling of the big deserted chamber with the checkerboard floor.

P-Switches Reveal Secret Doors

If you don't dive into the coins when the P-Switch is on, you'll see a door on the platform to the left that leads to a secret room!

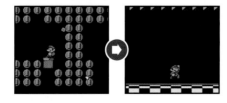

Claim Your Tanooki Suit

Enter this room by going through the door that appears when you hit the P-Switch. Go down the pipe here to find another giant "?" Block, which contains a Tanooki Suit!

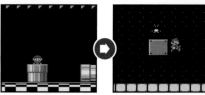

The Ultimate 1-Up Factory!

This room contains a P-Switch inside a mountain of Blocks! Activate it to collect over 100 coins before the magic wears off. Enter the bottom door and immediately press Up again. You'll return to this room with everything back in place. Do it again and again!

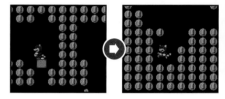

Power-Up to the Max!

You can get the Tanooki Suit as we just explained, or you can repeatedly get the Power-Up in the room with the lava (reset it by entering and leaving the room). The map shows where the pipe to Boom-Boom is. Once you can fly, get up there and take care of him!

World 7-6

You must fully master the use of the Directional Lifts to reach the top of this world. Unlike other vertical worlds, a fall in this one may land you on spikes!

Charging Koopas!

Go left from the start to reach the stairs. When you're about halfway up, a pair of Koopas will charge! You know what to do: Jump over them, or stomp and kick!

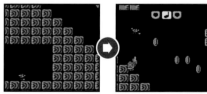

Take a Shortcut

Before you hit your head on the pipe above, jump up and around it. The Directional Lift you were on will continue upwards. You can remount and ride it to the halfway point of the world.

It Will Fall Conveniently

Don't worry if you don't catch this Power-Up right away. It falls down where it can easily be collected.

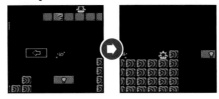

Side Step the Piranha Plant

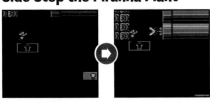

Stand on the edge of the Directional Lift as you go through this Piranha-guarded gap.

World 7-7

Imagine an unbroken field of hundreds of indestructible Munchers, stretching farther than the eye can see. How would you cross such an obstacle? With Starman's help, of course!

Catch Starman at the Last Second

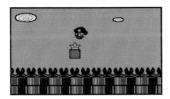

Hit a "?" Block with a Starman in it so Starman goes right. Follow Starman as he bounces along, then grab him just when you think your invincibility is about to wear off!

You'll Need Some Time Here

Hopefully you were able to get that last Starman close to this one, so that there's time to get the Starman here. You can waste precious seconds of invincibility negotiating the overhang!

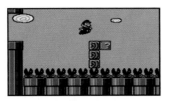

World 7-8

Since this world is overgrown by Piranha Plants and Fire Flowers, Fire Mario is best equipped to handle it. His firepower can easily wilt these wicked weebs!

Time Your Jump Carefully

Make your jump when both plants are fully extended here!

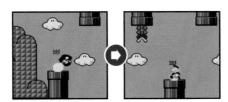

Make a Magic Note Block Appear

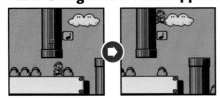

Jump up by the right side of the pipe to reveal a Magic Note Block that takes you to Coin Heaven.

Pardon Me, Ptooie

When the Ptooie moves out of the way, go down the left hand pipe here to find a Hammer Bros. Suit!

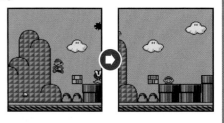

Fiery Walking Piranhas!

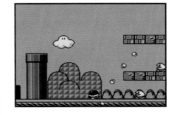

These monstrous, mutant, fire-spitting Piranhas cannot be eliminated by hitting them from underneath. Use firepower or hammers to defeat them. Remember that Hammer Mario is fireproof when he ducks!

World 7-9

Distinguished by its length, you must really watch your timer on this one. Don't go after bonus items unless you have plenty of seconds. Among the items available here are three Fire Flowers and a 1-Up.

Toss These Blocks

You can grab these Ice Blocks and toss them out of the way as you fall. Climb back up and jump off the edge again. This time, enter the passage and collect your bonus.

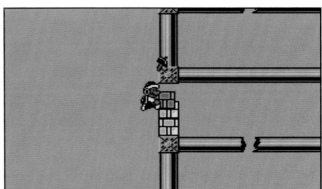

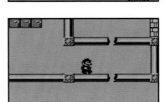

An Invisible 1-Up

Most players miss the 1-Up in the center of these coins. To collect it, duck and jump in the middle, under the space between the coins.

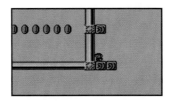

A Fork in the Path

The bottom passage here leads to a 1-Up and some bonus coins. The upper route leads to the end of the level. Don't go for the 1-Up unless you have plenty of time.

Road to Nowhere

Although it might be fun to run around outside the pipe maze, there isn't anything to be found and it just eats up precious seconds on the clock.

World 7 Fortress #2

This Fortress can be a real terror. There are lots of Piranha Plants, Thwomps, Boo Diddlies, and Roto Discs. Precise jumping is essential. Wear a Hammer Brothers Suit if possible.

B Button Run and Jump

From the starting position, begin running while holding the B Button when the Piranha Plant is fully extended. By the time you land on the pipe, it will have already retreated.

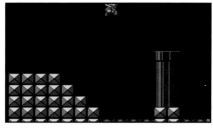

Get Your Friend, Starman

It can be extremely helpful to collect Starman here. Just don't fall in the lava trying to do it, and watch out for Boo Diddly!

Dupe Boo Diddly

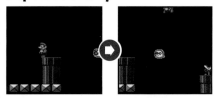

Draw Boo Diddly nearby, facing away from him. When he gets close, jump over him.

Piranha Plant Squeeze Play

To get through this gap, jump when both Piranhas are fully extended. If you delay on the pipe, duck so the upper one won't get you!

Just Run Through

Use the B Button dash to run through here, but don't jump to the next pipe until Thwomp is resetting.

Jump Up and Dive In

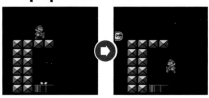

To get to the end pipe, jump up and then curve around the overhang as you fall.

World 7 Airship

Ludwig von Koopa's Airship is the Koopa fleet's flagship. It doesn't have any cannons, but it's loaded with tricky jumps and Bolt Lifts, and manned by Ludwig's scurvy crew of Rocky Wrenches.

The Lower Platforms Are Stable!

Go ahead and jump onto these platforms to get across here, but be wary of the rocket flames.

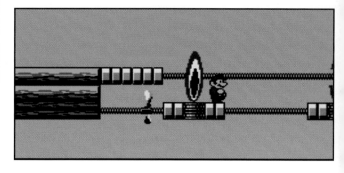

Collect The Power-Up With Ease

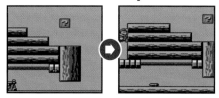

Hit this Bolt Lift from underneath to make it move left, then use it to give yourself a boost up to the Power-Up.

Skip These Nutty Bolt Lifts!

You can make it from platform to platform here without using Bolt Lifts, if you use the B Button jump.

Think About It...

You might want to use the Bolt Lifts here, because it requires perfect timing to get over the gap with a B Button Jump.

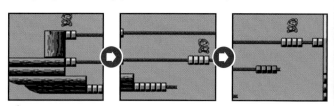

Ludwig Von Koopa: Second-In-Command!

"Vee shall see if you can defeat me, Mario. I combine all the attacks of my younger brothers and sister—I am the ultimate Koopaling! I see you trembling, Mario. Vy don't you just go home?"

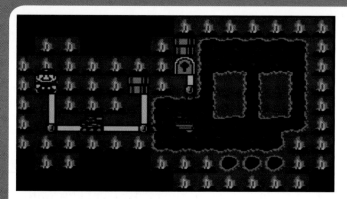

World 8 Big Tanks

Bowser's pulling out all the stops in this last world, and the challenge has never been greater! A parade of Koopa's finest tanks fills the air with flying lead. You must use fancy footwork to evade the hail of bullets!

Bob-omb Lobbers

These stubby cannons fire Bob-ombs as projectiles. Wait until the Bob-omb explodes and then make a dash for it. Always be watchful of cannon fire; some of these are almost like machine guns!

Leap Quickly

Jump when you see the end of the gun's barrel. If you wait too long, Rocky Wrench hurls his Ninja Throwing Wrench and makes it hazardous to leap!

Propeller Peril

You can't destroy these propellers, but you can stand on top of them. You must work fast to get this Power-Up!

Bring Out The Big Guns!

This giant cannon shoots two huge bullets in rapid succession. Either jump on its barrel or duck quickly!

A Wimpy Tank Commander

You'll be surprised to see a lone Boomerang Brother in the command tank. You've made it this far, so don't let him get you. He should be easy compared to the tanks.

World 8 Battleships

A finer trio of battleships has never graced the seas. Like everything else in Bowser's underworld, these ships are armed to the teeth.

Dangerous 1-Up!

To get this 1-Up, stay on the right of the screen and, as soon as you can, run down to it and make it appear. Collect it as you duck in front of the gun barrel.

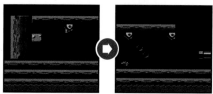

Swim Under The Ships!

It takes practice, but Mario can actually swim under these battleships! The trick is to get just under the boat, but not too far.

Captain Boom-Boom

An old sea dog of Boom-Boom is waiting for you in the battleship's cabin. Send him to Davy Jones' Locker!

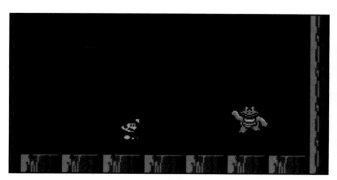

World 8 Hand Traps

This flame-lined bridge leads further into Bowser's underworld! It looks safe to cross, but no sooner do you step onto it than a monstrous hand reaches out to grab you and takes you to a mini-world. If you're lucky, you can make it through without being snatched, but you may want to hesitate on the bridge and get captured on purpose; for each trap, you'll get a Super Leaf if you finish!

Hammer Bros. Hand Trap

You must defeat all the members of the Hammer Bros. family here to make it to the goal. These guys should be a piece of cake by now!

Podoboos Hand Trap

Make it over a broken bridge harassed by Podoboos, and you deserve a Super Leaf! Actually, it's a pretty easy stage if you take your time.

Three-Up Pipe

Charge up your P-Meter at the beginning of the world, and fly to this pipe Raccoon Mario. Inside are three valuable 1-Ups! Charge up again and fly to the end of the stage.

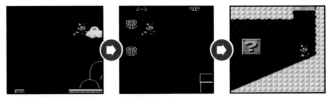

Fish Hand Trap

A swarm of attacking Cheep-Cheeps makes this the most challenging of all the Hand Trap stages; it's also the longest. Use the B Button run to get through, and don't be distracted by the meager coins in the "?" Blocks.

A Hidden Escape Route

Make this Invisible Block appear so you can easily escape this Bullet Bill firing range.

World 8 Airships

These mini-airships are the fighter planes of the Koopa's Air Force. They move faster than the Koopalings' Airships, so the screen scrolls at top speed.

A Mega-Tough Jump

Pick up the Koopa and release him as you hold him over a pipe. Get a running start, make a small jump onto the Magic Note Block, and immediately jump again while pressing Up.

Take Out Rocky

Try to stomp every Rocky Wrench, as this keeps stray wrenches from hitting you at an awkward time.

Stand On The Engine

It's best to stand on the rocket when you're jumping from ship to ship. Concentrate!

World 8-2

This world, like all of Bowser's underworld, is tough. But, there is a secret passage (to beat all secret passages) that takes you through to almost the end of the stage.

Take A Swim In Quicksand?!

Jump into this quicksand pit and go down. Trust us: you'll be okay. Both the pipes you see take you to a spot near the end of the stage.

World 8-1

After all that military hardware Bowser threw at you, you'll be glad to see a normal world. But this stage is extremely tough to complete unless you're Raccoon Mario.

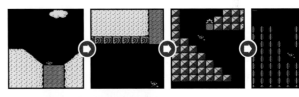

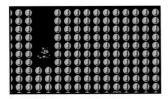

Hit The Switch Block And Dive!

Raccoon Mario can easily fly at the start. Go straight up, hit the P-Switch and go down. Look at all those silver coins!

Double Jeopardy!

When you come out of this pipe from the secret room, you'll be surrounded by Piranha Plant fire. If you jump up as they fire, they aim high and you can run by when they retreat.

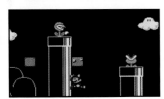

Try To Power-Up

If you're not already powered-up, you'd do well to get an item as soon as possible. This one is difficult to collect.

World 8 Fortress

Wow! If you thought the other Fortresses were tough, wait until you get a load of this one. The pinnacle of Koopa's crafty engineering, this Fortress boggles the mind with its two sides and multiple traps! Explore it thoroughly.

Lava Room: Get Back Up To The Power-Up

If you go through the third door as Small Mario, you may think there's no way you can get to that lone "?" Block. But if you go through the door under the power-up, Invisible Blocks appear and create a bridge. Now just get past Thwomp.

Blue Room: Secret Room 1-Up

If you're desperate for 1-Ups, here's a tricky one to find. Hit the P-Switch and hurry through the door under the "H." There's a secret door on the platform to the right of the conveyor. Go in for a 1-Up!

Lava Room: Repeated Item Collection

You can go in and out of this door and collect the Power-Up item multiple times. Just don't go for it unless the Thwomp is resetting.

Blue Room: Thumb Your Nose At Thwomp!

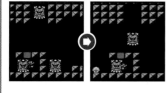

This Thwomp traps you in this area by the door, impeding your access to the "?" Block above. You can inch close enough to hit the "?" Block, revealing a 1-Up, without getting hit by Thwomp. Wait there and the 1-Up will come to you!

Blue Room: Another Secret P-Switch Door

Hit the P-Switch, go left, and enter the door. Next, go down and to the left, then through the door. You'll see three Blocks to the left: the one on the far-left contains a 1-Up!

Lava Room: Collect The 1-Up First!

The gap in this area is sealed by Invisible Blocks if you try to jump

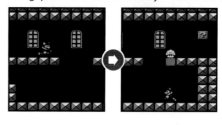

through it. The right-most Invisible Block contains a 1-Up. Be sure to get that one first, so it falls down where you can collect it.

Blue Room: Secret Door To Multiple Power-Ups

Activate this P-Switch and a door appears on the conveyor belt. It leads to a room with a "?" Block that contains a Fire Flower. If you'd rather have a Super Leaf, go through the lower door and head to the left.

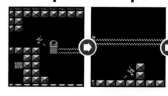

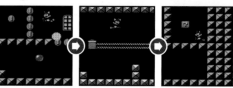

Lava Room: How To Get To Boom-Boom

With all of these secret doors, you might have guessed that the exit is also hidden. Hit this P-Switch and skip the door on the conveyor. The door on the small ledge to the extreme right leads to Boom-Boom. Once you enter, squat under the spikes and take him out!

World 8 Super Tank

A rolling juggernaut of cannons and Bob-ombs manned by six of Bowser's crack Rocky Wrenches is the only thing preventing Mario from entering the Castle of Koopa. The Princess is waiting for you!

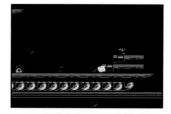

Don't Panic! (Easier Said Than Done)

Things begin flying fast and furious right here, at the front of the Super Tank. Keep cool and hold down the B Button as you jump.

It's Raining Wrenches

Six Rockies wait for you here, throwing wrenches at various heights. Avoid jumping if possible: you might lose control.

Shade To The Right

Although it's not totally safe (no place on the tank is), your best bet is to stay on the right side of the screen. Don't go to the very edge, though.

You're Almost There!

Take it slow now. Don't do anything rash. Just let these cannons fire and then get on their barrels. Next stop: Boom-Boom and then Castle of Koopa!

World 8 The Castle of Koopa

It's been a long and difficult fight, but you've made it to Bowser's creepy looking Castle of Koopa. A long time has passed since Mario and Bowser first met. You've seen how Mario has changed since then. Now find out how time has treated Bowser! Get moving!

Bowser is a vain creature, and the statues he set up in his own image shoot laser beams from their mouths! Run past them or jump over them!

Bowser's Fortress is like a maze—if you take the wrong path, you'll end up back at the beginning! One hint: always opt for the high road.

Stay on this Donut Lift until you see an opening to the right, then jump for it. If you miss the opening, you'll fall into a bottomless pit!

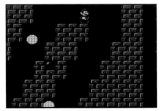

This stairway can be tricky. Crouch on the step near the hub of the Roto-Disc to avoid its whirling attack.

There are precious few Power-Ups in the Castle of Koopa. Be sure to get the 1-Up that's in the hidden block against the right wall at the top of the second set of stairs—you'll need it! Squat and jump on top of the Block the 1-Up was in, and if you're not small, you can go through this wall!

Try to make your way up as high as you can on these Donut Lifts. It will be to your advantage. In any event, be careful: these lifts are the only thing between you and a bath in molten lava!

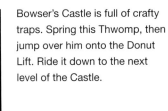

Bowser's Castle is full of crafty traps. Spring this Thwomp, then jump over him onto the Donut Lift. Ride it down to the next level of the Castle.

Are your palms sweaty yet? Not to make you nervous, but those are flames from Bowser's bad breath coming at you. Don't worry, though—you're almost there! Think fast and jump quickly to avoid them!

Congratulations! You've reached the door to Bowser's Chamber! Do you think you're ready? You'd better be, because you're on your own from here! Up and at 'em! The Mushroom Worlds are depending on you!

COUNSELORS' CORNER

Sometimes, as gamers, we find ourselves at the ends of our abilities to complete a game. It's okay, it happens to all of us. That's where the Counselors come in. Masters of all things gaming, the Counselors have compiled a list of tips and tricks for getting through some of the trickiest sections of your favorite NES games.

METROID
How do I defeat Ridley and Kraid?

There are several ways to defeat Ridley and Kraid. A few strategies we've found can be very effective. The Wave Beam is the strongest beam, and it has a wide area of fire. Stand where the shots from Kraid or Ridley don't hit you, and use the Wave Beam. You may be able to shoot from below, but don't stand in the lava for a long time. Another good method is to use the Freeze Beam to stop enemy fire and then shoot your opponent as his shots thaw. Use the beam or the missiles for this. However, the missiles aren't effective unless used at close range. You can also use Bombs while you're very close, but it requires a lot of energy. Choose your method by using whatever weapons you have in your possession.

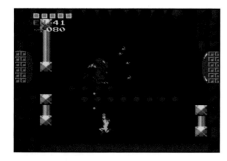

SUPER MARIO BROS. 3
Where are the Warp Whistles?

We got a lot of questions about the Warp Whistles, so we cover them here.

The first Whistle is in World 1-3. Make your way to the first white background block and defeat Koopa. Then, while standing on the block, crouch down for five clicks of the in-game timer. This causes you to fall through the block and land behind the scenery.

Run quickly to the end of the stage. Make it to Toad's House, and he gives you the Whistle.

Find the second Whistle in the World 1 Fortress. This one requires a Raccoon Tail. As soon as you reach the first door in the Fortress, double back and fly through the opening in the ceiling. Find a ledge above the screen, to the right. Run to the right as far as you can and press Up when you reach the end. This causes you to fall into a chamber with a chest that holds the Whistle.

The third and last Whistle is on the Map Screen of World 2. Get the Hammer from a Hammer Bro. and use it on the upper-right rock. This opens a path that eventually leads to the Whistle.

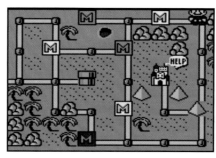

Use a Hammer on the upper-right rock in World 2 to find the path to the Whistle!

Use the Whistles like you use any item on the Map Screen. Press the B Button to open the inventory box, select a Whistle, and press the A Button to activate it. A Whirlwind takes you to the Warp Zone. Using a Whistle in World 1 enables you to warp to World 2, 3, or 4. Use a Whistle in World 2, 3, 4, 5, or 6 to warp to World 5, 6, or 7. Use a Whistle in World 7 or 8, or in the Warp Zone itself, to end up in World 8.

STARTROPICS
How do I get through the Ghost Village?

One of the most challenging sections of this epic adventure is the battle through the tunnel in the Ghost Village of Chapter 3. Here are a few pointers:

Power Up

Fight your way to the first long room in the tunnel and go through the gate to the north to reach a room with Double Small Hearts. Collect the Hearts and climb the stairs to exit the tunnel, then return to the tunnel and collect the Hearts again. Continue to loop around in this manner until you fill all your Hearts. Now you're ready to take on the challenges ahead.

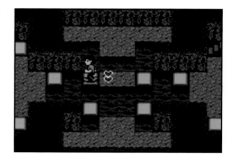

Collect the Double Small Hearts in a room near the entrance, then leave, come back, and collect the Hearts again.

Whack-A-Jelly

After you make your way through the tunnel for a while, you may encounter a dead end. Chances are you've been to a room with a stairway in the northeast corner and a Jelly just south of the stairway, next to the wall. The stairway leads to a tunnel exit, but a secret passage behind the Jelly leads to the rest of the tunnel. Defeat the Jelly and walk through the passage.

Maxie Battle

The giant ghost in this tunnel is all that stands between you and the mechanism that drains the Ghost Village lake. Use a Rod of Sight to make it visible and vulnerable, then pelt it with shots from the Bola. Aim for Maxie and avoid the Minies and fireballs. You should be able to knock it out with some practice.

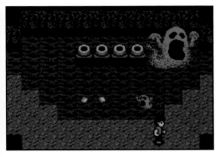

Hit Maxie with shots from the Bola.

How do I enter the tunnel in Captain Bell's Memorial?

Captain Bell was a crafty character. He made sure only those who were in on the secret of his Memorial had access to the Channel Tunnel. When you enter the Memorial, flames block the entrance to the tunnel. These flames can be extinguished, though, if you play the right tune on the gigantic pipe organ in the Memorial. One resident of the island knows the tune.

After talking to the people of the village and Chief Bellcola, you learn that Pete the Parrot is a direct descendant of Captain Bell's parrot. Pete helps you with the puzzle of the Memorial if you give him a gift, and there's nothing Pete likes more than a fresh Worm. Journey to the eastern side of the island and get a Worm from Bait, the young fisherman, then return to Pete with the Worm. He relays to you some words from Captain Bell. They are "Do Me So Far, Do Me." At first, this seems like a nonsense sentence. Notice, though, that every word relates to a musical note. The Pipe Organ in the Memorial has seven Keys corresponding to the scale "Do, Re, Mi, Fa, So, La, and Ti." The clue is telling you to hit the Keys corresponding to "Do, Mi, So, Fa, Do, and Mi," in that order. Play this tune, and the fires vanish!

Pete's hint: Hit the Keys in this order: 1, 3, 5, 4, 1, 3.

How do I reach the geyser in the Hermit's mountain?

Po knows how to reach the Hermit—in the Hermit's mountain, that is. You find a clue in his poem that talks about raindrops. At the heart of the mountain is a room with a pool, but no door leads into the room. You guessed it, there's a secret door! In the room to the right of the geyser is a Looper. Defeat the Looper and walk through the left wall of the room. Once you reach the hidden pool room, jump onto the white water, and it becomes a geyser that jets you upward to the top of the mountain. In a cave above the clouds resides the Hermit with his Scroll containing the magic chant.

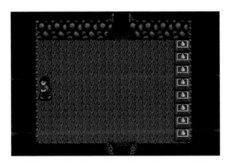

Walk through the wall, even though you don't see a shadow.

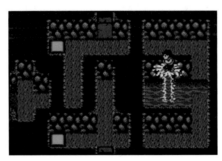

Jump onto the patch of white water. The geyser gushes, carrying you upward!

THE LEGEND OF ZELDA
How do I rig the money-making game?

You'll walk away with a bundle to purchase valuable items if you can outsmart the proprietor of the money-making game. Obtain a Bomb and at least 10 Rupees. Walk on-screen left of the starting point and Bomb the wall to reach the hidden cave. Pause the game by pressing the Start Button on Controller 1; then, on Controller 2, press the A Button and Up on the Control Pad. This Quick End maneuver allows you the option to Save, Continue, or Retry. Save the game and start again, then enter the cave, play the money-making game, and use the Quick End maneuver once more. If you win the money-making game, save your progress. If you lose, retry and use the same 10 Rupees for another chant to win. Earn up to 255 Rupees!

ZELDA II: THE ADVENTURE OF LINK
Where is the hidden town of Kasuto? How do I find the Magic Key?

"The Wizard got all of the people of Old Kasuto together. He said, 'There are too many ghosts here. Go east.' They went east past the three rocks, looked over their shoulders, and saw the ghosts following them. The townspeople were smart. They knew that some ghosts couldn't go through caves. They went north to a cave, and when they went through, they found a sandy beach and a clump of trees. They built a new town amongst the trees to hide from other ghosts that might happen by, and have lived there ever since."

Follow the path of the townspeople of Kasuto, and use the Hammer to chop down trees and reveal the location of the hidden town.

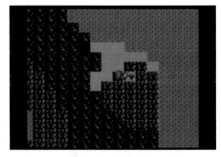

Use the Hammer to clear this area in search of the hidden town.

Once you find the hidden town of Kasuto, you discover within the town the last Magic Container, a new spell, and the Magic Key. If you have seven Magic Containers, you find someone here who gives you an eighth Container. Once you reach this level of magical expertise, you meet someone else who teaches you a spell. The spell, when used somewhere in the town, is the key to finding an item that helps you traverse the remaining palaces.

STARTROPICS

STARTROPICS
A test of island courage!

Developer:
Nintendo IRD

Director:
Genyo Takeda

Designer:
Makoto Wada

Programmer:
Masato Hatekeyama

Composer:
Yoshio Hirai

Original Release Date
December 1, 1990 NES US

A LETTER FROM UNCLE STEVE

"Dear Mike,

I am sorry I did not write you sooner, but I just returned from a long voyage in the islands in search of lost ruins and artifacts. I was very pleased to find your letter upon my return. Boy, time sure is flying by! Last time I saw you, you were just starting school…and now, 15 years old, an honor student, and captain of your high school baseball team!

I think it's a great idea that you visit me during your vacation. I'm sure that you'll enjoy the tropical islands, the blue water, and the friendly people you'll find living under the Southern Cross. You can even take a cruise in my super submarine, Sub-C.

I have enclosed some pictures and a map of C-Island for you. Hope to see you soon, and give my regards to your family.

Sincerely,

Uncle Steve"

A meteor shower over tropical C-Island triggers the disappearance of your uncle, the brilliant archeologist Dr. Jones, from his remote island Laboratory. This letter is all our protagonist, and Dr. Jones's nephew, Mike, has left of his uncle. Now it's up to Mike to locate his missing uncle and solve the mystery of the meteor storm.

CHAPTER 1 PRELUDE

Coralcola is the only village on C-Island. The villagers know a lot about island lore and the creatures that lurk below the surface. Talk to all of them before you begin your search for Dr. J (That's Dr. Jones's name to the locals). You learn important clues about his disappearance.

Coralcolans are friendly, and some of them know about the events that led to Dr. J's disappearance.

Coralcola

The most important resident of the village is Chief Coralcola. He is a good friend of Dr. J's and a wise man. Begin your journey by entering his hut.

Chief Coralcola divulges some important clues about Dr. J's disappearance and provides a valuable item. He sends you on your way.

Master the Yo-yo

A Yo-yo may seem like an unlikely weapon, but the Chief's Star Yo-yo has a long string and a powerful sting. With it, you can lash out at the enemies underground, and it will always come back. Since the Yo-yo slices through obstacles and stretches over gaps, it's easy to defeat creatures from a safe distance.

The keeper of the Star Yo-yo is Chief Coralcola. He gives it to you so that you can face the dangers ahead.

If you haven't talked to all the villagers, the guard blocks the Island Tunnel.

Once all the villagers know you, the guard lets you enter. Many dangers await beyond the tunnel stairs.

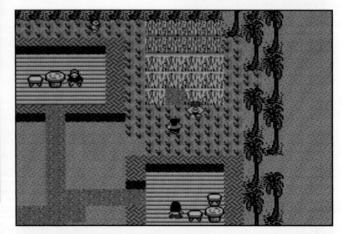

"I'm glad that you could make it to our island, Mike. I am Chief Coralcola. The news of your uncle's disappearance is very disturbing. His assistant says that he was captured by aliens. This may have something to do with recent sightings in the night sky. I'm counting on you to get to the bottom of this and save Dr. J. Take the powerful Star Yo-yo and fight your way through the tunnel to Dr. J's Lab. You'll find help there."

"I am the Shaman of Coralcola and sister of the Chief. I will provide you with support so that you may complete your journey. There are many challenges that await you in the underground tunnels. Recent meteor showers have caused a disturbance in the creatures below. Be careful, Mike."

The Island Tunnel

The only way to get to Dr. J's Laboratory is to pass through the tunnel at the edge of the village. The creatures in this tunnel are weak compared to what lies ahead.

Jellies Are No Problem

Jellies move slowly, so watch their movements and attack while they aren't moving toward you.

Magic Items

Small Hearts
Some enemies leave behind life-replenishing Single Small Hearts after you defeat them.

Stars
Stars appear after you beat some enemies. Collect five to earn a Small Heart.

Potions
Use this powerful medicine to fill your Hearts when your Life Meter is low.

Get the Right Angle

Jellies move left and right. Approach them from below and knock 'em out.

Hit the Switch

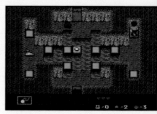

The Gate connects to a hidden Switch. Jump on the Tiles to trigger the Switch, and jump on the Switch to open the Gate. Before jumping to the Gate, beat the Rattus from the other side.

Jump on the upper-right Tile in this room to uncover the Switch that opens the Gate.

Tunnel Traps and Tools

Gate
Gates separate many of the tunnel rooms. Open them by finding a Switch or by defeating the right enemies.

Hidden Hole
Like Gates, Hidden Holes open after a Switch has been hit or enemies have been beaten. They blend into the wall before they're opened.

Tile
Tile-hopping plays a big part in the underground exploration. Some Tiles can be used as safe spots, and some trigger items and Switches.

Footprint
When you hit a Trigger Tile, a Footprint appears. It's important to know when you trigger something out of sight.

Switch
Once you uncover a Switch by hitting the right Tile, use it to open a Gate, Hidden Hole, or Treasure Chest.

Treasure Chest
Treasure Chest often contain special items. Find and trigger the correct Tiles to open them.

Work Around

Walk to the right in this Rattus-filled room, then Tile-hop to the left.

Straight Up

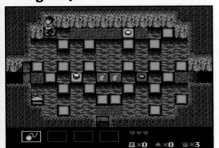

The rooms to the left and right are dead ends. Hit Tiles until you uncover a Hidden Hole on the north end of the room.

No Key Needed

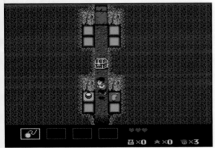

The only way to move to the top half of this room is to open the Treasure Chest that blocks the way. Hit the Tiles to trigger the Treasure.

Open the Treasure Chest, collect the Fire inside, and move on!

Special Weapon: Fire

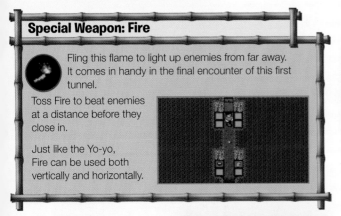

Fling this flame to light up enemies from far away. It comes in handy in the final encounter of this first tunnel.

Toss Fire to beat enemies at a distance before they close in.

Just like the Yo-yo, Fire can be used both vertically and horizontally.

Stop Motion Attack

Noctos move quickly and unpredictably. Take cover as they fly across the room, then hit them when they stop momentarily.

Wait until the Noctos stop, then give them a piece of your Yo-yo.

Enemies

Jelly
The slowest of the tuneel dwellers is no match for the fast Star Yo-yo. Take them out before they have a chance to catch you off guard.

Looper
As soon as these snake-like creatures see you, they charge. Get ready!

Nocto
The winged Noctos stop to rest after flying. That's your time to strike.

Rattus
These fast movers change directions quickly. Stand back and let them come toward you, then let 'em have it before they scurry away.

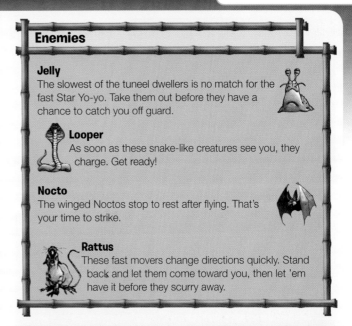

Surprise Attack

A Jelly makes a beeline for you as soon as you enter the room. Plan for an attack, and swing the Yo-yo out to the right as soon as you enter the room.

The Tile on the left opens the Hidden Hole on the right.

Potion Power

Hidden Holes lead to Potions, which refill your health when things are looking grim. Just don't enter the third Hidden Hole, as it holds certain doom.

Mixed Company

Exit the Hidden Hole Potion rooms, then unlock the Hidden Hole at the northern part of the double-wide room. Both Noctos and Loopers lurk in this next room. Beat the Noctos without crossing the Loopers' trail.

Take on the C-Serpent

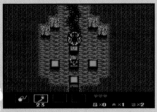

Send out Fire as soon as the C-Serpent opens its mouth.

Jump to the side to avoid the fireballs.

The huge C-Serpent blocks the exit of the Island Tunnel. Save the Fire for your encounter with this creature. When the C-Serpent opens its mouth, hit it with Fire, then jump out of the way of its fire counterattacks. Jump back in front of the scaley beast and repeat this method to defeat it. The C-Serpent picks up its attack speed, so be ready!

Find Help in the Laboratory!

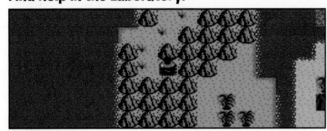

You've cleared the Island Tunnel! Points totaled depend on your performance.

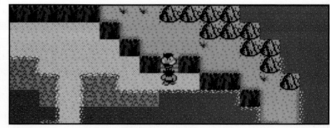

Baboo is just outside the Lab. Talk to him before you enter.

Now that you've made it through the Island Tunnel, find Dr. J's Laboratory and meet his assistant, Baboo. He tells you what he knows about recent events in the night sky and their connection to Dr. J's disappearance.

Dr. J's Laboratory

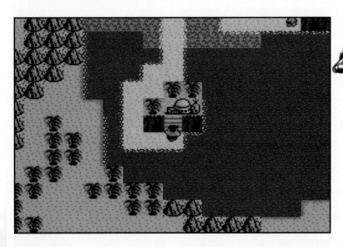

"Nav-Com here, reporting for duty. As soon as you enter the access codes you got from Baboo, I will be able to activate the Sub-C's auto-detection and submergible systems. I recommend an easterly direction to begin."

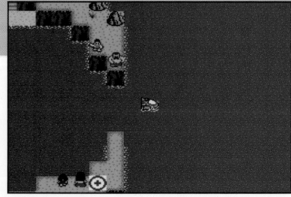

Dr. J's Laboratory is equipped with all the latest in tropical archeological gear, including the amazing Sub-C. This super cool mini-sub cruises quickly and has the capacity for other useful features, if you can find the access codes. The Sub-C's onboard robot, Nav-Com, helps you get where you're going.

Set sail in the high-tech Sub-C on your adventure to find Dr. J.

CHAPTER 2 — DOLPHINS

A mother dolphin approaches. She seeks your help.

The young dolphin has been captured by Octo the Huge. You'll find Octo to the east.

On the open sea, you find a distressed dolphin whose cub has been captured by the tentacle terror, Octo the Huge. If you save the young dolphin, the mother assists you in your journey.

> "Qui! Quy! Please! You're my only hope. Octo the Huge has captured my cub. You've got to find him before it's too late!"

Lighthouse Island

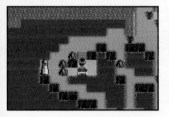

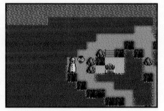

The maze-like Lighthouse Island has hidden passages both above land and below. Explore carefully to find a way to Octo's underground lair. Talk to the residents for clues.

Lighthouse

Talk to the Lighthouse Keeper for clues about island exploring.

The Lighthouse Keeper knows a lot about the island, but he's not very talkative. When you speak to him twice, he rewards your persistence by telling you an island secret.

Walk Through Weak Walls

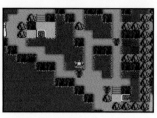

Look for bubbles while searching for underwater passages.

Push against land barriers to see if you can go through.

A good explorer tries everything. If you push up against barriers, you might discovers a way to get to remote areas of the island.

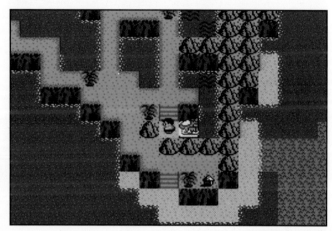

There are hidden passages in the island waters. Test the walls by hitting them with the Sub-C.

The Lighthouse Keeper's House

The Lighthouse Keeper's wife tells you about a bottle she saw on the east beach. This could be a clue.

Find the wife of the Lighthouse Keeper in their home near the south beach. Talk to her for clues about a hidden passage on land.

Message in a Bottle

Get the Submersible System access code from a bottle on the beach.

After you talk to the Lighthouse Keeper's wife and find a passage to the east beach, recover a bottle with a message from Dr. J. The message includes a code for the Sub-C.

 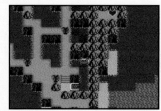

The Sub-C's Submersible System allows you to dive in one place and end up somewhere else. Use the dark areas in the water as indicators for where you can dive.

Passage to a Big Heart

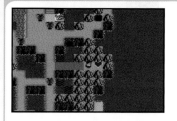

One of the mountains is not as solid as it looks. Somewhere nearby lies a secret passageway to a Big Heart!

Collect the Big Heart and add to your Energy Meter.

Octo's Lair

Mud-O-Fish, Spinistars, and other slimy creatures occupy Octo's hole. Blaze a trail with the Yo-yo and burn those creeps with a blast of power. The fight really begins here. Stay on your toes.

Mud-O-Fish Fillet

About halfway across this narrow lane, a Mud-O-Fish crawls onto the surface. Hit it with two quick Yo-yo lashes.

Tunnel Trap: Up/Down Tile

A few tricky Tiles move in and out of the water. Avoid getting dunked by hitting those Tiles only when they're dry. As soon as you see them emerge, jump and jump again.

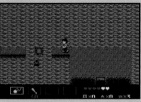
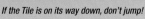

If the Tile is on its way down, don't jump!

Special Weapon: Baseball Bat

You find a new weapon in this room—a Baseball Bat. Swing away with this sensational enemy-swatting weapon. It's slow but strong.

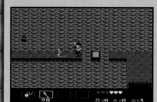

The circular swing of the Bat is effective against enemies that move diagonally.

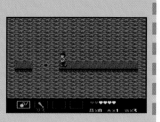

Knock out the Noctos

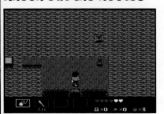

Use the Yo-yo or Bat to beat the Noctos.

Several Noctos attack at once here. Wait until they stop moving before you fight or use the Bat. It may pay off to save your swings.

Look Before You Leap

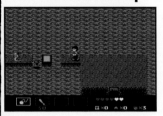

Wait for the Looper to retreat, jump when the Tile is up, and get ready to fight the Looper when you land.

If you jump as soon as you reach this area, a charging Looper on the other side may take you by surprise. Wait until the Looper starts to slither away before you move.

Dual Mud-O-Fish Attack

While you fight one Mud-O-Fish, a second emerges from the other side. Work quickly and watch out.

Pinch Hit

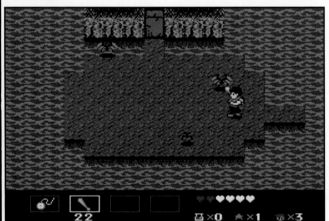

Use the Bat to hit the bats, but go easy and save your swings.

Knock some sense into the Noctos with a few well-placed swings.

Swing and Connect

It's hard to line up the Yo-yo with the Spinistar. Use the Bat to wipe it out.

Hit the Print and Back Up

Wait for the Up/Down Tile to emerge, and plan your jump so that the next Tile is clear of Octots.

Back up to reach the Switch and eliminate the Gate.

Advance toward the Gate and eliminate the Octots if they get too close. When you hit the Tile in the middle, a Footprint appears with no visible Switch. Move back to the right to find the Switch. Hit it and move on.

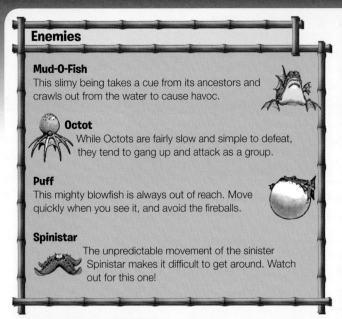

Enemies

Mud-O-Fish
This slimy being takes a cue from its ancestors and crawls out from the water to cause havoc.

Octot
While Octots are fairly slow and simple to defeat, they tend to gang up and attack as a group.

Puff
This mighty blowfish is always out of reach. Move quickly when you see it, and avoid the fireballs.

Spinistar
The unpredictable movement of the sinister Spinistar makes it difficult to get around. Watch out for this one!

Study Your Surroundings

Collect the items and jump on the Tiles to reveal a Footprint.

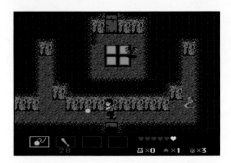

The Footprint in the left area triggers the Switch in this right area.

Make it to the Gate by moving all the way to the left side and entering a secret passage that leads to the right. Find the entrance to the passage by looking on the ground for shadows.

Deal with a pesky Looper to reach the Tiles. The only way to get the Looper to slither out of its hiding place is to cross its path. Step in, then step back and slay it with the Yo-yo when it approaches.

Single-Swing Strikeout

Before you enter this next room, equip yourself with the Bat. Now run in and head straight for the center of the Spinistars. Before they move in on you, swing and defeat them all with one quick roundhouse sweep.

Hop to Safety

 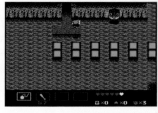

Puff's shots are low. Jump to avoid them.   *Clear the area of Octots to open the Gate.*

This long stretch is prime Puff territory. There's no way to beat Puff. Hop to the end quickly and jump over Puff's powerful fireballs. Defeat the Octots to open the Gate.

Trouble Free Power-Up

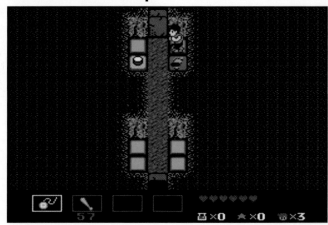

The Double Small Hearts in this room are yours for the taking. Hit Tiles to open the Gate.

Lucky Pick

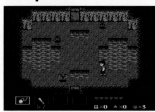 

Defeat the right enemy to clear the way.

Sometimes you have to defeat all the enemies in a room to open a Gate or Hidden Hole. Occasionally, though, you have to beat only one key creature to move on.

Magic Items

Double Small Hearts
While Single Small Hearts sometimes appear after you defeat enemies, groups of two are intentionally scattered throughout tunnels to add to your Energy Meter. Perhaps Dr. J left them behind for Mike to find?

Snowman Doll
The only place to find the mysterious Snowman Doll is on Octo's Lair. Use its magic to temporarily freeze your enemies. It's particularly useful for keeping Octo in place.

This next room contains a couple of Loopers and Noctos. One of the Loopers charges you as soon as you enter. Defeat it to trigger the Gate on the south side of the room. Beat it and move!

Clear the way by hitting the charging Looper.

Take the Potion and hit the Tile to find the exit on the right. This takes you back to the beginning of the circle, so hit the Switch and get moving. The dolphin cub is waiting for you!

Circle Left
Before you enter the secret passage on the right wall, go around this circle of rooms to get a Potion.

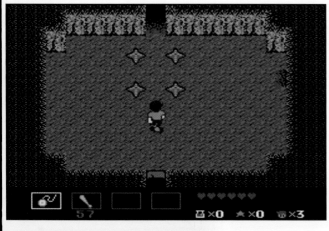

This next room is empty. Move on to the left.

Get the Treasure

After heading through the hidden passage on the right side of the room filled with Spinistars, hit all the Tiles to open the Gate and get the useful Snowman Doll.

Close Quarters

Eliminate the Octots and avoid the fierce fire of Puff. There's not much room to move, so think fast.

Conserve your energy. The big battle is still to come.

The Dolphin!

The captive dolphin cub is here. Defeat Octo and free him.

Shake Hands with Octo the Huge

The incredible eight-legged terror, Octo the Huge, has taken a cue from his squid relatives by arming himself with rapid-fire Ink Pellets. Most of the time, Octo is safely out of Yo-yo range. Occasionally, though, he swims in for a closer look. Jump over the Ink Pellets, but don't stray too far to the left or right. When Octo swims in, freeze him with the Snowman   Doll and pelt him until he thaws.

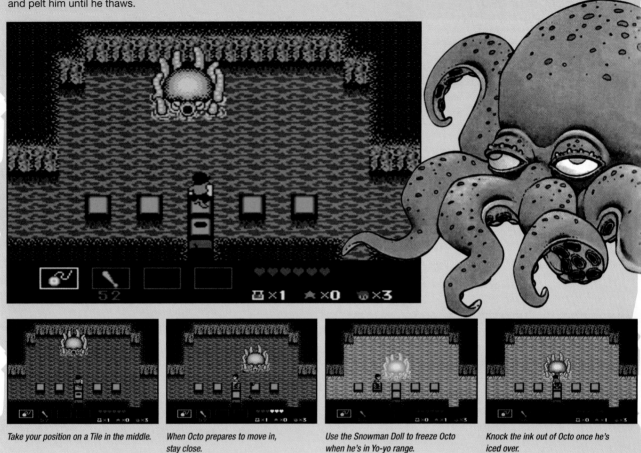

Take your position on a Tile in the middle.

When Octo prepares to move in, stay close.

Use the Snowman Doll to freeze Octo when he's in Yo-yo range.

Knock the ink out of Octo once he's iced over.

The Dolphin's Been Saved!

Now that the terrible menace, Octo, has been put to rest, the young dolphin joins his mother, and you continue on your journey to save Dr. J. In appreciation for your courage, the mother dolphin guides you around the reefs of Lighthouse Island.

The dolphins lead the way through the reef.

CHAPTER 3   STORM AND CALM

The dangers of Coralcola and Lighthouse Island are behind you. Now, even more difficult challenges lie ahead. A violent storm tosses the Sub-C into a coral reef. You're landlocked until you find a way to repair it and sail on to continue your search for Dr. J.

Coconut Cure

In the hut closest to shore, you find an old man who offers you a tast of life-saving Coconut Milk and points you in the direction of Miracola.

The Tunnel of Miracola

A short but dangerous tunnel lies between you and the village of Miracola. Fight your way through, and you may find someone at the Sub-C.

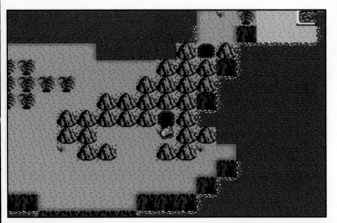

Wrong Way Out

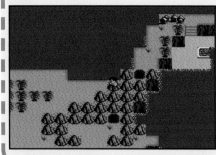

If you take the wrong exit from the tunnel, you end up on the wrong side of the hills. Go back to the tunnel entrance and start from the beginning. Take the other path to arrive in Miracola.

Enemies

Dodo
The small but strong birds of this island chain are slovers. Knock them with the Yo-yo before they have a chance to get close.

Ninja Monkey
The athletic Ninja Monkeys can surprise you with their quick moves. Keep on your toes when you see these characters, and seek out a safe spot.

Bonehead
As you may guess, Boneheads aren't known for their brains. They charge when you cross their path. Be prepared for a fight.

Treasure Trip

The Treasure Chest in the center of the room may seem out of reach, but you can reach it with a little finesse. Hit one of the corner Tiles, and a Trigger Tile appears in the water. Hop onto the Trigger Tile and jump to the center. The Treasure Chest opens to reveal a Bola. Use it to knock out the Dodos and keep moving.

Special Weapon: Bola

The Bola is a swift weapon that can be thrown a great distance. Find a safe spot with a clear shot at the enemy, then fire.

Toss the Bola across the water at unsuspecting enemies. Aim carefully—you only have a few shots.

Clear the Way

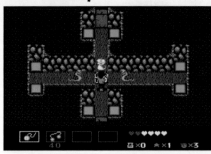

The Loopers in this room can't slither past the Treasure Chest in the room's center. Before you think about opening it, take out the top Looper with a few shots from the Bola, then Tile-hop to open the Chest and run straight up as the other Loopers head away from the center of the room. Open the exit by hitting the Tiles near the top of the room.

Ya Gotta Have Hearts

Hit the correct Tiles in this room, and a set of Double Small Hearts appear in the center. Study the movement of the Up/Down Tile where the Hearts rest, and jump quickly as the Tile is on its way up. After you grab the Hearts, hop off the Tile before you take a plunge.

Don't Move!

When you enter this room, stop and stand near the Gate. The Boneheads don't approach, and a few swift shots from the Yo-yo fend off the Dodos. Once the Dodos are gone, deal with the Boneheads. Stay on the other side of the water from these odd birds and reach them with the Bola or Yo-yo.

Choose Wisely

There are two exits from this tunnel. One leads to the village, and the other leads back to the shore. If you choose the wrong exit, you have to start the entire tunnel over from the beginning. The correct path is the northern passage. Jump on the Tile closest to the eastern door to light the room. Now jump on the Tile just above that to reveal the Switch to open the door.

Miracola

Miracola is a mysterious village. Its inhabitants are not very friendly to outsiders right now—not since the village Chief's daughter fell under a 100-day sleep. Unless you can find a way to help the Chief's daughter, the Miracolans won't help Mike.

After you visit the Chief, visit her by finding a hidden entrance in the north side of the Chief's hut.

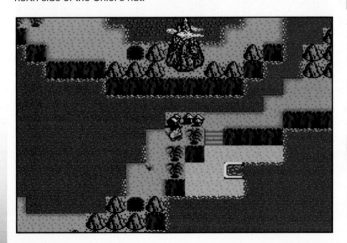

Answer the villager's question, keeping in mind that you are in Miracola, and the guard in front of the Chief's hut allows you to enter.

Bananette has been asleep for 100 days. Journey to the other side of the island and seek a cure for this strange malady.

"Welcome to Miracola, Mike. We Miracolans are very handy when it comes to repairing sea vessels. Before we can help repair your Sub-C, though, please find a cure for my daughter, Bananette. She has fallen asleep and will not wake without a spell from the Hermit on the mountain."

Magma's Molten Tunnel

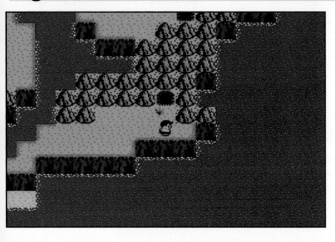

To help the Chief's daughter, you must travel through the deadly Magma's Molten Tunnel. Things get tricky from here on out.

Looper Leap

A set of six Loopers wait here to cut Mike off at the pass. Head straight up the center and jump up as each pair of Loopers charges, then move up before they can charge again.

Beat the Boneheads

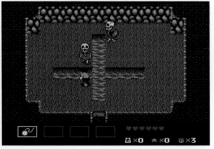

Use the water here to your advantage by hitting the Boneheads from the other side. When they jump over, run away and repeat the process.

Dark Room

The lights are out, but somebody's home. Watch the Loopers' movements to determine where the land ends and the water begins, then blast 'em with your Yo-yo and move on unharmed.

Heart Hideaway

On the west side of this long, dark room, there's an opening to the south that you may miss if you don't look carefully. Hop to the hidden chamber and collect the valuable items it holds. You need all the help you can get in this treacherous tunnel. There's still another floor to go, and a meet with the fiery fiend, Magma the Fierce. Save the Potion for when you encounter this horrific hothead.

Triple Play

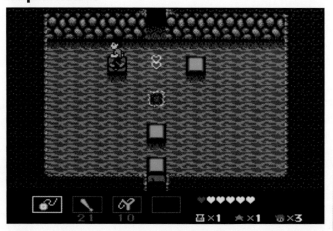

Three pesky Gadflies hang out in this room. Knock them for a loop with the Bat before they attack, then hit the Tiles on the bottom of the room to open the Gate at the top.

Helpful Hearts

If you need to fill up your Life Meter, hit the Tiles on the sides and collect the Double Small Hearts that appear on the Up/Down Tiles.

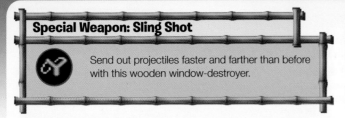
Freeze the Flies

There's a Stop/Slow on the lower row of Tiles. Trigger it to the left and collect it to the right, then clean the clocks of the frozen Gadflies.

Hit and Hop

Mad Muddy attacks when you get to the Trigger Tile on the side. Whack Muddy with your Yo-yo and hop straight up to avoid the mudballs he sends your way, then hop to the left and open the Gate before Muddy returns.

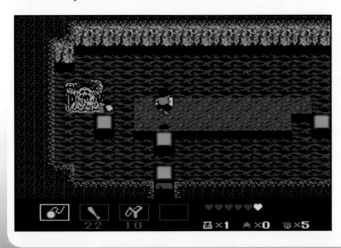

Don't Dive

Brave the attacks of Mad Muddy and the Gadflies in this room. If you need Hearts, go around to the left first, but stop before you hit the mud. From there, work around the right side and hop to the exit.

Magma the Fierce

The molten mass of this fiery fiend absorbs shots from your weapons without taking damage. The only way to extinguish his flame is to stick him into the muck.

Jump to find the Trigger Tiles that break Magma's link with the surface.

Find one Switch to the left and another to the right side of Magma's perch.

No Admittance

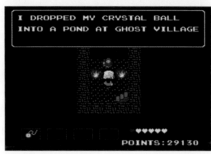

The warriors of Shecola know the secret of getting to the west side of the island where the Hermit lives. Only women are allowed to enter the castle to speak to the warriors. Find a way to trick them into letting you in.

Queen Shecola admits only women into the castle. Search the grounds to find a solution to this dilemma.

A Fortune Teller lives in a chamber on the side of the castle. She helps you enter if you find her Crystal Ball in the Ghost Village.

Ghost Village and the Ghost Tunnel

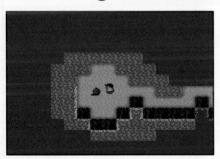

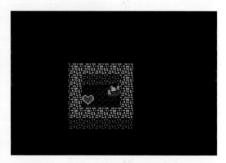

On your way to the Ghost Village, find a Big Heart in a hidden underground passage. The extra energy is invaluable in the coming fight.

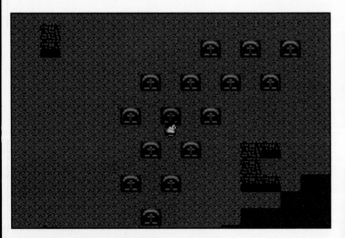

The entrance to the Ghost Tunnel is not immediately visible. Find it by walking into the headstones around the Ghost Village. Once you find the right headstone, note that it is a slightly different color from the others. Crawl down below and get ready for a challenging battle.

Bonedog Bonanza

The Bonedogs won't know what hit them if you play it safe and knock them with the Yo-yo from one of the Tiles in the water. It may take a little longer to get them this way, but it saves Hearts.

Heart Haven

After you collect these Hearts, you're forced to exit the tunnel and start from the beginning. Keep collecting them until your Life Meter is full, then move on.

Jump Quick

As soon as you enter this room, jump over the small section of water to avoid being hit by an invisible enemy.

See the Sights

When you get into this room, use the Rod of Sight to see a band of Minies flying back and forth. Blast them with a few hits from the Yo-yo so you don't have to avoid them when you hit the Tile and double back to the Switch.

Another Set of Hearts, Another Exit

Don't head through the south exit of this room unless you want a set of Double Hearts and are willing to start the dungeon over again. Going into this room forces you back out into the Ghost Village.

The Rod of Sight Sees All!

Use the Rods of Sight here as well to unveil hidden Minies. Defeating all the Minies unlocks a passage in the east side of the room. Find a set of Double Hearts in this east passage.

Slug It

Don't climb the stairs unless you want to exit the tunnel. Instead, take out the Slime and crawl through the passage where the Slime was. This one is easy to miss.

Rods of Sight? All right!

Use the Rods of Sight in this room to uncover more Minies. Defeating all of them unlocks a passage to the south that helps you

avoid unnecessary damage if you decide to go for the Double Hearts. What's inside the south passage? Two sets of Double Hearts! Not bad, huh?

Watch for Fire

The blasts of the Mini-Volcano in this room are few and far between. You should be able to avoid them easily as you open the Gate.

Magic Items

Rod of Sight
The extremely useful Rod of Sight makes ghosts visible and vulnerable with a flashbulb-like burst of light.

Lantern
For a few valuable seconds, the Lantern allows you to make your way around a normally dark room. Use it sparingly.

Take the Low Road

Before you ultimately go through the wall on the right side of this dark room, explore the area you can reach by hopping through the Hidden Hole at the bottom of the room.

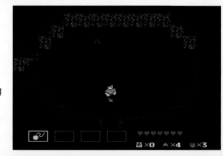

More Minies!

Use the Rods of Sight in this room to reveal more Minies. Defeat them to open a passage on the east side of the room. Hit the Tile on the bottom-left side of the room to uncover a Lantern—you want that for the upcoming rooms.

Light It Up

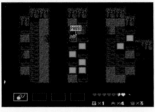 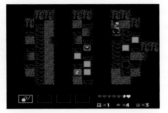

This series of three small rooms is dark when you enter, and unless you have a Lantern, they are difficult to clear. Use a Lantern and pause the game to keep the room lit while you plan your strategy. Once you feel confident in your ability to clear the room, resume the game and time the Up/Down Tiles so that you stay afloat.

Out of Reach

As soon as Mr. Armstrong breaks out of the ground, jump to an area above or below him and approach him from the side. This allows you to defeat him without getting pelted.

Get out of Here!

When you enter this room, go straight up and avoid any contact with the Muumus and Mini-Volcanoes. Water appears to surround you, but there is dry land ahead.

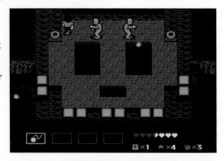

Dead End

The room to the right of the skull room is a dead end. All that results from entering this room is a possible loss of valuable energy. Quick! Get out!

Safe Spot

In order to avoid any unnecessary damage, jump to safety on one of the side Tiles and wait for the Muumus to get within Yo-yo distance. Or find the hidden Stop/Slow and get them while they're frozen.

Fight for Sight

 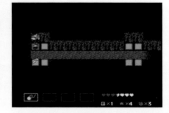

If you are low on Rods of Sight, take this short detour and fight off Mr. Armstrong. Hit the Tiles after Mr. Armstrong bites the dust to grab a Rod.

Enemies

Bonedog
These curious canines may seem incomplete, by they still take a bite out of you if you get too close.

Skull
Even though they are bodiless, Skulls have no trouble hopping around and making your life difficult.

Minie
Unless you have the Rod of Sight to uncover these ghosts, they float around unseen and unharmed.

Muumu
It takes a lot of Yo-yo power to persuade these mixed-up mummies to go back to where they came from.

Mr. Armstrong
The long limbs of Mr. Armstrong come up from the ground when you least expect it and toss handfuls of rocks.

Dimhag
Bearing more than a casual resemblance to Wizzrobes from *The Legend of Zelda*, Dimhags emit strong magical bursts.

Bounce Back

Dimhag alert! Wait for these merciless magicians to conjure up a blast, then turn their magic against them with a Magic Mirror. The Mirror only lasts a moment. Time it right.

Special Weapon: Magic Mirror

Reverse the magic blasts of the Dimhags by shielding yourself with the Magic Mirror.

Minie Haunt

A Minie waits in one corner of this room. You could easily pass it by. Use a Rod of Sight and defeat the Minie for a pleasant surprise.

Maxie Attack!

It's not apparent that Maxie is in the room until you use a Rod of Sight to reveal this enormous ghostly entity. As soon as you see it, avoid the Minies and aim for it with a round of Bolas. Use the Bolas sparingly, though. You have only a few of them, and the Bola is the only weapon that reaches Maxie.

Unless you use a Rod of Sight to reveal Maxie and the Minies circling around, you'll be hopelessly attacked by an invisible enemy

Don't waste your Bolas on Minies. Avoid these pests and aim for the big ghost.

Smash Maxie with the fiery Bola and step quickly to avoid the Minies and blasts from the Mini-Volcano. The only weapon that reaches Maxie is the Bola. Aim carefully.

When Maxie is damaged, it quickens its pace and becomes a more difficult target. Don't be hasty, or you risk wasting shots.

Drain the Lake!

Once you reach the lake stopper, hit the head Tile three times to make water pour from the skull. The Ghost Village lake drains, and you easily recover the Fortune Teller's Crystal Ball from the lake bed. Good job!

Shecola

Using the Fortune Teller's magic lets you enter Shecola and find out the secret of the West Tunnel.

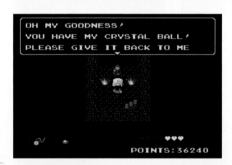

Return to the Fortune Teller with the Crystal Ball. She'll help you.

"Welcome, Warrior! Let me replace that outdated Yo-yo with something much more powerful!"

Talk to all the Shecolans. The warriors give you clues about the journey ahead, and the queen grants you a new weapon. You're then tasked with finding a Hermit who holds the key to waking Bananette, the Miracolan Chief's daughter.

The West Tunnel

This is a short tunnel, so there isn't too much to worry about here. Use the hint from the Shecolans to create a bridge across this gap. This allows you to move on and face a short battle to the other side of the island. Keep searching for the Hermit.

 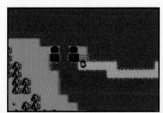

The Hermit's Mountain

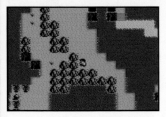 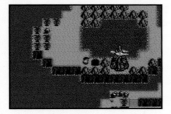

Finally! You make it to the side of the island where the Mountain Hermit lives. Now, of course, you face the chore of getting to the top of the mountain. Fight on, and find out what challenges lie ahead.

Po Knows the Mountain

The eccentric poet, Po, has been up to see the Mountain Hermit on many occasions. In his poem, you find a clue on getting to the top.

Talk to Po for a clue on scaling the Mountain. He knows exactly what will push you to the top.

Phantom Tiles

Some Tiles appear only if you faithfully leap out into the water. At the last second, the Tiles rise from below and save you from a mishap.

Boneheads from Abroad

A couple of straggling Boneheads have made it to the west side of the island. Just as you've done before, take on these Boneheads from the other side of the water.

Keep Hopping

Trap: Sink Tiles

You learn quickly that white Tiles start to sink as soon as you land on them. Approach these Sink Tiles with caution and jump off them immediately.

Treasure Trick

The Treasure Chest on the right side of this room looks unreachable. You can get it, though. Just jump off and have faith!

Look Out!

Froppas leap from the muck in this room and jump in your way. Look out!

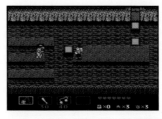

Mad Muddy

Hit Mad Muddy with a couple of quick lashes as soon as you get close to him.

Stomp the Tiles

Stomp the Tile on the left to make Hearts appear. Now get the Stop/Slow on the right Tile and freeze the Up/Down Tiles when they are up.

Touchy Tiles

You find Up/Down Tiles and Sink Tiles in this room. As soon as you land on the Sink Tiles, they start to submerge. Jump straight up and down on them and wait for the Up/Down Tiles to go up. Hop to the Hidden Hole on the left side of the room for a set of Double Hearts and a Potion; the right side of the room is the way to go next.

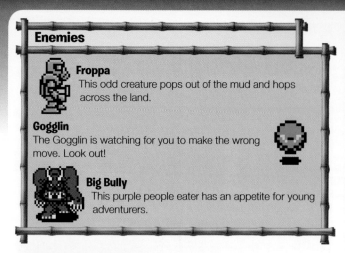

Enemies

Froppa
This odd creature pops out of the mud and hops across the land.

Gogglin
The Gogglin is watching for you to make the wrong move. Look out!

Big Bully
This purple people eater has an appetite for young adventurers.

Stand in the Center!

Defeat a handful of Froppas to exit this room. Head to the center and attack them as they approach you. This is the safest location to defend yourself from.

Get the Gogglin

The Gogglin is a single-minded creature. As soon as you hit it, the Gogglin makes a beeline in the direction the shot came from. Jump to the side and hit it again as it zips by. With some practice, you should be able to defeat it without being harmed.

Remember Po's Poem

Po's poem explains what you must know to get to the top of the mountain without any climbing gear. A geyser can push you up to the top. Find a way to get to it. Notice there is no Gate to the geyser. Look for a hidden passage in the room to the right of the geyser.

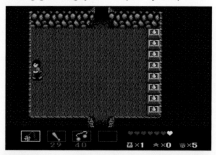

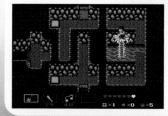 

At Last! The Hermit!

You've got the Scroll! Now, run back to Miracola and free Bananette from her long sleep.

The Hermit makes his home in a cave at the mountain's peak. Get the Scroll with the magic chant from him and hurry back to Miracola. Bananette is waiting!

A Miracle in Miracola

Chant the spell from the Hermit's Scroll. Banenette awakens from her trance. The Miracolans rejoice and repair the Sub-C!

"Good Morning! Did I miss breakfast? I'm starving!"

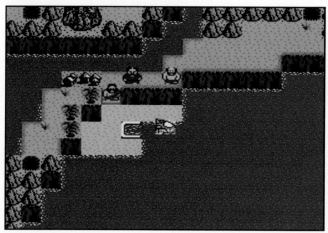

You saved Bananette! Now you can leave Miracola as a hero and, with a repaired Sub-C, continue on with your search for Dr. J.

CHAPTER 4 — CONFESSION

Tunacola

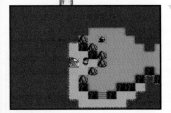

The unique shape of this island may have significance. Perhaps large fish and similar creatures frequent the area?

As you sail, you discover an island with a unique shape. Dock to find out if the villagers have any clues. Since islands are far apart in this area, anyone sailing with a vehicle less equipped than the Sub-C has to stop here for supplies.

Perhaps you should sail to the east and catch up to the mysterious C-Islander. C-Island is a small place—it might be someone you know.

Tunacola is a small fishing village with friendly residents. If they have seen anything out of the ordinary, they tell you. A few of the Tunacolans are among the oldest people on the island.

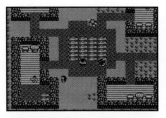

Fish grow big around here. If Dr. J weren't missing, you might think about dropping a line to see just how big they are.

Following the observances of one of the Tunacolans, it's a good idea to sail eastward and see if you can find something.

The Belly of a Whale

As you travel eastward, a Whale swallows the Sub-C. You heard that they grew big around here, but this is ridiculous!

Baboo! Dr. J's assistant is the C-Islander who was searching for you. While you were in Miracola, he was swallowed by this Whale.

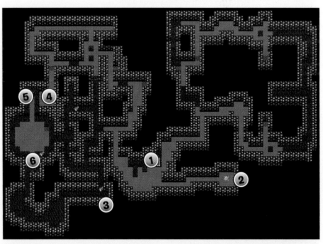

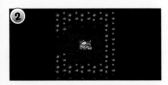

This place is a maze, but nothing an experienced adventurer like Mike can't handle.

Baboo dropped a Lighter somewhere in the Whale. With it, you can light a fire and force the Whale to sneeze you out. Search for it.

Reach the Lighter by heading north as far as you can, then heading west. Wrap around south until you reach the spot shown in the screenshot above. Push through the wall here, head south until you dock, then head east, and the Lighter is yours!

The Crafty Dr. J

Dr. J wasn't about to take chances, not with intergalactic evil afoot! He hid his code inside the letter that came with the game's instruction manual. Dipping the letter in water displays a three-digit set of numbers. But what could they be used for? Try inputting the numbers "747" into the C-Sub and see what happens. Wait... Could it be...? The frequency to Dr. J's radio! A pretty crafty trick, huh?

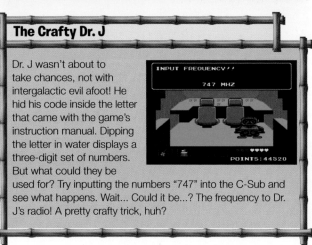

CHAPTER 5 CAPTAIN BELL

You're still shaking the salt water from your shoes after the Whale episode when you come across yet another obstacle. This one is in the shape of an ancient Ship that blocks a strait between halves of an island. Where to now?

Bellcola

Enter the village to discover some way around the giant ship blocking the strait.

Bellcola was named after a sailor who long ago anchored his Ship in the middle of the strait to block an invading fleet.

This villager has a clue that may help you figure out how to befriend Pete the Parrot.

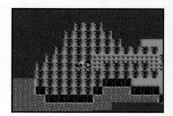

Chief Bellcola hints that talking to Pete the Parrot is a good idea. Pete is the descendant of Captain Bell's parrot. He could have a clue.

"I am Chief Bellcola. I can see that you'd like to sail through the straits. Pete the Parrot may be able to help."

"Braaack! Braaack! No gift, no chat! Braaack! No gift, no chat!"

```
NO GIFT NO CHAT/
NO GIFT NO CHAT/
```

The greedy parrot doesn't talk without a gift. This fisherman on the east side may have what Pete wants.

Captain Bell's Memorial

That's some Pipe Organ! Apparently Captain Bell was a fan of the instrument. If you know the right tune, you might play your way into the underground passage. Perhaps Pete could hum a few bars.

Navigate the passages on the lower-east side of the ocean to get to Captain Bell's Memorial. Stop off at the hut on the northeast side of the island and talk to the fisherman who inhabits it. He gives you a special gift that might just get Pete to part with the secret of Captain Bell's Memorial.

This part is a bit tricky. According to the song Pete teaches, the correct key order is as follows: 1, 3, 5, 4, 1, 3. If you make a mistake at any point, leave the Memorial, then come back.

After Captain Bell saved the island from pirates, the people built this memorial based on his plans. Some say it holds the secret of the Ship.

Solve the mystery in the Memorial and extinguish the fire blocking the underground passage.

A Big Heart waits in the passage. You may have to search for it, though.

Captain Bell's Cave

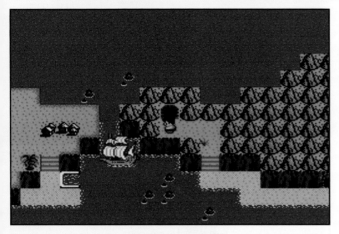

Enter the cave and fight to the machine that can sink the Ship.

Captain Bell designed this cave to drive pirates away from the mechanism that keeps his ship afloat. The traps he set are ingenious. Nevertheless, getting through this cave is the only way to sink the Ship.

Hidden Hearts

Find a couple Double Small Hearts in a hidden passage to the right of the entrance stairs. Not a bad way to start this area off, huh?

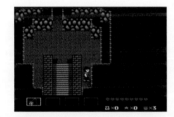

Earthquake!

When you reach the center, the ground shakes and Tiles begin to sink. Jump over the gap on the left to give yourself more time.

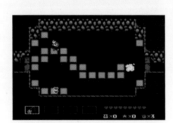

Get the Point?

Arrows shoot out of the walls as you run across this room. To avoid them, either jump out of the way or keep running.

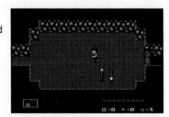

Jump and Run

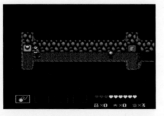

When you hit the Silver Ball, it slides back and forth. Jump as it approaches and run to the other side.

Which Route to Take?

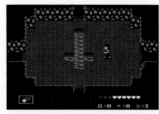
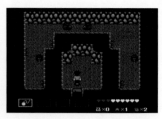

Three different paths await exploration. Ultimately your quest leads you down and to the left, but to get there, head up through a passage on the left wall, then down from the next room. Continue left from here.

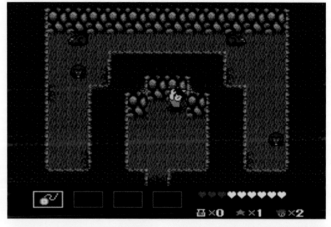

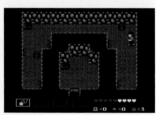

The north room is particularly tricky. Stop on the spot in the top-right corner of the small alcove of the room you enter from. Fall through the floor and deal with the deadly gauntlet of Pencil Traps. Head through the stairs in the bottom-right corner of the room, then head north and stop when you're in-line with the secret path to your left. Head through the path, then step left once, south once, then left, and head through the secret passage to exit the room.

Whew! That was brutal!

Another Ground Shaker!

The Tiles break in a spiral pattern in this earthquake chamber. Jump straight to the left and look for a Trigger Tile there.

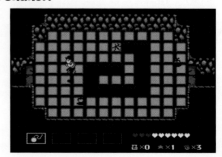

Strike!

Captain Bell was a bit of a bowler. When his giant Megaton strikes, it knocks down everything in its path. Use the alcoves in this hall to avoid this destructive orb.

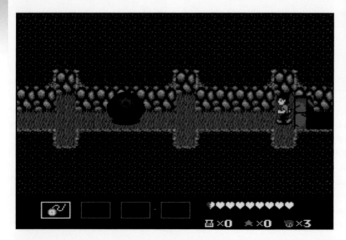

You also find a Magic Mirror in this room, if you're up for a bit of investigating.

Crossroads

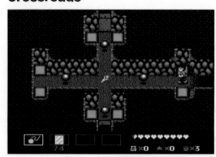

You locate another set of crossroads after fighting through Muumus and a Looper. The northern path leads to two sets of Double Small Hearts, but you have to jump along Sink Tiles to survive.

The western room leads to a Bat and eventually a Potion. Use a Rod of Sight in this room to track down a wandering Minie.

The path you ultimately want here is to the south, so if you don't need a Potion, a Bat, or a couple sets of Double Hearts, feel free to head south.

Minie Madness

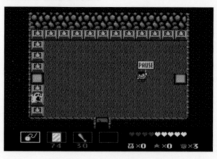

When you reach the room with two Big Bullies, use a Rod of Sight to uncover a hidden Minie. Defeating the Minie opens a passage on the left side of the room.

Twice the Trouble

The dual attack of the Silver Balls in this room keeps you jumping. Hit the second one so that it moves with the first.

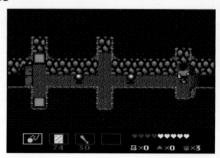

Sharp Attack

The Pencil Traps push up from underground to put holes through Mike. Avoid them and keep running.

Double Danger

Arrows and an Up/Down Tile combine for a serious situation here. Stay out of the Arrows's way until the Tile is on its way up. Now jump!

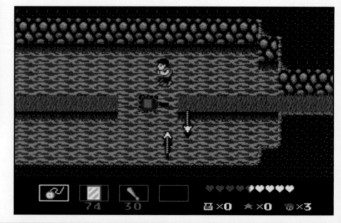

Gutter Ball

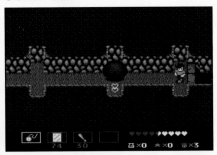

This Megaton is even faster than the first. It comes right back at you after it passes. Slap it with the Yo-yo to temporarily freeze it. When it comes rolling back, freeze it again.

Go for the Ghouls

Knock out all the Pirate Ghouls and Loopers, including the ones across the gap, and the Gate opens.

Sink It!

This room houses the mechanism required to sink the Ship, but you need to use a couple of secret passages to reach it.

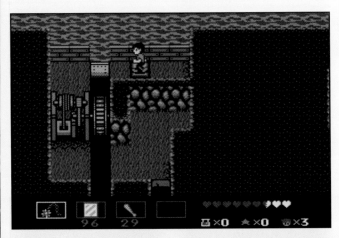

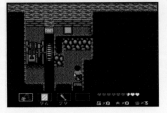

Enter through here...

And head through here to reach the Switch.

Enemies and Traps

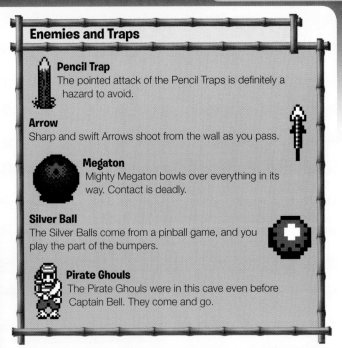

Pencil Trap
The pointed attack of the Pencil Traps is definitely a hazard to avoid.

Arrow
Sharp and swift Arrows shoot from the wall as you pass.

Megaton
Mighty Megaton bowls over everything in its way. Contact is deadly.

Silver Ball
The Silver Balls come from a pinball game, and you play the part of the bumpers.

Pirate Ghouls
The Pirate Ghouls were in this cave even before Captain Bell. They come and go.

Captain Bell's Ship Sinks

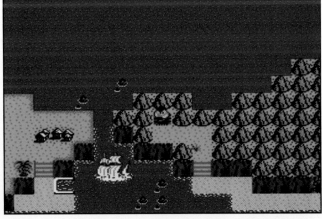

Another chapter ends, and once again, you sail off in search of Dr. J. What could possibly be next?

With a hull full of water, Captain Bell's Ship heads for Davy Jones's Locker and clears the way for the Sub-C.

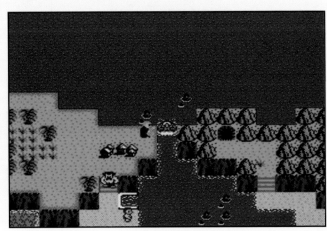

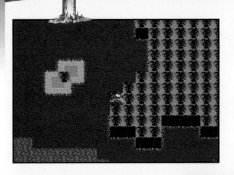

Search the maze-like island chain carefully and thoroughly.

Nav-Com finally has a lock on Dr. J. Pilot the Sub-C through a maze-like series of islands and zero in on his location. A close signal doesn't necessarily mean you're on the right track. Search everywhere, and keep an eye open for secret passages.

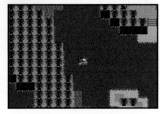

Several secret passages exist in the islands. Look for the bubble on the shore.

Howdoyadu-Cola

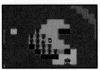

This small village is on the first island you come to after finding a secret passage.

You learn from a Howdoyadu-Colan that there is a Big Heart on one of the islands. Keep searching and you're bound to find it.

Special (and Not So Special) Items

The Big Heart in this island chain is just as useful as ever. The Big Apple, though, seems to be here only to add flavor.

Search for the Lost Ruins

Dr. J was exploring the underwater ruins in this area. That must be where he's held captive. Nav-Com still has a lock on Dr. J's location. If you keep trying new passages, eventually you find him.

There may be a special item on this island. Dock the Sub-C and take a look.

There's a series of underwater passages in this chain. Some of them lead to important locations.

"We're closing in on Dr. J's location. I have a positive ID that he is in the Lost Ruins."

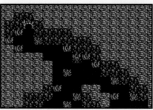

Once you zero in on the Lost Ruins from the surface, dive down and explore them from below. You're getting close to Dr. J's location.

Long Jump

Once inside the ruins proper, you run into this room. Grab the Anklet and take a long leap to one of the Tiles. A Tile appears in the middle of the water. Jump to it and open the Treasure Chest for Double Small Hearts.

Magic Item: Anklet

The magic power of the Anklet lets you jump the length of two Tiles. Beware, though: it only works in the room where you found it.

Muumu-Go-Round

Hop on the biggest gap between the Muumus and follow them around until the Treasure Chest opens. Jump to the center for a perfectly safe place from which to defeat the Muumus.

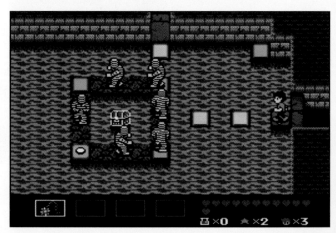

Giant Turboss

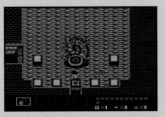

The Giant Turboss has an attack similar to that of Octo the Huge. This time, though, you can't freeze the action. Jump left and right to avoid the shots, and when it moves in, hit it hard.

Jump left and right to avoid the shots, but don't stray too far to one side.

When the Giant Turboss closes in, hit it with multiple shots.

Three-Way Entry

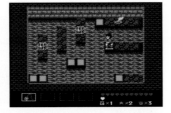

Three secret passages lead into this room. Enter through the bottom passage first and hit the Tile, then leave and re-enter through the top passage. Next, collect the Anklet and drop down to the area in the middle. Open the Chests and move on!

Special Weapon

Wonder Horse Hide
Baseball has been very, very good to you. First you get the Bat, and now the Baseballs.

Spikes
You can really dig in with this super set of cleats. Use them to hit several enemies at once.

Spike 'Em

The Squidos are too numerous here to deal with individually. As soon as you get the Spikes, use them to take out all the Squidos before they get close. You'll have Squidos on a stick, right quick!

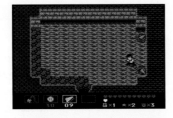

Heart Frenzy

There are several sets of Double Small Hearts in this room. Be careful to avoid all the enemies and collect all the Hearts, and you can really clean up.

Muumu Mania

Muumus are abundant here. If you have Spikes, use them to hit all the Muumus at once. If you don't, try to get the Muumus to follow you, then turn around and attack!

Enemies

Armet
These small creatures are like miniature versions of the Giant Turboss. Likewise, they're only a fraction of the threat.

Squido
The Squidos only make a cameo appearance in the Ruins. Knock them with the Spikes and get on with it.

Break Broken Joe

Direct from Easter Island, Broken Joe has taken his show on the road. His weak point? His wide-open mouth. As soon as he opens wide to send out a squiggly, tongue-like attack, jump straight up to avoid it and pitch a handful of Horse Hides right into his strike zone.

Jump to avoid contact with Broken Joe's tongue-like attack.

Throw as many Horse Hides as you can into Broken Joe's open mouth. It's his only weak point.

Big Rock

The mysterious meteor in the Lost Ruins may have something to do with recent events in the night sky. There are three holes of equal size in the rock. Items may have been removed from it after it landed.

Max Hearts!

Other Big Hearts disappear after you pick them up, but this one is special. If you pick it up and head past the Big Rock and into the Big Rock Tunnel, you can leave the Big Rock Tunnel and head back to the Big Heart's location and pick it up again! Use this trick to max out your Life Meter, because the next tunnel is an absolute beast!

There's a strange message on the Big Rock that you can't read. Maybe someone with experience in deciphering messages of this nature would have better luck.

Before you fight through the next tunnel, grab the Big Heart on the right side of the Lost Ruins.

The Big Rock Tunnel

Walking straight up from the entrance of this challenging tunnel leads into a dead end. Look for a secret passage in the right wall of the entry.

Enemies and Traps

Dagger Trap
Just like Pencil Traps, these sharp blades punch up from underground. They're almost unavoidable.

Fuzz
While they don't cause any damage directly, the Fuzz temporarily take your weapon away.

Rocky
The stone-like Rockies are invincible as they walk across the room. You can defeat them only when they hit a wall.

Hoodoo Doll
The sinister Hoodoo Dolls attack in four directions at once. Stay away from them and fight from a distance.

Biter
These land fish are easier to defeat than the Mud-O-Fish. Take them out with a couple of hits.

Urchin
Urchins act exactly like the Silver Balls in Captain Bell's Cave. Hit them, and they move back and forth.

Special Weapon: Asterisk

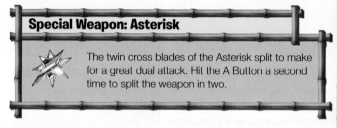

The twin cross blades of the Asterisk split to make for a great dual attack. Hit the A Button a second time to split the weapon in two.

Avoid the Fuzz

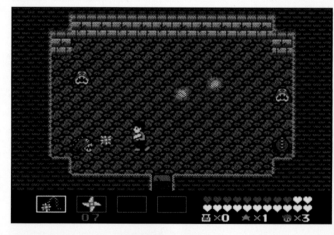

Coming into contact with the Fuzz causes you to lose your ability to attack for a few seconds. Run from it and aim for the other enemies.

Split 'Em

Instead of trying to get close to these Loopers, blast them with the Asterisk. It splits and takes out two Loopers at once.

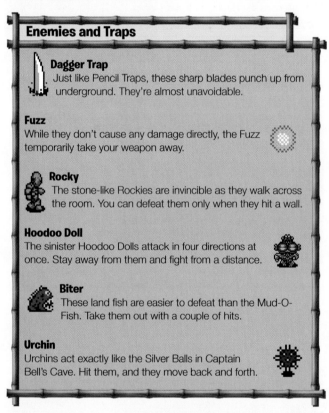

Up and Around

There's nothing of note in this room. Walk around the wall on the right side and jump back into the lower room to find a secret passage.

Hoodoo Voodoo

The Hoodoo Doll fires in four directions. Use the Asterisk if you can, and stay as far away as possible. Direct contact is deadly.

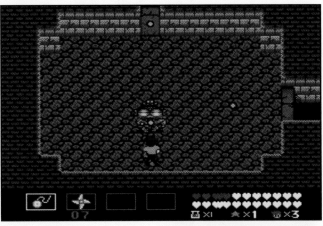

Skip It

Don't bother with the enemies in this room. As soon as you enter, head for the left wall and find a secret passage to the next room. You can get through without taking any damage.

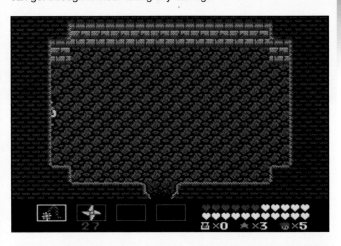

On the Side

Use the Asterisk while facing left or right to take out the Loopers. Avoid hitting the Urchin until it's necessary. Once the room is clear, you can exit without a problem.

Knock out Rocky

Rockies are vulnerable to your attack only when they hit a wall. Get out of their way as they charge, then send out an Asterisk when they get close.

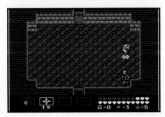

Dark Passage Bonus

In the unlit hallway leading to the Statues of Twin Sumocho, find a secret passage by testing the left wall. It leads to a room with Double Small Hearts and a Treasure Chest!

The Statues of Twin Sumocho

The weapon of choice against this duo is definitely the Asterisk. Stay near the center

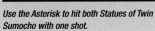

Use the Asterisk to hit both Statues of Twin Sumocho with one shot.

Jump out of the way of the Statues' fire and collect another Asterisk if you need it.

"Mike! You found me! I was beginning to think that I would never get out of these Ruins alive. Aliens have taken the three Crystals that were imbedded in the meteor that landed here. You've got to board their Ship and retrieve the Crystals!"

Mike's Journey Continues...

Dr. J tells Mike the importance of taking the three Crystals back from the aliens, and like a true hero, Mike volunteers. To complete his journey, he must board an alien craft and challenge an alien overlord.

We've shown you the ropes and told you how to get a complete Life Meter. You're ready to take on anything that's thrown at you! Go get 'em!

DR. MARIO

Developers
Nintendo R&D1

Director
Shigeru Miyamoto

Producer
Takahara Harada

Composer
Yukio Kaneoka

Release Date
Original Release Date: June 27, 1990 Famicom JP;
October 1990 NES US

SUMMARY

Medical alert! Microscopic monsters are out in force to take over the lab of the famous plumber-turned-practitioner, Dr. Mario. You've got to set things straight by manipulating Dr. Mario's special vitamin capsules and making matches to obliterate the menace. It's strategic fun for one or two players!

DR. MARIO'S DIAGNOSIS

Mario tosses capsules into the bottle in an attempt to stomp out the viruses that have taken over. It's up to you to control the capsules so that their colors line up with the colors of the germs. A vertical column or horizontal row of four same-colored capsules and/or germs disappear—problem

solved. When the bottle is clear of germs, you move on to the next emergency. If the capsules pile up to the top of the bottle, though, the patient's a goner.

Capsule Control Capsules

Capsules move just like pieces in other puzzle games. Slide them left, right, and down using the Control Pad, and rotate them with the A and B Buttons.

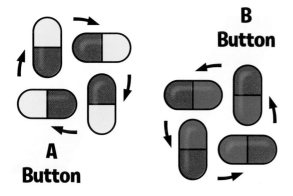

Look at the Big Picture

When four capsule colors and viruses line up in a row, they disappear and make room for other colors to fill the space. Examine how placement of each capsule affects the colors around it, so that when you make matches, you drop the right colors in the most advantageous spaces. Some placements result in multiple matches.

This drop results in a lineup of three yellow capsules and viruses.

Make a two-color match in one move with this placement.

Three at a Time

With some practice and patience, you can set up the capsules so that three lines disappear in a single move.

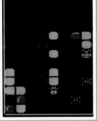

A triple play comes in handy in a two-player game.

Plan Ahead

Dr. Mario always keeps one step ahead of the game by holding up the next capsule he plans to toss. Consult with him while you're playing to better plan where to place each capsule.

What's up, Doc?

Finish It Off

When you're down to just one germ, don't worry about how your moves affect the rest of the bottle. Concentrate on making a match to eliminate the bug.

De-bug the bottle.

Work from the Top Down

Since the capsules drop from the top, it's a good idea to clear away the highest viruses first. That way, you open up maneuvering space and give yourself room to work into the lower areas. If the viruses are very high, consider making horizontal matches.

Clear away the highest viruses first to make room for maneuvering.

Think Before You Stack

If you can't find a perfect match for a falling capsule, place it to the side so that you have space in the middle to manipulate other falling capsules. Wherever you stack, always look for both horizontal and vertical matching opportunities.

Don't let the capsules stack up in the middle. | *This virus is difficult to reach.* | *After some completions, the field is clear.*

Fill the Space

Since the capsule control in this game is very much like the control in other vertical puzzle games, some techniques work here like they do in other games. One such maneuver is sliding pieces to the left or right into open spaces. That way, you fill spaces sideways that are surrounded on three sides. This is important to remember when the stacks have grown so high that you can no longer places capsules on top.

Rotate the capsule and slide it in with a quick move to the right. | *Work it in and match the colors.*

An expert eye can catch inventive ways to make matches. | *Work it in and match the colors.*

Two Can Play This Game; Doctors Duel over Dexterity

The best way to play is with two players in an all-out, split-screen, simultaneous battle! Race against another budding doctor to get your name in the medical journals. With the right moves, you can upset your opponent's research and move on to critical acclaim.

Double Trouble

Line up your capsules so that you make two matches with one move, and your opponent receives two capsule-halves.

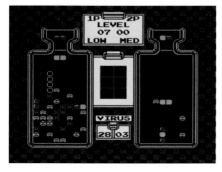

Make a double to bury the other player in unexpected pieces.

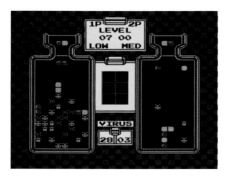

You can keep playing, while the other player has to wait for the two yellow halves to fall.

Try for a Triple

If you arrange three matches with one move, three colors drop down into the other player's bottle. That could mess up anyone's plans!

Make the Match Even

If one player is more experienced that the other, you can make the match fair by individually choosing Virus Level and Speed.

DR. MARIO'S MED SCHOOL

Study and practice are the keys to success. When you face off with another potential *Dr. Mario* champ, you must play with precision and speed. Not only are you obliterating viruses in your own bottle, you're also aiming to slacken your opponent's pace by sending over colors. The way to do this is by making doubles and triples. Doubles send over two colors, triples send three, and practice makes perfect. Dr. Mario recommends that you practice the methods of making winning moves on your own, until you're ready for a two-player game with a competitive edge.

Clinic 1: Prepare a Practice Field

In this practice session, the object is to learn how to set up and carry out double and triple scores. To clear the bottle for practicing, start with a low Virus Level. Play to a point where only a few capsules remain stacked to either the left or right edge and near the bottom of the bottle. While practicing, use the capsules shown in the examples and set the others out of the way.

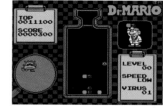

Rid the screen of all but one virus.

Dr. Mario's Diagnosis

Be careful not to eliminate all your viruses while practicing.

Clinic 2: Doubles

The key to making multiple matches is to arrange sets of three same-color capsules and to wait for an opportunity to complete those sets with a single move. Here are two examples of two-set matches.

Example #1

This is a basic vertical double. Stack two three-of-a-kind matches end to end and wait for a capsule with both colors.

Start the stack with a double blue. | *Stack three blues high.* | *Then start stacking yellows.* | *Finish the setup and wait.* | *Yellow matches first, then the blue drops; you've scored a double!*

Example #2

Remember that you can make matches both vertically and horizontally. Here's an example of a double horizontal match.

  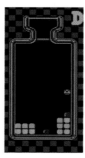 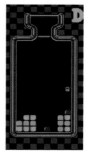 

Start with a blue-and-yellow capsule. | *You need either a double-yellow or more blue-and-yellows to set up the bottom match.* | *Keep it going.* | *Complete the setup.* | *When the next blue-and-yellow capsule falls, you make both matches simultaneously.*

280

Clinic 3: Triples

Triple-match scores are similar to doubles, but they take more precision and time to set up. The results are worthwile, though, since your opponent is pelted with a three-color shower. When you follow these examples, remember to set capsules that don't fit into the scenario to the side.

Example #1

Just like the first double example, this multiple match is vertical. The twist is that now there are three colors in the equation.

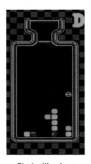

Start with a base of yellow-and-red capsules.

Another yellow-and-red capsule would make for a perfect double, but wait it out for a triple.

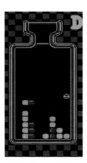

Build blue onto the yellow and set up a red match.

A blue-and-yellow capsule sets off a chain reaction. In this scenario, the area clears completely once the matches are made.

Example #2

In most triple scores, you incorporate both horizontal and vertical matches. This enables you to bring a wider array of capsules into your scheme.

A horizontal yellow match creates the first part of the setup.

Begin to stack red capsules, but leave a space for the blue match.

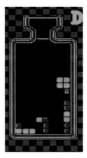

Blue is the next color to build up.

All the matches have been set up. Now wait for the trigger.

Blue matches first. Then red falls, and yellow makes three!

Dr. Mario's Board Exam

It's time to check up on your ability to recognize multiple score setups and see if you qualify to be a full-fledged doctor. Examine the following situations, then take a look at the next capsules to come into play, and decide where they should go in order to score a double or triple. Think about setting up near completions of the same color and then arranging for the last capsule to make the matches. The answers are in the next tip box.

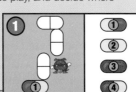

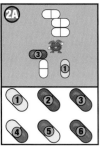

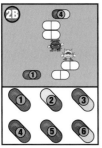

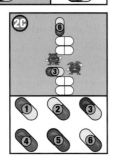

Here Are the Results

If you haven't figured out the answers to Dr. Mario's Board Exam, study them here and try to work out a few more examples on your own. Understanding doubles and triples gives you an advantage in competitive situations.

Practice, practice, practice. Even when you understand the principles of multiple matches on paper, the only way to really master the methods is by making up a practice field in a one-player game and trying out double and triple scores. When they become second nature, try out your skills in a two-player game.

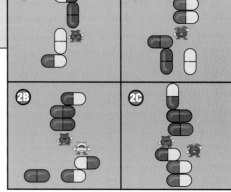

If You Find Triples Easy, Try a Quadruple!

It probably won't ever happen in a playing situation, but you might try to find a way to score a coveted quadruple while practicing. Give it a try, and keep fine-tuning your *Dr. Mario* skills.

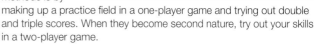

KIRBY'S ADVENTURE

Developer:
HAL Laboratory

Director:
Masahiro Sakurai

Producers:
Satoru Iwata, Shigeru Miyamoto, Takao Shimizu

Designer:
Masahiro Sakurai

Composer:
Hirokazu Ando

Original Release Date:
March 23, 1993 Famicom JP; May 1, 1993 NES NA

A CRISIS IN DREAM LAND!

Light-years away, on a tiny star not visible from Earth, is the magical, peaceful place known as Dream Land. The beings that inhabit this wondrous world live a blissful existence that centers on eating, sleeping, and playing. Their carefree customs include the traditional after-lunch feast nap. After they awaken from their nap, the Dream Landers discuss their dreams and fervently hope that each other's fondest wishes come true.

One day, a young Dream Lander named Kirby awakens from his after-lunch nap feeling terrible. "What happened?" he wonders to himself. "I didn't have any dreams during my lunch nap!" This lack of dreams leaves Kirby feeling very uneasy. After talking to some of his friends, he finds that the problem is much more serious than he had thought, for they had not experienced any dreams either! "Something must have happened to the Dream Spring!" they exclaim in unison.

The Dream Spring is a magical well that is a reservoir for all the dreams of the inhabitants of Dream Land. Dreams also flow out of the Dream Spring and envelop Dream Land, granting all sleeping beings enjoyable dreams.

Legends tell that the Dream Spring was created by a magical artifact known as the Star Rod. The sparkling star on the tip of this scepter is a fragment of a star that landed in Dream Land in the distant past. The Star Rod now provides energy to the Dream Spring and serves as the very symbol of Dream Land.

The lack of dreams makes everyone in Dream Land feel restless and irritable. The joyful laughter that once resounded throughout Dream Land can no longer be heard at all. Things are bleak. Kirby, the roly-poly hero of Dream Land, boldly announces his intention to investigate the Dream Spring and find the cause of all the trouble.

Upon reaching the Dream Spring, who does he find but King Dedede, bathing in its magical waters! In the past, King Dedede caused mischief in Dream Land by stealing all the Dream Landers' food and sparkling stars. Now, in the middle of the Dream Spring, in place of the Star Rod, sits Dedede, covered with bubble bath!

"So, you're up to your old tricks again, eh, Dedede?!" Kirby accuses.

"What are you talking about, young pudge ball?" Dedede looks surprised. "I thought I'd do everyone a favor by—"

"No, no, no!" Kirby shook his head. "I won't listen to your tricks! What have you done with the Star Rod?!"

"Oh, that old thing," Dedede says nonchalantly. "I broke it into seven pieces and gave each piece to one of my friends…"

What was Dedede thinking?! Kirby wonders. Before hearing any more of what Dedede has to say, Kirby sets off on the long trek to gather the pieces of the Star Rod and return them to the Dream Spring. Hopefully, he can return the sparkle to the Dream Spring so that the people of Dream Land can again enjoy their happy midday naps.

COPY ABILITIES

What makes Kirby special is his ability to swallow enemies and steal their powers. Read on to see all the Copy Abilities Kirby can steal!

Normal
Hit the Down Arrow when Kirby has an enemy in his mouth to copy the enemy's special ability!

Back Drop
Kirby uses a powerful wrestling technique to defeat his opponents.

Ball
Kirby rolls into a smooth ball. If you hold the A Button, he jumps higher!

Beam
Kirby fires a beam like that used by some enemies. This is an easy weapon to use.

Crash
This power defeats all enemies on the screen, but you can use it only once.

Cutter
Kirby throws a series of cutters that return like boomerangs.

Fire
Kirby breathes fire. Enemies beware, or you're gonna get burned!

Fireball
Kirby turns into a flying fireball. Jump and attack in a flash of fire!

Freeze
Kirby creates a shield to freeze enemies. He then knocks away the frozen blocks.

Hammer
This weapon is very powerful. Use it on stubborn bad guys to clear your path!

Hi-Jump
Kirby jumps many times higher than usual. Jump and dive-attack to beat the enemy.

Ice
Kirby can freeze enemies with his cold breath! He can then throw them into others!

Laser
Kirby fires a laser beam that bounces off slopes. Try it in many places!

Light
Dark areas are spooky. Light lets Kirby set off fireworks. It works only in the dark.

Mike
Kirby sings his favorite song three times. I wonder why that song hurts enemies…

Needle
Lots of needles, just like a porcupine's, come out of Kirby. This is a great defense!

Parasol
Open your parasol and take a nice walk! Do you think this might have other uses, too?

Sleep
…Please…   …A little more…
…Let me sleep…   …Please…

Spark
Kirby creates fireworks-like sparks from his body. This is a great defense!

Star Rod
Make the final effort. Shoot the star to defeat the final enemy!

Stone
Kirby's body turns into a solid rock. In this form, he cannot be hurt by enemy attacks.

Sword
Use the sword to defeat enemies. If you attack in midair, Kirby spins and slashes.

Throw
Kirby grabs an enemy and tosses it away like a shooting star. Use an enemy to beat others!

Tornado
Kirby spins and bumps away his foes. Hold the B Button to spin into the air!

UFO
Hold down the B Button to charge, and then let go. You can attack four different ways.

Wheel
Kirby turns into a wheel and moves at super speed. But watch for obstacles and excess speed!

VEGETABLE VALLEY

LEVEL 1

Level 1-1

Copy Abilities

This first stage is perfect for getting the hang of Kirby. It's a straightforward level without any tricks or real challenges to give you a hard time. Try out each of the Copy Abilities you find to get a feel for them, and you'll have a strong start for the rest of the game.

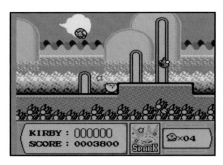

Crane Fever

Use the buttons to move the crane and get a Kirby. A big one's hard to get, but worth it!

Use the A Button to move the crane claw. Position the claw directly over one of the stuffed Kirbys, then release the A Button. A small plush is worth one 1-Up, while the big one is worth two.

We suggest you chase after the big ones at all times. If you get directly over one of them, you pick it up almost every single time. Grabbing one big Kirby is worth as many 1-Ups as two small ones, so there's really nothing to lose.

Beam

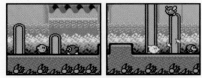

Waddle Doo is your go-to for Beam.

Beam creates a slow-moving whip of energy balls that damage or defeat any foes it touches. This solid ability allows Kirby to maintain distance from enemies while also dealing a fair amount of damage.

Fire

Hot Head lives up to its namesake; suck it up for Fire!

Fire allows Kirby to breathe fire onto enemies. The range is pretty short, but this Copy Ability deals a lot of damage if used tactically.

Spark

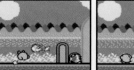

Shock Sparky when you suck it up, and steal its thunder!

Known as a more defensive power, Spark allows Kirby to create electricity that appears around him and damages any enemy foolish enough to approach him.

Level 1-2

Copy Abilities

There are a lot of new abilities to get and try out here. We explain the new powers as you go along.

You see a lot of the spiky ball enemies called Gordos in the first area of this stage. Handle them in one of two ways: either destroy the Star Blocks above them and let them fly away, or fly over them; either method works. Just don't touch them—Gordos really pack a punch!

Cannons, known as Shotzos in Dream Land, are devious. In addition to blasting out cannonballs, most Shotzos you encounter track Kirby. Never stay in a Shotzo's sights for long, and always find a way to put either distance or an obstacle between the Kirby and the cannonballs the Shotzo fires.

Cutter

Cutter gives Kirby the ability to throw out blades that return to him if they don't hit anything first. It's not a particularly powerful Copy Ability, but its range allows you to keep your distance from enemies, which is never a bad thing in this game.

Sir Kibble is the wielder of the boomerang-like Cutter ability.

Miniboss: Poppy Bro Sr.

Eventually you run into this guy: Poppy Bro Sr., a bouncy, smiley pyrotechnician who specializes in throwing bombs at his enemies.

His jumps seem unpredictable and hard to avoid, but if you race to the middle of the screen and duck while he's not throwing bombs, he's pretty easy to take down. Wait for him to throw a bomb your way, suck it up, and spit it back at him.

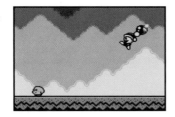

Crash

Poppy Bro Sr. and Bomber are the primary sources of Crash.

Crash doesn't work like other Copy Abilities. Where Cutter, Fire, Beam, or Spark can be used until you give up or lose the ability, Crash is a one-time, single-use power, and for good reason! When used, Kirby explodes across the screen, either defeating or dealing massive damage to any enemies unlucky enough to be caught in the explosion.

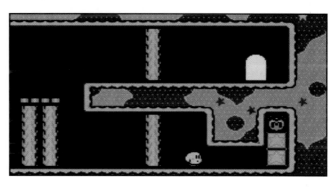

Kirby is a food fanatic. He likes food so much that eating anything he loves refills his health a couple of bars. But there is no food that gives Kirby a bigger health boost than a Maxim Tomato. Eating one of these bulbous fruits refills all of Kirby's health, which can really come in handy on tougher stages.

Single-Use Edibles

You may see a healing item and think, "Oh cool! I can use this over and over if I lose a life!" Unfortunately, that's not the case in *Kirby's Adventure*. There are several items and minigames that can only be used a single time during a sitting. Once you grab a healing item, it's gone for good, or until you turn the game off or get a Game Over.

Sword

If you see a Sword Knight, suck it up to give Kirby a sword!

Sword is an ability that gives Kirby exactly what the power states: a sword. This is a close-range Copy Ability that does a solid amount of damage, but puts Kirby close to danger at all times. If you have this ability in hand, use it with care.

Level 1-3

Copy Abilities

This stage begins with a barrage of Shotzos. Thankfully someone was foolish enough to put most of them on Star Blocks. Destroy or suck up the Blocks under a Shotzo, and it plummets into the pit below. This keeps the first part of this level from becoming something of a war zone.

Fireball

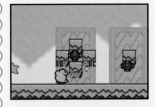 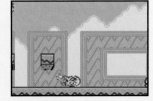

The quick and aggressive Flamer is your source for Fireball.

Fireball is a pretty interesting ability that can really deal damage if used properly. When it's used, Kirby turns into a fireball and rockets forward, damaging any enemy in his path. While in fireball form, Kirby doesn't take damage from most enemies, so not only do you move fast, but you're safe from harm as well. Not a bad deal if you ask us.

This stage features your first bout of swimming in the game. Swimming can be tricky, as it not only changes how Kirby moves, but it disables almost every available Copy Ability. Though there are a few exceptions (Sword being one of them), most of your underwater attacks involve spitting water at enemies. This requires you to be very close to an enemy to hit it, so be very careful when attempting to attack while underwater.

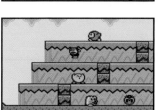

Find another Maxim Tomato in this stage once you reach its final area. Look for the small hill with the Hot Head at the bottom.

Level 1-4

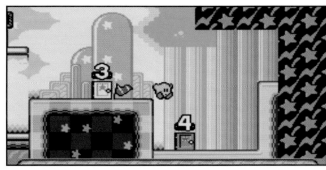

Copy Abilities

Miniboss: Mr. Frosty

Mr. Frosty is one of the easier Minibosses in the game. He's slow-moving and telegraphs his attacks thoroughly. His two main modes of attack are to throw ice blocks at you and to charge at you. Suck up the ice blocks and shoot them back, and simply jump over his running attacks.

Once he's been defeated, suck him up to get the Freeze Copy Ability.

Freeze

Suck up Mr. Frosty after defeating him, and Freeze is yours!

Freeze is a handy ability that allows Kirby to freeze any enemies that step into his freezing aura. Some enemies take more time in the aura than others, but if it can be damaged, it almost certainly can be frozen. Kick a frozen enemy, and it rockets forward, damaging any enemy it hits.

Needle

 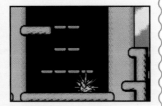

Sharp and dangerous, Togezo is your go-to for Needle.

Needle is another defensive Copy Ability that Kirby can use to ward off attacking foes. When Kirby activates this ability, long, pointed spikes jet out of his back, damaging any enemies that haphazardly walk into them.

You have your first encounter with the Invincibility Candy in this stage. If Kirby eats this sweet treat, he becomes completely invulnerable to all enemy attacks temporarily. On top of that, just about anything he touches is defeated immediately. Don't linger! This bonus only lasts a short amount of time.

Vegetable Valley Boss: Whispy Woods

Your first Boss fight of the game is one fans of *Kirby's Dream Land* will recognize right away. Whispy Woods definitely isn't a hard Boss, but if you let him, he can certainly dole out some damage.

Whispy Woods only has two attacks: dropping fruit from his branches and blowing out puffs of air. Getting hit by either of these damages Kirby, but you can easily reverse Whispy's fruit attack. Simply suck up one of the pieces of fruit that fall from his branches and spit it back at him.

His other attack can't be used against him, unfortunately. If you see Whispy purse his lips, fly into the air and wait for him to stop spitting. Just don't stay in the air for too long, or you might get hit by a piece of his fruit, should he decide to attack with it.

It doesn't take many attacks to defeat Whispy. Once he's finished fighting, grab the piece of the Star Rod to be transported to Level 2: Ice Cream Island.

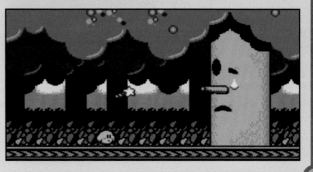

ICE CREAM ISLAND

Level 2-1

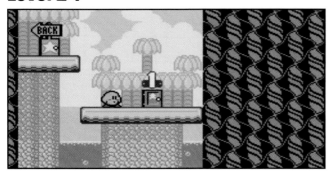

Copy Abilities

Watch your head! This area is littered with coconut trees. If you get near one of them, the coconut hanging from its branches falls—and explodes! A new Copy Ability in this stage helps with falling projectiles, but for now take your time and suck up the coconuts one at a time.

Head through the first door you come across to find a Waddle Doo hanging from a parasol. Sucking up the parasol grants you the Parasol Copy Ability, which helps protect you from those falling coconuts.

Parasol

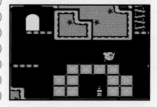
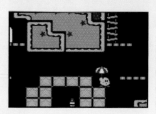

Suck up a Parasol to be granted its power!

Parasol is a very simple power. You can swing the parasol, float with it, and it automatically protects you from overhead attacks—provided you're not swinging it, of course. It's not a particularly strong Copy Ability, but it does have excellent utility.

Be careful as you approach the end of the first area. There's a new type of enemy that *Kirby's Dream Land* fans are sure to

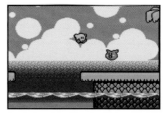

remember. Scarfy looks joyful and innocuous at first, but the second Kirby tries to suck it up, it transforms into Mutant Scarfy and begins chasing Kirby aggressively. After a moment, Mutant Scarfy will explode.

Tornado

This windy rogue is Twister; suck him up and Tornado is yours.

Tornado allows Kirby to spin so fast that he bounces around the area he's in. He damages any enemies he comes into contact with, but at the cost of being largely uncontrollable. Kirby is invulnerable while spinning, so use the ability when in a tight spot.

Egg Catcher

Press the buttons to make Kirby's mouth open. Eat the eggs—but not the bombs!

This is a challenging minigame. King Dedede will throw out eggs along with bombs, and your job is to eat 30 eggs. The more eggs you eat, the better you prize, but if you eat a single bomb, your minigame is over.

Hold Kirby's mouth open with the B Button, and keep a constant lookout to avoid eating a bomb. While you're learning the minigame, it's better to miss out on some eggs for the sake of not eating a bomb. Once you're more experienced, be a bit more daring, but for starters, making it to the end with as many eggs as possible nets you a solid prize.

Level 2-2

Copy Abilities

There are a lot of new abilities to get and try out here. We explain the new powers as you go along.

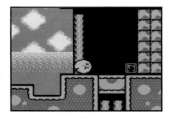 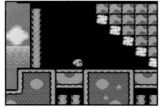

You encounter your first real Bomb Block at the start of this stage. Bomb Blocks, when attacked, destroy set blocks and obstacles. What a Bomb Block destroys is never random, and while they can open new paths for you, sometimes they cause you problems. Always pay attention to the spark produced by a Bomb Block, and when you see one of these explosive cubes, take a quick look at your surroundings to gauge what the Bomb Block might destroy—or unleash.

You get to choose from three different Copy Abilities as you approach this level's Miniboss: Spark, Fire, and Sword. We find that Fire is a good match against most Minibosses, but pick the power you're most comfortable with to get the most out of it.

Miniboss: Grand Wheelie

Grand Wheelie is one of the easier Minibosses in the game. Despite being a sentient wheel, it doesn't move particularly fast, and it only has two real ways of attacking: spitting out normal-sized Wheelies, and driving into you. When it spits out smaller Wheelies, suck them up and spit them back at Grand Wheelie. You can tell when it's about to shoot out a Wheelie when it topples over onto its side.

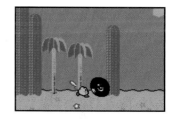

Wheel

Wheel turns Kirby into just that: a wheel! A fast-moving wheel impervious to most damage so long as he contantly moves. This power is perfect for long stretches of unbroken land and for motoring through several weaker enemies. In the right hands, Wheel is downright devastating.

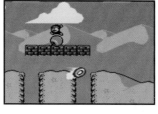

We suggest you dump any powers you have and suck up Grand Wheelie for its Wheel Copy Ability. You can drive through the rest of this level with little effort—and it's a great time!

Level 2-3

Copy Abilities

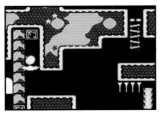 

Sword just isn't going to cut it…   *Beam will do the trick!*

In the second area of this level, you come across a Bomb Block high above your head. You need a power that can reach it in order to destroy the wall of blocks and reach the door. We suggest using Beam, which you can find in Level 2-2.

Once inside the room, find a UFO and a Maxim Tomato. Quickly drop your current Copy Ability and suck up the UFO to get the UFO Copy Ability, arguably the best Copy Ability in the game!

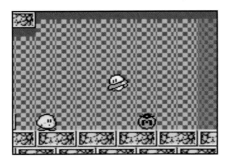

UFO

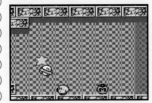 

UFO is the ultimate Kirby Copy Ability. When Kirby sucks up a UFO enemy, he transforms into a UFO himself and has the ability to fly everywhere effortlessly. If that's not rad enough, you can also swing a Beam attack, or charge up and fire a powerful projectile. The only downside to this power is once you finish a level, you lose UFO, which we think is just too sad.

Ice Cream Island has a fair amount of water areas, which you already know are terribly limiting when it comes to Kirby's Copy Abilities. One power in particular really helps in these areas, and that's Sword. Sword works in the water almost the same as it does on land, giving you a nice sweeping motion with your attacks, instead of that pitiful spritz of water from Kirby's mouth.

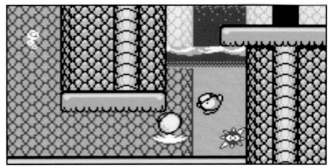

Destroy this Bomb Block…   *To find this 1-Up!*

After the first swimming area of this stage, fly straight up to find a Bomb Block. Destroy this Block and follow the path it uncovers to find a 1-Up!

✦✦✦✦✦✦✦✦✦✦✦✦✦✦✦✦✦✦

Miniboss: Meta Knight's Knights

Meta Knight is a hard character to pin down. On one hand, he throws Invincibility Candy to Kirby, but on the other, he calls his flunkies to take Kirby out. Is he friend or foe? Tough call… Well, there's no use ruminating over this dilemma, especially when you've got a slew of Knights to combat.

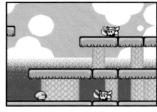

We personally find fights with Meta Knight's crew much easier as normal Kirby. Any of these Knights can be sucked up with little effort, and spitting one into another defeats them both at the same time. Take your time, and this fight will be easy.

✦✦✦✦✦✦✦✦✦✦✦✦✦✦✦✦✦✦

Crane Fever

Use the buttons to move the crane and get a Kirby. A big one's hard to get, but worth it!

Level 2-4

Copy Abilities

As you jump across the clouds of the first area, be on the lookout for this door. When you come across it, enter it and head to the bottom

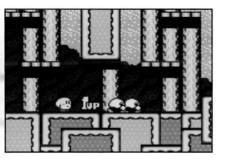

of the room to find a 1-Up. Climb up the room's right side to reach the door leading back to the clouds.

Shortly after you leave that corridor, you encounter a Maxim Tomato surrounded by Star Blocks.

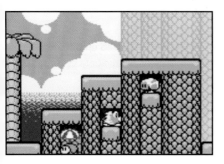

You get another opportunity to pick your power at the start of the next area. The powers up for grabs this time around are Stone, Fire, and Parasol. As always, we suggest Fire, especially

because you're about to fight a rather stationary Miniboss, but the choice is yours to make!

Stone

Stone is the ultimate defensive ability. When Kirby uses Stone, he quite literally becomes a stone! This protects him from all damage so long as he stays in stone form. He can also use Stone while on hills to slide down them and damage any enemies in his path. When it comes to attacking, you really only have one choice, and that's to jump into the air before transforming. Any enemy unfortunate enough to walk directly under you is crushed by Stone Kirby.

Miniboss: Mr. Tick-Tock

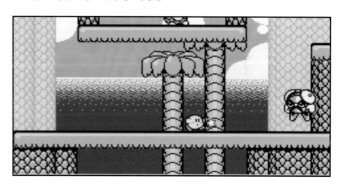

Mr. Tick-Tock isn't much harder than Grand Wheelie. That being said, Tick-Tock does have a few tricks up his sleeves—er…bells?— that you should know about.

This attack is safe to move in on.   *This is the one you should hang back on.*

Tick-Tock's main method of attack is ringing his eardrum-damaging bells. If Kirby is near and is hit by either the notes or sound waves Tick-Tock produces, he takes damage. If Kirby doesn't have a power, he can suck up the music notes and use them to attack Mr. Tick-Tock. Be careful, however, because when Tick-Tock starts ringing, he might surround himself with the aforementioned sound waves, which can't be sucked up and damage Kirby if he's too close. When he starts ringing, pause for a moment and see what attack he's performing, then rush in and do your work!

Once you've defeated Mr. Tick-Tock, suck him up to gain the Mike Copy Ability.

Mike

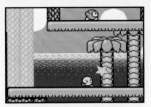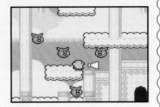

Mike is similar to Crash in that it is a limited-use power that damages every enemy on-screen. Kirby can only use Mike a total of three times (the star above Kirby's remaining lives displays the number of uses left), so use them wisely!

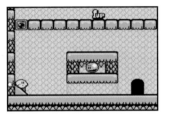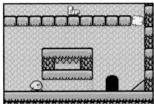

You run into another new Copy Ability in this stage, one that is quite different and useful. Laser allows you to shoot a laser beam from Kirby's hands, which is cool, but there's more to it than shooting projectiles. If Laser is fired at a slope, like the slopes in the bottom-left and -right corners of this room, the laser beam redirects based on the angle of the slope. In the case of the slopes in this room, the laser beam directs up into those Bomb Blocks above Kirby, allowing that 1-Up to drop. Pretty handy, huh?

Museum

Here is a colorful display of enemies with special abilities. Eat the one you want! You can find Laser and Fire here.

Arena

Two fighters go in, but only one leaves. Eat a Tomato and an ability for a win!

Your opponent for this Arena is Mr. Frosty. Keep your distance and wait for him to throw ice blocks at you. Suck up the blocks and slap a "Return to Sender" on them to make short work of the slippery walrus.

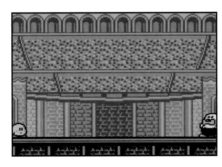

Level 2-5

Copy Abilities

Be careful while an enemy parachutes with a parasol.

But be especially careful when the parasol has been released!

Watch your head! Several enemies in this first area of Level 2-5 parachute down on parasols; one of those enemies is our favorite cannon, Shotzo! Enemies hanging from parasols are hard to predict, but that's not the only challenge here. Some of the parasols double back after the enemies release them. They angle toward Kirby and explode when they hit the ground. If you thought the enemies were unpredictable, get ready for the parasols!

Before you head through the door at the end of this area, head a little farther right to find a healing soda. Normally we'd recommend

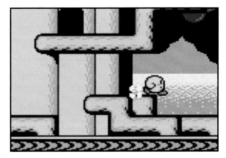

not drinking sodas you find on the ground in the middle of an island, but we insist you do it this one time, specifically if you're missing a couple of bars of health.

Sleep

Suck up Noddy to get Sleep.

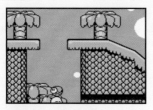

Though maybe you should just pass on it…

Did you think all Copy Abilities worked to Kirby's benefit? Unfortunately, Sleep proves that definitely isn't the case. This power does only one thing: makes Kirby fall asleep. It's a single-use power that, when used, forces Kirby to sleep, taking control of him away from you temporarily. Use it for a laugh, but never use it when there are enemies nearby.

When you reach the area containing Noddy (the enemy that gives the Sleep Copy Ability), drop down and follow the lower path for a healing item, avoid more Noddys and some Gordos along the way. The healing item is worth the trip.

Hi-Jump

Hi-Jump allows Kirby to leap into the air at a rapid pace. Any enemies Kirby jumps toward take damage, and Kirby is largely invulnerable during his jump. It functions similarly to Wheel, but instead of going horizontal, Kirby leaps vertically. Use it carefully and you can get a lot out of it. Use it recklessly and Kirby will end up dropping it.

Once you complete this area, you end up in an area in the sky, full of buildings on clouds. Notice all the buildings have windows, but

amongst these windows is an imposter! Jump and press Up to send Kirby through the would-be window like the door it actually is! What's inside? A Flamer enemy that yields the Fireball Copy Ability!

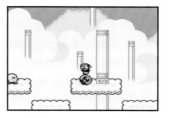

After completing the cloud village area, you come to a tall area covered in Star Blocks. Suck up one of the Starmen here to get Hi-Jump (if you didn't have it), then start jumping! Jump until you reach the door at the top of the area, then head on through.

As soon as you go through the door, Poppy Bro Jr. greets you, riding on a Maxim Tomato. If you were hurting for health before now, you're in luck!

Ice Cream Island Boss: Paint Roller

Paint Roller is an interesting Boss in that most of its attacks come from enemies it paints into existence. It skates from canvas to canvas, damaging you if you are in its path. Maneuvering

gets trickier, as Paint Roller spontaneously changes its path from one canvas to another, so be constantly ready to avoid it. Your best bet is to hover in one corner of the room until it comes to a stop.

You can suck up and swallow some of the enemies and items Paint Roller paints to attack you for a Copy Ability. Consult the following list of items and their corresponding powers:

A baseball: Ball Copy Ability

A lightning cloud: Spark Copy Ability

A parasol: Parasol Copy Ability

A bomb: Crash Copy Ability

A car: Wheel Copy Ability

Ball

Use the Ball Copy Ability to turn Kirby into a bouncy, rubber-like ball. He bounces off things and jumps higher than normal. It's hard to attack enemies with this power, so we suggest using it exclusively for traversal.

With the exception of the bomb, we suggest you spit all items at Paint Roller, instead of using the Copy Ability. Paint Roller moves around a lot, making it pretty hard to hit. Shooting stars at it deals the most damage, with the few opportunities you safely get.

3 BUTTER BUILDING

Copy Abilities

Level 3-1

In the second area in this stage, find a Bomb Block in the bottom-right corner of the room. Hit it to advance, but watch your head! There are two Rockys above that come crashing down as soon as you hit the Bomb Block.

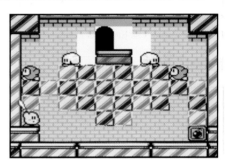

Miniboss: Mr. Tick-Tock

Find Mr. Tick-Tock in the next room. Keep your distance to figure out whether he's using a sound wave attack or shooting out musical notes. If the latter, get in there and attack! You can defeat him in no time!

Find your first Switch of the game in this stage. What are these mysterious giant Switches? Let's focus on hitting it first, then all will be made clear.

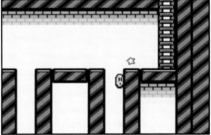

Two narrow pits lie directly below the Switch—except they aren't pits! Drop down the right hole to find a couple of Star Blocks. Suck up those Star Blocks to uncover a door. Enter that door and BOOM! The Switch is yours! Well...almost. You need to go through another door, but after that, it's all yours!

So back to what a Switch actually does. There are Switches hidden all over the remaining levels of Dream Land. When you manage to hit a Switch in a stage, you unlock a minigame for that level. In the case of this Switch, you unlock the Arena back on the Level Screen.

How to Find Switches

Some Switches are a real challenge to track down. So how do you know if one is hidden in a stage? Simple! When you complete the stage, the door flashes as if it's an unplayed level. If you see any doors flashing for stages you've already completed, that means there's more to discover!

Arena

Two fighters go in, but only one leaves. Eat a Tomato and an ability for a win!

Hit the Switch in Level 3-1 in order to unlock this minigame.

As a refresher, Grand Wheelie only has two attacks: driving into Kirby and throwing out smaller Wheelies to attack. When it charges toward you, it does so at a pretty slow speed, so dodging shouldn't be an issue. Keep your distance to avoid pretty much all of its attacks. When it falls over, it releases a Wheelie in your direction. Suck it up and spit it back at the Grand Wheelie to damage it. Repeat this process to defeat Grand Wheelie.

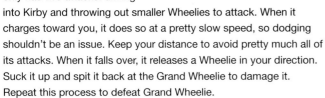

Level 3-2

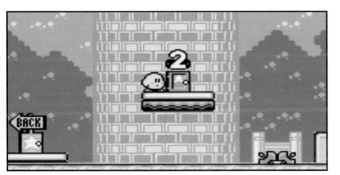

Copy Abilities

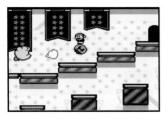

At the top of the first area awaits a most curious sight: Poppy Bro Jr. riding atop a Maxim Tomato. If you were hurting for health, here's your chance to undo that damage.

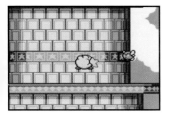

After leaving the first area, rotate a tower by running to the right. Easy enough, right? Well, it would be if it weren't for all the enemies that appear as you spin the tower. To avoid taking a lot of damage, be patient and careful.

In the next area, fly up the left side of the shaft until you see a Rocky fall on the right, then switch sides and fly up the right to avoid a second Rocky on the left.

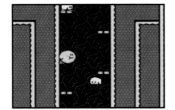

You find a Togezo near the top of this room, which you can suck up for Needle power. Use Needle in the next room to destroy a Bomb Block right above where you enter the area. The Bomb Block uncovers a path to another room, which leads to Grand Wheelie.

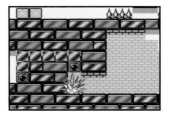

Take this opportunity to fight and defeat Grand Wheelie for its Wheel Copy Ability, as it helps you in this area. Once you have Wheel, drive through the rest of the area.

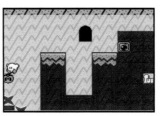

Getting the Power-Ups in the next room is a real challenge. Drop Wheel—you won't need it for the rest of the stage—and suck up one of the Pengis to gain Ice and shoot it at one of the Bomb Blocks while moving toward it. As soon as the Blocks disappear, fall toward the Power-Ups. Hold Down to gain a little more speed. If you're lucky, you'll get your hands on them. If not, they plummet into the pit below.

Ice

Though it shares an element with its cousin power Freeze, Ice has as much in common with Fire as it does Freeze. Instead of creating a freezing aura around Kirby, Ice allows Kirby to breathe freezing breath. Similar to Freeze, this freezing breath turns enemies into ice blocks for Kirby to kick, but that's where the similarities end.

Miniboss: Bugzzy

All that stands between you and the end of the level is Bugzzy, a monster beetle that is one of the hardest Minibosses you face in the game. Bugzzy's favorite method of attack is grabbing his enemies in his giant mandibles and slamming them to the ground. It's because of those mandibles that we told you to drop the Wheel power before this point; Wheel isn't invulnerable to Bugzzy's

grab attacks. Keep far away from Bugzzy at all times. Wait for him to unleash some small beetles to attack you. Suck those up and spit them out at Bugzzy to damage him.

Suck up Bugzzy after you defeat him for the Back Drop Copy Ability.

Back Drop

When Kirby sucks up enemies, instead of drawing them into his mouth, he pulls them into his hands to perform the devastating Back Drop attack on them. This only works on enemies Kirby can suck up, but once he's got one in his clutches, it's as good as done when the Back Drop hits.

Level 3-3

Copy Abilities

In the first area, while climbing down the ladder, take it slowly and stop just above each pair of empty squares. Bronto Burts flies up and hits you if you're in between the ladders as you descend.

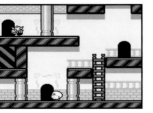

After the ladder, watch your head to avoid falling Waddle Dees. If you fall too far, the Waddle Dees reappear as you fly up, so make your ascent careful and calculated.

The final area of this stage is a bit tricky. It's a tower with two sides: a red side and a blue side. Hop back and forth between sides to make it out of the level.

Find a Maxim Tomato in the middle of the blue side of the tower. To reach it, go through the fourth door on the red side of the tower. For a 1-Up, go through the third door on the blue side.

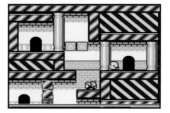

Museum

Here is a colorful display of enemies with special abilities. Eat the one you want! You can find Hi-Jump this time.

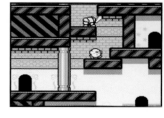

To reach the exit for this stage, climb to the top of the red side, then head through the door you find there. Hop through a couple more doors, and you're on your way out.

Level 3-4

Copy Abilities

★ ★ ★ ★ ★ ★ ★ ★ ★ ★ ★ ★ ★ ★ ★ ★ ★ ★ ★

Miniboss: Meta Knight's Knights

This a fairly simple stage that mostly focuses on fighting Meta Knight's crew. As we suggested before, use normal Kirby to suck up each Knight and spit it at the others. The fight is over before you know it.

At the end of this stage, you encounter a wind tunnel full of Shotzos, Gordos, and a handful of Power-Ups. Move slowly and carefully to avoid taking damage while also grabbing the goodies. It's a pretty dangerous area, but nothing you can't handle.

★ ★ ★ ★ ★ ★ ★ ★ ★ ★ ★ ★ ★ ★ ★ ★ ★ ★ ★

Quick Draw

When the enemy draws, press the A Button. If you press it too soon, you get a penalty!

Level 3-5

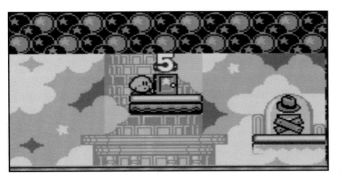

Copy Abilities

What luck! You find an Invincibility Candy in the bottom-right corner of the starting room in this stage. Grab it and start running! You need

it for the next area, which is another spinning tower. This time there are even more enemies, which are no trouble for Hyper Kirby.

Miniboss: Bonkers

Bonkers looks intimidating, but once you learn his patterns, taking him out is effortless. Like Grand Wheelie, Bonkers loves to charge

and throw things at Kirby. Unlike Grand Wheelie, Bonkers also loves to jump and slam his hammer down. When he slams his hammer, he often produces a star, which Kirby can suck up and spit at Bonkers. Also use the coconuts he throws as weapons against him.

Once you defeat Bonkers, suck him up for Hammer power.

Hammer

 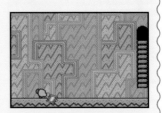

Hammer is one of the strongest and most useful powers in the game. It functions similarly to Sword in that Kirby simply swings a weapon around. The difference here is Hammer's damage outmatches Sword's, allowing Hammer to excel in close-range fights.

 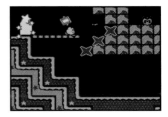

An interesting function of Hammer outside of combat is its ability to pound pegs into the ground. Test this ability in the next room. Fly up to the peg to the right of the stage exit door and pound it into the ground to free the Maxim Tomato and 1-Up.

Level 3-6

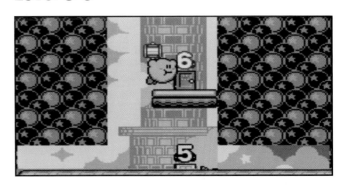

Copy Abilities

Be very careful in this tunnel. There are several Bombers here, and normally you just stay in the air when they explode to avoid damage, but you have a hard job pulling that off in these narrow spaces. You can use Laser at the start of the stage to

fight them, but you should also have enough time to get in close and suck them up when you see them.

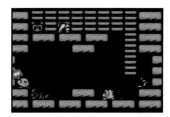

If that tunnel beat you up, take comfort in knowing the next area has a Maxim Tomato out in the open and ready for Kirby's consumption.

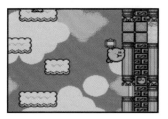

As you scale the tower, keep an eye out for a set of Star Blocks built into the side. Destroying them reveals a door. Once you enter, spot the Bomb Block sitting above you. Hit it to reach the other side of the room, but be quick! Blocks form in the middle of the room, barricading the door. To get across before the blocks appear, hit the Bomb Block, then immediately fly across the top of the room to the door.

Find another Switch just past the door. This Switch opens the Egg Catcher Minigame for this world.

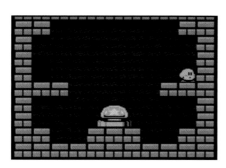

After you climb the tower, you enter a very dark area. Be careful here, because all sorts of enemies lurk in the darkness. The only way to lift the darkness is with a bright enemy called Cool Spook.

Find these luminescent spectres in this room—trust us, you can't miss them. Once you see one, suck it up and swallow it to gain the Light Copy Ability. This single-use power lights up any darkened rooms like this one.

Egg Catcher

Press the buttons to make Kirby's mouth open. Eat the eggs—but not the bombs!

To unlock this stage, hit the Switch found in Level 3-5.

Butter Building Boss: Mr. Shine and Mr. Bright

This is one of the tougher Bosses in the game, because you fight not one Boss, but two! Mr. Shine and Mr. Bright are a sun and moon that usually feud with each other, but when it comes to Kirby, they make amends and team up to give the creampuff what for.

Each enemy takes turns fighting with Kirby directly, while the other hovers in the sky. The hovering enemy shoots projectiles, which produce stars for Kirby to suck up. We suggest bringing a Copy Ability into this fight. We

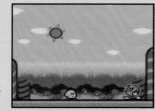

find Sword and Hammer are particularly useful against these two. Just don't go in empty-handed, because it can be really hard to grab a star from an attack—and dangerous.

While Mr. Bright (the sun) is in the air, he shoots out a flurry of beam attacks directly at the ground while slowly moving toward Kirby. This attack produces stars, but watch out for Mr. Shine's position, because he loves to roll at Kirby, which can block your ability to grab a star.

Mr. Shine attacks while in the air by calling down a storm of stars all around the map. Thankfully Kirby can suck up these stars, and they are generally easier to get ahold of than the ones from Mr. Bright's attack. Don't worry about Mr. Bright blocking your chance to get stars since he mostly likes to jump around. He charges at you from time to time, but this attack is pretty easy to spot.

We tell you all this in case you lose your Copy Ability during the fight. Really, if you bring in a power and go to town, you should be just fine.

LEVEL 4 · GRAPE GARDEN

Level 4-1

Copy Abilities

Find the UFO Copy Ability in the third area of this stage. UFOs abound here!

Push up where Kirby is to find a secret room.

And you find a Switch inside!

At the end of the next room, find a secret room in the wall of Star Blocks blocking your passage to the door. Find a Switch inside that unlocks the Crane Fever Minigame on the Level Screen.

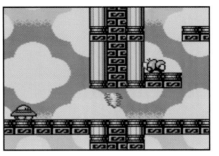

Unfortunately, the Star Blocks aren't hiding any other secrets, so head through the door to the next area after you're done here.

This next area is positively packed with Twisters, and the path is narrow, so take it nice and slow to get through unscathed. Twisters bounce quickly and randomly, so figuring out where they'll go while on the warpath is tricky.

Crane Fever

Use the buttons to move the crane and get a Kirby. A big one's hard to get, but worth it!

To unlock this stage, hit the Switch in Level 4-1.

Level 4-2

Copy Abilities

On the right side of the third area of this stage, find a tower of Star Blocks. Clear them out to find a door leading to a Maxim Tomato.

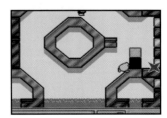

Near the end of the stage, a soda sits between two sets of spikes. As tempting as it might be to grab it, especially if you're low on health, ignore this one outright. It's too difficult to reach that soda unscathed. You're better off moving on.

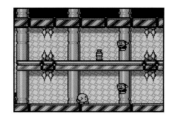

Miniboss: Poppy Bros. Sr.

Our old friend Poppy Bro Sr. is back, but this time he's brought another Bro. Two Poppy Bros may seem intimidating, but the same strategy from last time works just as well here. Stay put in the middle of the room and duck down when the Bros start jumping back and forth. When one throws a bomb, suck it up while avoiding the other bomb, then let one of the Bros have it! Take out one of them, and the fight becomes much easier.

Quick Draw
When the enemy draws, press the A Button. If you press it too soon, you get a penalty!

Level 4-3

Copy Abilities

Grab Fire.   *Light the fuse.*   *Get in the cannon.*

You encounter a trapped Hot Head right at the start of the stage. Suck it up for Fire power—you need it for this next part. Once you have Fire, head up the hill until you find a piece of rope sticking out of the ground. Except it's not just any rope, it's a fuse! Use Fire on that fuse, then run to the right. Find a cannon just below the fuse. Hop in the cannon and wait for the fuse to burn up. Once the spark reaches the cannon, Kirby shoots into the sky to snatch a 1-Up!

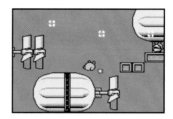

You hop from blimp to blimp in this next area. The strong winds up here constantly push you to the right, and flying to the left is much, much slower. If you're not careful, the wind blows you into enemies and obstacles pretty easily.

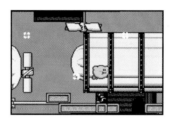

If you drop to the bottom of the area and head right, you eventually run into a blimp with a door. If you have Hammer, bust open some boxes in there to gain access to a Maxim Tomato.

 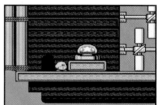

Keep heading to the right while flying on the bottom of the screen to encounter another door. A Switch inside uncovers the Museum in the Level Screen.

Museum

Here is a colorful display of enemies with special abilities. Eat the one you want! Sleep and Ball are your powers for this Museum—not a great spread, but at least you have access to other powers in other Museums.

Arena

Two fighters go in, but only one leaves. Eat a Tomato and an ability for a win!

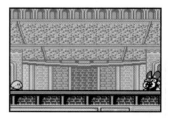

Bugzzy's your opponent for this Arena, which means you get Back Drop if you defeat him. As a reminder, keep your distance from him at all times and wait for him to send smaller beetles after you. Suck those up and shoot them back at him to deal him damage.

Level 4-4

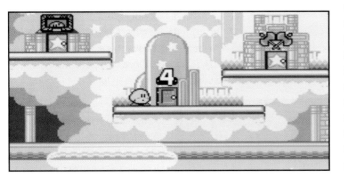

Copy Abilities

In the third area of this stage, you arrive at a set of slopes and a Wheelie trapped in a small alcove. Grab the Wheelie and start racing down the slopes!

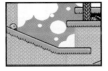 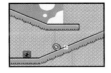 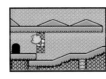

You encounter a Bomb Block on the second slope. Race through it, but don't stop there! From here on out, it's a race against a spark produced by the Bomb Block! Bring your Wheel A-game to stay ahead of the spark.

Ultimately your goal is to reach the bottom of the area and head to the door on the left side of the screen. A 1-Up waits for you as a prize for getting first place.

You come to another "Pick Your Power" section before the next Miniboss, but we suggest you forgo taking either of these powers. The next Miniboss is challenging, and being close to him is dangerous. You're better off fighting him as normal Kirby than with any of the Copy Abilities you have access to right now.

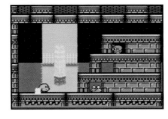

Miniboss: Rolling Turtle

Rolling Turtle is quite similar to Bugzzy in the way he fights. If he gets close, he grabs you and throws you across the room. Stay as far away from him as possible. When he hops into the air while spinning, he throws a turtle in your direction. That's your moment

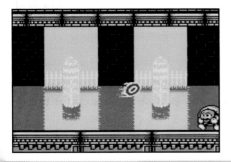

to strike! Suck up the turtle and shoot it back at Rolling Turtle to damage him. Repeat this process until Rolling Turtle has been defeated, then suck him up to gain the Throw Copy Ability.

Throw

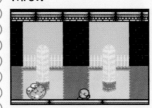 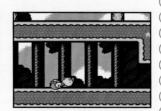

Throw is similar to Back Drop in that Kirby sucks up enemies, but instead of slamming them backward, Kirby throws them forward. How is this different from Kirby sucking up and spitting out enemies? Well, for starters, Throw does more damage, but the real difference is that you can angle Kirby's throws upward, instead of just throwing straight.

Level 4-5

Copy Abilities

At the start of the stage, Meta Knight throws an Invincibility Candy to Kirby, which you should accept graciously. Hyper Kirby lasts until just before the first door in this area, provided you race over there as quickly as you can.

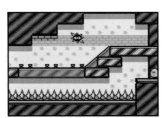

The room behind the first door leads you to a 1-Up if you head all the way right. A wall seems to block you on the far right side, but that's an illusion. Walk right through the wall and drop down to the lower part of the room. From here, head left until you find two Star Blocks stacked on top of each other. Destroy both blocks to uncover a door, then head through the door to find a 1-Up.

Miniboss: Meta Knight's Knights

Face off against Meta Knight's cadre of Knights once again! You know how to deal with these masked maniacs now. Go get 'em!

Before you finish the level, traverse the Deadly Gordo Gauntlet. Move carefully and watch the Gordos' movement patterns to avoid taking damage here.

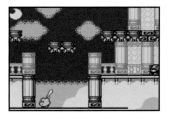

Level 4-6

Copy Abilities

Miniboss: Mr. Tick-Tock

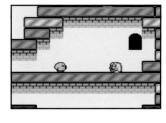
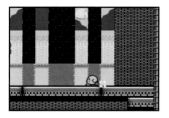

Face off with Mr. Tick-Tock once again! A Hot Head lurks just before the door leading into Tick-Tock's room. We highly suggest you absorb it for Fire power, which works really well against Tick-Tock.

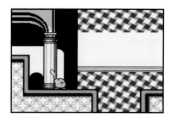
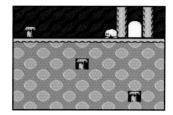

The next room is pitch-black, and the only way to raise the brightness level is to swallow another Cool Spook and use the Light Copy Ability. Head left to encounter a previously unseen door. Inside the door is a Switch, which unlocks the Grape Garden Warp Station.

After leaving the dark room, you enter a room with three pegs and a single Rocky. Absorb the Rocky for Stone power, then hit the left peg, the right peg, then the middle peg to unlock the 1-Up.

Grape Garden Boss: Kracko

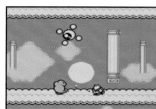

The fight with Kracko doesn't begin as soon as you enter the door, at least not in the usual sense. Start by sucking up the Starman and swallowing it for Hi-Jump, then leap up the screen until you run out of real estate. Kracko eventually catches up and begins the fight in earnest.

Hi-Jump is effective against the cycloptic cloud. Leap through him while angling yourself diagonally, so that you can fall away from Kracko after completing your jump.

Kracko's attacks are pretty easy to dodge. He charges at you, doubling back and basically circling the screen. If you're in either corner when he does this, you can avoid damage with little issue.

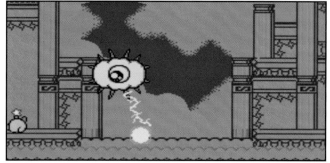

Kracko also shoots a continuous stream of lightning at the ground while moving toward Kirby. Either fly over Kracko or jump through him with Hi-Jump.

His final attack simply involves Kracko conjuring a Starman that jumps in Kirby's general direction. Suck up the Starman if you lose your Hi-Jump, or get out of the way.

LEVEL 5 — YOGURT YARD

Crane Fever

Use the buttons to move the crane and get a Kirby. A big one's hard to get, but worth it!

Hit the Switch hidden in Level 5-1 to unlock this stage.

Level 5-1

Copy Abilities

About halfway through the first area of this stage, you come across a tiny door. To reach it, go back a little ways, and fly under the clouds and over the Shotzo. A 1-Up and a couple of Rockys wait inside.

You start the next area falling past a multitude of enemies. Stay in the center to avoid taking damage. When you hit the row of Star Blocks, destroy them to find a hidden lower area. A door there contains another Switch. To uncover the door, destroy the tallest row of Star Blocks.

The Switch unlocks the Yogurt Yard Crane Fever.

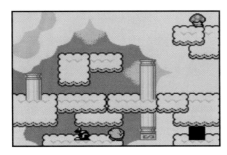

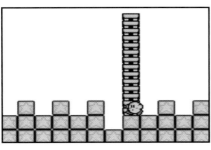

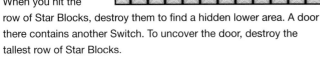

Level 5-2

Copy Abilities

When you come to this door, make a point to go through it. When you first enter the area, you'd be forgiven for assuming you came through that door, but really it's just a clever way to hide a 1-Up. Head on through and claim it as your own!

★★★★★★★★★★★★★★★★★★★★★

Miniboss: Bonkers

Bonkers makes another appearance in this stage. Watch for those coconuts, and send them right back at him!

★★★★★★★★★★★★★★★★★★★★★

Egg Catcher
Press the buttons to make Kirby's mouth open. Eat the eggs—but not the bombs!

Museum

Here is a colorful display of enemies with special abilities. Eat the one you want! This time, your free Copy Abilities include Stone and Tornado.

Level 5-3

Copy Abilities

Shotzos positively load the first area of this stage. Be bold and charge through! If you fly straight up the middle, you'll be fine. Just don't pause, even for a moment, or you risk taking a hit!

Eventually you come across a Wheelie. If you don't aleady have a Copy Ability, suck it up and use Wheel for this area. There's a whole lot of road to cover here, and a whole lot of enemies that try to stop you. Wheel makes quick work of traversing this area.

Drop the Wheel power once you enter the next area. It doesn't do you a lot of good here.

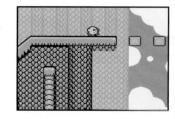

At the end of the Star Block bridge ahead, find two Star Blocks stacked on top of each other. Clear them out to find a door. Inside are two pegs, a Rocky, a Maxim Tomato, and a 1-Up. Use Stone to pound the pegs down, but be warned: the Maxim Tomato is perfectly safe, but the 1-Up will plummet into a hole the peg creates. Use Stone Kirby to drop rapidly, grab the 1-Up, then quickly break away from stone form. The timing here is extremely tight, so maybe practice midair transformations before trying the real thing.

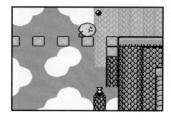

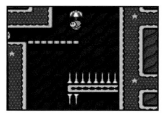 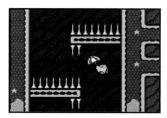

Grab the parasol in this room. This whole area is just one long chamber of spikes and the parasol will make navigating this treacherous terrain.

Level 5-4

Copy Abilities

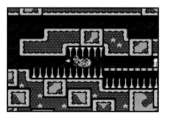

As you start this stage, you run into a Flamer enemy. Suck it up to get Fireball power. This area is full of narrow corridors layered with spikes; Fireball helps you get through these tunnels unscathed. If you can hang on to your Fireball power through most of this area, you eventually get the chance to grab a 1-Up.

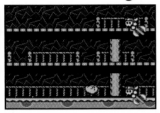

Miniboss: Meta Knight's Knights

If you manage to carry Fireball all the way to this point, you're in luck! Fireball is particularly devastating against Meta Knight's squad.

When you reach the waterfall area in this stage, look out for the small passage where water is pouring out (use the screenshot above to point the way). That's not just any ol' water passage; it's a door! And inside is another hidden Switch! Head through the door in the middle of the room and hit the Switch to unlock the Arena for the Yogurt Yard.

As a side note: if you're wondering how to make that 1-Up yours, get to the left of it and suck it up through the platforms!

Arena

Two fighters go in, but only one leaves. Eat a Tomato and an ability for a win!

To unlock this Arena, hit the Switch hidden in Level 5-4.

You know him. You love him. Bonkers is back for another fight! Knock him out, and his Hammer Copy Ability is yours!

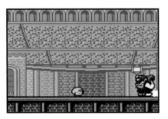

Level 5-5

Copy Abilities

Stay low in the first area of this stage. You eventually come to a door with a cannon, a Hot Head, and a Starman inside. This is clearly a puzzle, but how do you go about solving it? You might be tempted to grab the Hot Head for its Fire power, light the fuse, then grab the Starman to jump through the Star Blocks, but unfortunately that order doesn't leave you with enough time to get to the cannon.

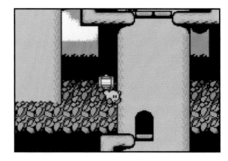

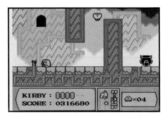

Instead, start with the Starman's Hi-Jump ability and leap through the Star Blocks to clear the way.

Drop Hi-Jump with the Select Button, then absorb the Hot Head and light the fuse. Use your cleared route to reach the cannon quickly.

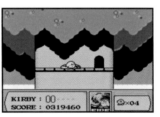

After all that work, you should get something nice, right? You aren't wrong. All that effort pays off, and you gain access to another hidden Switch! Hit this one to unlock the Yogurt Yard Quick Draw Minigame.

Miniboss: Fire Lion

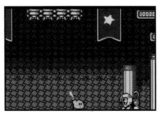

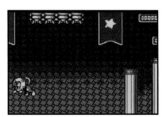

This Miniboss can be a real heel. He grabs you like Bugzzy and Rolling Turtle, charges at you faster than Bonkers and Grand Wheelie, and he likes jumping almost as much as the Poppy Bros. Nervous yet? Don't be, but don't underestimate this ferocious feline either. He tears Kirby into pink fluff if he's allowed to.

One of his favorite strategies is to trick Kirby into flying while he charges toward our favorite creampuff. His aim here is to get Kirby in the air so he can leap and smack him. Be careful to avoid getting caught in this clever trap.

continues

Miniboss: Fire Lion - continued

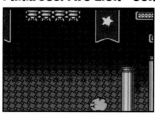

The time to strike is when he face-plants. He leaps into the air on occasion and comes down straight onto his face, producing a star in the process. Suck up that star and hit Fire Lion, then wait for your next opportunity.

Once you finally defeat him, absorb him for Fireball.

Watch out for Bounders climbing up and down the trees in this area. As you approach the trees, they attempt to fall on your head. A Laser Ball at the start of this area helps— shoot the slopes, and the beam bounces upward toward the Bounder—but what helps the most is patience. Approach a tree, wait for the Bounder to fall, defeat it, then move on.

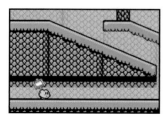

Quick Draw

When the enemy draws, press the A Button. If you press it too soon, you get a penalty!

To play this minigame, hit the Switch hidden in 5-5.

Level 5-6

Copy Abilities

You find another hidden Switch, but to grab it, you need Hammer power. Thankfully the Arena has Bonkers, who gives Hammer power when absorbed. Head over, fight him, and grab his Hammer power before starting this stage.

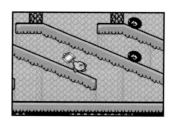

Getting the Switch requires you to carry Hammer through most of the stage without losing it. By now you are likely acutely of how easy it is to lose a Copy Ability. The easiest way to avoid losing a power is to avoid taking damage, and the easiest way to do that is to avoid fighting altogether. This is a real challenge in this stage, especially in the first area. A ton of Wheelies ride up and down lots of slopes here. Rushing through this area is almost guaranteed to get you hit. Very slowly move through to see if a Wheelie appears from off the screen before transitioning to the next slope.

Enter the first door you encounter in the third area of this stage to find a strange arrangement of blocks surrounding six Star Blocks. This is what you need Hammer for. Swim up and destroy the green blocks at the top of this arrangement to reach the Star Blocks. Destroy those two to find a door that leads to the hidden Switch in this stage. Hitting that Switch unlocks the Star Station for Yogurt Yard.

Yogurt Yard Boss: Heavy Mole

Heavy Mole is a different Boss fight than you've seen up to this point. The entire time you fight it, it constantly digs to the right side of the screen. If you don't constantly keep up with it, you can get left behind and potentially lose a life. When Heavy Mole digs upward, you lose a life if you fall to a point off the screen. Take special care to watch your footing.

Heavy Mole doesn't really have any attacks aside from opening its back hatch and shooting projectiles at you on occasion. Its digging tools do damage if they touch you, but that's only if you get too close.

To damage Heavy Mole, simply suck up its projectiles and spit them back at it. All in all, though this is a different kind of Boss fight, it's mechanically simple. That doesn't mean it's not a challenge, but you know exactly what you're up against once you get into the fight.

LEVEL 6 ORANGE OCEAN

You've probably encountered a Mix Copy Ability by now, but in case you haven't, Mix is what happens when you suck up two or more enemies with Copy Abilities at the same time. The powers mix, and you get a random power to replace them. Though, in reality, it's not as random as it might appear. Certain combinations of enemies increase the likelihood of certain powers being produced. In this case, sucking up the Flamer and Sparky gives you a high chance of getting Hammer, which is a power you need to hit the hidden Switch in this stage.

Level 6-1

Take Hammer through the first door you encounter up ahead, and use it to break the block barricading the door in the bottom-middle area of the room. Head through the door to find the hidden Switch for this stage, which unlocks Orange Ocean's Museum.

Copy Abilities

Miniboss: Rolling Turtle

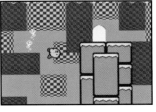

Going through the first door you find in this stage leads you to Rolling Turtle, in what is arguably one the toughest rooms in the game for fighting a Miniboss. The shallow water is just high enough to prevent you from sucking up the rocks he throws, and from jumping over his attacks easily. Since this fight only yields the Throw Copy Ability, we suggest avoiding it altogether. Throw is not worth the effort and risk it takes to get it. The only real benefit to having Throw in this stage is the ability to get a 1-Up, which we believe isn't work the risk either.

The final area of this stage is very challenging. Leaping, flying, and running enemies attack Kirby at every turn. Move through this place slowly, and take out each enemy one at a time.

Museum

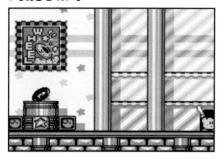

Here is a colorful display of enemies with special abilities. Eat the one you want! On display in this Museum? None other than Wheelie!

Access this Museum by hitting the Switch in Level 6-1.

Level 6-2

Copy Abilities

To get the soda in this screenshot, bring a Copy Ability into the stage. Puffing up with air and spitting it out at the Bomb Block doesn't give you enough time to reach the soda.

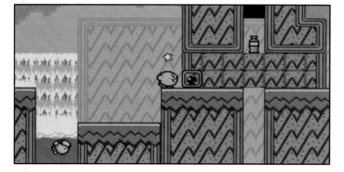

Another important element to this particular area is the black square above the soda. You may have already guessed, but that's actually a door. Upon entering the room, stand completely still. A Rocky falls from the sky and crushes you if you try to get the 1-Up too soon. Suck up the Rocky to get Stone power; you need it to reach the hidden Switch in this stage.

In the middle of the cloud area is a door. Enter with Hammer or the Stone power you found earlier and pound the peg down in the center of the room. This grants you access to the hidden Switch, which unlocks the Arena for Orange Ocean.

Be careful when exiting. The Sparkys in the room prior are right there waiting for you, regardless of whatever door you exit the Switch room from.

This area of the stage is jam-packed with Copy Ability enemies. Right from the start you find Fireball and Tornado, and at the end of the area you find UFO! Find a Maxim Tomato at the bottom too!

Arena

Two fighters go in, but only one leaves. Eat a Tomato and an ability for a win!

Hit the Switch in Level 6-2 to unlock this Arena.

Fire Lion is back and as ferocious as ever. Keep an eye out for its air attacks, don't let it grab you, and be ready for when it smashes its face into the ground— that's your time to strike!

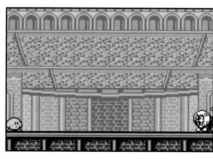

Defeating and absorbing Fire Lion nets you Fireball.

Level 6-3

Copy Abilities

★★★★★★★★★★★★★★★★★★★★★

Miniboss: Bonkers

Bonkers returns in this stage, and it's a good thing too! To get the hidden Switch in this stage, you need his Hammer power. Find Fireball in front of the door leading into the stage's second area. Fireball works well against Bonkers, so to make the fight go quickly, grab it on the way in.

★★★★★★★★★★★★★★★★★★★★★

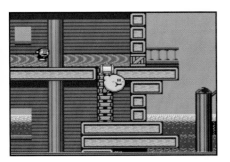

After defeating Bonkers, absorb him for his Hammer power. Head right, and destroy the crate to the right of the top of the ladder.

Head to the right and drop down. Follow the path left until you see a Bomb Block. Hit the Bomb Block to flood the lower area of the ship. Walk over to where the Bomb Block was, and press Up to head through an invisible passage. Hold Down

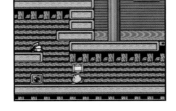

immediately after emerging. There's a 1-Up directly below you in the next room, and you don't have a chance of getting it if you aren't holding Down as soon as you enter.

Getting Hammer Back

If you lose Hammer at any point, head back through the door you entered the area from and then re-enter the area to make Bonkers reappear. You have to fight him again to get Hammer once more.

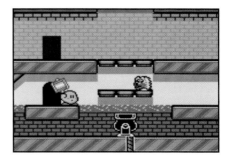

Defeat the Sword Knight, then push up while standing on the block he was on. You enter another hidden room, this one containing a Maxim Tomato and a Laser Ball. Suck up the Laser Ball to get Laser power, then head back out and go through the passage on the left. Use Laser to shoot the slanted corner on the right side of the room, just above the fuse. This lights the cannon fuse, so jump into the cannon immediately afterward.

After all these steps, after going through all this, your reward is worth it: a hidden Switch that unlocks the Crane Fever in Orange Ocean.

Once back outside, you come to a part of the ship with two doors. When you enter, you encounter a wall that separates you from a 1-Up. The trick is to ignore the doors and go through the windows instead.

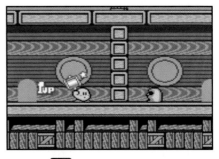

Crane Fever

Use the buttons to move the crane and get a Kirby. A big one's hard to get, but worth it!

Hit the Switch in Level 6-3 to unlock this Crane Fever.

Level 6-4

Copy Abilities

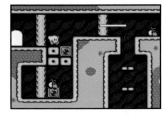

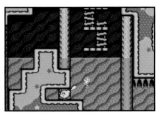

In the second area of this stage, you find a handful of Bomb Blocks and a small collection of 1-Ups. You need a power that can attack downward to destroy the first Bomb Block. We suggest you use Freeze, which you can find in Level 5-1. It's a bit of a trek to get back there, but as soon as you get Freeze, pause the game and exit the level, then race right back here. You get a whole mess of 1-Ups for your trouble.

Another tricky hidden passage conceals the Switch for this stage. Use the screenshot to find exactly where it is. This location is in the bottom-right corner of the second area. Enter the narrow path and push Up when you reach the end to find the Switch. Hitting the Switch unlocks the Egg Catching Minigame for Orange Ocean.

Coconuts cover this narrow area. Grab the parasol from the prior area before flying up this mess. The parasol deflects the coconuts, allowing you to safely reach the top.

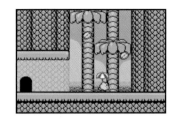

Egg Catcher

Press the buttons to make Kirby's mouth open. Eat the eggs—but not the bombs!

Hit the Switch in Level 6-4 to unlock this minigame.

Level 6-5

Copy Abilities

This stage hides another tricky Switch. After traversing several areas, you eventually come to a mountain with a Bomb Block near its summit. Destroying the Bomb Block uncovers a fuse. Head up a little farther to find another Bomb Block; this one uncovers the cannon the fuse is connected to.

The obvious goal here is to light the fuse, then jump into the cannon in time to be shot out of it, but this is much, MUCH easier said than done.

To complete this challenge, both Bomb Blocks must be destroyed before you light the fuse. Get Fire to light the fuse from the Hot Head at the base of the mountain. As soon as you light the fuse, fly back up and immediately double-tap the Right Button to make Kirby run. Two enemies on the slope can undo your plans if they hit you. Don't attack either of them. Jump over both of them without flying and keep on running. If you do everything right, you land in the cannon with just enough time to spare.

If at any point you make a mistake, head to the start of the area, go through the door, and come back to reset the room.

Quick Draw

When the enemy draws, press the A Button. If you press it too soon, you get a penalty!

To unlock this Quick Draw, hit the Switch hidden in 6-5.

Level 6-6

UFOs, which wait in the next area, work splendidly for breaking ice blocks. Grab one, then fly back to the first area of the stage and break open the ice blocks. Inside you find—you guessed it!—another hidden Switch. Hitting this one unlocks the Orange Ocean Star Station.

Eventually you come to a room with two doors to choose from. Which door should you go through? Well, the bottom door leads to a pair of Mr. Frostys, but after that it's a pretty simple trip to where the paths converge.

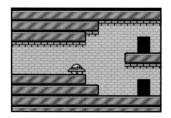

The top room, on the other hand, leads to a pair of Poppy Bros Sr., then to a room with an Invincibility Candy, and eventually a 1-Up, but only if you have Fire, Fireball, or UFO power. The choice is yours which door to use. Both paths inevitably converge on Meta Knight's squad.

Copy Abilities

In the first area of this stage, run to the right until you find an opening in the ground. Drop down and fly to the left. Find a small passage with a door barricaded by ice blocks. To break through, you need another power, which, as luck would have it, you can find in the next room.

Miniboss: Meta Knight's Knights

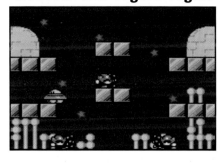

No matter what path you take, you end up fighting Meta Knight's squadron of Knights. Use normal Kirby to suck each of them up and spit them out at each other, making short work of them.

Orange Ocean Boss: Meta Knight

It's finally time to take on Meta Knight and discover whether he's actually friend or foe. A sword in the center of the room gives Kirby permanent Sword power for this fight. Meta Knight wants a duel between equals and refuses to fight until he's certain Kirby agrees to these terms.

Meta Knight fights like Fire Lion in that he loves to trick you into moving in certain directions. He also charges toward you quickly and deflects your attacks with his sword. If that's not bad enough, he often follows up your attacks with a counterattack. He's a real challenger, so to beat him, be ready for anything.

There isn't really a trick to fighting Meta Knight. Dodge his attacks, then immediately follow up with a flurry of your own. It takes practice and skill to best him, so don't worry if you lose lives against him. You can do it!

LEVEL 7 RAINBOW RESORT

Two blue blocks keep you from reaching the door, but those aren't a problem. Head back until you find a Flamer enemy, then absorb it for Fireball power. Head back up to the door and use Fireball to break the blue blocks to the right of the upper right door. What's through the door? A hidden Switch that unlocks Rainbow Resort's Crane Fever Minigame.

Level 7-1

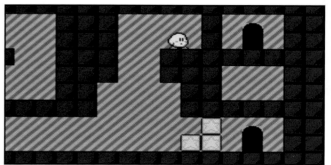

Copy Abilities

When you reach this room full of Star Blocks, you can find a hidden Switch if you know what to look for. Start this room by making your way toward the Sparky and Hot Head, then grab one to speed up the Star Block-destroying process. When you see a Waddle Doo, suck it up for Beam power; this makes fast work of destroying the Star Blocks.

Crane Fever

Use the buttons to move the crane and get a Kirby. A big one's hard to get, but worth it!

Track down the tricky Switch in Level 7-1 to unlock this minigame.

Level 7-2

Copy Abilities

Near the end of the area, you come across a trio of Waddle Dees in a small alcove on top of the Star Blocks. If you jump up and use Beam in their alcove, you actually destroy some of the deep blue blocks that make up the area. You can clear a path in the blue blocks all the way up to the door in the top-right corner of the area.

Welcome to the Tower of Minibosses! This place is positively packed with Minibosses—in fact, you face every Miniboss you've fought throughout the game in this stage. The same strategies work, but we give you a brief refresher for each enemy you encounter. It's a tough climb, but you can do it!

Miniboss: Poppy Bro Sr.

The first challenger is Poppy Bro Sr., whom you should be all too familiar with. Stand in the middle and watch out for his jump attacks.

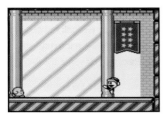

Suck up his bombs and throw them right back. Once he's defeated, absorb him for Crash power, which makes the next Miniboss that much easier.

Miniboss: Mr. Tick-Tock

Tick-Tock isn't particularly fast, but he still charges at you. Wait for him to release music notes while ringing his bells, but watch out for the sound waves he produces.

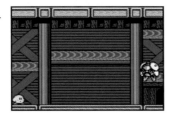

Once Tick-Tock is down, absorb him for Mike power, which makes the next Miniboss easier.

Miniboss: Mr. Frosty

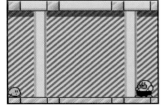

Mr. Frosty is slow and easy to defeat. Wait for him to throw an ice block at you, suck it up, then shoot it right back at him. It's that simple.

After beating him, absorb him for Freeze power.

Miniboss: Bonkers

Bonkers produces a star when he slams his hammer down, but you can also use his coconuts against him. He's not too challenging, and absorbing him gains you Hammer power. However, we advise against using it for the next Miniboss.

Miniboss: Rolling Turtle

Stay away from Rolling Turtle at all costs and wait for him to throw out a boulder. Suck up those boulders and shoot them back at him, which is your primary method of attack against this challenging foe.

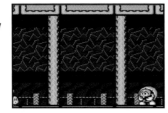

Absorbing Rolling Turtle nets you Throw, but we suggest you don't use it for the next Miniboss.

Miniboss: Bugzzy

Just like Rolling Turtle, stay away from Bugzzy at all times. Wait for him to send out his little beetles, suck them up, then shoot them back at this beastly bug.

Bugzzy grants Back Drop when absorbed, but that's not very useful for the next Miniboss.

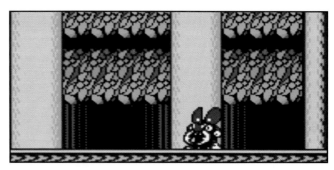

Miniboss: Fire Lion

To wrap things up, you fight Fire Lion. You likely remember how tough Fire Lion is, so be ready for the worst. Watch out for his face-plants, so you can grab a star and spit it back at him.

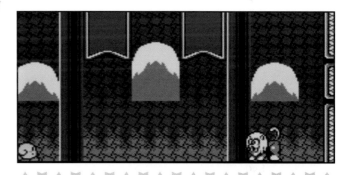

Level 7-3

Copy Abilities

This level is short and sweet to make up for that fantastically challenging Miniboss tower. Nothing significant troubles you in this stage. Head on through at a leisurely pace to catch your breath before the next level.

Level 7-4

Copy Abilities

The Twizzies in the starting area of this stage are out for Kirby and persistently chase him until Kirby defeats them or they make contact with the pink puff. Take it slow through this area to avoid getting overwhelmed by several Twizzies at once.

This first area is a veritable zoo of Copy Ability enemies. You have plenty of options to choose from.

Level 7-5

Copy Abilities

Bombers litter the first area in this stage. You have no hope of defeating them all before they hit the ground, so employ a different strategy. Bombers damage everything that touches the ground or a platform, but Kirby doesn't have to worry about being hurt by their explosions if he's in the air. Fly on through this first area.

A challenging fuse-and-cannon section lies near the end of the stage. In order to light the fuse and successfully make it into the cannon, absorb one of these Bombers and carry Crash all the way to the fuse. That's no simple task, but it must be done to reach that cannon!

Miniboss: Grand Wheelie

One more Grand Wheelie fight for the road! Wait for Grand Wheelie to shoot out smaller Wheelies, suck them up, and shoot them back.

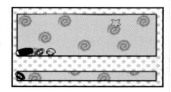

If you're carrying Crash to the fuse, this fight presents more of a challenge. Press Select to release Crash every time Grand Wheelie shoots out smaller Wheelies. Suck up the Wheelie, shoot it back, then quickly reabsorb Crash. Repeat this until Grand Wheelie is defeated.

Pay close attention to the background to get through this area safely. Whatever direction the shooting-star emblems point toward reflects the direction the invisible wind tunnel pushes Kirby as he crosses them. If a star points up, Kirby launches up. If it points down, he's forced down. This can make getting over pits quite tricky. Add to that the Sparkys and Flamers waiting across several of the pits, and you've got a deadly obstacle course.

Take it slow and jump toward the Flamers to bait them into attacking Kirby, then immediately pull back.

Now to the main event: the cannon and fuse. If you brought Crash all the way over here, this is the easy part. Line Kirby up with the fuse as close to the left side of the screen as possible, use Crash, then immediately hop into the cannon.

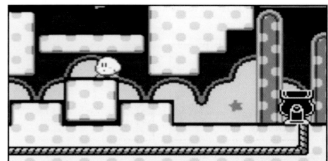

For your trouble, you net four 1-Ups. Not a bad haul for all that effort!

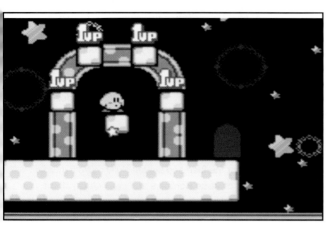

Level 7-6

Copy Abilities

This stage is a real treat for *Kirby's Dream Land* fans, because it acts as a sort of abridged version of that game, taking Kirby back through his old haunts.

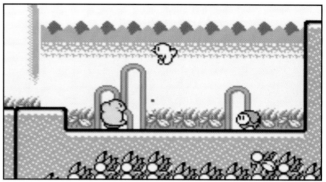

The hidden Switch in this stage is pretty tricky to find. When you reach the door to finish the stage, instead of heading through, fly up to the moon. The moon is actually a secret passage that leads to the Switch. Hitting the Switch unlocks the Star Station for Rainbow Resort.

Rainbow Resort Boss: King Dedede

Dedede looks simple enough, but don't underestimate him; he's a real challenger! Several of his attacks drop stars, but he attacks so fast and furiously that it can be hard to reach them. He also has a ton of health, so this fight requires careful health management as well as skill. Every bar is precious, so don't make any risky moves if you want to see this fight through to the end.

Keep your distance at all times, because Dedede has a habit of springing toward you unexpectedly. He also sucks things up just like Kirby—or in this case, he sucks KIRBY up!—and if you're near him when he starts inhaling, you're definitely going into his belly.

He also inflates like Kirby and flies around the stage. Don't fly when he does this. He is faster than an air-filled Kirby, and he almost always hits you. Instead, stay on the ground and wait for him to hit the ground. He bounces back up a little bit, which gives you a chance to run past him to the other side of the screen.

FOUNTAIN OF DREAMS

It turns out that Dedede didn't take the Star Rod out of the Fountain of Dreams to harm Dream Land; he did it to protect it! Hidden inside the dreams of Dream Land's inhabitants was a creature of pure darkness known only as the Nightmare. It's up to you to save Dream Land by defeating the Nightmare and putting the Star Rod back where it belongs.

Nightmare

The Nightmare first appears as an orb, and the battle takes place in the sky. Kirby's only method of attack uses the Star Rod to throw stars at the Nightmare, so this fight plays out a lot more like a shooter than the Kirby you're used to.

This fight is simple mechanically: shoot stars at the Nightmare and don't get hit by its dark stars. They are pretty easy to see coming and dodge well in advance. The fight is made trickier by an unseen timer ticking down for the entire exchange. As the battle between Kirby and the Nightmare rages on, they fall closer and closer to the ground. If Kirby touches the ground, he loses a life, and you start the fight over. Make each shot count, and don't dawdle! Time is not on your side!

Once you defeat the Nightmare's orb form, the fight is far from over. He reveals his true form as the Nightmare Vampire! This is where the fight really begins.

To defeat the Nightmare Vampire, use the Star Rod to shoot stars into the glowing parts under his cloak. He keeps them covered until the moment he attacks; that's when you strike! He teleports across the room before pretty much every attack, so you don't get a lot of time to damage him when he reveals his weak point.

All in all, the Nightmare Vampire isn't hard if you are quick and accurate. Take your time learning his patterns; there's no hurry this time, and his moves are easy enough to dodge. Shoot the Star Rod several times whenever you see the Nightmare Vampire's weak point to deal extra damage. You've got this!

Challenge Mode

After completing the game, you unlock Challenge Mode, which lowers your total health to three bars and removes your ability to save the game. For the most die-hard of Kirby fans only.

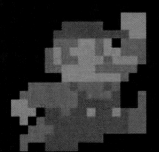

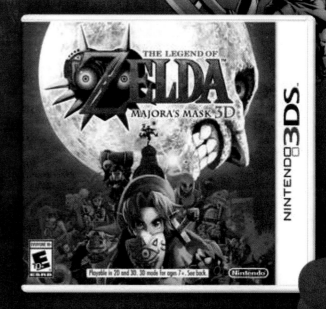

NES PERIPHERALS

We all know the standard NES setup, the Control Deck, controllers, Zapper, and a game or two, but did you know that the NES was supported with a boatload of other hardware? From arcade sticks and circle pads to four-player controller adaptors and light guns, the NES had a wider variety of peripherals than pretty much any other console on the market—it even had a robot that would play games with you!

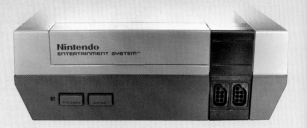

R.O.B.

R.O.B. (or your Robotic Operating Buddy) was created as a means to show retailers that the NES was more than just a gaming machine. Retailers were unnerved by the idea of putting more game consoles on store shelves, since they had become a very hard product to sell during that time. R.O.B. was meant to show retailers that their machine was, in fact, an "Entertainment System" as the name implied. It only worked for two games on the NES, but the plan clearly worked.

NES Max Controller

The NES Max was a variant on the standard controller that had a circlepad in place of the Directional Pad. The controller had more of a boomerang shape, as opposed to the rectangular look of the regular NES controller. It also had a Turbo function that could be used for rapid fire in-game.

NES Advantage

Nintendo went back to its roots with this controller—a joystick with two massive buttons for A and B and a flat bottom, perfect for placing on a flat surface and emulating the arcade experience. The controller also had turbo buttons, which made shooting games a breeze. As an added bonus, the Advantage also had a "Slow" button, which rapidly paused and unpaused the game, giving it the appearance of moving in slow motion.

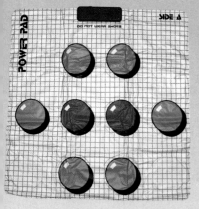

Hands-Free Controller

This controller was created to allow Nintendo fans with disabilities to play the NES. Players moved characters in-game with a chin-controlled joystick, which was used as the Directional Pad. Players would sip and puff into a straw-like device attached to the controller to use the A and B Buttons.

Power Pad

The Power Pad was part of Nintendo's ideology of making the NES more than a game console. It was used as a way to keep gamers active and also bring other non-gaming family members into the mix. Most of the games that were made for the Power Pad were fitness- and physical exercise-related.

Zapper

The Zapper was a light gun for the NES that allowed players to play games with shooting gallery mechanics. Games like *Duck Hunt*, *Hogan's Alley*, and *Wild Gunman* provided different motifs, but still ultimately focused on firing the Zapper at targets on the screen.

▶ NES Four Score

The Four Score was a controller bay that allowed for four total NES controllers to be plugged into the NES. This allowed for a total of four players on any games that supported it. The Four Score also had Turbo toggles, so all controllers plugged into the Four Score could benefit from Turbo buttons.

▶ NES Satellite

Like the Four Score, the Satellite enabled four-player gaming on the NES. Where the Satellite differentiates itself is in its wireless functionality. The Four Score was wired to the NES, but the Satellite had an adapter that plugged into the NES and sent a signal to the actual control bay where the controllers were plugged in.

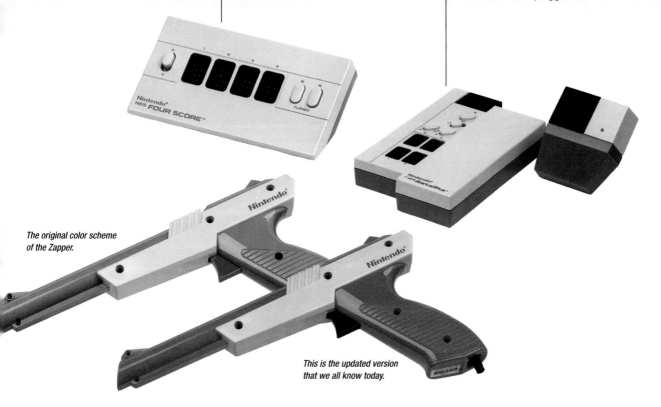

The original color scheme of the Zapper.

This is the updated version that we all know today.

319

PLAYING WITH POWER:
NINTENDO NES CLASSICS

Written by Garitt Rocha and Nick von Esmarch

Maps for *Kid Icarus*, *Metroid*, *Super Mario Bros.*, *The Legend of Zelda*, and *Zelda II: The Adventure of Link* created by Rick Bruns (www.nesmaps.com).

DK/Prima Games, a division of Penguin Random House LLC
6081 East 82nd Street, Suite #400
Indianapolis, IN 46250

Standard Edition: ISBN: 9780744017779

Collector's Edition: ISBN: 9780744017670

Printing Code: The rightmost double-digit number is the year of the book's printing; the rightmost single-digit number is the number of the book's printing. For example, 16-1 shows that the first printing of the book occurred in 2016.

19 18 17 16   4 3 2 1

001-305002-Nov/2016

Printed in the USA.

Thank you. But our Princess is in another castle!...Just kidding! Ha ha ha! Bye bye.

Prima Games Staff

VP & Publisher
Mike Degler

Editorial Manager
Tim Fitzpatrick

Design and Layout Manager
Tracy Wehmeyer

Licensing
Christian Sumner
Paul Giacomotto

Marketing
Katie Hemlock

Digital Publishing
Julie Asbury
Tim Cox
Shaida Boroumand

Operations Manager
Stacey Ginther

Credits

Senior Development Editor
David B. Bartley

Lead Designers
Dan Caparo
Tim Amrhein

Layout Team
Carol Stamile
Julie Clark
Areva

Production
Angela Graef

Editorial Team
Serena Stokes
Jennifer Simms

Acknowledgments

We'd like to thank everyone at Nintendo for their outstanding support and cooperation on this project, especially Jeremy Krueger-Pack, Emiko Ohmori, Teresa Wong, Kanani Kemp, Tim Bechtel, Todd Buechele, Ryan Dean, Connor Reed, Brian Harris, Chris Kuehnberger, Masayaki Oyata, and Roger Harrison. Your collective time and talent have helped make this book great.